VIEWERS LIKE YOU?

VIEWERS LIKE YOU?

HOW PUBLIC TV FAILED THE PEOPLE

LAURIE OUELLETTE

COLUMBIA UNIVERSITY PRESS NEW YORK

Columbia University Press

Publishers Since 1893

New York   Chichester, West Sussex

Copyright © 2002 Columbia University Press

Library of Congress Cataloging-in-Publication Data
Ouellette, Laurie.
Viewers like you? : how public TV failed the people /
Laurie Ouellette.
p.   cm.
Includes bibliographical references and index.
ISBN 0–231–11942–9 (cloth : alk. paper)—
ISBN 0–231–11943–7 (paper : alk. paper)
1. Public television—United States—History.
2. Elite (Social sciences)—United States—History.
3. Ideology—United States—History.   I. Title.
HE8700.79.U6 O94 2002
384.55'4'0973—dc21
2002025745

Columbia University Press books are printed on permanent
and durable acid-free paper.
Designed by Chang Jae Lee
Printed in the United States of America

C 10 9 8 7 6 5 4 3 2 1
P 10 9 8 7 6 5 4 3 2 1

CONTENTS

ACKNOWLEDGMENTS   VII

INTRODUCTION
*The Cultural Contradictions
of Public Television*   1

CHAPTER ONE
Oasis of the Vast Wasteland   23

CHAPTER TWO
The Quest to Cultivate   67

CHAPTER THREE
TV Viewing as Good Citizenship   105

CHAPTER FOUR
Something for Everyone   141

CHAPTER FIVE
Radicalizing Middle America   175

EPILOGUE
*Public Television, Popularity,
and Cultural Justice*   217

NOTES   229
INDEX   265

ACKNOWLEDGMENTS

Viewers Like You? was made possible by the support
of mentors, colleagues, and friends. At the University
of Massachusetts, Amherst, Justin Lewis introduced
me to critical studies of popular culture and cultural
studies of policy and showed me how to connect my
interests in these areas. He supervised the dissertation
from which this book evolved, and I am grateful for
his intellectual generosity and encouragement. Susan
Douglas, Lisa Henderson, and Carolyn Anderson offered many helpful insights and suggestions as dissertation readers. The Graduate School at the University
of Massachusetts, Amherst, also supported this project with a dissertation fellowship.

Tom Conners and Karen King at the National
Public Broadcasting Archives helped me locate a
wide range of historical material and provided courteous assistance with photocopying and videotape
duplication. The staffs at the Wisconsin State Historical Society, the Minnesota Historical Society, the Library of Congress, and the Museum of Television
and Radio in New York always were helpful, even on
short notice. KTCA in St. Paul, Minnesota, made its
membership guides and early programs available to

me, and the Corporation for Public Broadcasting provided access to early studies of the public television audience.

Many individuals offered support as I was transforming my dissertation into a book. I thank my colleagues in the Department of Journalism and Media Studies at Rutgers University, particularly Bill Solomon for his careful readings of the manuscript. Toby Miller invited me to speak about public television and its imagined audience at New York University and offered theoretical clarity at a crucial stage. James Hay read an early draft of chapter 3; his thoughtful comments prompted me to clarify public television's relationship to the professional middle class. I am especially indebted to Patricia Aufderheide for her sage assistance during the revision process. Pat's keen understanding of both public television and the dynamics of social change made her the perfect reviewer. She demanded complexity, and her optimism was contagious.

At Columbia University Press, I thank Ann Miller for her early interest in my dissertation and encouragement during the revision process. John Michel guided the manuscript to fruition with the utmost patience and professionalism. Chapter 3 is a significantly revised and expanded version of my article "TV Viewing as Good Citizenship? Political Rationality, Enlightened Democracy and PBS," which appeared in *Cultural Studies* 13 (January 1999): 62–90.

I could not have completed this book without the support of family and friends, particularly Susan McKenna, Katherine Sender, Jocylyn Geliga Vargas, and my sister, Jeannine, a consistent source of inspiration and amazement.

My deepest appreciation goes to my husband Harry, who read every word with the critical eyes of a journalist and a regular PBS viewer. His unwavering faith in this book—and his willingness to make it a priority—sustained me more than words can say.

VIEWERS LIKE YOU?

Why would you say to some poor worker out here
with three kids, "We're now going to take your
money and tax you for a program that you may
never watch?"
—Newt Gingrich, January 1995

Vulgarity is the lack of experience in things
beautiful. In its own modest and halting way,
public television has something to offer.
—Bill Moyers, April 1995

INTRODUCTION:
THE CULTURAL CONTRADICTIONS
OF PUBLIC TELEVISION

In January 1995, Newt Gingrich threatened to "zero
out" federal funding for public broadcasting. According to the Republican Speaker of the House, taxpayers were being forced to help subsidize a cultural
welfare program for well-heeled elites. A few months
later, the working-class Conner family on *Roseanne*
tuned in to PBS. Why? To subvert the expectations
of the A. C. Nielsen Corporation, the TV ratings
service. In the episode, the sitcom characters had
been chosen to participate in the ratings as a Nielsen
family and are eagerly anticipating their chance to
"help shape the culture of America." When a company bureaucrat arrives at their home to verify socioeconomic information, however, their pride is
shattered. Angered by his condescending remarks
about their modest neighborhood, unsophisticated
tastes, "required educations only," and probable addiction to commercial television, Roseanne de-
nounces the ratings as a scheme to blame people like
the Conners for lowbrow television shows. She also
suspects the Nielsen company of colluding with advertisers and budget-slashing politicians to keep
"have-nots" in their unenviable place, at the bottom

of the socioeconomic hierarchy. With her usual gusto, Roseanne decides to disprove the snobbery and undercut the "conspiracy" by watching only respectable television on PBS.

Beyond impressing Nielsen's number crunchers, Roseanne hopes that a "cold turkey" switch to public television will uplift the Conners, a project that is obviously doomed. Numerous jokes hinge on Roseanne's dogged attempt to supervise her family's awkward and sometimes hilariously uncooperative viewing of conventional public television shows, from slow-moving educational documentaries to public lectures "live from Yale." Before long, Roseanne quietly relents. By the end of the episode, she is deeply engrossed in a commercial channel's marathon showing of *The Beverly Hillbillies*, the top-rated 1960s sitcom about poor, illiterate mountaineers who discover oil and become millionaires. Roseanne realizes that she identifies with the fish-out-of-water hillbillies because they cannot adjust to the sophisticated ways of their "betters." In light of her epiphany, the family's short-lived upgrade to public television seems all the more amusing and far-fetched. For the Conners and, by implication, for the sitcom's viewers at home, PBS will remain a respected but ignored presence on the TV dial.

Public broadcasting may have been saved from the congressional chopping block, but the cultural contradictions pointed out in *Roseanne* remain unresolved. While commentators debated one another in the editorial pages, the popular sitcom negotiated a "bottom-up" perspective on the brouhaha in Washington, playing on the social, cultural, and moral distinctions ascribed to public television in the United States. For Roseanne, the PBS logo stands for intelligence and good taste as well as for an institutional mission that transcends popular entertainment, relaxation, and the sale of consumer goods. When the Conners actually watch PBS, however, this high-minded image is humorously skewered. Public television is shown to be a medicinal antidote to the pleasurable programs found on less prestigious commercial channels. For the Conners, its "worthwhile" programs are the cultural equivalent of cod-liver oil.

Public television is still understood to signify "class," defined as education, taste, sophistication, and prestige. Roseanne coaxes her reluctant family to swallow edifying doses of public television because she wishes to raise their social standing. She is determined to prove that people who are derisively labeled as hedonistic and uncultured are misjudged, as evidenced by the Conners' newfound capacity to appreciate the finest, "smartest" programs that television has to offer. And yet the assumption that people lacking university diplomas, white-collar professional jobs, overstuffed bookshelves, museum memberships, *New York Times* subscriptions, and similar signs of upper-middle-class cultural identity *are* an abnormal audience for prime-time public television is so taken for granted in our collective imaginary that it cinched the comedy and the moral of the story. Standing in for uncultured lower-class Middle America, the Conners return to the popular programming supplied by commercial broadcasters, leaving public television to the cultural elites they simultaneously resent and admire.

Although the Conners did not subvert the expectations of the Nielsen company, the episode did show that people's cultural tastes and preferences are circumstantial, not innate. Roseanne's short-lived embrace of public television arose from her desire to enter the respected social universe that it represents. While this space, or *habitus*, the term used by sociologist Pierre Bourdieu, may seem accessible to anyone by just a flick of the remote control, the Conners cannot sustain their new-and-improved TV-viewing regime. They are compared with another sitcom family, composed of nouveau riche hillbillies who also lack the learned "cultural capital" to negotiate newly upscale surroundings. The representation of public television on *Roseanne* evokes Bourdieu's argument that class is more than an economic category or relationship between the "haves" and "have-nots," in the classic Marxist sense. Class is a socially constructed identity shaped by social and cultural factors such as family origins, education, professional status, gender, ethnicity, geography, and lifestyle.[1] The Conners are shown to be inherently "wrong" for PBS, not simply because they are modestly fixed, but also because their high-school diplomas, Sears catalog furniture, and admitted fondness for beer, contact sports, and rowdy daytime talk shows clash with the respected cultural habitus that public television represents.

Roseanne pokes fun at public television from a populist vantage point that finds its programs dull, authoritative, erudite, and dreary. This episode also shows, by example, that "mass appeal" television genres like sitcoms can be meaningful and enlightening when they connect with the everyday lives of viewers. However, the story line does not question the value system that finds "mass culture" unworthy of public investment. The sitcom characters, who appear on a broadcast network currently owned by the Disney Corporation, accept the relegation of popularity to the commercial market, as epitomized by the closing statement "God bless Ted Turner." Following Bourdieu, policy analyst Justin Lewis argues that patterns of funding public culture are not, in fact, as natural or obvious as this episode would have us believe. Live theater is not inherently more deserving of public resources than are sitcoms—or televised lectures, ballets, symphonies, or educational documentaries. The tendency to assume otherwise, says Lewis, demonstrates the extent to which "arbitrary" cultural distinctions legitimated by ties to dominant classes and academic canons limit the scope of what is considered appropriate for public investment.[2]

The convergence of Newt Gingrich and *Roseanne* seems strange at first blush, considering the Speaker's conservatism and the sitcom's feisty working-class heroine. The meeting of minds speaks to the "sense-making" discourses that have surrounded public television since its formation in the 1960s. As the most recognized face of the interlocking U.S. public broadcasting system, PBS represents a liberal mission to bring "quality" and "enlightenment" to an otherwise "crass" and commercialized television culture.[3] Unlike the commercial channels, it promises "excellence and diversity" without commercial interruptions or concerns for profitability. The meaning of these terms is made clear by "The Promise of Television," a PBS documentary that gives high honors to public television for bringing classical music, serious theater, and "thoughtful conversation" to the airwaves. Public television is also praised for cultivating tastes, sharpening minds, enlarging expectations, and putting viewers "in touch" with great thinkers, artists, and performers. Insisting that people ought to turn on their TV sets "to be engaged, not just indulged," the documentary maintains that public television addresses its viewers as developing human beings and responsible citizens, not as consumers addicted to "time-wasting" amusements.[4] The paradox discovered by the Conners that the superlatives ascribed to the "oasis of the wasteland," to use public television's own terminology, acknowledge its limited appeal. That is, with the exception of its popular children's programs, public television is situated above popular culture, billed as "better" TV for unusually discriminate "viewers like you." It secures cultural distinction—and invites recurring charges of elitism—by defining the public that it exists to serve against a negative image of an indiscriminate mass audience glued to uncivilized afternoon talk shows, insipid sitcoms, cops-and-robbers dramas, sensationalistic tabloid news, and formulaic movies-of-the-week.

Similar tensions underscore public television's own characterization of its expected adult audience. Officially, public television promises "universal service" to everyone in the United States. When conservative accusations to the contrary gain currency, public television executives present statistical evidence to prove that the public television audience "mirrors society as a whole." When PBS journalist Bill Moyers debated conservative columnist

George Will on *Nightline* during the controversy of 1995, his defense of public broadcasting hinged on precisely such evidence. Skeptics argue that dem-
ocratic-seeming figures are inflated, as does independent research indicating
that children's programs like *Sesame Street* draw the majority of "ethnic and
downscale" families, whereas the prime-time public television audience is
disproportionately white, educated, and upper-middle class. Institutional
claims of audience inclusiveness are further contradicted by a less visible
marketing discourse in which the coveted public television audience is construed as "more affluent and highly educated than the general population."
According to one audience profile used to secure corporate underwriting,
most public television viewers "earn more than $40,000 per year and nearly
60 percent are business professionals, managers or owners." The dissonance
between the promise of universal service and the portrait of the "selective"
and upscale public television audience that circulates institutionally and in
popular representations like *Roseanne* points to incongruencies at the heart
of public television's mission. So too does the tension between "image sur-
veys" showing that most people consider public television to be more educational, serious, tasteful, and important than commercial television, and
ratings figures indicating that on any given evening, 98 percent of the people
who watch television ignore PBS's programs.[5]

How did public television become a contested sign of democratic
progress and cultural exclusivity? Why does public television occupy such an
elevated—and deeply marginalized—place in television culture? How was
the audience for public television envisioned during its formative years? And
what are the stakes in cyclical political disputes over its future? *Viewers Like
You?* asks these questions from a cultural studies point of view, drawing from
archival research and social and cultural theory to understand public television's conflicted relationship with the people it claims to serve and represent.
Excavating a wide range of original sources, including government hearings,
TV criticism, institutional and corporate records, audience profiles, publicity, viewers' letters, journalistic commentary, and iconographic PBS programs, this book traces the social construction of what broadcast reformers
called a "chance for better television." Analyzing the intersection of discourse, the "public interest," and cultural power, my study analyzes the "archaeology of ideas" that gave shape and purpose to public television and
made its mission susceptible to unresolvable contradictions and perennial
culture wars.[6] Following the call to put "policy into cultural studies," it denaturalizes the taken-for-granted boundaries that divide popular culture and
public culture in the United States and provides a critical perspective on debates over public television today.

Public Television and the Culture Wars

Public television has been long been contested by critics on Right and the Left. President Richard Nixon declared the first victory in the culture wars when he vetoed its congressional funding in 1972, just three years after PBS made its national debut. Nixon believed that public television was too liberal and supportive of "antiestablishment" viewpoints. Setting a discursive pattern that continues to this day, the president's advisers and supporters explained his veto in broader populist terms that accused public broadcasting of perpetuating "East Coast cultural elitism." The White House was not suggesting that PBS embraced popularity, nor was it questioning the commercial foundations of U.S. broadcasting. Rather, Nixon wanted public television to make education its priority, as "educational" stations had done in the 1950s and 1960s. Reforms pressed in the name of the people had little to do with closing the cultural gap between "public" television and the commercial programs that most people preferred.

Despite Nixon's early interventions, critics on the Right have continued to fuse cultural, geographical, and political complaints about its programs in a long-standing attempt to reform and dismantle public broadcasting. During the Reagan and Bush administrations of the 1980s and early 1990s, politicians and media critics (some funded by wealthy conservative foundations) argued that public television's financial dependence on the government made it arrogant, liberal, and tolerant of "subversive" ideas. As commercial cable and satellite technologies developed and upscale channels began to provide commercially viable, "quality" and educational programs, conservatives also said that public television's mission was redundant.[7] Proponents of this free-market view asserted that whatever the people wanted from public television—including its best-known children's programs—could survive on commercial channels or on viewer support and the sale of merchandising tie-ins. Conservative responses to public television began to seep into popular culture as well. The 1980s sitcom *Family Ties* pitted a former 1960s radical who managed his local public television station against his ultraconservative, Reagan-worshiping son. Like the bleeding-heart liberal father, public television was presented as a reservoir for "do-good" values that were comically out of step with the changing times.

Whereas public television has survived chronic conservative attacks, its claim to noncommercialism has not. By 1995, the system could barely be called "public" in economic terms. Just 14 percent of its overall budget came from the federal government, a percentage that dipped to 11.6 in 1999 and continues to decline. Corporate sponsors were compensated with credits resembling advertisements, and private contributions from viewers kept the system afloat, as they continue to do today. Nonetheless, when a Republican majority swept Congress that year, another round of culture wars came to the fore. Upon his election as Speaker of the House, Gingrich immediately announced his intention to abolish federal subsidies for public broadcasting. His pledge to eliminate the "little sandbox for the rich" coincided with the Republicans' Contract with America, a campaign to "privatize the Left" by eliminating Aid to Families with Dependent Children (AFDC) and most of the other social welfare programs created during the 1960s. Joining conservative ideology to populist rhetoric, Gingrich and his supporters contended that public television emerged from the same liberal "public interest" milieu that gave rise to radical cultural movements and an expanded welfare state to become an upper-middle-class entitlement.[8]

Following this argument, many conservative critics characterized public broadcasting as a liberal Great Society relic that benefits the sort of people who attend Ivy League universities, live in penthouses, and spend their holidays in Europe. "Stop subsidizing the tastes of the upper-middle class," demanded a spokesperson for the Project for the Republican Future, a conservative reform group. Ending public funding would wage war "not on the poor but, rather, on the cultural elites at the public trough," reiterated the vice-president of the Heritage Foundation, a prominent conservative think tank. While the sums at stake were small, conservative critics argued that the principle spoke "volumes to the American public that Congress is back on their side against the cultural elites, the radical social engineers, and the buttinski bureaucrats who insist on telling a self-governing people what is best for them."[9] In Washington and in the media, conservative opponents established themselves as the people's ally in the war against public broadcasting by demanding to know why the hardworking taxpayers should fund public culture imposed from above. PBS should be forced to operate in the commercial marketplace—or else the people who want it should pay for it themselves, said the reformers, some of whom made well-publicized donations to their public television stations to underscore its privatized future.

Unlike other social welfare programs targeted by Republicans, public broadcasting was not easily dismantled, precisely because its supporters tend to be vocal and well placed. Liberal politicians, commentators, and loyal viewers mobilized by their local stations defended public television as an outpost of quality, civility, and public service in a sea of cultural mediocrity and commercial excess. Those who opposed Gingrich's plans for public television defended its contributions to culture, education, and democracy and rebuked charges of elitism by highlighting its special benefits to people who could not afford cable and satellite services.[10] According to this recurring argument, public television served "haves" and "have-nots" by bringing opera to the hinterlands, enlightening the citizenry, educating children, combating delinquency, uplifting the disadvantaged, preserving cultural standards, and infusing prime-time television with a level of quality unsurpassed by for-profit cable venues. For most supporters, public television deserved government support to sustain its presumed social, aesthetic, and moral differences from mass culture. The defense adopted what political economist Nicholas Garnham calls an "idealist" approach to cultural policy, in which

> public intervention, in the form of subsidy, is justified on the grounds (1) that culture possesses inherent values, of life enhancement or whatever, which are fundamentally opposed to and in danger of damage by commercial forces; (2) that the need for these values is universal, uncontaminated by questions of class, gender and ethnic origin; and (3) that the market cannot satisfy this need.[11]

New York Times writer Max Frankel's assertion that "market culture is an inadequate culture" typifies the idealist rationale for public television. According to Frankel, without some form of government subsidy—including tax breaks for philanthropists and other private patrons—there "would be no great universities, no great libraries, no great museums, no grand opera or basic science." For him, public television is an extension of "great culture," and its existence confirms the "civilized conviction that not everything of value can be popular." Frankel defended public television from conservative claims of redundancy by insisting that the expanded commercial marketplace was "unable or unwilling" to deliver the superior programming it alone provided, including "mature" music, dance, sophisticated news analysis, and legitimate theater "beyond the soaps."[12] Also adopting an idealist view, Tom Shales of the *Washington Post* opposed privatization on the grounds that it would "cheapen" public television. Shales bristled at the prospect of *Masterpiece Theatre* being "peppered with ads for underarm deodorants and adjustable beds," comparing the notion with "billboards and neon signs between the paintings in the National Gallery of Art." For Shales, as for many defenders, unleashed commercialism was inevitable for a "mass appeal" medium like commercial television but wholly unacceptable for a respectable cultural institution like PBS.[13]

Commentators characterized public television as a venue for legitimate culture and lobbied for government support on those grounds. Senator Robert Byrd (D-West Virginia), an avid supporter on Capitol Hill, typified the extent to which concerns about its privatization intersected with social judgments about commercialized mass culture and its audience. For Byrd, public broadcasting deserved federal support because it offered discriminating viewers an alternative to lowbrow television while simultaneously attempting to uplift the inadequate tastes, behaviors, and morals of "other" people. In his testimony to Congress, Byrd gave the following summation of public television's development and role as the antidote to the "vast wasteland":

> From the beginning of the adulteration of television, thoughtful people have sought alternatives to the trash and vulgarity that have increasingly contaminated the airwaves of this miraculous medium of communication. And, to the relief of millions of thoughtful Americans, in time, "educational television" laid the foundations for today's public broadcasting stations. As a result, the public television network grew, children in our inner cities and in rural states like West Virginia and eastern Kentucky could be reached by television images that stretched their imaginations, taught them stories by great authors, exposed them to initial concepts in science and arithmetic, and challenged them with mainstream values such as telling the truth, respecting other children, obeying their parents, and becoming good citizens. At the same time, the Public Broadcasting System . . . increasingly filled the voids left by the commercial networks when they turned their backs on the people in our society who crave good music, who hunger for good drama, who desire to see good public debates on important questions of our times.[14]

Although Congress did not pull the plug on public broadcasting, the dispute that Gingrich initiated forced policymakers to contemplate the purpose of "public" alternatives to commercial broadcasting at the dawn of a new media age. While supporters and opponents disagreed about the continued need for public television—or any type of government-supported public culture, for that matter—they did agree that popular culture was best left to the machinations of the commercial market. On the one hand, for supporters like Byrd, "mass appeal" programming was rightfully banished from public television, justifiable only in children's shows like *Sesame Street* with proven educational track records. On the other hand, for Gingrich, the commercial marketplace was inherently democratic because unlike public television, it "gave the people what they wanted." The liberal defense hinged on the promise of cultural uplift, whereas the conservative opposition rested on the presumption of consumer sovereignty. Even though the speakers were new, their arguments were borrowed from well-established discourses, or what Michel Foucault calls routinized patterns of thinking and speaking about important subjects.[15] As Foucault has demonstrated, discourses are productive forces that help shape the institutions and policies of modern societies. Public television's cultural priorities and the terms of its earliest conservative critique were defined during the 1960s and early 1970s. *Viewers Like You?* situates public television and its proclivity to culture wars within this "discursive formation" because it provides the clearest context in which to analyze the contested "meanings of cultural policy from the perspectives of social and cultural theory."[16]

Culture, History, and Public Television

The critical literature on U.S. public broadcasting is incomplete and—like the subject it addresses—deeply marginalized in media and cultural studies.[17] Although the existing research scrutinizes the high-level institutional operations and political economics of public broadcasting, it says very little about its cultural dynamics or everyday implications. The earliest studies chronicled the emergence and conflicted nature of public broadcasting from an official perspective that attributed its existence and its troubles to interlocking agencies and powerful individuals. Against this descriptive paradigm, critical interpretive studies began to address the commercialization of public television, the ideological biases of its programming, and its failure to achieve democratic public-service goals. Public television's "decline" at the hands of corporations and structural conservative forces is now the principal preoccupation of critical studies of U.S. public broadcasting.

The common argument in this scholarship is that accelerated corporate funding—triggered in part by conservative reforms—has eroded public television's performance in the prioritized spheres of advocacy, citizenship, and public affairs. Corporate involvement is generally protested against the backdrop of a less commercialized "golden age," characterized as the interval between the passage of the 1967 Public Broadcasting Act and Nixon's interventions. Because public television was more receptive to experimentation and progressive programming during this tumultuous period, scholars tend to chart its history as a series of subversions and declines. Forced to depend on corporate sponsors and pledge drives for economic sustenance, public television lost the ability it once had to "provocatively challenge the status quo," according to James Ledbetter in *Made Possible by . . . the Death of Public*

Broadcasting in the United States.[18] From Ledbetter's perspective, public television's shortcomings are ideological, and because of its compromised funding structure, public television adopted the narrow ideological worldview of corporate sponsors and private donors. For critics like Ledbetter, public television's normative relationship to popular culture and everyday life—a phenomenon that predated its corporate co-optation—is irrelevant.

In *Public Television for Sale*, William Hoynes also contends that political economic pressures have undermined public television's capacity to nurture democracy by providing an electronic "public sphere" that is receptive to critical viewpoints. Like Ledbetter, Hoynes is mainly concerned with the bourgeois, masculine sphere of "serious" news and public affairs. He does not contemplate the class and gender connotations of these favored forums for "information exchange," and he cares little about sitcoms, soap operas, daytime talk shows, music videos, TV movies, or any popular genre, for that matter, believing them to be "fictional" distractions that are presumably unworthy of critical contemplation or public subsidy. Hoynes's approach to public television drew conceptually from Nicholas Garnham, an important figure in the earlier European debate over "public service versus the market." Updating theorist Jürgen Habermas's argument that democracy depends on rational discussions carried out in public forums, Garnham argued that public television is inherently more democratic than commercial channels are because it serves all citizens, regardless of their purchasing power, and addresses TV viewers as "rational beings" instead of consumers of toothpaste and automobiles. Garnham was worried about the uncertain fate of state-owned institutions like the British Broadcasting Corporation—the original backbone of broadcasting in Europe—in light of deregulation and heightened private competition. The United States, however, took the reverse approach in that it developed commercial broadcasting as the dominant system, using public television as a belated supplement. Glossing over these different policy traditions and their cultural implications, Hoynes champions public television as the singular exception to an otherwise shallow, trivial, consumerist, and distracting television culture. From this vantage point, he protests public television's submission to market mechanisms aimed at pleasing corporate funders and donors who prefer prestigious entertainment like *Masterpiece Theatre* and *Antiques Roadshow* to the somber "public sphere" he advocates. Public television's narrow classification of worthy pleasure is less important to Hoynes, because any slippage into mass culture is problematic. For him, commercial pressures have distracted public television from its principal task of transmitting "the kinds of imagery and information that fundamentally prepare the public for its role in a democracy."[19]

Corporations used PBS for upscale "ambush" marketing purposes, blurring the lines between consumers and citizens and audiences and publics, concurs Patricia Aufderheide in her critical studies of public broadcasting. For Aufderheide, however, the undemocratic consequences have less to do with ideology, distraction, or cultural "crassness" than with public television's conventional focus on delivering "programs to audiences" instead of mobilizing publics to contemplate issues and solve problems in their communities. Public television should consider itself "anti-television," she argues, prioritizing the medium's capacity to facilitate grassroots activism and collective organizing over the privatized spectatorship cultivated by commercial broadcasters. Aufderheide favors the independent documentaries created under the auspices of the Independent Television Service, public television's most progressive, experimental, and—significantly— marginalized wing. While few and far between, these programs come the closest to an alternative approach to public television that is committed to bridging social conflicts, combating consumerism, building communities, activating disadvantaged and exploited citizens, and fostering the "common good." For Aufderheide, the realization of public television's democratic potential will require a fundamental reinterpretation of the medium. Her utopian vision is defined against TV's established role as an everyday leisure pursuit and conveyer of popular meanings, information, and entertainment to the home. While Aufderheide's commitment to progressive justice is commendable, her call for "anti-television" characterizes public television as a means to greater ends that have little to do with enriching television culture on its own terms. She also relegates the mediated cultural environment in which most people live to the commercial market and, in so doing, accepts public television's idealized place outside this domain. The radical overhaul of television that Aufderheide advocates does not challenge—and, in many ways, solidifies—the taken-for-granted divide between popular culture and public culture in the United States.[20]

Willard Rowland is one of few scholars to note the "contradictions of popularity and publicness" that keep public television in this narrow but contested cultural space. Rowland has observed that public television's right to existence in the United States is tenuous, caught between the expectation of avoiding cultural overlap with "mass appeal" commercial broadcasting and the promise of universal service that comes with reliance on tax-based resources. Likewise, he notes that public television is awkwardly situated between the notion that the people need "enlightenment" from above and the democratic access implied by its claim to "publicness." Rowland's critical lens does not extend beyond the official policymaking process and the institutional conflicts inside public broadcasting, however. He does not consider the broader cultural context that gave rise to such contradictions or the routinized "discourses" on which they depend. Nor does he contemplate the cultural policy implications of the "paradox of popularity," partly because he presumes that any attempt to develop a popular public television system that would address "large collectivities" is an inherently exploitative endeavor and a misuse of noncommercial resources. Like Aufderheide, Rowland idealizes authentic publics over "passive" audiences and presumes that these constructs are mutually exclusive. Sharing the negative view of mass culture that permeates critical studies of public broadcasting, Rowland ultimately advocates firm boundaries between public culture and popularity. In his later work, Rowland and his colleague Michael Tracey protest the extent to which market forces have undermined European public broadcasting, citing as evidence its willingness to support noncommercial game shows and soap operas with "no obvious" public-interest rationale. Like his contemporaries, Rowland equates popular culture with trivial pursuits and designates public television for more important purposes.[21]

Despite raising important concerns about the commercialization of public television, scholars gloss over its complex cultural dynamics—or treat them as economic by-products. While conservative reformers lobby for privatization, the typical response of the Left has been to protest the taint of corporate underwriting but defend an idealized vision of public television as a democratic counterpoint to the commercial "marketplace of ideas." In academic and advocacy contexts, the need to address citizens who "require information to participate fully in the nation's political and cultural life" is conceptualized against both accelerated commercialism and corrosive infotainment.[22] The public to be activated or radicalized by public television is pitted against the "passive" television audience ensconced in the distracting rituals of privatized leisure and consumption. The conceptual divide between public and popular culture is not questioned. At its worst, leftist criticism conflates concerns about corporate control over television with an unexamined, patronizing view of popular taste, thereby reproducing unexamined judgments floating in the discourse of the "vast wasteland."

Cultural studies has made this conflation problematic, for several reasons. First, as Lewis observed, we live in an era of "priorities, not ideals." Critics may not approve, but "popular domain organized by the free market" is the culture in which most people live.[23] Second, even though noncommercial television alternatives created in the name of "quality" or the "public interest" may be theoretically available to all, they are not necessarily universally beneficial. As cultural studies scholar Ien Ang has shown, we cannot assume that public broadcasting is inherently democratic just because it may not have any market pressures. In her studies of European public broadcasting, Ang draws attention to what Foucault calls the "art of effects," or what, in another context, one early public television supporter called the "great power to affect the behavior of individuals and groups."[24] For Ang, public-service philosophy is different from the impetus to "win" an audience for advertisers or corporate underwriters, but it is not always less controlling. Cultural institutions like the British Broadcasting Service are rooted in what Raymond Williams called a paternal logic, committed to transmitting "values, habits, and tastes" so as to uplift the populace according to standards determined by the "ruling majority."[25] As Ang points out, there is a fine line between enlightenment and social management when television's noncommercial purpose is to reform the public in order that it "better perform [its] democratic rights and duties." Ang contends that European public broadcasting's adoption of market principles in the wake of heightened commercial competition cannot be dismissed as merely co-optive in the traditional leftist sense. The audience's refusal to cooperate with traditional public-service aims when popular alternatives became available can be considered unruly or even resistant, says Ang.[26] Public television in the United States was belatedly conceived as a corrective to commercial television's established role; thus, its history brings different tensions and potential outcomes to the debate over "public service versus the market" in the United States. Ang's theoretical work has provided a starting point for making sense of U.S. public television's particular priorities, contradictions, and discontents.

Viewers Like You? is written from a cultural studies perspective that recognizes the constructed nature of aesthetic hierarchies and rejects the essential distinctions among television viewers, citizens, and publics. Popular culture is contradictory, and it can overlap with democracy, citizenship, and politics in unpredictable ways. However commercialized and hooked into the "circuits" of ideology and commodity production, popular culture also has "its base in the experiences, the pleasures, the memories, the traditions of the people," Stuart Hall contends. Public television's positioning as the demarcated opposite of popular television speaks to the "ordering" of aesthetics, morals, and social practices critiqued by Hall and other scholars.[27] For cultural studies, the divide between public culture and popular culture is not obvious or inevitable but, rather, the subject of critical investigation. Conservatives who charge public television with cultural elitism and other sins against taxpayers wish us to believe that publicly supported television is unwarranted. Liberals often adopt a trickle-down approach to public television on the untenable grounds that "better" culture is universally beneficial.

Critics on the Left have overlooked the social bases of cultural ideals that cannot be reduced to political economic forces and constraints. This book takes a broader approach by questioning why public television became the "oasis of the wasteland" instead of a popular democratic channel and proposes that we can learn from this history as we enter the new media age.

Culture Studies and Public Television

Former PBS president Lawrence Grossman once admitted that when the "history of American television is written, public television will be largely a footnote."[28] To understand why even supporters acknowledge public television's marginalization, we need to move beyond protesting corporate influence while also resisting the temptation to invert cultural hierarchies.[29] U.S. cultural studies has virtually ignored public television, partly because it has little bearing on the routines of everyday adult life, but also because its status as serious and distinguished television makes it less prone to the transgressions that attract scholars to popular, commercialized programs. Since popular television in the United States is controlled by the culture industries, this presents cultural studies with a conundrum when analyzing alternatives to what the free market offers. Therefore, cultural studies of television have, until recently, prioritized textual negotiations and audience interpretations at the expense of policy issues.

There are good reasons to acknowledge the contradictions of commercial culture and the creativity and resilience of people cast as passive victims of the television apparatus. However, as Charlotte Brundson observes, what may be lost on this route to cultural democracy are the possible demands placed on television institutions. The "problem of always working with what people are, of necessity, watching," she argues, "is that we don't really ever address that something else—what people might like to watch." Unless the "recognition of the creativity and competencies of the audience" is linked to demands for "programming which is adequate to the needs, desires, and pleasures of these audiences," cultural studies risks "reproducing the dominant paradigm."[30] I share Brundson's perception that cultural studies needs to be particularly cautious about landing in the same conceptual camp as the conservatives who celebrate the cultural democracy provided by the commercial market. Cultural studies has not found ways to address Newt Gingrich when he crusades to reject the concept of public culture and claims that indeed, popular conservative ideologues like Rush Limbaugh *are* public broadcasting.

The drama of the culture wars has overshadowed U.S. public television's contradictory relationship with the people, a relationship that cultural studies is best positioned to address. The progressive, pluralistic, and participatory promises that surrounded the national creation of public television distanced it from the openly paternalistic European public broadcasting systems critiqued by Williams and Ang. However, these discourses coexisted with anxieties about the quality of television and its imagined audience. The impetus to create "better" TV intersected with concerns about the decline of cultural standards in an age of heightened mass production and consumption. Likewise, attempts to conceive and develop democratically enabling television often brushed up against fears of mass political apathy and minority "deviance." The move to disseminate televised education was simultaneously humanitarian and indicative of elite worries about the twin problems of unproductive leisure and popular taste. Pluralist promises of cultural diversity were inflected by the assumption that well-educated taste cultures and influential opinion leaders were least served by prime time's homogenous programming. In the United States, public television was positioned to mobilize *and* reform the imagined public, activate *and* guide the citizenry, enlighten *and* classify TV viewers according to unquestioned hierarchies of knowledge and power. The people were not asked what they might like to see on public television, for their judgments and behaviors were implicitly held responsible for the very "TV problem" that public broadcasting was created to solve. Across policy, institutional, and cultural contexts, public television was envisioned *for* the people, not *by* the people, because its democratic potential was perpetually contingent on their transformation as subjects.

Tony Bennett's approach to public culture as a "reformer's science," a phrase he uses in reference to the famous reformer Matthew Arnold, is especially useful for making sense of these contradictions. Complementing Bourdieu's sociology of culture, Bennett attends to the historical and subjective dimensions of cultural policy. His studies develop the cultural implications of Foucault's analysis of administrative power by showing how early libraries, museums, and rational recreations merged with progressive intentions as well as "governmental" attempts to shape and guide the populace. Bennett does not deny that these late-nineteenth-century prototypes of public culture represented significant gains. But the new "cultural technologies" also sought to develop and fine-tune the morals, behaviors, and tastes of patrons while differentiating the cultivated upper-middle class from the working class rank-and-file.[31]

In this sense, notes Jim McGuigan, they went beyond the "hardware" needed to transmit culture and information, to the "machinery of institutional and organizational structures and processes that produce particular configurations of knowledge and power."[32] For Bennett, these were "reforming endeavors" rooted in a "normative view of culture bequeathed" by Arnold's crusade to maintain elite cultural standards and restore social order to a turbulent industrial society by diffusing the "best that has been thought and said."[33] What Bennett calls "look and learn" campaigns were not conspiratorial schemes but, rather, complex cultural responses to unstable capitalist democracies.[34] His careful work demonstrates that long before the conceptualization of public television in the United States, cultural reformers were deeply concerned with the "art of effects." The historical development of public alternatives to commercial mass culture traversed humanitarianism as well as taste management and social control. Bennett connects the birth of cultural institutions like museums, their "political rationalities" or reform logics, and contemporary policy debates, providing a useful framework for analyzing public television. Although public television operates with its own reform logics, it also appeared at a historical moment when modern cultural and democratic ideals were perceived as being seriously undermined. It was conceived at a time when anxieties about cultural standards were pronounced, and the conflicting demands of the consumer economy (selfishness, hedonism, pleasure) and the political order (discipline, rationality, responsibility) noted by cultural theorist Toby Miller were particularly acute. Miller proposes that these tensions present a perpetual dilemma for the modern democratic capitalist state, which requires "training" subjects to meet conflicting roles and requirements as consumers as well as citizens.[35] Since commercial television was central to the consumer economy, even though its programs were charged with undermining culture and democracy, public television became a repository of largely corrective strategies.

From this vantage point, it matters that anxieties about mass culture, mass audiences, and mass movements accompanied the formation of public television, helping define its mission to shape and guide cultural and social change. Indeed, its potential to do so was what made a public alternative possible in a nation previously committed to free-market principles in broadcasting. Commercial television's "mass appeal" output, coupled with the cancellation of prestigious but poorly rated cultural and public affairs programs, alarmed the intelligentsia of the 1960s, prompting the Federal Communications Commission chairman Newton N. Minow's "vast wasteland" speech and sparking demands for federal intervention beyond the existing "educational" stations dotting local landscapes.[36] In this pre-cable era, many reformers, social scientists, TV critics, and philanthropists lobbied in the name of a superpower democracy undermined by mass ignorance, consumerism, and trivial TV shows yet imagined public television as a much-needed niche for university-bred intellectuals and college-educated cultural "minorities."

The Great Society's concern with raising the nation's quality of life, combating the "cultural depravation" of the poor, and improving people's capacity for excellence in all spheres of social life tempered this contradiction, prompting high-level thinking about TV's ability to educate and enlighten broadly and particularly to assist disadvantaged populations. President Lyndon Johnson and advocates at the U.S. Department of Health, Education and Welfare promoted public broadcasting as a conduit for informal education, cultural enlightenment, and self-improvement. In this atmosphere, benefactors at the Carnegie and Ford Foundations stressed the universal benefits of "quality" television not tied to the principle of audience maximization in their pursuit of federal funding for a public television.

Demands for equal rights, countercultures, and civil disobedience—coupled with elite fears that society was breaking down because of these disruptions—triggered additional hopes and aims. Public television's potential to address angry, marginalized, and disenfranchised populations and its capacity to mediate conflicts, restore liberal pluralism, and facilitate social order became concerns for reformers who had initially envisioned public television as a solution to mass cultural malaise. The "TV problem," the interventionist spirit of the Great Society, and the turbulence of the late 1960s provide the historical backdrop for charting public television's contradictory impulses and susceptibility to marginalization and culture wars.

The Cultural Contradictions of Public Television

Viewers Like You? contextualizes contemporary debates by revisiting the period when public television was conceptualized and, in the words of the Carnegie Commission, "embedded in the national consciousness."[37] It traces the "sense-making" discourses that gave shape and meaning to public television across policy, institutional, and cultural contexts. Because there is no "master" discourse to explain public television's course, I organized the book thematically, analyzing the design of five principal ideals: excellence, cultivation, citizenship, pluralism, and advocacy. These case studies are united by my focus on tensions among progressive promises, classifying tendencies, and governmental aims.

Chapter 1 traces the discourse of the "vast wasteland" and its enormous influence on public television in the United States. I examine the factors that positioned public television as a corrective to indiscriminate TV viewing, including the corporate claim that television was a "cultural democracy" for which viewers were responsible and the precedents for reform established by educational television. Setting the stage for the remainder of the book, this chapter explains the dual cultural reform logics that warranted and guided the creation of public broadcasting. In so doing, it shows how the desire to reach educated viewers and uplift the mass audience converged to establish public television's taken-for-granted cultural boundaries.

Chapter 2 reconsiders the discourse of "equality of opportunity," showing how public television's promise to level socioeconomic hurdles with a televised display of knowledge and culture positioned differently imagined viewers. Comparing public television's quest to cultivate across children's programming, the "social and personal development" genre for disadvantaged adults, and prime-time public television, this chapter shows how the promise of class mobility brushed up against the limits of meritocracy and claims of cultural distinction. *Sesame Street* and job-training programs created in response to race rioting positioned "have-nots" in relation to what social scientists called the "culture of poverty" thesis. To attract a disadvantaged audience to educational messages, both used mass culture techniques as necessary lures. Prime-time public television sought to raise the level of television culture, which forbade similar strategies but attracted sponsors hoping to find the "class audience" within the mass. I show how corporate America, instead of co-opting public television, reached formerly unknowable "influentials" by supporting an interpretation of "better" television that was widely shared by reformers, philanthropists, executives, critics, and well-educated viewers.

Chapter 3 looks at the discourse of "enlightened democracy" and its relationship to news and public affairs. I situate public television's attempt to transform television viewers into active citizens in the broader context of the "TV problem" and the turbulence of the late 1960s. Fears that commercial television news ill served "opinion leaders" and sensationalized protesting and conflicts contributed to public television's focus on credentialed experts and print-derivative formats. While progressive in many respects, efforts to expand legitimate and "rational" opportunities for participation in democracy via televised hearings, town halls, and simulated debates also worked as exclusionary devices and "governmental" mechanisms of training and control. Finally, this chapter shows how the construction of "enlightened democracy" via public television drew from social scientific discourse, including the influential theory of the "two-step flow" in which information allegedly trickles down from "primary influentials" to the mass public. In so doing, this chapter both denaturalizes and critiques the assumption that enlightened citizenship is necessarily anti-thetical to popular television and its imagined audience.

Chapter 4 examines the discourse of pluralism, showing how the promise of "something for everyone" was constrained by both the official denial of class difference and the normalization of whiteness. The chapter looks at the construction of public television's unquestioned cultural "center" within policy discourse and compares the much heralded debut of PBS programs steeped in upper-class European cultural associations with the rapid rise and fall of popular "minority" programming for blacks. Both strains blended mass culture with literary, pedagogic, and high cultural traditions and goals. While white programming was conceptualized and billed as superior television devoid of any racial connotations, black programming was marginalized and subject to cancellation as the nation stabilized. Class and whiteness also were normalized by public television's membership and fund-raising cultures. Instead of dismissing these ventures as quasi commercialism, I show how they provided new rationales through which public television could temporarily indulge popular rituals, pleasures, and modes of participation—but only in upscale, white, and consumerist terms.

Chapter 5 analyzes public television's first encounter with conservative culture wars against the backdrop of formative experiments in "advocacy" television. Both conservatives and left-leaning advocates and producers drew from a fictional portrait of Middle America in the political struggle played out around public television. As a result, provocative, oppositional, and often arrogant PBS programs emanating from New York City and other major metropolises became the focal point of conservative remediations, supported by local stations that also preferred a less controversial, land-grant approach to educational broadcasting. Looking at the records of WNET in New York City and KTCA in Minneapolis-St. Paul, I show how geographical disputes over public culture shaped and were shaped by an authoritarian-populist discourse advocating conservative reforms in the name of the common person. Even though some critics have dismissed localized approaches as trivial and apolitical, this chapter shows how the land-grant philosophy forced public television to broaden its understanding of "good" TV and its imagined audience. Likewise, I argue that the attempt to "radicalize" Middle America emanating from large urban stations failed to generate public support because it privileged, and attempted to diffuse, intellectual tastes and cultural competencies.

Throughout this book, I often use the terms PBS and public television interchangeably, even though the Public Broadcasting Service is technically not a television network but, rather, a connecting agency managed in part by its affiliate stations. PBS was established in 1969, two years after Congress passed the 1967 Public Broadcasting Act. The Corporation for Public Broadcasting was charged with dispersing congressional funds, while PBS managed the national interconnection and planned and publicized the National Program Service. PBS was both more visible and more involved in daily programming decisions, and it quickly became the most recognized icon of the public broadcasting system, which includes several national agencies and more than 350 stations across the states. For most people, the PBS logo is virtually synonymous with public television. Therefore, to avoid bureaucratic intricacies that have little to do with my cultural focus, I have treated PBS like a cultural institution as well as a shorthand reference to public television at the national level.

Finally, a note on my background. I became interested in the public television culture wars during the early 1990s as a media critic for an alternative press. While the objections emanating from the Right and the Left differed, it struck me that the tendency to blame singular causes like "cultural elitism" or "creeping commercialism" for public television's malaise cut across political lines. These one-dimensional conceptual frameworks struck me as profoundly limiting, as did staunch defenses of public television based on its status as "worthwhile" television or its alleged cultural and educational benefits for all citizens. When I decided to pursue a Ph.D. in cultural studies, I found the critical vocabulary that I could use to articulate my unresolved questions about public television and its cyclical discontents. In late 1994, as I was preparing a dissertation proposal on the cultural politics of public television, Newt Gingrich launched another contentious debate over public broadcasting. I realized that the most recent explosion of discourse about public television echoed the very debates I had covered as a journalist and critic some years before. The episode was new, but the terms for discussing public television were virtually the same. To understand why, I delved into the cultural history of public television in the United States. What began as "supplementary" research soon convinced me that patterns of thinking about and contesting public television were set into motion during its formative period, the late 1960s and early 1970s. While supporters and opponents debated public broadcasting in Washington, I embarked on a five-year study of archival records, including oral histories, press clippings, audience studies, speeches, station-membership guides, promotions, congressional hearings, and early PBS programs.

As I pieced together the cultural formation of public television, I realized that my project was intertwined with my personal history as well. I am contradictorily positioned by the discursive frameworks this book analyzes. I grew up in an upwardly mobile, blue-collar family that gained access to higher education because of Great Society programs. Since I was a child of the 1960s who acquired legitimated "cultural capital" secondhand through the educational system, I am deeply familiar with the contradictory promises, cultural distinctions, and reform logics that coalesce around the diffusion of "excellence." Instead of viewing promises of excellence, uplift, diversity, and citizenship as inherently progressive or elitist, I have tried to understand the historical forces that gave rise to these cultural reform discourses, television's role in triggering them, and their residual impact on public television today. Since I grew up in Minnesota and live in New York City—spatial locales with historically conflicting approaches to public broadcasting—I have taken the places I know best as twin case studies for reconsidering the geographical dimensions of the public television culture wars. Finally, while I critique the Left's mistrust of popular culture, I share its concern with commercial control over cultural production and support struggles for social and economic equality. Indeed, my alignment with progressive causes has intensified my curiosity about the "golden age" of public television celebrated by other scholars who bring different intellectual, generational, and social backgrounds to their work. *Viewers Like You?* is an attempt to reconcile idealist hopes for "better" TV with the contradictions of public TV as it currently exists. I hope that by critically unraveling the cultural construction of public television, this book will pave the way for a broader debate over the purpose of public television today.

Masses was a new word for mob, and the
traditional characteristics of the mob were
retained in its significance: gullibility, fickleness,
herd-prejudice, lowness of taste and habit. The
masses, on this evidence, formed the perpetual
threat to culture.
—Raymond Williams, *Culture and Society*

Walter Lippmann stated the justification for
noncommercial educational television in 1959
when he wrote that it should be a network which
can be run as a public service, and its criterion not
what will be most popular but what is good.
—McGeorge Bundy

CHAPTER ONE

OASIS OF THE VAST WASTELAND

In 1992, the Corporation for Public Broadcasting
published a retrospective of milestones, accolades,
and vintage photographs to celebrate the twenty-fifth
anniversary of public broadcasting in the United
States. Grandly entitled "From Wasteland to Oasis: A
Quarter Century of Sterling Programming," the report constructs a triumphant narrative of undisputed cultural progress. Following the passage of the
1967 Public Broadcasting Act, public television arrived on the airwaves, providing worthy alternatives
to what FCC Chairman Newton Minow, in his 1961
speech to commercial broadcasters, famously called
a "vast wasteland." Leaders in government, education, business, and culture supported the national intervention in television, spurred by the realization
that "Americans were making an enormous mistake
to let the law of the least common denominator set
the sights of broadcasting." Fortunately, public television has salvaged a slice of television from the dust-
bin of civilization and continues to improve both the
medium and society as a whole.

Although it is presented as self-evident, this
chronology draws from a long history of reformist

thinking about the problem of mass culture and the purpose of public alternatives. The report presumes an obvious distinction between barbarous, shallow, hackneyed television programs commercially geared to the indiscriminate millions, and civilized, edifying, sophisticated television programs requiring protection from the perils of popularity. The opposing metaphors used to symbolize this contrast tend to glorify public television as a confined space for "good" television in an otherwise debased, superficial, unsophisticated, and otherwise destructive cultural environment. The colossal divide between the "vast wasteland" and its redemptive "oasis" informed the cultural formation of public television in the United States and remains a well-rehearsed justification for its contested survival. In the words of scholar Robert Avery, the binary constitutes public television as a site for cultural and intellectual "quality" against the "crass" majority culture mass-produced and consumed in a "system of commercial free enterprise." But *is* a public cultural alternative that rests its "sterling" reputation on the degradation of "majority" television a democratic way to determine cultural policy?[1]

The perch claimed by public television can be traced to complaints about commercial television's "lowness" that arose with the medium and grew more vociferous as it fully "massified" in the late 1950s and early 1960s. Waged most ardently by intellectuals, critics, and professional reformers, the terms of this discontent seeped into journalism, social science, TV criticism, and policymaking. Within this discursive formation, Minow's allusion to T. S. Eliot's poem *The Waste Land* typified the conflation of commercial control over television with its disparaged cultural level and perceived obligation to unqualified "majority rule." The FCC chairman's 1961 lecture to the National Association of Broadcasters did not question the capitalist engines of broadcasting as much as it scolded the industry for subverting the public interest by pandering to the tastes and desires of the mass television audience.[2] While Minow's plea for programmatic upgrades within the existing commercial broadcasting system was unsuccessful, the specter of the vast wasteland hastened the appearance of PBS on the TV dial and provided the reference point for its cultural dos and don'ts.

Despite the cultural import of Minow's speech, its impact on public television has not yet been addressed. Most critical historical accounts protest the system's dependence on corporate funders in the wake of conservative pressures dating back to the Nixon administration. According to this established narrative, beset by political opposition and funding shortfalls, PBS succumbed to a "safely splendid" marketing logic that stymies controversial programming.[3] While the "creeping commercialization" thesis does bring important political economic constraints to the table, it downplays the importance of culture and ideas. Pointing fingers at corporate America, scholars have ignored the broader discursive formation grounded by Minow's influential metaphor, and the social/cultural image it helped construct for public television.[4] In the United States, public broadcasting's raison d'être was to manage the "TV problem" as it was conceived by experts and tastemakers, not to provide a popular-democratic alternative to capitalist cultural production. Contrary to the major public service systems operating in Europe, the Public Broadcasting Service was envisioned as a corrective cultural supplement, and its marginalized role was both legitimated and compounded by its comparative prestige. Just as bourgeois culture needs the "low-other" to define its high status, according to cultural theorists Peter Stallybrass and Allon White, the superlatives ascribed to the "oasis" required the presumed mediocrity of the "vast wasteland" and its lowest-common-denominator mass audience.[5] This "ordering and sense-making" schema positioned public television against the grain of popularity, making it both attractive to upscale sponsors and vulnerable to conservative protests waged in the name of the common person. Focusing on only these consequences, however, puts the cart before the horse. To make sense of public television from a cultural studies perspective, we need to revisit the historical impetus to guide and manage the taste culture from which it sprang.

This chapter examines the discourse of the "vast wasteland" in order to rethink the logic of an oasis amid the ruins. Drawing from archival research and cultural theory, I argue that the high/low opposition conveyed by these metaphors has shaped public television's normative relationship with the people that it claims to represent. Public television was defined against a negative assessment of popular commercial television, regardless of what program was shown from one hour to the next. The distinction hinged on what cultural studies scholar Ien Ang calls the ideology of mass culture, or the assumption that programs geared to large numbers of people must be shoddy, cheap, manipulative, indulgent, and silly.[6] Three patterns that cut across philanthropic, social scientific, journalistic, and policy discussions of the "TV problem" are telling in this regard: the denigration of popular genres as trivial and low, the claim that the mass audience was responsible for the wasteland, and the assumption that better television would inevitably be crafted from above. Together, these conjectures warranted a "public" television alternative with an ambivalent view of the people, for its reform logic hinged on their presumed failures as cultural arbiters.

(De)Constructing the Television Problem

The binary that separates public television from Minow's vast wasteland is the logical conclusion of the "unresolvable" cultural tension that historian Michele Hilmes observes at the very heart of U.S. broadcasting. On one hand, the private corporations that controlled radio were held accountable to a liberal public service ethos dominantly interpreted as the transmission of legitimated knowledge and culture with a capital "C." On the other hand, broadcasting was a corporate business that profited from the sale of advertising and, therefore, the ritualized listening of the "feminized" mass audience. When popular entertainment became the leading conveyor of the mass movement of merchandise, radio became the target of critical contempt and a broadcast reform movement orchestrated mainly (but not exclusively) by private foundations, university educators, and well-placed citizen groups. As Robert McChesney shows in his chronicle of its peak in the early 1930s, the bid to recast radio as a noncommercial venture—as it had been, in its earliest years—was blunted by corporate lobbying campaigns that pledged public service compliance while demonizing "haughty" broadcasting reformers and the high-quality, uplifting programs that they championed. Public broadcasting was finally authorized three decades after the 1934 Communications Act sanctioned private control as the American way. When the new medium of television emerged at the center of postwar culture and society, the residual tension between high cultural expectations and the drive to manufacture popularity resurfaced with a vengeance.[7]

Some doomsayers deemed television an instant threat to civilization. Other critics lamented the apparent passage of commercial television's "golden age," when they could find operas and symphony performances (NBC had its own orchestra), live plays, documentaries, arts programming, education, and expert discussions of public affairs outside what became known as the Sunday morning "egghead" hour. The television networks had initially broadcast high culture alongside popular programs like variety shows and situation comedies adapted from radio formats, partly to lure monied viewers to buy television sets. But the most prestigious commercial programs—*Playhouse 90*, *Studio One*, opening night at the Metropolitan Opera, *See It Now*—were underwritten by single sponsors hoping to reach upscale viewers or were sustained by the networks themselves as a public-service gesture. Such fare was phased out as TV set ownership mushroomed and commercial broadcasters realized that they could maximize revenue by selling multiple advertising spots within standardized serial entertainment filmed in Hollywood. By the late 1950s, the operational goal was to attract the largest possible audience and smooth its flow from one program to the next.[8]

At a time when the clever ratings instruments now used to differentiate "desirable" viewers according to consumer demographics had not yet been implemented and ninety-eight cable channels were the stuff of science fiction, competition for gross numbers among the three major networks shaped the television culture beamed into everyone's homes. In the eyes of some observers, television addressed an uncultivated crowd at the expense of an intelligent and cultured minority. For others, the pressing issue was that a potentially edifying medium had become another crude amusement in the service of hawking soda pop and shaving cream. According to one commentator, "We have triumphantly invented, perfected, and distributed to the humblest cottage throughout the land one of the greatest technical marvels in history, television, and have used it for what? To bring Coney Island into every home."[9]

The complaints about commercial television that gained influence and legitimacy in postwar America shared an aversion to mass culture compounded by the pressing but largely unacknowledged contradictions of postwar capitalism. Broadcasters' quest to maximize profits was sanctioned by the ideology of free enterprise, and yet this same quest spawned prime-time television programming that mocked America's claim to pluralism and undermined the cultural authority of the educated white male bourgeoisie. Commercial television was perfectly in sync with the "fun morality" noted by alarmed sociologists of the day, and as such it helped circulate the values (enjoy! indulge! spend!) of the burgeoning consumer economy.[10] The medium's cultural association with hedonistic entertainment, passive relaxation, and mental escape clashed with high hopes for enlightened democracy, the macho image of a world superpower, and the credo of hard work and self-improvement ascribed to the American Dream. The discourse of the vast wasteland managed these intersecting tensions without addressing their messy origins, by presenting the "TV problem" as a cultural malady closely aligned with—and perhaps caused by—a fictional construction of the mass audience. The discursive formation grounded by Minow's metaphor undermined popular debate about television by situating policy decisions within the expert-governed boundaries of quality and audience comportment, not unlike the postwar debate over mass culture documented by historian Jackson Lears.

According to Lears, the economic boom of the 1950s led the nation's intellectuals (critics, academics, policy advisers, professional thinkers) to new pressing problems that coalesced around the quality and homogenizing effects

of mass culture. Although liberals were most apt to discover a "national purpose" in these issues, the fixation cut across political lines. Cold war ideology encouraged "consensus" among economic elites, intellectuals, and philanthropists, creating what Andrew Ross called a "discursive climate that
equated social, cultural and political difference with disease." The growth of
public universities and the related expansion of the white-collar professional middle class, composed of college-educated people who worked with
knowledge instead of "making things," made it easier, Lears believes, to dis-
place "questions of power" onto treatable cultural symptoms. Intellectuals of
various stripes took the level of mass culture as demonstrable proof that the
upwardly mobile people needed (and perhaps secretly wanted) the "direction of a cultural elite."[11] Vance Packard summed up this critical sentiment
in his 1959 book *The Status Seekers: An Exploration of Class Behavior in America*. According to Packard,

> In modern America, where especially at the consuming level the
> masses have to a large extent become the dictators of taste, we have
> to endure the horrors of our roadside architecture and billboards;
> our endless TV gun-slinging; our raw, unkempt, blatantly commer-
> cialized cities; our mass merchandising of pornographic magazines;
> our faceless suburban slums-to-be; our ever-maudlin soap operas.
> Voices have been crying out for the restoration of some kind of elite
> that can set standards and make them stick.[12]

Similar thinking prompted the 1960 President's Commission on National Goals to declare that American mass culture was in a state of emer-
gency. The report *Goals for America*, prepared for the outgoing Eisenhower
administration, contained a scathing assessment, "The Quality of American
Culture," by August Heckscher, president of the 20th Century Fund, a New
York City philanthropy. Heckscher zeroed in on the "TV problem" and took
commercial broadcasters to task for undermining the public interest by pandering to an "audience eager for fourth-rate material." Echoing Packard's
conflation of accelerated consumerism with mass taste, he asserted that the
burgeoning postwar affluence had not spawned higher levels of cultural sophistication in the mass public. On the contrary, Americans had become a
"great mass prepared to listen long hours to the worst of TV or radio." Para-
doxically, if the hoi polloi were setting the sights for broadcasting, as
Heckscher claimed, the mass market was simultaneously "virtually abolish-
ing" class distinctions, rendering the United States too close to communism
for this cold war critic.[13]

The "TV problem," as Michael Curtin argues in his revisionist study of the golden age of network documentary, emerged just as social scientists and cultural critics were embracing American pluralism as the "distinguishing difference between free societies and totalitarian ones." Mass culture—especially prime-time commercial television, was not easy to reconcile with this theory. But Heckscher's distaste had nothing to do with television's presentation of prosperous white middle-class suburban families as the national norm, to the exclusion of everyone else. His dismay at seeing everyone offered the "same culture" on their television sets was rivaled only by his alarm that "women at different levels of income dress indistinguishably" and that the "most luxurious housing units boast the same dish washing machine available in almost any worker's home."[14] This defensive response to cultural homogenization spoke to the loss of class differences and, implicitly, to the enormous social authority they bestowed on "tasteful" people like Heckscher.

The year after *National Goals* appeared in paperback, John F. Kennedy arrived in the White House, and his reform-minded appointee to the Federal Communications Commission declared television to be a "vast wasteland." Newton Minow, a Northwestern University-educated lawyer, brought to the regulator's chair a mixture of liberal idealism and Camelot's cultural tastes. While his intentions were humanitarian, both his famous speech and his overall concerns about television culture mirrored Heckscher's diatribe in crucial ways. Minow also glossed over thorny issues like private ownership and commercial sponsorship, treating "screaming, cajoling and offending" advertisements mainly as cultural offenses, not unlike the Highway Beautification Act later championed by Lady Bird Johnson to curb the "visual pollution" created by tasteless outdoor billboards.[15] Minow also drew from the ideology of mass culture in his plea for better programs, implying that "assembly line" entertainment catering to a mass audience was, by its very nature, mediocre, uninteresting, and banal. Minow's ideals illustrate sociologist Pierre Bourdieu's claim that the ranking of culture is indirectly related to the ranking of people in capitalist democracies. This process is not seamless, conspiratorial, or even necessarily conscious, but it does bear on what is deemed "obviously" worthy, tasteful, and sophisticated and what is not.

In 1961, good culture was closely aligned with a social world defined by upper-middle-class family networks, prestigious universities, and generational privilege, much as it is today. As Bourdieu explains, culture embraced by those who hold a disproportionate amount of social, intellectual, and cultural power tends to be universalized as the national ideal. The savviest cultural connoisseurs do not necessarily own factories or gargantuan trust funds, but they are socialized from infancy into the restricted knowledge, tastes, and dispositions that define what Bourdieu calls a legitimated social space or "habitus." For post-Marxists like Bourdieu, class is more than property, income, and occupation; it is also constructed and lived through a "whole set of subsidiary characteristics" having to do with culture and lifestyle, geographical origins, family connections, gender and race, and educational credentials. While presented as obviously superior according to commonsense criteria, the definition of good television promoted by reformers like Minow was socially and historically bound to urban, upper-middle-class, white Eurocentric, university-bound, and, very often, masculine experiences. Officially available to anyone, it favored those with the required "cultural capital" to belong, which constructed an aura of innate sophistication around television's most visibly disaffected.

The upwardly mobile middle classes could also acquire socially legitimated cultural capital through the expanding public education system, but this relationship was taken to be pedagogical, not "natural." For those lacking both inherited and educational channels of access, culture was enshrined with the symbolic equivalent of a barbwire fence. Despite progressive dreams of harnessing broadcasting as an instrument of mass public uplift, most people were socialized by their habitus and subordinated place in society to prefer what Bourdieu calls the popular aesthetic, or accessible images and narratives that do not require a studious or detached "contemplation" to appreciate and that reward everyday knowledge and allow for visceral responses like emotion, laughter, and suspense. The "denial of lower, coarse, vulgar, venal, servile" enjoyment implies an "affirmation of the superiority of those who can be satisfied with the sublimated, refined, disinterested, gratuitous, distinguished pleasures forever closed to the profane," writes Bourdieu. "That is why art and cultural consumption are predisposed, consciously and deliberately or not, to fulfill a social function of legitimating social differences."[16]

When socieoeconomic inequalities exist, the "best" culture can never be made accessible to everyone, argues Bourdieu. The content of "high" culture can and does fluctuate over time, explains Stuart Hall, but its hierarchical relationship to "low" culture always validates the heritage and competencies of society's powerful groups. Likewise, what is broadly accessible is less valued, partly because it is not restricted to cultural and intellectual elites. In the United States, the glitch in Bourdieu's influential theory is that the culture industries have colonized and mainstreamed the popular aesthetic in their quest to maximize profits. As Hall pointed out, the commodification of popular culture in its "mass-cultural, image-mediated, technological forms" has not fully displaced Matthew Arnold's European-inflected definition of culture, but it has steadily eroded its ideological influence. In the late 1950s and early 1960s, commercial television became the most visible display of this capitalist contradiction. In this context, traditionalists like Heckscher protested the collapse of cultural distinctions, and Minow struggled to reconcile culture with commerce.[17]

Liberal reformers who protested the quality of the vast wasteland did not advocate public ownership of broadcasting. When Minow told private broadcasters that they must serve the public interest to justify their use of publicly owned airwaves, his goal was to improve the medium's cultural performance. Minow's displeasure with the "steady procession" of amusements that he saw populating prime-time commercial television was partly filtered through cold war anxieties about national defense. In his "vast wasteland" speech, for example, he cited political chaos in the Congo and "communist tyranny" in the Caribbean as public-interest dilemmas that warranted the subordination of profits to advance the cultural frontier. Minow was mainly concerned with issues of quality, however, and it is telling in this regard that he also singled out the most popular TV genres of the early 1960s—situation comedies, soap operas, Westerns, and quiz shows—as the principal signs of cultural malaise. Minow did not invent such thinking: By the time he declared TV a "vast wasteland," the medium was already coded as feminine and low, partly because it was closely associated with formula, repetition, spectacle, emotion, fantasy, mass distribution, and "assembly line" production, the basic characteristics of what has long been derided as mass culture.[18] According to Lynn Joyrich, complaints about television's crass commercialism tended to belie gender anxieties as well. Since commercial television addressed "all viewers" as potential consumers, it also constituted them as feminine to the extent that consumption and femininity are historically bound. For a society that was "desperately trying to shore up traditional distinctions," says Joyrich, television's implicitly feminine mass appeal address was not only contradictory but potentially "destabilizing" as well.[19]

If Minow's speech channeled these broader tensions and anxieties, the regulator's own social background also came to bear on his thinking about cultural policy. According to broadcast historian James Baughman, Minow came of age in a well-educated family that favored "prestige" programs like *Omnibus*. His subjective tastes were, in other words, much closer to the programs doomed to cancellation than those born of commercial broadcasting's attempt to attract large audiences. Minow was also influenced by TV critics who championed the "golden age," particularly Jack Gould of the *New York Times* and Norman Cousins and Robert Lewis Shayon of the *Saturday Review*. As Baughman observed, these men looked down on popular television programming, which they saw as a victim of Hollywood's lowbrow, standardizing tentacles. Following their lead, Minow dismissed popular genres instead of proposing creativity, diversity, and noncommercialism *within* them. When Minow told broadcasters that they must present a "wider range of choices, more diversity, more alternatives," he did not mean an expanded repertoire of popular programs. Rather, for Minow, as for the critics whose opinions he shared, better television meant *upgraded* programs imbued with educated and masculine connotations, like legitimate plays and panel discussions.[20]

Minow did not acknowledge the upper-middle-class, white, and largely male habitus from which he spoke. He promoted instead an unexamined, undebated, and seemingly universal understanding of the public interest, arguing that "it is not enough to cater to the nation's whims—you must also serve the nation's needs." The "public interest" to which he referred is not, however, obvious, for it is a deeply subjective construct.[21] For Minow, what the people *needed* was maturation and cultural uplift, a paternalistic premise that cast them as infantile and flawed in their constitution as a mass audience. Implicitly held responsible for commercial television's cultural shortcomings, the public was thought to require "protection, regulation, and rule," not a participatory role in the medium's governance. This is a textbook example of what television theorist John Hartley calls protective "paedocracy," or the regulatory flip side of the "pleasure regime" that orients commercial broadcasting.[22]

Just as for Raymond Williams, for whom there were no masses, only ways of "seeing people as masses," Hartley approaches television audiences as institutional "fictions" created and circulated by the television industry and its regulatory bodies for their own institutional purposes. To maximize profits, commercial broadcasters often imagine hypothetical viewers as childlike, says Hartley; they are especially apt to paedocrize "in the name of pleasure" when courting the largest audience possible. Broadcasters harness the popular aesthetic with broad appeals that cut across social and educational differences, so that popularity is organized around inclusiveness and pleasure, not pedagogy or exclusion. Instead of judging popular television on aesthetic grounds, Hartley stresses the controlling and corporatized dimensions of the paedocratic regime.[23] He rejects cultural hierarchies without alternately celebrating the commercial marketplace—thereby providing a useful conceptual model from which to recognize the programs condemned by the discourse of the vast wasteland as popular—in a paedocrized and corporatized form.

Regulatory institutions like the FCC often infantilize television viewers, too, by "speaking about and for them," according to Hartley. Minow's vast wasteland speech did the same by casting the mass audience as immature, uncultivated, and therefore unable to distinguish between wants and needs. Television was corroding the public interest as defined by educated officials, for "given a choice between a Western or a symphony, most people will watch the Western." This argument *presumes* the tawdry and corrosive status of the Western and ascribes the correct taste to those who prefer the symphony. Not choosing the "best" was taken as a sign of an undeveloped character, not as evidence of cultural and educational difference. Such thinking was part of the discourse about television during the 1960s, and as such it came to bear on the social construction of PBS. Why consult the public when, as one critic lamented, it "chooses—again and again and again—the frivolous as against the serious, 'escape' as against reality, the lurid as against the tragic, the trivial as against the serious, fiction as against fact, the diverting as against the significant"?[24]

The tendency of the mass audience to choose "wants" over "needs" was treated as a discipline problem that could be managed by regulators and broadcasters. Assumptions about television's lowness intersected with anxieties about its promotion of amusement over respectable activities like work and learning. Constructing an analogy that ascribed these problems to the fictionalized mass audience, Minow argued that if parents and teachers followed "ratings," children would be spoiled by ice cream and holidays. Class and gender were, once again, implicit parts of this troubling portrait of the collective id. As Curtin notes, the valorization of the "productive labor" in watching educational television programs over the "passive consumption" ascribed to popular entertainment correlates with stereotypical renditions of the lazy, feminized masses: consider Joe Sixpack glued to the TV set, or the archetypal housewife, in bathrobe and curlers, addicted to soap operas. Commercial broadcasters were not being asked to discipline university professors or corporate CEOs; nor was *New York Times* TV critic Jack Gould referring to sophisticated male newspaper readers when he opined that the "mass audience can be childlike; it will generally choose candy over spinach." *TV Guide*, though, dutifully informed its readers that they stood accused of gorging on "popcorn and candy" instead of selecting a "nutritious meal." The solution echoing across these venues blamed issues pertaining to cultural production and control on viewer self-discipline, as epitomized by the headline "Not Until You Finish Your Vegetables."[25]

The discourse of the vast wasteland ignored commercial television's failure to serve every minority except one: college-educated people with "respectable" tastes. People who shared Minow's criticisms of television tended to be "well-heeled upper-middle class," not just in cultural representation but in sociological terms as well. Although "expert at mobilizing a PTA, they made for a minor constituency, an elite," says Baughman in his examination of Minow's reform tactics. Conspicuous by their absence were "members of the working class or racial and ethnic minorities who, while arguably victimized by television, evinced little displeasure with the medium." Minow's vast wasteland speech was just the most famous example. Social scientific studies and public opinion polls also reported that the "most literate and alert Americans" were least happy with television. In all these discursive forums, the issue of commercial control over television culture was displaced onto the class and gender implications of television's acquiescence to "majority rule."[26]

In 1965, *Newsweek* declared that television had become a "boob tube" because the tastes of its "most ardent viewers don't run to the *Partisan Review*." Sophisticated people had "no choice but to shun their set," especially when "Westerns and comedies were offered." Beneath this contempt for "others" were unstated concerns about television's negative impact on the educated middle class. Stallybrass and White noticed that moments when the low especially troubles the high speak to repressed anxieties in dominant social groups, a discovery that seems to explain the fanfare surrounding Gary Steiner's 1963 social scientific study *The People Look at Television*. Funded by commercial broadcasters, the study garnered enormous media attention and was even excerpted in three installments by *TV Guide*. In it, Steiner contended that people with college degrees and higher incomes were more apt to associate television with low culture and laziness. When asked what kind of people the "programs on the air today are designed for," many such respondents cited the indiscriminate mass audience, a category populated by "people who just go to work, come home, and vegetate." Steiner also found that the tendency to distinguish between "me and other people" rose sharply with education, as did the tendency to "find something redeeming" about favorite programs that justified watching them. Compared with "average" people who found pleasure and relaxation in TV viewing, this "disaffected" minority was characterized as deeply anxious. According to Steiner's profile,

> As a middle-class, striving American, he more acutely feels the need to spend time usefully than his less ambitious counterparts; and his formal schooling has placed a high value on reading and serious study. This combination attaches more than a little uneasiness to the hours he spends being entertained without effort by materials he regards of little intrinsic worth. If he could only learn something—historical, political, scientific, cultural—that would justify this otherwise unproductive use of time.[27]

In addition to articulating differences between the mass audience and the selective audience, Steiner's study reported a "perplexing gap" between what disaffected respondents said they wanted from television and what they watched. Many, he asserted, did not choose culture and information over popular entertainment when it was offered, a pattern that led him to propose that the critical segments of the television audience were not nearly so selective as their survey responses suggested. These contradictions—and the inability of social scientists to explain them—suggest that during the 1960s, educated middle-class identity and television were perceived as being antithetical. At the same time, it could be that the sophisticated cultural minority constructed by critics and social scientists felt that it too was falling prey to the lapses of taste and character ascribed to the mass television audience. Why else would *Newsweek* take pains to distinguish its readers from the "low others" held responsible for the vast wasteland? Television's faults were perhaps also its forbidden pleasures, and not just for the scapegoated millions.[28]

The Perils of Cultural Democracy

In 1965, *CBS Reports* tackled a related issue. In a documentary called "The Ratings Game," William Henry, Minow's successor at the FCC, confessed that ratings had more clout in commercial broadcasting than the federal regulatory agency did. Four years after Minow's vast wasteland speech, prime-time television was still dominated by formulaic amusements like *Petticoat Junction, Gilligan's Island,* and *The Beverly Hillbillies.* Network executives claimed they were merely "giving the people what they wanted," as proven by the figures supplied by the A. C. Nielsen company, the nation's preeminent TV ratings service. In cultural studies, broadcast ratings are considered to be a social construct used by the television industry and its associates in the commercial advertising industry to define, manage, and therefore control the audience. Scholars who accept ratings figures as a measure of something tangible stress their narrow reportage of the "commodity audience" for programs that the commercial television industry, based on its own market assumptions and projections, has been willing to provide. In policy and popular discourse, however, ratings treated very differently. At the peak of the "TV problem," commercial television's reliance on ratings was said by network executives and appalled critics alike to have spawned a "cultural democracy."[29]Since public television also was conceptualized in this discursive milieu, we should consider the "cultural democracy" argument and its legacy.

"The Ratings Game" typified journalistic and policy discussions of the ratings by pitting the discourse of the vast wasteland against the corporate defense of "cultural democracy." Both discourses spoke *for* the people, a pattern duplicated by the documentary, which interviewed credentialed experts and executives only. The program began with the question of accuracy, which was defined as the extent to which the statistical samples of the Nielsen company and other ratings agencies sufficiently measured the "right" kind of people. This had been an issue since 1959, when popular quiz shows were discovered to be rigged. Although the ratings were not implicated in television's deceit, the scandal brought the genre into the spotlight and raised questions about who watched the fraudulent programs. Between 1963 and 1964, a subcommittee of Congress held hearings on the ratings industry to assess the validity of its statistical measurements, reported the documentary. According to one congressman interviewed, the sample was suspected to contain too many "uneducated people" who watched a lot of television. From this point of view, ratings gave to the "heavy viewers" concentrated in the "bottom 60 percent of the population in educational and socio-economic standing" a disproportionate influence over television culture. Compounding this concern were the data-gathering techniques accused of overrepresenting the working class and the indigent poor. According to an *Atlantic Monthly* exposé, congressional investigators discovered that field researchers working in "apartment areas" tended to approach the building's janitors because they, unlike white-collar professionals, were usually at home during business hours. Even more disturbing to some critics was the discovery that the families chosen to represent the TV-viewing preferences of an oil-rich Oklahoma town with "large professional populations and three colleges" lived in "slum housing" and subsisted on government relief.[30]

In the CBS documentary, executives defended the TV ratings in populist terms. Characterizing themselves as followers of the popular "vote," they aligned the commercial broadcasting industry with the common people against snobbish elites. Arrogant critics are really saying that "nobody in their right mind could watch those kinds of programs," proclaimed a typical executive interviewed by the program. A. C. Nielsen himself insisted that the ratings were impartial and democratic to the extent that they offered every home in the United States an "equal opportunity" to get into the "representative" statistical sample. "We are merely counters of the ballot box," asserted the founder of the leading ratings company; any inaccuracies had been fixed with scientific expertise and technological advances, a point that was reiterated visually by footage of rows of gleaming steel machines tallying a representative sample of viewers' choices. For critics who accepted the new-

and-improved veracity of the ratings but protested the cultural outcome of the audience sample's "vote," the crux of the problem became, Is the majority suitably equipped to govern television culture? For the critics and reformers interviewed, the answer was obviously no, a stance that made it easy for commercial broadcasters to charge their detractors with unbridled cultural elitism.

Minow, for example, protested what he called the problem of the "slide rule," or television's tendency to favor "crowd pleasers" over better but less popular programs. Other critics complained that the ratings had killed good plays, symphony performances, and serious public affairs programs, the very genres that Minow had unsuccessfully pushed as FCC commissioner. Commercial broadcasters had two responses to their critics. The first was to argue that even when "people say they want" such programs, they do not actually watch them, a claim made in the ratings discourse as well as social scientific studies like Steiner's *The People Look at Television*. The second response was to hold up ratings measurements as a facilitator of cultural democracy in television. Comparing the ratings with the election of political candidates, the vice-president of CBS contended that in a cultural democracy, as in a political democracy, there is "nothing wrong with finding out what the people want." Television's disgruntled critics betrayed a "serious distrust of a people in a democracy," echoed another broadcast executive. "Why," he demanded to know, should a "committee at the top" dictate what is shown on television? By equating ratings with people's democratic participation, the industry's spokesmen obscured their own powerful role as the commercial shapers of television culture.

Industry discourse reflected a broader historical pattern. According to television historian William Boddy, since the 1950s, commercial broadcasters had been casting their critics as haughty elites who looked down on "plain folks," a discursive strategy drawn from corporate lobbying campaigns against the broadcast reform movement of the 1930s. As the "TV problem" intensified, so did the myth of cultural democracy and, with it, the demonization of "antidemocratic" television reformers. The broadcast industry reconstructed the fictionalized mass audience as empowered decision makers, defying and replacing the patronizing and childlike portrait constructed by Minow with an image of an empowered body politic. While it sounded respectful, this corporate rationalization provided no "real voice for audiences to speak within the institution," to use Hartley's argument.[31] By aligning itself with a "voting" majority of its own construction, the industry justified in populist terms its enormous cultural power, as well as its marketing strategies.

The fiction of the culturally franchised mass audience concealed the controlling nature of commercial broadcasting, and the industry's arguments spilled over into cultural forums. The intellectual magazine *American Mercury* agreed that in the case of commercial television, "the leaders of the nation do exactly what the people want them to do." *TV Guide* reported that if television was a "belt-line assemblage of repetitive inanity," it was because viewers liked it that way. Having accepted industry fiction, others pondered the consequences. In a book devoted entirely to the pressing question *Can You Give the Public What It Wants?* media critic Edgar Dale worried that the "cultural democracy of the majority" would bring about a cultural tyranny of the people. Other commentators phrased their concerns about cultural democracy in political terms. Some agreed with Edward R. Murrow, the famed journalist, who claimed that the medium's trivial amusements jeopardized "the virtue of the republic if not the security of Western democracy."[32]

High-level complaints about the cancellation of prestigious but poorly rated news shows like Murrow's *See It Now* were harder for the industry to dismiss as cultural elitism. Baughman proposes that the broader anxieties accompanying such complaints signaled a "crack" in the liberal corporate faith that commercial broadcasters could both be "good entrepreneurs" and serve the public interest. The myth of cultural democracy had also implicated the feminized, lowly masses in what Toby Miller calls the "conflicting demands" of the consumer economy (selfishness, pleasure, indulgence) and the political order (ethics, discipline, civic duty). In this context, public television could—for the first time in the nation's history—be justified as a device to uplift the people while serving the opinion leaders displaced by the people's hedonistic programming choices. To meet these dual imperatives, it would have to be the cultural opposite of commercial television, for the restoration of democracy hinged on the assumption that mass wants and public needs were diametrically opposed. Taking his ideological bearings from Minow's wasteland speech, one educational broadcaster characterized the "public-interest problem" as an overabundance of light entertainment caused by the people's insatiable demands for enjoyment. Typifying the discursive milieu in which public television emerged, he explained that

> we are in trouble as we unconsciously confuse the interests (tastes) of the public with the public interest, which is what broadcasting, under law, is charged to serve. For the public interest has little to do with our appetites and desires, however widely shared. It has everything to do with our needs, as human beings and citizens of this

democracy. In both realms our whims and appetites must be sub-
ordinate to our needs and duties.[33]

The "TV problem" spawned dual cultural reform logics, both of which
informed the commonsense priorities subsequently ascribed to public television. The first reform logic advocated the national development of a public-
service alternative to commercial television on the grounds that it would bypass the tastes and expectations of the indiscriminate mass audience and
operate at a higher level. At an intellectual summit to address the problem of
mass culture, which was attended by philosopher Hannah Arendt, social scientist Paul Lazarsfeld, and NBC president Frank Stanton, among other
prominent guests, the famed author and Kennedy adviser Arthur Schlesinger
Jr. urged the federal government to "rescue" a portion of television because
"soap opera and give-away" shows made more money for stockholders than
"news and Shakespeare" did. Conceding that since "horse opera sells more
autos than Ed Murrow, then the advertiser has to go for horse opera," John
Fischer, the editor of *Harper's* magazine, promoted the creation of a nonprofit national broadcasting authority to be run by a board of distinguished
directors which might include the "president of Harvard, the heads of the
Carnegie and Rockefeller Foundations, and the director of the Metropolitan
Museum." The proposed authority would plan "public-service" programs,
narrowly defined as in-depth news, serious music, and good theater. Under
the arrangement, which drew high praise from public officials, civic leaders,
and mass-culture critics like David Reisman, people who were "not interested" in superior public-service offerings could simply "turn to a Western on
CBS or a song-and-dance number on ABC."[34]

Walter Lippmann's declaration that there was something fundamentally wrong with U.S. television policy is another example of elevated cultural
reform logic. Writing in his *New York Herald Tribune* column in the wake of
the quiz show scandal, the influential social critic called commercial television a "prostitute of merchandising." His main complaint, however, was that
a "superb scientific achievement" was being misused at the expense of "effective news reporting, good art and civilized entertainment." For Lippmann, culture was an exception to the free-enterprise system he supported.
Taking the quiz deceit as an opportunity to decry commercial cultural standards, he proposed that "the people at Harvard and Yale and Princeton and
Columbia and Dartmouth" find a way to run a public-service network that
would show "not what was popular but what was good." Presuming that
good television as he envisioned it would never attract a substantial or inclusive viewership, he reasoned that it would make "up in influence what it

lacked in numbers."[35] Lippmann articulated what many critics had proposed, namely, that quality was incompatible with quantity. From this perspective, the principal problem with commercialism was the cultural degradation spawned by the industry's desire to serve large and presumably indiscriminate audiences.

Lippmann's template for public-service television was so unapologetically arrogant that it had little chance of attracting either federal funding or broad bipartisan political support. However, the elevated reform logic epitomized by his column coexisted with another, more pedagogic vision that promised to extend the benefits of public broadcasting, effectively serving the people by improving them. Like the proverbial chicken and egg, the question was which came first, an audience naturally predisposed to appreciate high culture or high-culture programming that viewers could be gradually taught to appreciate. The decision makers' opinions split right down the middle. Minow believed that the people could be uplifted by the cultural upgrades he championed, and the president of the American Council for Better Broadcasts proposed that "the surest way to get programming of higher quality and taste is to have audiences with better taste." Throughout the postwar period, social scientists at Columbia University's Bureau of Applied Social Research maintained that the level of popular taste could be raised with increased exposure to the best, despite the critical contempt generated by NBC president Pat Weaver's "Operation Frontal Lobe," a short-lived attempt in the 1950s to insert bits of cultural enlightenment into popular television entertainment. While those who defended the instructional capacities of the mass television audience were arguably more humanitarian, the pedagogic reform logic they espoused presumed that cultural authorities (like themselves) should and could manage popular taste by merging behaviorist strategy and cultural expertise.[36]

With the emergence of Great Society programs and rhetoric in the early 1960s, this presumption gained an egalitarian component, in which raising taste by diffusing high culture was fused to the democratic promise of equal opportunity and improved quality of life for *all* Americans. "Many people are not rejecting the best—they simply had never had the opportunity to choose it," said one such supporter. This promise tempered the Lippmanesque vision and attracted people like Senator (and later President) Lyndon Johnson, a former Texas schoolteacher who advocated education but was no cultural intellectual, to the cause of public broadcasting In 1964, FCC Chairman William Henry and Education Commissioner Francis Keppel, whose father had promoted the dissemination of Great Books in the 1930s as the president of the Carnegie Corporation, declared in a speech to educational broadcasters that it was time to overcome "our electronic Appalachia." We "must find ways to make the medium serve one of its highest and most natural uses—as a means of eliminating cultural poverty"—by making culture and enlightenment "available to everyone," not just an elite.[37] Significantly, although Lippmann's overtly elitist vision and Great Society-infused pedagogic reforms had different aims, both called for the creation of a public-service alternative operating against the grain of popular appeal. For practical reasons, both also hinged on the national expansion of "educational television," a spattering of low-budget stations licensed to communities, universities, and school systems across the states. Since public television was built from the remnants of the ETV (educational television) system, we now will take a brief detour to reconsider this mostly forgotten blip in the cultural history of American television.

The Classroom in the Parlor

In the 1950s, ETV stations pioneered what we now call distance education, providing televised instruction to schools and colleges and vocational courses to adults. These services have survived in many locales, assisted by modest federal resources. ETV also broadcast quasi-instructional cultural and public affairs programming, providing the only alternative to commercial television until the national formation of the Public Broadcasting Service. Like public television, it was conceptualized and created for the people, not by them. The system did not emerge from popular demand but, as even educational broadcasters conceded, was "forced into being" by private foundations, reformers, and educators hoping to rescue television from the ravages of commercial entertainment. In the late 1930s, the FCC granted limited space on the outer reaches of the FM radio band to universities, setting a precedent for noncommercial educational channels. In the late 1940s, reformers organized to extend to television this land grant of the airwaves. The Rockefeller Foundation and the Institute for Communication Research at the University of Illinois convened university broadcasters, mass communication scholars, and representatives from the U.S. Department of Education to conceptualize "educational television." Under the leadership of social scientist Wilbur Schramm, the participants devised a "curriculum" stressing liberal arts and sciences, great works of literature, and the transmission of wisdom, knowledge, and expertise. Although they did not define their work as such, advocates devised a way to mitigate the cultural contradictions of postwar capitalism. At the core of their vision was a move to validate the legitimated habitus while addressing the mass audience as pupils instead of children at recess. ETV was conceptualized as the "second chance" for television, or the "panacea that would make it possible for the educators to preserve civilization."[38]

Supporters were not calling for a popular-democratic alternative to commercial control over broadcasting. Instead, the impetus was to develop television as an educational technology for cultivating knowledge and cultural excellence. This was as true of the left-leaning political economist Dallas Smythe as it was of the Ford Foundation, ETV's main benefactor. In 1950, Smythe published an influential critique of U.S. television policy in which he defined the public interest against the backdrop of commercial programs charged with "triteness, ineptitude, vulgarity, and pandering to addicts of formula entertainment on a tawdry level." Characterized in this way, the TV problem called for protective paedocracy, not public input, for as Smythe explained, the "parent and the operator of a popular art agency have a common responsibility." Smythe's 1951 analysis of "One Week of Commercial Television," a study carried out at the Waldorf Astoria Hotel by a team of volunteers who admitted to "hating" the programs they meticulously documented, was used to support their reservations to the FCC about an educational channel. Funded by Ford and publicized on the front page of the *New York Times*, the study brought scientific credibility to subjective complaints about television's mediocrity. Taking the idealized cultural tastes he shared with many fellow educators and philanthropists as an objective measure of the public interest, Smythe protested the absence of classical music, a lone educational program, and an overall negligence to "enduring art and literature." Anticipating the discourse of the vast wasteland, his study called for a parental authority to redeem television culture.[39]

The Ford Foundation also envisioned television as a conduit for culture and adult education, a vision accountable not to the public but to the priorities established by its white, male, upper-class trustees. Like other philanthropies created to spend tax-exempt fortunes amassed by industrial capitalists, the automaker's philanthropy wielded considerable power and influence in postwar society. Beyond defining and orchestrating the "public good" with the foundation's impressive checkbook, its prominent executives shaped national policy as informal advisers and government appointees. In the late 1940s, flush with a hefty allowance of Ford Motor Company stock, the foundation embarked on a multifaceted campaign to develop "mature, wise and responsible citizens who can participate intelligently in a free society."[40] Its mission was "governmental" in the cultural sense theorized by Tony Bennett. Drawing from Michel Foucault's view of administrative power, Bennett defines governmentality as subtly shaping, guiding, and reforming people (including those of us who internalize such directives) toward manageable ends, whether that means uplifting popular taste or encouraging desired habits, behaviors, and morals. The social management inherent in cultural governmentality can be traced to Matthew Arnold's promotion of the pursuit of the "best" culture over "doing what one's ordinary self likes" so as to improve taste, instill discipline, and prevent "anarchy." Under the auspices of its Fund for Adult Education, the Ford Foundation instituted a modern version of Arnold's vision. The foundation helped develop and fund adult discussion groups, recordings, pamphlets, radio programs, and films, coupling cultural guidance with broadcast technology so as to enlarge the "abilities of persons to choose the good in the best order."[41]

The foundation was deeply unimpressed with the cultural level of commercial television and initially intervened with *Omnibus* (1951–1956), created by its Radio-Television Workshop. *Omnibus* coupled light entertainment with edifying segments designed to promote classical music, dance, literature, drama, philosophy, history, and science. Attracting viewers with popular appeals, it sought to cultivate their capacity for sophistication and good taste. With his genteel demeanor and British accent, host Alistair Cooke brought refinement to the program, but he also addressed the imagined viewer as a tentative and possibly resistant pupil, prefacing uplifting lessons with soothing promises like "this won't hurt a bit." *Omnibus* strove to make legitimated culture accessible to upwardly mobile television viewers who were, presumably, more comfortable with the popular aesthetic. A typical segment entitled "Isn't Opera Grand" promised to reorient people "who think of opera as a formidable figure as the mother-in-law"; another spiced up an educational lecture on the U.S. Constitution with musical numbers, dramatic reenactments, and costumes. *Omnibus* was ridiculed for its "midcult" tendencies and showbiz flair by high-culture purists like the influential art critic Dwight MacDonald, who also wrote an influential *New Yorker* essay and book on the Ford Foundation. They need not have worried, for the hybrid program survived only four years, despite solid Ford Foundation backing and a proven ability to attract upscale commercial sponsors, or "subscribers," as Cooke discreetly called them. After bouncing from one network to the next, *Omnibus* was canceled when no one would risk a plunge in the evening's ratings to broadcast the program. To Ford, the debacle proved that "commercial TV did not provide a dependable vehicle for high-quality cultural and informational programming on a continued basis."[42]

This is how ETV became, by default, the Ford Foundation's principal hope for "mature" television. According to his biographers, Henry Ford believed strongly in enlightenment for all, as he showed by distributing *McGuffy's Readers* to workers in his plants in Detroit. Before his death, the inventor of the assembly line reportedly harbored a vision of ETV stations "singing like a beacon over the country to show the light to others." In 1952, when the FCC agreed to reserve spectrum space for educational channels, his charity helped get the "classroom in the parlor" off the ground. Millions of dollars were pumped into ETV station development and programming via the auspices of the Fund for Adult Education, supervised by a one-time marketing executive named C. Scott Fletcher. Raised in an academic family devoted to "the cause of education almost like missionaries," Fletcher recalled "going to the theater and opera" as a routine similar to attending church. After a stint at the Studebaker Corporation, he served as president of Encyclopedia Britannica films. Believing that every home would eventually have a sound motion-picture projector, Fletcher promoted educational films in his position as a trustee of the Committee for Economic Development, a coalition of business elites devoted to strengthening the postwar free-market economy. In speeches like "Capitalism Versus Totalitarianism," he promoted the marriage of audiovisual media and liberal adult education as a boon to commercial enterprise, claiming that educational films in particular could help prevent labor strikes, discourage "collectivism," and produce learned and appreciative citizens of the free world. "We know that enlightenment is only partial in our time . . . we must bring more weapons to bear on ignorance."[43]

Fletcher got the opportunity to put his vision into practice at Fund for Adult Education, using the Ford Foundation's sizable bankroll to develop television as an educational force in the home. The optimism he brought to his philanthropic post epitomizes the love-hate relationship with television that spoke to long-standing progressive dreams of using mass culture for uplifting ends, filtered through the ideological peculiarities of the cold war. According to Michael Curtin, what "elevated the critique of TV to a particularly lofty level of concern among American leaders was that TV's shortcomings might be turned into assets. That is, the same medium that was used to mesmerize the masses might transport them . . . to understand social concerns."[44] In a 1947 speech entitled "Maintaining World Peace Through Mass Communications," delivered to the Advertising Federation of America, Fletcher pitched the union of adult education and mass media in remarkably similar terms: "A basic idea can be disseminated until, like the process of chain reaction in the atom bomb, it can permeate all groups widely and bring about positive social action." Ironically, the basic idea that he was most keen on propagating was freedom.

ETV's mission, as shaped by the Ford Foundation and National Educational Television (NET), conflated the "problem" of mass culture with anxieties about communism. Good taste and the "free world" were inextricably bound in the promotion of an educational technology that could guide the American people in their duties as cultural connoisseurs and responsible citizens. This coupling ran through NET's most lavish educational programs, including a noteworthy documentary called "The Face of Russia" (which aired around 1960). Filmed on location in the Soviet Union with a sizable Ford grant, the documentary is completely devoid of the "pinko" sentiments that conservatives have long ascribed to public television. To the contrary, it solemnly educates TV viewers about the horrors of modern Marxism. While a male voice of authority converses off screen, the camera lingers on the strange ways of a clearly misguided land. Blaming socialistic totalitarianism for "brainwashing" the citizenry and also cultural homogeneity and hideously bad taste, the program concludes by ridiculing the cookie-cutter surroundings, "gaudy" tastes, and the overweight bodies of the Soviet masses.[45]

Fortunately, the push for "quantity over quality" had not yet produced a "faceless mass of interchangeable units" in the United States, explained Max Lerner, professor of American civilization at Brandeis University, in another NET program called *The Age of Overkill* (1962). Sitting on a desk in a book-lined study, Lerner lectured on the free world's answer to mass culture in a telling episode called "Power Elite and Creative Elite." While mass culture was indeed a pressing problem, all was not lost, for a minority within the mass had an enlarged capacity for "excellence." This "creative elite" would serve as cultural guardians, leading the nation toward uplift, much as educational television would.[46]

National Educational Television valorized the sophisticated, college-educated, intellectually oriented, implicitly white minority who protested television's cultural mediocrity while engaging its upwardly mobile aspirants in a pedagogic and frequently disciplinary relationship. *New York Times* TV critic Jack Gould presaged the dynamic when he urged educational channels for "minority tastes," meaning those held by the sorts of people who read national newspapers, read good books, and patronized art museums. When KCET-Los Angeles coined the station slogan "I Love Lucidity" in the early 1950s, it anticipated attracting viewers who were considerably more learned and sophisticated than *Lucy* fans—or who agreed that they ought be striving toward such goals. Only when John F. Kennedy took office in 1961, however, did ETV gain substantial ground as a "cultural ambassador to the nation's homes." Camelot and the rhetoric of the New Frontier brought unprecedented prestige to intellectuals, and in this context Ford's checks grew larger.

Meanwhile, the 1957 *Sputnik* embarrassment prompted Congress to chip in by funding the development of new stations in the name of national defense. While supporters were declaring that ETV television was for a "People Who Will Travel to the Moon!" television viewers were still mostly ignoring the classroom in the parlor, precisely because the programs so closely mimicked the staid classroom experience, filled with facts but devoid of pleasure.[47]

ETV was a decentralized system composed of local stations, whereas educational television was a shared cultural form, developed by educators who took as their principal models the "lecture, textbook and training film."[48] Preserved kinescopes and videotapes at the Library of Congress and the Museum of Radio and Television look and sound much like adult versions of the authoritative, black-and-white instructional filmstrips I remember seeing as a schoolgirl. Most ETV programs minimized television's unique capacity for orality and visuality and instead came across as unadorned and slow-moving interpretations of the written word, which led some enthusiastic critics to declare ETV to be "the greatest stimulus to culture since Gutenberg started setting type."[49] The print-derived aesthetic was not confined to no-budget lectures delivered in front of gray curtains. NET's national programs, which were delivered to the stations via the U.S. mail, also came across as erudite, serious, complex, and subdued—the exact opposite of the pleasure, fantasy, formula, and spectacle promised by commercial broadcasters. The look defined educational television, communicating its distinction from mass culture as much as a descriptive NET brochure promising a serious play, the rehearsal of a string quartet, or a lecture on the atom.

Whereas *Omnibus* was scorned for sugar-coating high culture, ETV did not "pander" to the mass audience, stylistically or otherwise. It could not, for beyond disseminating socially approved knowledge and tastes, its rationale was to discipline the fun morality that underpinned the burgeoning consumer culture. While the commercially sponsored networks moved merchandise, ETV's governmental mission was the "maturation" of the individual, noted the *Saturday Review*'s TV critic Robert Lewis Shayon, an avid supporter. Whereas commercial entertainment was condemned by critics and reformers for indulging "mass wants," ETV insisted that viewers learn, strive, pay attention, and, eventually, turn off the set and "do what has been suggested." *Spotlight on Opera* typified the disciplinary mode of address found on many ETV programs. In one episode, the tuxedoed master of ceremonies introduced the program with the command: "Don't do what you just wanted to do . . . turn the knob and switch to another station." Like the social scientists who believed that their laboratory experiments could improve popular taste, NET programs were mandated to "provide a stimulus" that contributed, "in the long run, toward a cumulative effect." Of course, the people could not be forced to cooperate in this agenda, and most apparently did not. According to *Channels of Learning: The Story of Educational Television,* the "quiet steps toward the making of an epoch" passed unnoticed by the enormous "audience of *Milton Berle, Sid Caesar* and the Roller Derby."[50]

NET continued to pitch ETV as an anecdote to the vast wasteland. In another 1964 brochure, the hub of the system promised to take Americans "out of our easy chairs and out of the stupors that mass entertainment has lured us into, and make us active and alive again." Despite such bold assertions, NET's intention was not to draw a crowd. Instead, ETV was conceived as television's equivalent to the "good library," geared to discerning individuals who visited with a specific purpose in mind and did not loiter. "A new kind of viewer seems to have been created by this new kind of broadcasting," reported *TV Guide.* "He turns to television, not to have fun but to work and to fill a need." Social scientists also valorized the "abnormally high percentage of college-educated viewers and professional and managerial families" who regarded educational television channels as exceptionally "purposeful" and "selective." For these viewers, ETV was deemed "respectable" because it did not "waste time," dealt with reality instead of fantasy, and had nothing "cheap, shoddy or in poor taste about it." Such claims routinely conflated "selectivity" with the social factors—education, socialization, gender—that, according to Bourdieu, guide people in their leisure practices and cultural choices. They also concealed the role of the culture industries in shaping leisure preferences. According to television historian Lynn Spigel, commercial broadcasters encouraged the habitual viewing habits scorned by critics by scheduling television programs to "punctuate" the rituals of family life and, in the process, maximize audience flow from one to the next. The "good library" ideal ascribed to ETV and later PBS ignored the social and corporate dimensions of established leisure practices and placed the onus for "purposeful" television viewing on the individual.[51]

Like the construction of the "TV problem," the discourse surrounding ETV constructed a hierarchy between licit and illicit leisure that carried over to commonsense thinking about public television. On the one hand, like formal learning, Good Television was valorized as active, redeemed by a positive association with work, self-improvement, purpose, and studious concentration. Bad Television, on the other hand, was deemed passive, associated with mindless pleasure, indulgence, and time wasting. From a cultural studies perspective, these binary categories are problematic, for several reasons. First, we all are active viewers who inevitably learn from the meanings circulated by television, including popular entertainment. Second, as sociologist Henri Lefevbre convincingly argued, the desire for distraction and temporary escape is not an individual character flaw. It is a broad social phenomenon that arises from the capitalist divide between labor and "free time." The tendency to avoid leisure that "appears to be educational" can be seen as audience resistance to overtime, as suggested by the non-ETV viewer who told researchers: "When I want to lounge around in the evening," this "crazy station . . . wants to give me a lecture." Finally, experiences of work and leisure are socially situated. For people with high-status white-collar jobs (i.e., lawyers, teachers, journalists, doctors, managers), work is "seen, and often experienced, as intrinsically rewarding, creative and important," observes Barbara Ehrenreich in her cultural study of the professional middle class. Professionals who gain mental stimulation and a positive source of identity from their work are also less apt to draw firm distinctions between work and pleasure. For laborers and female workers confined to the home, however, work tends to be less prestigious, more "monotonous," and rewarding mainly in the sphere of consumption.[52] The discursive construction of ETV obscured these social differences by validating the impetus to view educational programs demanding concentration, work, and productivity and condemning the desire to watch entertainment associated with unproductive relaxation and escape.

Despite being called "educational," ETV programs were also distinguished by content and style and were addressed to viewers with a formal education well beyond the typical high-school level. Acknowledging this bias in *TV Guide*, New York City's station manager confessed to giving priority to television viewers "who are well along the ladder, people who can make immediate use of the materials we give them. He told the magazine that his station was well aware of losing the least-educated segment of society by putting on a string quartet but thought it far worse to "alienate" sophisticated viewers "with too primitive a music program, beginning with somebody holding up an instrument and saying 'This is a violin.'" NET programs were especially apt to come across as the videotaped equivalent of graduate school. Highbrow and dense, "Basic Issues of Man" (1960) was a typical experiment in liberal adult education produced for NET with Ford funds by the University of Georgia. The point of "The Return of Prometheus" was to combat the public's "confused and fearful attitude" toward science. Coupling off-screen narration with vignettes performed by actors, it profiles a fictional scientist who is subtly compared with the Greek god Prometheus while a male voice reads a ponderous lecture filled with unexplained references to philosophers.

Invitation to Art (1960), produced for NET by WGBH-Boston, also presumed that its viewers had knowledge of the topic at hand. Filmed with a single camera on location at the city's Museum of Fine Arts, the show consists of a suit- and tie-clad male instructor with a pointer delivering an unedited lecture on the Impressionists. The solemn talk is laced with unexplained references to dozens of paintings as well as intimidating words like *misanthropic* and *enigmatic*. For those unfamiliar with artistic canons and intellectual terminology, the advanced lesson offered little opportunity for learning. *Pablo Casal's Master Class at Berkeley* (1961), produced by the University of California and also distributed by NET, similarly consists of an hour-long long shot of the famous cellist teaching protégés in a poorly lit gymnasium. The unedited practice session provides no introduction of the "master" to viewers unschooled in classical music and no narration to contextualize the event. From time to time, a male voice breaks the tedium to name specific techniques and pieces of music, but only in specialized jargon unfamiliar to most people (e.g., "the first movement of the Brahms Cello Sonata no.1 in E Minor").[53]

As the "TV problem" accelerated, the overtly instructional tenor of programs like these was gradually phased out. Why? For one thing, social scientific discourse continually reported that the ETV audience—while "well placed," according to sociological criteria—was tiny and sporadic. For another, Minow's failure to upgrade the vast wasteland put the hopes for better television on the existing noncommercial "educational" stations. In the mid-1960s, NET attempted to reposition itself as a "fourth network" known for quality cultural and informational programs, not pedantic lessons delivered by tweed-coated professors. The order came from the Ford Foundation, whose new president envisioned ETV more as a superior program service than an electronic schoolroom. McGeorge Bundy, a liberal intellectual and Boston Brahmin, had been a professor and dean at Harvard University before planning Vietnam War strategy as special assistant for national security affairs to Kennedy and Johnson. After graduating from Harvard, he helped his mentor Walter Lippmann update *The Good Society*, a 1937 blueprint for a "welfare market" state. For Bundy, noncommercial television, like the "strong government" he advocated, was perfectly compatible with liberal capitalism.[54]

After Bundy's arrival at Ford, NET attempted to revive the golden age of television by funding live drama, performing arts, concerts, sophisticated treatments of current events, documentaries, and prestigious BBC imports like *The Age of Kings*, a series of Shakespeare plays. While pursuing the good over the popular, as Lippmann had advised, NET continued to stress the benefits of ETV for the less fortunate, insisting that "few by few, through accidental or unintentional exposure, they will come to realize that the 'finest' is indeed the best."[55] At the same time, Bundy joined the chorus arguing for the national expansion of ETV. Ford's checkbook was not bottomless; NET programming was limited to around ten hours per week; and distribution by mail was both slow and cumbersome. ETV was still a long way from the public-service network that Lippmann advocated. In the mid-1960s, the discourse of the vast wasteland, the uplifting spirit of the Great Society, and the precedent set by the creation of the National Endowments for the Arts and Humanities created a moment hospitable to federal involvement. Once dismissed as unnecessary and un-American, the prospect of a national public broadcasting system gained credence, within boundaries. In 1966, its conceptual blueprint was crafted by a study group assembled by the Carnegie Corporation, another prominent philanthropy. By 1967, Congress had chartered the final solution to the "TV problem" in the form of the nonprofit Corporation for Public Broadcasting.

Blue-Ribbon Solution or Caviar Television?

The idea for a private corporation to be funded by public subsidies came from the Carnegie Commission on Educational Television, a "blue-ribbon" panel of prominent national business, educational, and cultural leaders. The commission and the public-private bureaucracy that it spawned exemplified what Thomas Streeter calls the "liberal corporate approach" to U.S. broadcasting policy. Streeter contends that the "social vision" that gave rise to U.S. broadcasting in the 1920s was "corporate liberalism," defined by a tendency to conceptualize the public interest as a component of capitalist principles, as opposed to an alternative value system. Unlike the policymakers critiqued by Streeter, the Carnegie Commission recognized the importance of noncommercial television. Yet the "public" alternative it championed was a complementary supplement to the dominant commercial broadcasting system, not a fundamentally different way of organizing television culture. The impetus, proposes Willard Rowland, was not to rethink the private commercial foundations of U.S. broadcasting but, rather, to maintain the legitimacy of that system by resolving its apparent "weaknesses and contradictions." Within the established parameters of corporate liberal ideology, a public-private intervention designed to correct the perceived cultural- and public-interest shortcomings of free enterprise in the domain of broadcasting made perfect sense.[56]

The creation of a private commission to address the "TV problem" was also compatible with the "liberal corporate approach" to welfare policy critiqued by many late-1960s activists. Richard Flacks, a former member of the Students for a Democratic Society, summarized these concerns when he argued that Great Society reforms were, by and large, designed at the national level by elites and experts, as opposed to publicly elected officials deliberating in open forums or grassroots constituencies. Flacks called this policy-making process "corporate" because corporations, philanthropies, and other representatives of "private interests" helped design government welfare policies, while the public institutions they created took cues from "modern corporation management." The process was also "liberal," Flack noted, because representatives from "special-interest groups" (including minorities and progressives) were consulted. Flacks's complaint was that change was negotiated and managed from above, not below.[57] The Carnegie Commission on Educational Television—which operated outside public jurisdiction in consultation with the corporate sector, academics, state officials, and representatives from unions and racial minority groups—is a classic example of the liberal corporate mode of governing that Flacks was describing.

The critical academic literature on philanthropy similarly argues that "private, high-level public-policy formation groups" constitute an unofficial and unaccountable branch of government in the United States. The Carnegie Corporation, according to scholar Frank Darknell, exemplified this unofficial governing role, "maintaining the interests of corporate wealth by underwriting studies and solutions" to social problems that might undermine the stability of the capitalist state. Founded by steel magnate Andrew Carnegie, the corporation was especially active in education and cultural policy, concerns that also spoke to its attempts to "govern" the social, cultural, and moral characteristics of the public. According to Ellen Condliffe Lagemann's history of the foundation, Carnegie associated his legendary donations to public libraries with the phrase "sweetness and light," a phrase he picked up from the influential reformer Matthew Arnold, whom he had once met at a dinner party. Like Arnold, the Carnegie Corporation valorized traditional high culture and, with it, the socially approved "habits and sensibilities" ascribed to the white, educated upper-middle class. Similar to the Ford Foundation, it believed that this culture and the character traits it might instill were "essential to character and taste" for all people, especially as society became more turbulent and "culture became more susceptible to commercial standards."[58]

The Carnegie Commission was the culmination of an "old boys" network that during the 1960s extended across private foundations, the Ivy League, the corporate sector, and the federal government, as even early public broadcasters concede. Oral histories of public television credit several prominent, well-networked individuals with suggesting a presidential commission to study ETV's expansion, including C. Scott Fletcher, who had retired from the Ford Foundation to consult for educational broadcasters, and wealthy banker Ralph Lowell, board chairman at WGBH-Boston and heir to the Lowell Institute, providers of public lectures to Bostonians for more than a century. Lyndon Johnson, who supported public broadcasting as an extension of his Great Society programs, evidently had no qualms about outsourcing its conceptual development to the private sector. John Gardner—Johnson's appointee to head the Department of Health, Education and Welfare and the former president of the Carnegie Corporation is said to have arranged for his former employer to undertake the study.[59] With virtually no public input, a prestigious commission was assembled to chart the terms of public broadcasting in the United States.

As *Broadcasting* noted at the time, the members—who were selected by Carnegie executives—were a "who's who list" filled with corporate CEOs, the former president of Harvard, the former head of NBC, and the ambassador to Switzerland. Novelist Ralph Ellison and Leonard Woodcock of the United Automobile Workers of America were on the commission as well, providing token representation of blacks and laborers. The commission had only one female commissioner, Oveta Culp Hobby, a corporate-minded Texan newspaper mogul with prior connections to Lyndon Johnson. The daily staff included Hymin Goldin, a professor at Boston College who had served on the FCC as a Republican appointee; Stephen White, a one-time commercial broadcaster and TV critic; and, as chairman, James Killian, a former president of the Massachusetts Institute of Technology. As the leading face of the commission, Killian embodied the Carnegie's Corporation's fetishization of educational credentials and technocratic expertise. Described as having vast "scientific knowledge in the communication field," Killian had been a science adviser to Dwight Eisenhower before accepting his managerial post at MIT. Characterized by the press as a renaissance man, he was reported to own a "prized" art collection, serve on the corporate boards of AT&T and General Motors, and have published scholarly articles advocating "science as a cultural force." In a speech made just before his appointment to the Carnegie Commission, Killian also demonstrated a strong commitment to the arts and humanities, which he promoted as essential to the "strength and welfare" of the United States.[60]

The Carnegie Commission solicited advice from four sources: cultural experts (professors, cultural figures, staffers at prestigious magazines like *Atlantic Monthly* and the *New Yorker*), government officials, ETV personnel, and commercial broadcasters. The discourse of the vast wasteland permeates

the oral and written statements of these well-educated and almost exclusively male advisers (race is not mentioned, suggesting the normalization of
whiteness). In a letter reminiscent of his earlier proposal for a noncommercial national broadcast authority, the editor of *Harper's* complained about
insufficient "programming for the minority," by which he meant people
with sophisticated tastes. Another professor of broadcasting testified that
"quality" had disappeared at the point at which commercial television decided it must draw a "crowd." Numerous advisers warned against "entertainment for a mass audience," believing it frivolous and—in the cautionary
words of Douglass Cater, special assistant to President Johnson—antithetical to the purpose of a "major social institution of defined character." Network executives, happy to surrender unprofitable high cultural expectations,
could not have agreed more. Philanthropist-turned-policymaker John Gardner and CBS board president William Harley agreed on public television's
principal purpose: both anticipated a "serious" complement to commercial
broadcasting, analogous to a university press. But there were objections:
Union leader Leonard Woodcock suggested that many people might welcome noncommercial entertainment, as did Franklin Patterson, president of
Hampshire College, who called for programs that were joyous and fun. Such
suggestions were difficult—indeed, impossible—to reconcile with public
television's cultural positioning as the respectable wasteland "oasis."[61]

The commissioners and their advisers also called on public television to
restore cultural pluralism, a goal that was presumed to be incompatible with
"mass appeal." With expert planning, it could provide a plethora of choices
to differentiated "subgroups," claimed supporters, some of whom envisioned public television as a stepping-stone to the options awaiting "pay TV"
subscribers. The social movements of late 1960s and the struggles over representational identity politics they spawned had very little impact on these
discussions. Before 1968, social class was the principal yet unacknowledged
"difference" that public television was poised to affirm. The Carnegie Commission's report made no mention of the word *class* in the economic sense
or in the social/cultural sense theorized by Bourdieu when it positioned public television as quality television for many small and specialized audiences.
These fragmented taste cultures did not, however, extend beyond the educated habitus associated with intellectuals and cultural minorities, a limitation made even more explicit by an unpublished audience profile of public
television's potential audiences.[62]

Demonstrating John Hartley's point that audiences are institutional creations, the "draft" document characterizes likely public television audiences
according to specialized tastes and needs. Despite the "fragmented" interests

ascribed to these hypothetical audience segments, the ideal beneficiaries of public television are termed an "elite 10 percent" on the basis of shared characteristics such as education, taste, and influence. The first potential audience was called the "intellectual elite," a "small and compact" subgroup composed of exceptionally well educated people. More affluent than average, this group was principally defined by its close association with professional occupations that "occupy the mind." Passionate about reading and discussing, its members would be served by news analysis, documentaries, discussions, and serious treatments of intellectual topics. Another subaudience was termed the "cultural elite," characterized as people interested in good "drama, fine and applied arts, music, ballet, dance." Though not quite as "narrow as the intellectuals," this taste culture was also presumed to be well educated and concentrated among society's "higher economic brackets." According to the profile, television "mirrored the theater or the concert hall" was its unmet priority. The "political audience," an "extremely influential" subgroup mainly concerned with the community's "soundness and welfare," was also characterized as well educated and disproportionately affluent. For its members, sophisticated news and discussions of civic issues were essential. Together, these constituencies for public television were said to comprise what the profile's author, Stephen White, called the "elite 10 percent" of the population.

Together, the subaudiences delineated by the Carnegie Commission's audience profile added up to an "elite" quite a bit larger than the tiny ruling class envisioned by Karl Marx. Typified more by university degrees and cultural competencies than by ownership or property, they spoke to the growth of the professional middle class reported by the news media during the 1960s and, with it, the expansion of "persons who like to think of themselves as intellectual and cultivated." What journalist Vance Packard called the "diploma elite" was growing in both influence and sheer numbers. Between 1956 and 1967, according to *U.S. News & World Report*, the number of bachelor's degrees awarded more than doubled in the United States. Master's degrees rose by more than 250 percent, while the number of Ph.D.'s more than tripled. It was simply taken for granted that public television would emphasize the cultural and informational needs of this societal niche. The question under debate was, would "better" programs cater to the cream of the crop or to the upwardly mobile? As *U.S. News* pointed out, with public education booming, the "elite role" once played by college graduates was increasingly being transferred to people with graduate diplomas.[63] This upping of the ante was reflected by the audience profile's treatment of potential public television viewers who felt the pressing "need for self-improvement." The ambivalence with which "self-improvers" were treated situated this potential audience among the newly minted, state university-educated middle class and its many aspirants. Sandwiched between the "elite 10 percent" and the unmotivated masses served by commercial television, this group was said to be looking for expert guidance on all matters, from culture to bridge instruction, French cooking, and "College of the Air." While most receptive to the official promise cultural uplift, people "bent on self-improvement" were also construed as a "threat" to quality. As theorized by the unpublished profile, if public television catered too much to this subaudience, it would probably "repel" the truly sophisticated intellectual, cultural, and political elite.

This arrogant assumption did not go unquestioned by the Carnegie Commission's advisers and consultants. But the contention over the audience for public television coalesced around the tension between serving the "elite 10 percent" and providing opportunities for universal self-betterment, not the logocentrism that underpinned the commission's thinking. One critic, for example, warned that the "average congressman" would not support public television unless it promised all Americans the chance "to improve and upgrade their minds." Implied by his statement, and others like it, was a practical concern: the suggestion that a supposedly nonexistent American ruling class—however diffuse and fragmented—was waiting to reap the benefits from television would have doomed public subsidies. Tellingly, the Carnegie Commission's published report, *Public Television: A Program for Action*, avoided direct references to the term *elite*. Public television was instead positioned as a "continuing learning experience" closely aligned to the quest for "self-improvement."[64] According to the lofty rhetoric of the report, public television would use broadcasting technology for "great purposes," bringing expert "analysis of art and philosophy, music and literature, science and technology" to the TV-viewing populace. Catering to individuals who yearn for "something they do not find in their everyday lives" and which they "cannot afford unless it comes to them free," it would be an agent of classlessness, not privilege.[65] If the unpublished profile characterized the "elite 10 percent" as the logical beneficiary of public television, *A Program for Action* repositioned elite knowledge and culture as potentially available to all Americans.

The audience profile also recommended "target audiences" for public television in an attempt to broaden its reach beyond the intellectual, cultural, and political elites. Ultimately, however, this attempt to orchestrate cultural pluralism merely defined these same privileged groups in different ways. Television viewers with unserved "specialized leisure tastes" were deemed analogous to the "discriminating" listeners of "better" FM radio stations, venues that featured classical music, news and analysis, drama, and "civilized conversation." Other target audiences, which included the "child in an intellectual household" and the "intellectual housewife," were similarly positioned in the upper-middle class. Clearly, public television's much touted service to "minority audiences" implied service to educated, upscale whites, and yet the very promise of cultural pluralism also opened the door to inclusional demands from less privileged groups. For instance, during one commission meeting, Leonard Woodcock proposed specialized programming for African Americans, a gap in commercial programming that the initial audience profile had ignored.

Reflecting the broader conception of minority culture implied by Woodcock's proposal, A Program for Action noted the geographical, cultural, and ethnic diversity of the United States when it advocated "excellence in the service of diversity." In so doing, the report promised expanded cultural "choices" to all TV viewers, including subordinated groups shortchanged by commercial broadcasting's white, middle-class homogeneity. At the same time, it situated the possibility of choosing "from an ensemble of transmitted alternatives" one that is "most appropriate" to individual "needs and interests" in the realm of socially acceptable consumption as defined by expert cultural planners.[66] A Program for Action might have promised something for everyone, but it was unable to transcend the narrow vision of good culture and appropriate leisure that framed the "TV problem." Unacknowledged class and racial privileges informed the very nature of the program categories (live plays, science specials, serious public affairs) that it proclaimed suitable for public television. Despite its positive acknowledgment of diversity, the Carnegie Commission's blueprint ultimately proposed greater selectivity to the critics of commercial television's mass cultural tendencies, situating pluralism squarely within the legitimated habitus.

Diversity and popularity were incompatible in this conceptual framework, for public television's purpose—never stated but continually implied—was to rise *above* commercial television's existing cultural level. This goal was made clear by the commission's unpublished audience profile. In that document, Stephen White acknowledged that the commercial networks had never offered a mass television audience "courteous treatment" and conceded that it was possible to "conceive of a noncommercial station which would offer exactly the same schedule as its commercial competitor but which would do it better in some manner." Such a service, he speculated, might present popular variety shows, sitcoms, and light entertainment without advertisements. But popular public television was an oxymoron incompatible with the prevailing expectations for the "oasis of the wasteland," so the possibility was dropped. A Program for Action called on public television to provide "all that is of human interest and importance," with the crucial exception of the "desire to relax and be entertained." The report constructed an obvious and seemingly impassable divide between public television and popular pleasure, much as critics like Lippmann and Minow had done. By defining the public interest in this way, the commission sanctioned the cultural hegemony of commercial broadcasters who claimed to serve the people's wants. In a gesture that simultaneously confirmed and approved its liberal corporate solution to the "TV problem," CBS president Frank Stanton pledged $1 million to the proposed Corporation for Public Broadcasting.[67]

In January 1967, *Public Television: A Program for Action* was published in paperback and hardcover, and the push for public broadcasting was catapulted into the media spotlight. The *New York Times* reprinted the report's "summary and recommendations" in full, and a professional clipping service hired to document its impact reported "top attention" in newspapers nationwide. Many reporters and commentators cheered the report as the long-awaited answer to lowbrow television. Such supporters tended to use the discourse of the vast wasteland to reiterate the faults of the fictionalized mass audience. To make the concept of public television meaningful, they defined it against what it was not: a service for unsophisticated "other" people. The *San Francisco Examiner*, for example, enthusiastically approved the recommendations made by *A Program for Action* on the grounds that "all private television networks have expended huge sums and energies in trying to elevate programming but usually, when they read the ratings, their ambitious efforts have been shunned and Joe Public is still back there gawking at *Bonanza* or *Gomer Pyle* and *Red Skelton*."[68]

The Carnegie Commission's report drew heady praise, but it also triggered opposition to what some opponents called tax-supported "caviar television." The commission's proposed 2 percent "excise tax" on TV sets provoked a heated debate that anticipated conservative attacks on public television. Even the Johnson White House had warned against the excise tax, predicting the "cost of supporting public broadcasting through an excise tax would be inequitably borne, primarily by the poor, who were probably the least interested in the passage of such a bill."[69] An independent consulting firm employed to assess funding possibilities for public television agreed that most people—a construct that presumably did not include grateful public television viewers—would "revolt" at such a prospect. The commission wanted the permanent revenue stream implied by the automatic tax, but its vision of public broadcasting was vulnerable to high-level conservative complaints that "self-selected guardians" were trying to create the television *they* wanted, at the people's expense. It was "an ingenious system of taxing the poor to furnish culture to the rich," declared one such opponent in a scathing editorial printed by the *Washington Post*. Why should Joe Q. Public be a "captive subsidizer of the noncommercial system?" asked another critic in the *Seattle Daily Times*.[70]

FCC commissioner Lee Loevinger's fierce objection to the "culture tax" echoed throughout media coverage of the report. Loevinger, a conservative who also opposed the regulation of commercial broadcasting, turned the discourse of the vast wasteland on its head by defending television as "the literature of the illiterate; the culture of the low-brow; the wealth of the poor; the privilege of the underprivileged; the exclusive club of the excluded masses."[71] "The common man has every right to be common . . . we shouldn't criticize the golden goose for not laying caviar," he told the *Milwaukee Sentinel*. "Let those who want it, or want to force it on others, pay for it themselves." Also equating prime-time commercial television with "cultural democracy," Carnegie Commissioner Joseph McDonnell, the president of Reynolds Metals, offered, for the record, his dissenting opinion. He told a Dallas newspaper it was unfair to tax the "mass of the public, whose program preferences determine what television we have," to provide another service we believe they should have as well. Even Jack Gould, an avid crusader for public television, worried that the excise tax implied a "reward" to the mass public who paid it and that service to this audience was antithetical to public television's purpose. The excise tax was thus rejected for a temporary appropriation, and to this day Congress must decide every few years, often amid considerable controversy, how much to give to public television. Critics still protest this lack of permanent funding, though without addressing the cultural dimensions of its failure to materialize in the 1960s. The Carnegie Commission favored the good over the popular, which made its template for public television antithetical to the democratic cultural gains it simultaneously espoused. Conservatives—not liberals or leftists—expressed the inherent contradiction most loudly from the outset, effectively claiming any populist opposition as their own. Today, the idea that "caviar television" is unfairly subsidized by the taxpayers lingers in the rhetoric of conservatives like Newt Gingrich, thereby keeping the "culture tax" in its place.[72]

Despite conservative opposition to what one critic dubbed the "New Deal" in television, most public commentators approved of the Carnegie Commission's push for "excellence, not just acceptability," in television programming. Johnson recommended public broadcasting in his State of the Union address; staffers at the White House and the Department of Health, Education and Welfare prepared legislation based on the commission's report; and Congress passed the Public Broadcasting Act within ten months. The legislation created the Corporation for Public Broadcasting and awarded temporary start-up funds. The congressional debate on the legislation was conducted within the discursive parameters delineated by *A Program for Action*. The discussion in the House of Representatives, which was overseen by Torbert MacDonald, a supportive Democrat from Massachusetts, drew from the ideology of mass culture to position public television as the opposite of popular programming. The presidents of the commercial networks testified that the "economic realities of commercial broadcasting made it impossible to produce and distribute educational and cultural programs which do not have mass audience appeal." Public television, in contrast, would emphasize quality over quantity. It would solve the "TV problem" by reconstituting good plays, educational documentaries, opera, symphony performances, and an "experimental program now and then." It would offer not a choice "between two or possibly three stations programming similar kinds of entertainment" but one between "programs of entertainment and programs of cultural worth," a typical supporter remarked. Implied but rarely stated were the lower-class, feminized connotations of mass culture, which formed the basis of public television's dos and don'ts. Public television would be "first class," but it would not compete for mass audiences or, with them, for advertising dollars, promised the Ford Foundation's McGeorge Bundy in his testimony to Congress. Articulating the very assumptions that had underlain broadcast reform discourse throughout the late1950s and 1960s, Bundy reasoned that

> commercial television is commerce first, and with the marginal exception it exploits only that part of the promise of television which gives the most assurance of the most profit. To the commercial networks, time is money, and they cannot give much of it away. It follows that noncommercial television must do the job that commercial television cannot do. Walter Lippmann stated the justification for noncommercial educational television in 1959 when he wrote that it should be a network which can be run as a public service, and its criterion not what will be most popular but what is good.[73]

Since quality was thought to be incompatible with "large numbers," public and commercial television were deemed the equivalent of apples and oranges. One would entertain the millions, as it had always done; the other would serve a selective "fragment" of the audience with tasteful and substantive fare. "We have to serve the greatest number of people in order to do our job," explained CBS President Frank Stanton. "They will be able to do types of special interest programming that we cannot do." While many supporters defined the "selective" role to be played by public television in terms reminiscent of the dominant hierarchies of cultural respectability, contradictory claims about public television's uplifting role tempered the appearance of elitism. Not competitive and geared to what Stanton called commercial television's "occasional" viewers, it would also expand the cultural universe of millions of Americans. Just as early radio broadcasts of the New York Philharmonic and Arturo Toscanini-conducted concerts had made "great music" familiar to the masses, John Gardner promised that public television would expose all Americans to "the best in our cultural tradition."[74]

Such a task was presumed to require the guidance of "men of culture and ability," elites who could give public television "direction that would conduce to leadership in good programming," in the words of the FCC's Rosel Hyde. "We must use our skill and knowledge to instruct and lead the people into a less anxious and more rewarding way of living," said another supporter who, like Hyde, presumed that only well-educated and cultured people like himself were suited for such responsibility. The myth of cultural democracy permeated such thinking, legitimating the assumption that public television must be carefully protected from the downward cultural pull of the mass audience. Since commercial networks were already believed to be catering to the people's unsophisticated and hedonistic wants, public television was characterized as a "whole other world" devoted to their rehabilitative needs. Only then could the profit motive and the public interest be simultaneously served, for the commercial broadcaster who "reasoned that he can sell more time" by avoiding the cultural equivalent of nutritious vegetables would no longer jeopardize cultural standards, or worse, the fate of democracy itself.[75]

Since entertainment was considered to be "plentiful" on commercial television, noncommercial public television would emphasize enlightenment, explained Carnegie Commission President James Killian. When pressed to explain the distinction, Killian conceded that educational material might be "made to appear" enjoyable and that certain forms of quasi entertainment for "specialized" audiences—by which he implied those with dignified tastes like tennis buffs—might be suitable for noncommercial presentation on public channels. Former TV news executive Fred Friendly, the Ford Foundation's high-profile television adviser, defined entertainment worthy of public subsidy in opposition to lowbrow "amusements" geared to a mass audience. Like many who testified, Friendly presumed that commercial broadcasting's willingness to pander to uneducated tastes and desires had undermined its public-interest capacities. He drew from class-coded descriptors to contrast public television with crowd-appeasing raunchiness and vulgarity, telling policymakers that "public television must not be permitted to become a honky-tonk midway of action games, violent fantasies, and contrived farces with fake laughter and applause, designed to appeal to the lowest common denominator all of the time." Reflecting similar concerns, the House version of the legislation forbade the Corporation for Public Broadcasting from funding public television programs designed to "amuse and for no other purpose," a clause that was eventually modified to allow for entertainment that coated "the philosophic pill with innocent merriment." Although the clause explicitly prohibiting amusement did not appear in the final version of the Public Broadcasting Act, its contemplation exemplifies the discursive formation in which public television was conceived. U.S. public broadcasting was conceptualized for the people, not by them, for its anticipated purpose was to combat the troubling consequences of their alleged cultural sovereignty.[76]

The Oasis of the Wasteland

In 1967, *Life* magazine announced the creation of a "wasteland oasis." Until the Public Broadcasting Service became operational, the slogan promised much but delivered little. Created to manage the satellite "interconnection" among local stations and distribute national programming, PBS began limited operation in 1969 to became the most recognized face of the new public broadcasting bureaucracy. For most people, the symbolic meanings and distinctions carried by the new PBS logo were themselves public broadcasting. The promotional discourse that accompanied PBS's full-fledged 1970 debut helped construct public television's cultural identity. Taking cues from television reform discourse, the wave of publicity drew from the ideology of mass culture to define public television as commercial television's opposite. For its part, PBS encouraged the binary. Critics and journalists received introductory press kits with the slogan "A Chance for Better Television" displayed in huge block letters on a blank TV screen, setting the tone for a media blitz that equated PBS with cultural progress.[78] Critics and journalists followed suit. "Almost overnight, a major new force in American television—public broadcasting—has sprung to prominence throughout the nation," declared *U.S. News & World Report*. In this article and countless others like it, public television was defined as good television, a noteworthy anomaly.[77]

Between 1970 and 1972, PBS's clipping service scoured major magazines as well as national and local newspapers, collecting mediated cultural responses to public television's belated arrival in the United States. It found lavish descriptors not commonly associated with the medium of television, including *quality, excellence, impressive, thoughtful, distinctive, sophisticated, absorbing, unique, intelligent, worthwhile, unique, educational,* and *meaningful.* Commentators proclaimed public television's superiority over mass culture, ignoring its claim to publicness and magnifying evidence of originality versus seriality, live performances versus tele-films, serious artistry versus formulaic programs "ground out" factory style. Speaking more to the cultural tensions that had triggered the "TV problem" than to the opening PBS schedule, which was modest and heavily derived from ETV, Jack Gould of the *New York Times* announced that a lowly medium "initiated by radio and imbued by Hollywood" had been virtually transformed. Many critics displayed similar tendencies, praising PBS not for what it offered but for what it was not. Finally, discerning viewers could find superior alternatives to "comedies, westerns, and whatnots" that "glaze the eye and mind," reported the Washington, D.C., *Evening Star. TV Guide,* a mass-circulation periodical geared to people who liked television, demonstrated the trend by giving the 1970 PBS schedule "honors" as opposed to the "commercial junk art." Even public television's most radical feature, its commercial-free format, was contrasted with lowbrow mediocrity, praised more as a signifier of cultural distinction than an alternative way to produce TV culture. According to one journalist, the lack of a "staccato pattern of a blurb every 10 minutes" was the perfect context for the dignified and thoughtful alternatives found only on PBS.[79]

Public television was also deemed a pluralist corrective to mass culture. *Reader's Digest* promoted public television as an escape from the "Giant American Homogenization Process." Implying that cultural diversity was for people with respectable tastes, however, the article praised public television for what it "doesn't have—soap operas, situation comedies, private eyes, Westerns." Public television's expected viewership was similarly defined against the mass commercial audience, as typified by a *Washington Post* article that contrasted the new "channel for the minority" with a common denominator that got "lower and lower." Public television is for intelligent people, not viewers of sitcoms, game shows, and cops and robber dramas, said other commentators. One such critic observed, "It is rare indeed when television contrives to make one think and succeeds at it . . . unfortunately such television will not cause much of a stir among masses of viewers."[80] Another *Washington Post* article relied on the familiar stereotype of the hedo-

nistic crowd doomed to wander the vast wasteland in order to establish public 'evision's cultural worth. The *Post*'s positive review of the 1970 PBS season ., pified the extent to which the extraordinary praise for PBS was based
on the ideology of mass culture to demarcate "good" and "bad" television
while also distinguishing enlightened viewers from passive and indiscriminate ones. According to the critic,

> [PBS] erupted with so much relevancy, success, quality, and sub-
> stance, I was afraid my television set wouldn't be able to stand it. . . .
> The first sprinkling of the noncommercial entrants uncorked some
> bold, giant strides toward making the TV set more than a dumb-
> dumb box of few-and far between good shows. Not that public tel-
> evision hasn't shown its quality colors in the past. The problem has
> been, though, the American public found it takes less effort to swal-
> low the slick and often insubstantial commercial programming than
> the more substantial but slower paced offerings from PBS.[81]

Along similar lines, *Look* characterized the probable audience for PBS
against the "millions of people who measure out their lives . . . in the brief
intervals between commercial messages." Like many mediated responses, the
article conflated television's commercialism with its lowbrow reputation.
Despite the magazine's large circulation, it cast the mass audience glued to
the shallow television programs it condemned as "other" people. The article
compared the selective "connoisseur" most apt to seek out "meaningful"
moments on public television with this portrait of the "dedicated" TV
watcher who quickly "sinks into familiar loyalties." It encouraged its readers
to identify with (or aspire to) connoisseur status, even when they lacked the
class markers ascribed to "selective" people or liked sitcoms or soap operas.
The print media's participation in the elevation of public TV made it difficult to challenge these terms. By placing public television on a cultural
pedestal, commentators discredited the notion that it might be both noncommercial and popular. Making this impossibility explicit, one satirist
speculated about what PBS would look like if it actually catered to the "man
in the street" who paid the bill for public broadcasting. Equating his wishes
with base instincts and desires, he supposed that

> for entertainment he probably would enjoy things like wrestling. For
> education, live reenactments of great moments in history, such as
> the St. Valentine's Day massacre. And adult movies. Sex may be only
> the second or third most important thing on the average viewer's

mind, but that's what would tear them away from those football games on commercial networks. Electric power to the people![82]

Unlike the masses, the anticipated audience for public television did not consider watching TV a habit, according to many journalistic forums. Selective viewers could find at least ten hours of "worthwhile watching" on public television, and who "wants to watch more?" asked a typical reviewer in the *Des Moines Register*. The TV addict with which the PBS audience was compared was given a face in a 1970 social scientific study reported by *Life* magazine. The research affirmed what the discourse of the vast wasteland had implicitly postulated: that it was mainly women, blacks, and working-class people with less education and income than professionals who were the "heavy TV viewers" (watched twenty or more hours a week), whereas the more acceptable "light viewer" was a highly educated white male.[83] Disregarding the vast discrepancies in social and cultural power, the article stigmatized heavy viewing as a behavioral problem not unlike the "negative and disturbing psychosocial characteristics" ascribed to the "heavy viewer" by mainstream academic research, according to Ien Ang. When critics claimed PBS as the channel for people who disliked watching television or watched it only occasionally, they were interpreting ideological cues circulated by social scientific studies like the one profiled by *Life*, as well as by broadcast reform discourse and PBS publicity. The same message extended across all these venues: public television's purpose was to serve the "purposeful" (light and selective) television viewer while attempting to occasionally "convert" the millions condemned for watching commercial television habitually and, presumably, indiscriminately.[84]

Press responses to the arrival of public television complemented the cultural reform logics from which it sprang. The template for "better" television negotiated by philanthropists and reformers was embraced and legitimated by critics and journalists who constructed cultural and moral distinctions between mass culture and PBS. The pervasiveness of these conceptual frameworks made alternative visions that did not hinge on the ideology of mass culture difficult to express. At worst, they encouraged well-placed individuals to claim public television as their birthright. Such was the case with a 1970 viewer letter addressed to the Corporation for Public Broadcasting. Reiterating the press's intersecting assumptions and derisions, the writer found it "frustrating and sad to note that [television] has become a morass of intrigue, violence, asinine drivel called comedy, and chap movies." Such fare might be "fine for those who choose to listen and watch such programs," but it was unsuitable for people of taste who "do not appreciate this kind of entertainment." Like reformers, this writer confused concerns about commercialism with anxieties about popularity while claiming that public television was meant for a slice of the population made up of selective people like herself.[85]

Rationalizing Public Television

The cultural tensions that led to the belated creation of public broadcasting in the United States eventually prompted commercial broadcasters to change their programming strategies. During the late 1950s and 1960s, broadcast executives defended their quest for maximum ratings as a form of "cultural democracy." Not long after PBS's debut, they decided that the huge audiences generated by top-rated programs like *The Beverly Hillbillies* contained too many lower-income, elderly, and rural people who did not interest advertisers. According to a 1969 Ford Foundation report on public television that predicated the dilemma, "It is ironic to contemplate that perhaps millions of dollars spent on advertising on commercial television are being wasted on people who can't afford to buy the products."[86] Alarmed by reports indicating that young, urban, upscale professionals with disposable income were "dropping out" of the mass audience, advertisers became willing to pay substantially more to pitch their products to the "right" people.[87] The commercial networks responded by basing the programs' ratings on a variety of consumer demographics, instead of numbers alone. To reach the desired viewers with money to spend, the industry supported commercialized versions of "quality" television.

Just as PBS was emerging as the channel for "selective" viewers, programs like *Mary Tyler Moore* and *All in the Family* appeared to redeem the vast wasteland in different ways. According to television historian Jane Feuer, these shows (and their cultural offspring) were praised for addressing topical issues, and they also were considered by critics to be more intelligent, complex, and "psychologically deep" than ordinary television. Like public television, commercially developed "quality" entertainment permitted well-educated viewers to separate themselves "from the mass audience and watch television without guilt." Unlike public television, it also provided familiar forms of popular pleasure in an approved package.[88] Whereas public television was narrowly positioned to serve the people's "needs," commercial broadcasters found ways to continue to capitalize on their wants.

Nobody expected public television to draw a crowd, but its grand and perhaps overstated promises became difficult to reconcile with statistical reports of its diminutive audience. Ultimately, the extent to which most people, including the "selective" and sophisticated minority, continued to choose commercial channels most of the time was framed as a success story. In 1971, the Corporation for Public Broadcasting's now-defunct audience research department proved in social scientific terms what TV critics had long contended, that public television's prime-time audience, though extremely small and sporadic, was also uncommonly well educated, professional, and upscale. These findings did not bode well for those who, like the president of the Corporation for Public Broadcasting, wished to convert people to public television, but the study nonetheless had several victories to celebrate. Public television was declared both a "selective" medium and a "qualitative" improvement because it encouraged better TV-viewing practices. According to researchers, people did not watch public television habitually or vegetate in front of the set. On the contrary, they "actively sought out" its programs and were less apt to be "distracted" by other activities or to feel as if they were "wasting time" when watching them. From this perspective, ratings that hovered between 1 and 2 percent of the television audience could be interpreted as a positive sign, for if nothing, else the figures proved that public television was not "addicting."Although hardly anyone was watching, public television was declared a "plug-free" medium because, as even *TV Guide* admitted, its "viewers watch selectively and are there by choice."[89]

Minow's metaphor cut across cultural and institutional contexts, providing the predominant terms through which public television was implemented and rationalized. The discourse of the vast wasteland compared popular appeal with cultural malaise, making it virtually impossible to conceptualize public television outside these parameters. Cast as a redemptive oasis, public television soothed a number of intersecting anxieties but posed no threat to commercial broadcasters, from which it inherited a narrow interpretation of cultural excellence and "public-interest" responsibilities. Envisioned as a world apart from mass culture, its contradictory promises made it vulnerable to the upscale niche-marketing tactics that concern leftist critics and the conservative backlash that is waged in the name of the common person. An early PBS fund-raising spot demonstrated how easily the cultural ideals circulated by broadcast reform discourse could be deployed to win private funds from "selective viewers." "Drop by drop we're doing our best to raise the level of television," explained an announcer, who requested donations to "keep TV beautiful" as water drops sent ripples though an opulent aquarium. Public television would need the help to survive the culture wars. Anticipating the populist terms of a conservative attack that would force reforms within a few years, an article from the *Charleston Gazette* jumped out among rave responses to the debut of public television: "Let TV Be Vast Wasteland," the headline scoffed, "Plurality of Voters Decide."[90]

Television is the technical means through which
it will be possible to meet a great many of the
objectives that must be attained if we are serious
when we speak of a Great Society.
—Testimony to the Carnegie Commission, 1966

CHAPTER TWO

THE QUEST TO CULTIVATE

In 1995, Newt Gingrich vowed to "zero out" congressional funding for public broadcasting. Following a
line of conservative reformers dating back to the
Nixon administration, the Speaker of the House stated the rationale for "privatization" in populist terms.
Why, according to his argument, should hard-earned
tax dollars subsidize a cultural service for elites who
can easily pay for it? In the ensuing policy debate, liberal supporters insisted that public television could
bring culture and knowledge to every home. Vice-
President Al Gore argued that programs like *Sesame
Street* teach millions of children, giving the disadvantaged among them a "chance for a better future." Another advocate pleaded with Congress to keep public
broadcasting alive so that troubled young people who
might turn to "drugs or gangs to fill their empty hours
and souls" could find uplifting alternatives on PBS.
Public television was also said to expand the cultural
and intellectual horizons of grown-ups. While some
local stations publicized adult literacy and instructional services, PBS president Ervin Duggan emphasized
PBS's prime-time history of bringing "great and beautiful upper middle brow moments" to the broadcast

airwaves for anyone to experience. For lower-income families unable to afford the cost of commercial cable, these high-quality broadcasts were deemed to be indispensable. This defense effectively turned around Gingrich's accusation, suggesting that conservatives who would deny the people their chance for culture, edification, and self-improvement were the real elitists.[1]

The promise of education, uplift, and universal access to the "best" has surrounded public television since its creation, tempering its exclusive image as the "oasis" of the vast wasteland. Public television inherited its cultural ties to education from ETV (educational television), which for years was the United States' only alternative to commercial broadcasting. In the 1960s, a national commitment to cultivating excellence and combating the "cultural depravation" of the poor infused broadcast reform discourse with pledges of "equal opportunity" and assistance for disadvantaged populations. President Lyndon Johnson and his advisers at the Department of Health, Education and Welfare advocated public broadcasting as a cultural technology for cultivating the self and envisioned benefits for all members of the Great Society. Reformers who expected public television to serve educated "minorities" also insisted that it would narrow the culture/knowledge gap separating the "haves" from the "have-nots." During the congressional debate over the 1967 Public Broadcasting Act, policymakers were promised an electronic version of the Land Grant Act, a TV channel that would do for "informal education what assembly line production did for the automobile." Public television would beam the accumulated wisdom of the nation's universities, libraries, and museums into millions of living rooms, however downtrodden. It would facilitate the people's desire for "betterment" by providing one and all an opportunity to "continue their education and cultivate their artistic tastes."[2]

These promises survive in residual form, helping protect public broadcasting from conservative accusations of elitism. When supporters propose that public television democratizes respected culture and knowledge, they are also implying that public television viewing can facilitate social mobility—something not said about ABC, Fox, MTV, or the Cartoon Network (although the products advertised on those networks promise a different route to mobility in the form of commodity consumption). Such claims situate public television as an instrument of meritocracy and, with it, the American Dream of rising above one's birthright. While most people approve of the "equal opportunity" that public television is said to represent, they are not necessarily well served by its uplifting priorities. This paradox is illustrated by the working-class Conner family on the sitcom *Roseanne*, who perceive public television as a rather dull channel for "classy" people but on one episode decide that watching its programs can make them equally "respectable." The desire for upward mobility that motivates the Conners is widespread, particularly in a nation that is supposed to be classless and where apparent class hierarchies are routinely attributed to individual, not social, differences. If public television can help dismantle social inequalities perpetuated by the uneven distribution of socially legitimated culture and knowledge, so much the better. Ultimately, however, the Conner family cannot connect with public television in any significant or sustainable way. Like most people, they value the hypothetical opportunities it presents to them but bypass its respectable offerings and instead choose the popular culture found on the commercial channels.

In the United States, public television has been pigeonholed as a channel for uplift *only* when it is watched by people like the Conners, who lack the education and cultural capital ascribed to its idealized audience. Promises of democratic access to the "best" have been made at the expense of cultural diversity and popular pleasure, partly because public television presumes to ameliorate (rather than acknowledge and program for) educational and class differences. While critics have documented the corporate-economic forces that constrain public television, the legitimating discourses that keeps it in this cultural place have evaded scrutiny. To move beyond the stagnant public television culture wars, we need to address obvious hurdles as well as commonsense goals and priorities that might seem "above reproach."[3] This chapter traces public television's cultivating ethos, looking critically at two long-standing assumptions that resurfaced during the debate triggered by Gingrich's proposal to "zero out" funding. The first assumption is that public television is an equalizer working against, not for, class hierarchies. The second is that public television's responsibility to "have-nots" is to solve social problems, ranging from educational inequality to poverty to delinquency. My intention is not to disparage the humanitarianism of these pledges but to unravel their contradictions and shortcomings as templates for public culture in broadcasting.

Cultivating the People

Public television's cultivating priorities have multiple origins and cultural manifestations, which makes a genealogical analysis akin to untangling a spider web. Its quest to uplift the people is partly rooted in what cultural historian Joan Shelley Rubin calls "self-culture," or the penchant for self-cultivating practices—attending public lectures, learning music appreciation, visiting museums, seeking out the great books—associated with educated (or upwardly mobile) middle-class social formations. Self-culture was promoted as a universal ideal by the cultural reformers of the late 1800s and their Progressive-Era successors. Against the backdrop of tumultuous industrial capitalist democracy, the promotion of self-culture intersected with broader hopes of uplifting and guiding working-class people, a task that included combating the perceived effects of commercialized mass amusements. As with Tony Bennett's study of the nineteenth-century public museums, the dissemination of respectable culture was bound to disciplinary logics not always recognized or even consciously construed. For many reformers, the point was not just to distinguish culture from amusements; it was also to create better individuals. According to Bennett, the "governmental" aims associated with self-culture included instilling character, uplifting taste, encouraging self-discipline, and, through these self-improvement strategies, preserving the future of civilization itself. The democratization of what the English reformer Matthew Arnold called the "best that has been thought and said" was, for this reason, believed to be contingent on enlightened individuals who had a genteel heritage and learned expertise.[4]

Early broadcast reform discourse was based on similar assumptions that planted the seeds for the cultivating ethos governing public television. According to Rubin, education was often cited as the principal rationale for the development of nonprofit radio because, in the eyes of genteel thinkers, without the "guidance of an educated minority, the majority would all too readily find itself entrapped in a . . . paradise of mediocrities." Joy Elmer Morgan of the National Committee on Education by Radio typified the wish to "improve the quality of thinking" of the masses by "exposing millions of people to the finest intellectuals." Appalled by radio's mediocre cultural content when in the hands of entrepreneurial barbarians, reformers like Morgan argued for "objective" cultural planning overseen by enlightened and cultured men much like themselves. Culture with a capital "C" was pivotal to the Darwinist progress they espoused, for as Morgan explained, it was what made "the difference between man and beasts, between weak and brutal people and a strong and noble humanity." "Education by radio" would not only preserve cultural standards and uplift taste. For idealists like Morgan who supported capitalism but shunned its cultural consequences, educational radio was desperately needed to curb the character flaws blamed for chronic unemployment and to control the "chaos" on the horizon of an increasingly turbulent capitalist democratic society.[5]

Self-culture's eventual mutation into entrepreneurial, mass-mediated "middlebrow" operations threatened to popularize legitimated culture to the point that some critics proclaimed them to be scandalous. As Janice Radway shows in her study of the Book of the Month Club, the expansion of the middlebrow as a cultural field in the 1920s and 1930s triggered an intellectual backlash that continues to reverberate in academic circles. Radway questions the motivations behind the backlash, showing how intellectuals confused complaints about commerce, purity, and cultural worth in their indignant attacks on "middling" tendencies. In fact, she says, the growing middle ground between mass and high culture facilitated the "reorganization of class in a consumer society." The promise of class mobility inherent in middle-brow culture and the "configuration of taste it cultivated and developed as a kind of social pedagogy" was integral to the class identity of a growing "frac-tion of professionals, managers, and information and culture workers" and to those who "aspired to the status of this class, to its work routines, and to its privileges." Public television appeared amid another surge of profession-al middle-class expansion and served a similar cultural function. Its perfec-tion of the middlebrow sensibilities favored in varying degrees by *Omnibus* and ETV resists one-dimensional claims of progress or elitism. Highbrow art critic Dwight MacDonald derided the merger of self-culture and television as a watered-down "mid-cult" geared to strivers. For others, the public televi-sion audience was a "self-made" elite defined by its capacity for work, taste, improvement, ambition, and intelligence.[6] Despite the differences in these perspectives, both situated public television in an expanding class formation defined by culture as much as economics.

The quest to cultivate can also be traced to North American anxieties about "productivity" versus play. In his cultural history of Coney Island at the turn of the twentieth century, John Kasson argues that reformers protest-ed mass amusements on the grounds that "all activities should be edifying and constructive," a premise that shaped reformist notions of "better" tele-vision as well. The productive activities associated with self-culture were val-orized over roller coasters and the like because they demanded continual learning and effort. The fun to be had at amusement parks and nickelodeons was suspect because in the minds of reformers, only hard work improved "the individual as well as society, curbing men's animal passions, which if unchecked would bring about social collapse." If this Calvinistic attitude was deeply moralistic, it also complemented the constitution of the American Dream, notes cultural historian Garth Jowett. Industrial capitalism's promo-tion of an ethic that "glorified work and demeaned pleasure and play" was buttressed by the promise of upward mobility for industrious behavior, says Jowett. Producer values valorizing hard work, self-discipline, deferred grati-fication, and future rewards became associated with "middle classness" even as these values eventually clashed with the consumer logic promoted by the mass media of radio, advertising, and Hollywood. Complaints that television bred passivity, unproductivity, indulgence, and sloth spoke to the residual tension typified by Wilbur Schramm's claim that television viewing ran counter to the American credo that a "person should be active, striving, achieving, trying to better himself." During the early 1960s, Schramm's social scientific studies indicated that ETV was more in sync with traditional "middle-class norms" than were its commercial counterparts. But the studies also reported that viewers, even well-educated groups, watched ETV only infrequently. This contradiction implied that at every level, producer values were losing ground to consumer culture. Nonetheless, Schramm claimed to have discovered a "self-made" elite in the viewership for educational television. ETV viewers might be few and far between, but they were in the audience by "choice," as evidenced by their willingness to use their leisure time to work, learn, improve, and achieve.[7]

Schramm's study *The People Look at Educational Television* set the stage for the social scientific construction of the public television audience. Without a critical framework to analyze his findings, Schramm relied on the discourse of meritocracy, or the presumption that U.S. society has no barriers. In a meritocracy, all individuals are said to have an equal chance of succeeding, with the most ambitious, intelligent, and talented rising to the top. ETV appealed mostly to the "gravitators," the "uncommon" types who hurry off to a lecture or the symphony after a full day's work, said Schramm. This "small minority" was also more apt to read serious newspapers, participate in civic events, take adult education courses, and demonstrate a "deep interest in cultural activities." According to Schramm, these individuals enjoyed a higher class status for the same reasons that they watch ETV; that is, they had a strong work ethic, ambition, self-discipline, deferred gratification norms, and a goal-oriented outlook. Inherited economic and cultural privilege has nothing to do with it, according to this analysis. People who watched trivial entertainment on the commercial channels simply lacked those values associated with purposeful and productive ETV viewing. What about those who stumbled on ETV and were not well-placed gravitators? According to Schramm's study, they must be "deviants" who mistakenly rate "themselves higher than the social status to which they objectively belong."[8]

U.S. public television inherited producer values and meritocratic claims from ETV. Its edifying priorities also spoke to the demands of the growing knowledge industry. As Todd Gitlin documents in his history of the 1960s, federal investment in education boomed with the GI bill and Great Society programs; between 1956 and 1967, the number of college degrees granted doubled and continued to grow. Public television was part of the national push toward a more educated workforce, a cultural technology meant to help combat what bureaucrats called the "poverty of the intellect." While commercial television was credited with moving merchandise, it was also believed to be stunting the smarts of a world superpower, a dilemma that prompted the U.S. Congress to help build the ETV system as part of the National Defense in Education Act. In 1962, the year after Newton Minow declared television a "vast wasteland," economist Fritz Machlup's influential book *The Production and Distribution of Knowledge in the United States* predicted that "education, of which culture is sometimes a tributary, will become the outstanding growth industry." According to Machlup, who cited ETV as an example of this trend, the information sector needed "knowledge workers" with education and intellectual skills. Public television was positioned as the thinking person's channel, a distinction symbolized by its programming and its call letters, of which the P was made to look like a human head. Although the formal "educational" label was dropped when public television went national, the flow of federal dollars was still expected to combat mass-produced entertainment's presumably negative impact on cerebral activity. As the president of the Corporation for Public Broadcasting (CPB), John Macy, explained, public television's counterpurpose was to "enlighten" the people.[9]

The progressive dimensions of this cultivating role came from advocates like Frieda Hennock, a Polish immigrant who, as the first woman appointed to the Federal Communications Commission, had promoted ETV. Remembered by her colleagues for her unpolished Brooklyn accent, non-Ivy League credentials, and gaudy clothing, Hennock advocated a "super university of the air" at a time when a four-year college degree was becoming an increasingly mandatory admission ticket to the middle class.[10] Lyndon Johnson's unpretentious teachers' college diploma and early work with underprivileged Texas schoolchildren brought similar credibility to his enthusiastic promotion of a "great network of knowledge" with dividends for all members of a changing Great Society. These are humanitarian intentions, for education is a human right and must be made equally available, but it does not mean that public television is capable of, or suited to, educational parity. In a society in which most adults consider watching television a welcome form of leisure, labeling public television as the cultural equivalent of night school has been profoundly limiting. And public television has not generated the broad enrollment envisioned by Hennock and Johnson, despite its claim to reach every demographic group in the United States.

A cultural product of the Great Society, public television is caught up in the paradox outlined by John Gardner's enormously influential 1961 book *Can We Be Excellent and Equal Too?* As the president of the Carnegie

Corporation, Gardner helped shape both postwar educational policy and public broadcasting. Later he became the secretary of the Department of Health, Education and Welfare under Lyndon Johnson. In both roles, Gardner advocated "discipline and tenacity of purpose" and the pursuit of excellence as a national goal. His blueprint for the Great Society urged the United States to attend to the motivational factors that "lead people to level off short of their full ceiling" and to "cultivate the idea and exercise of excellence in every man at its disposal." According to Gardner, this was especially crucial in a democracy in which the people had the power to influence the "deterioration of standards, the debasement of taste, shoddy education, vulgar art, cheap politics" and the "tyranny of the lowest common denominator." Advocating the cultivation of excellence as a public good and as a disciplinary measure, Gardner explained that

> in an era when the masses of people were mute and powerless it may have been possible for a tiny minority to maintain high standards regardless of their surroundings. But today the masses of people are neither mute nor powerless. As consumers, as voters, as the source of public opinion, they heavily influence levels of taste and performance. They can create a climate supremely inimical to standards of any sort.[11]

Gardner was the first to concede that those who "actually achieve excellence will be few at best." The vast majority, he suggested, "lack the qualities of mind or spirit that would allow them to conceive excellence as a goal, or to achieve it if they conceived it." Still, he insisted that "many more can try to achieve it than they do now." What about those people who were denied the chance to pursue excellence? At the Carnegie Corporation and in Washington, Gardner promoted measures to ensure equality of opportunity, subject to a "sorting-out" process to identify the best and the brightest.[12] Gardner acknowledged that the meritocracy he envisioned was a competitive business: Despite the introduction of opportunities, the Great Society would still be a pyramid with a limited number of spaces at the top. His vision was perfectly illustrated by the following scenario from Vance Packard's 1962 book *The Status Seekers: An Exploration of Class Behavior in America*. As Packard explained,

> One way to picture the situation graphically is to imagine a host of people strung along a trail up a mountainside. Some have given up the idea of climbing higher and have pitched their tents. But many

would like to climb still higher. At several points the trail becomes precipitously steep, and so narrow that only a few people can pass at a time. Between these difficult passages are broad, gentle inclines where large numbers of people can spread out as they climb or rest. Some few will be finding the climbing beyond their capacity and will be retreating down the mountainside.[13]

Like Gardner's *Excellence and Equal Too?* public television promised to cultivate self-improvement and equality of opportunity in the spirit of the national interest, to the extent that socially legitimated culture and knowledge would be displayed for everyone who wished to see and hear. But like the book, this mission rejected full egalitarianism, which Gardner saw as the path to cultural mediocrity or, worse, communism. The implicit assumption was that public television would cultivate and serve the most talented and ambitious individuals and that meritocratic competition would weed out people like the Conners who proved unwilling or unable to achieve the excellence it offered. The presumed fairness of the system has been thoroughly analyzed by cultural studies scholars, who claim that democratic capitalism merely "pretends" that everyone has an equal opportunity to scale the pyramid or watch a ballet instead of *The Beverly Hillbillies*. Drawing from Pierre Bourdieu's critical sociology of culture, John Fiske contends that people who successfully reach the "peak of the pyramid" begin with hidden advantages. Beyond economics, they often have access to the approved knowledges, tastes, and aesthetic dispositions that Bourdieu calls "cultural capital." Schools are more apt to reproduce than erase this leg up, says Fiske, because classifying processes that purport to measure the "natural talent" of individuals promote "middle class values and reward middle class students."[14] From this critical perspective, the "educational system transforms social hierarchies into academic hierarchies and, by extension, into hierarchies of 'merit.'"[15]

In the 1960s, the decade that gave birth to public television, this tendency was challenged. The "discovery" of the poor, the civil rights movement, and the social uprisings of the era all cast doubt on public schools as meritocratic laboratories. The War on Poverty, Project Head Start, and the federal investment in full educational opportunity promised to remedy the situation, particularly for children. Consistent with the discourse of meritocracy, socializing disadvantaged children to compete in the academic realm was conceptualized as the preferred route to social change, and gains were made. Many people became educationally mobile because of Great Society programs. Yet the structural inequalities persisted, obscured by the promise that the playing field had been leveled. As Lyndon Johnson explained, there was "no need to contemplate schemes of economic redistribution" as long as rich and poor alike had access to education.[16]

Public television's relationship with "have-nots" was conceptualized in relation to liberal thinking about remedying educational inequality and, with it, systemic poverty. As Barbara Ehrenreich showed, the heightened attention to the problem of poverty in the 1960s often was humanitarian. It also was troubling, for it cast the poor as "others" who were presumed to be suffering from what anthropologist Oscar Lewis termed the "culture of poverty." For Lewis, whose thesis informed many "equalizing" Great Society educational programs, the poor were characterized by some seventy cultural traits that separated them from mainstream (i.e., Western-educated, middle-class) society. Among the attributes ascribed to poverty were lack of ambition, inability to defer gratification, undeveloped work ethic, living in the present moment, "hopelessness and despair," and indifference to self-improvement. Since these flaws were believed to be passed down, reformers advocated "changing the environment of the young" to break the cycle of poverty. However well meaning, the antipoverty programs that arose from this conviction were paternalistic, "based on a very deeply rooted ethnocentrism" in which the poor have to be lifted to "our level," in the words of activist Casey Hayden. Hayden and many other critics protested a dynamic that mirrored public television's quest to cultivate: Instead of "people changing institutions to meet their own needs and desires, people are shaped to meet the needs of those with power."[17] For better or worse, public television's uplifting promises intersected with broader thinking about the alleviation of educational inequality and poverty. In his testimony to the Carnegie Commission, William G. Harley, president of the board of CBS, summed up the potential contribution of public television to the Great Society, quoting U.S. Commissioner of Education Francis Keppel to explain why public television must adopt the educational aims that commercial television, which had "profitability as its major motivation," was unable to pursue. Public television, Harley explained, was suited to provide "educational opportunity to every child in America" and to bring "educational resources to bear directly on problems in our communities as an *indispensable social instrument*" (emphasis mine).[18]

Such goals were conceptualized quite differently for different social groups, particularly children and adults. To restore equality of opportunity, children's programming on public television had to reach a disadvantaged audience that cut across class and race differences, which led to experiments with multicultural popular aesthetics. Prime-time PBS, though, could not simultaneously be popular and symbolize the pursuit of excellence; it had to be superior to the mass culture it was supposed to improve. The gap between the large and diverse child audience for public television and its smaller, more "selective" adult counterpart was explained in meritocratic terms. According to Gardner's blueprint for the Great Society, people are not "equal in their native gifts [or] their qualities of character [or] their motivation," which means that they will "not be equal in their achievements."[19] If public television could help reconstitute equality of opportunity for children, regardless of their social background, its limited appeal to mostly well-educated, white adults could be—and often was—confused with the competitive individualism that Gardner and other liberal thinkers espoused.

James O'Connell, Johnson's telecommunications adviser, recommended passage of the Public Broadcasting Act in precisely these terms. Combining the call for universal excellence with a "sorting-out" process that favored social and cultural leaders, O'Connell explained that

> the march is on to bring more knowledge—bringing better physical and mental health—less crimes—less poverty stemming from educational deficiencies. . . . Obviously this can only be done by inspiring and motivating people toward the higher goals of self-improvement—to swim upstream—not float downstream—to seek the higher values of growing knowledge along with the diversion and entertainment which is now so plentifully available and at least to achieve a better balance between the two. Whereas inherently commercial television to be successful has had to develop the talents of followership and the ratings of the mass tastes of our public for diversion, [public television] must develop the talent for leadership—for innovation and for "incentovation."[20]

Public television's uplifting promises did not emerge spontaneously but bore the imprints of several, intersecting influences, including self-culture and its middlebrow successors, the push for excellence and knowledge in the 1960s, the discourse of meritocracy, and the "culture of poverty thesis." In other words, multiple ideas coalesced around the historical formation of U.S. public television, injecting the quest to cultivate with particular—but not always visible—aims and unresolvable contradictions. This becomes more apparent when we revisit three early strands of programming that claimed to democratize culture and knowledge in different ways: the debut of *Sesame Street*, the rise of the "personal and social development" programming for disadvantaged adults, and the 1969 PBS presentation of *Civilisation*, a BBC documentary that was critically praised for "glorifying the box" with intellectual depth.

Television for a Great Society

In 1971, *Reader's Digest* reported a positive development in U.S. television. A public channel had been introduced, promising to be the "most stimulating educational venture in history." The proof was *Sesame Street*, which debuted in 1969 to become the best-known program on public television. Because *Sesame Street* still attracts a broad following of children and grateful parents, it is often used as a liberal trump card in the public television culture wars. In 1995, for example, supporters rallied against conservatives who were trying to "kill Big Bird."[21] *Sesame Street*'s origins in the antipoverty programs of the 1960s were reclaimed to disprove conservative charges of cultural elitism. It was a powerful strategy that in many ways stymied debate about public television's prime-time priorities. While scholars have debated *Sesame Street*'s educational "effects" for years, their behaviorist lens cannot explain the appeal of the "chance for a better future" promised by Al Gore and other supporters.

The Carnegie Commission's influential 1966 report *Public Television: A Program for Action* reflected the Great Society's concern with equality of opportunity, particularly for poor children. The report recommended that "special attention" be paid by public television to the educational needs of preschoolers, particularly those "whose intellectual and cultural preparation might otherwise be less than adequate." Shortly after its publication, the Carnegie Corporation hired Joan Ganz Cooney—a University of Arizona journalism major and the producer of several documentaries about poverty for New York's ETV station—to investigate public television's potential "exploitation" as a vehicle for preschool education. Her study "The Potential Uses of Television in Preschool Education" foresaw a television classroom that could help facilitate the National Education Association's proposal that children be "given the opportunity to enter school at public expense at age four." In addition, Cooney believed that television could deliver preschool education with modern technological efficiency for a nominal cost. Based on the Cooney's study, the Children's Television Workshop (CTW) began operation in 1968. Under her direction, the workshop created and produced *Sesame Street*, named for the "magic door to knowledge" evoked by the "Open, Sesame" command in *Arabian Nights*. The goal was to use television to boost the "intellectual and cultural growth" of preschoolers, especially those who were disadvantaged economically. According to Cooney, *Sesame Street*'s equalizing mission was a direct response to antipoverty initiatives and urban race rebellions. "The cities were burning and people were focusing on the poor in America," she explained during a *Sesame Street* retrospective. "Our efforts to help poor children seemed like a good way to channel all the grief and confusion that abounded at the time."[22]

During its formative years, *Sesame Street* received 50 percent of its funding from the U.S. Department of Health, Education and Welfare. The remainder came from the Carnegie Corporation, the Ford Foundation, the Corporation for Public Broadcasting, and corporate donors. The show was set in a Harlem neighborhood studio and had a racially diverse human cast and Jim Henson's now famous Muppets. *Sesame Street*'s lesson plans included basics like letters, counting, and spelling, as well as trickier subjects like cognitive development and "social interaction." In social scientific lingo, the program's overall goal was to narrow the "achievement gap" among youngsters, compensating for "differences in learning opportunities" by disseminating "what middle class children would otherwise learn from a rich diet of books and records and vacations and parental conversations overheard."[23] In other words, *Sesame Street* would distribute across class and race lines the cultural capital common to middle-class families, ensuring that preschoolers entered the kindergarten meritocracy on even terms. With coverage on the front page of the *New York Times* and favorable attention from newspapers and magazines, *Sesame Street* quickly became a cultural symbol of the War on Poverty. Just as social scientists of the era believed that they could "devise policies to eliminate poverty in all but the most extreme cases," CTW's psychologists and consultants lent credence to journalistic claims that the show would help poor children hidden in "big city ghettos, Indian reservations and Appalachian enclaves" succeed.[24]

Unlike prime-time PBS, *Sesame Street* was modeled after the illicit tastes, consumer sensibilities, and leisure practices ascribed to the mass audience. Cooney admitted looking to Madison Avenue for techniques might be used to sell "skills and knowledges" instead of products. CTW researchers, meanwhile, confirmed what commercial executives understood: kids liked "fast action, catchy music and cartoons" more than grown-up talking heads or slow-moving fairy tales. *Sesame Street* appropriated the popular aesthetic as developed by the culture industries, using cartoons, films, snappy jingles, humorous skits, and appearances by celebrities, musicians, and sports figures with instructional goals "sponsored" by letters and numbers. *Sesame Street* takes "advantage of what children like best about TV," said *Time* magazine of the format. CTW's ambivalence about the vast wasteland it mined was revealed, however, in segments that worked as entertainment for children and as parody for knowing adults. In one early episode, the Muppets star in a mock television game show, complete with a superficial host named Guy Smiley, a cheering studio audience, and dim-witted contestants who become hysterical when they win silly prizes. The skit pokes fun at a disparaged genre and its feminized, working-class audience yet trades on its familiar pleasures to make learning (in this case, counting) fun for children.[25]

Whereas prime-time public television was expected to serve small and fragmented adult audiences, *Sesame Street* strove for mass appeal. CTW conducted experiments to ensure that "every element" in *Sesame Street* said to every preschooler, "This is for you." While Cooney often insisted that all kids were "conditioned" by commercial television, the child test subjects came from day-care centers in poor areas. The children were shown episodes and monitored by researchers for signs of boredom or distraction. Based on these "tip-offs," the programs were altered. The "edu-tainment" approach contradicted everything that public television symbolized, and some commentators condoned it only as a means to attract disadvantaged children to "uplifting" knowledge. Children from the slums, "where a TV set is the only outlet to a better world, need nontraditional education," explained one middle-class parenting magazine. Others commentators expected children eventually to graduate from *Sesame Street*'s popular format. Writing in *Reader's Digest*, an analyst for the U.S. Department of Education predicted that "growing up with the electronic *McGuffey's Reader*," or the televisual equivalent of the nineteenth-century primer, would lead to greater use of public television as a "channel of adult culture and education." Some critics could not accept *Sesame Street*'s mass cultural format for any reason. The TV critic for the *San Francisco Chronicle* typified this appalled response, arguing that "the fact that it was said, 'We're trying to reach disadvantaged homes most of all,' is no excuse for lowering teaching standards so perilously close to the vulgarity from which their audience seeks to escape through education."[26]

In the midst of these debates, CTW took an unusual step for public television by developing audience-building strategies that emphasized low-income areas. Flyers were posted; social service and community organizations were enlisted; schools and day-care centers were contacted; and volunteers went door-to-door in urban areas to attract poor and minority viewers. In 1970, *Sesame Street* went on national tour as part of these intensive audience-building strategies, offering free performances to generate a following in low-income and inner-city areas. At the height of the promotional blitz, there was even talk of communal *Sesame Street* "viewing centers" in housing projects and supermarkets. In 1971, CTW commissioned a polling firm to measure the payoff. The much-reported study reported a sizable *Sesame Street* viewership among the urban poor, thus affirming CTW's attempt to build a cross-class, cross-race viewing constituency. Soon after, the Educational Testing Service studied *Sesame Street*'s "effects" and reported that disadvantaged preschoolers who regularly watched the program had "sharper" cognitive skills than those who did not. While contested among academics, the scientific proof became part of *Sesame Street*'s progressive aura, confirming its promise to catapult children out of poverty. "The study has vindicated TV—it can teach, and teach well," explained Cooney. "Parents cannot do what *Sesame Street* did . . . only the public television system can achieve such results," remarked another typical supporter. The praise tapped into liberal hopes for social equality, but it also conveyed the idea that only public television could elevate individuals from their structural circumstances. As radical educator John Holt observed at the time, *Sesame Street*'s virtually impossible quest was to cure "learning deficits" with television, a premise that obscured huge inequities in school funding and institutionalized teaching methods that favored the white middle class. There was another important issue at stake as well: If *Sesame Street*'s alleged success with poor children warranted popular entertainment *as a means to an end*, what about inequalities among grown-ups?[27]

The news media magnified *Sesame Street*'s boon to antipoverty initiatives, downplaying the social and economic forces noted by Holt, and accentuating the miraculous coupling of education and technology. Drawing from the culture of poverty thesis, commentators insinuated that the show "saved" poor preschoolers before they internalized the character flaws ascribed to impoverished adults. "The plumbing may be primitive, books nonexistent, but almost every tenement walk up and farm shack has at least one heavily watched television set," said a typical *Newsweek* profile. "Theoretically, the ideal viewer is poor and culturally deprived. Actually, the show catches the preschooler almost before his society does," observed *Time* magazine in a similar piece. The assumption—rarely stated but always implied—was that proof that learning took place was necessary for public television bureaucrats to justify *Sesame Street*'s mass appeal. The program bore the PBS logo because it educated, not because "millions of youngsters watched and enjoyed" it. Because of *Sesame Street*, educational children's programming became the principal exception to the credo stated by the CPB president, John Macy, that public television must avoid popularity. When it comes to prime-time PBS, however, there was "no way public television can play the numbers game . . . and look good."[28]

With its black, white, and Latino cast, *Sesame Street* also promoted interracial respect and cohesiveness. For white supporters like TV critic Les Brown, it was the "most naturally integrated show on television." If racial "peace and harmony ever visit this country," Brown declared, "*Sesame Street* may be one of the reasons why." For this reason, some public TV stations in the South refused to broadcast early episodes. Some black leaders were also critical of *Sesame Street*, on the grounds that its uplifting promises smoothed over racial and economic inequalities. The antisocial Muppet Oscar the Grouch, who voluntarily lived in a trash bin, was especially controversial because he was perceived as the symbolic representation of the urban ghetto. "*Sesame Street* is telling a black kid that it's perfectly normal for you to live in a garbage can if you keep it clean," one minister complained to *New York* magazine. In fact, *Sesame Street*'s first episodes were obsessed with cleanliness, feeding stereotypes about the culture of poverty. One episode, built around the theme "where you live has to be clean," illustrates sweeping, dusting, washing dishes, and personal hygiene. In another, the once-resistant Muppet Ernie discovers the joys of bathing and tells the audience that "everybody in the world ought to take a bath. Then they'd be happy." If some parents found such advice a helpful socialization tool, the poor inner-city black community often had grounds to read it differently. According to a black organizer, instead of worrying about tidiness, the "cat who lives in the garbage can should be out demonstrating and turning over every institution, even *Sesame Street*, to get out of it."[29]

For many white public television viewers, supporting *Sesame Street* was the symbolic equivalent of participating in the War on Poverty. But just as the program enabled middle-class whites to embrace the troubles of the multicultural inner city from a mediated distance, *Sesame Street* tended to encourage volunteerism but maintain dominant power/knowledge hierarchies. In New York, WNET sponsored promotions to bring *Sesame Street* to poor neighborhoods. Humanitarian noblesse oblige permeated coverage of the events in *Image*, the viewer "membership" magazine sent to people who made financial contributions to the station. One 1971 article profiles the Lamars, a white, college-educated couple congratulated for donating a twenty-two-inch color television to a Harlem day-care center. The gift was described as "the latest human relations project" for the volunteer-oriented residents of a "comfortable suburban community." The previous year, they had gone to Newark, New Jersey, for an urban street clean-up campaign. This discourse framed the black urban poor as "others" to the sympathetic white middle class understood to comprise public television's audience. It presumed that society was basically sound and that a television show, like litter removal, could redress apparent inequalities. "It's not the personal glory that's important here . . . the need for TV sets at these centers is so great," said Mrs. Lamar, while a prominent photograph depicted the humanitarian couple watching *Sesame Street* with black toddlers.[30]

While *Sesame Street* symbolized equality of opportunity, it was not conceived as a benefit for disadvantaged kids alone. With industry demands for knowledge workers on the rise, the mandate to prepare all young children for academic success came not only from the Department of Health, Education and Welfare but also the private foundations who supported *Sesame Street*. Corporate donors funded the program to impress influential opinion leaders and middle-class parents with disposable income. Xerox sponsored a costly preview on commercial television; Mobil Oil paid for the printing of *Sesame Street* magazines; and General Foods and Quaker Oats sponsored weekend reruns in major cities. Combining its sponsorship of *Sesame Street* with middle-class anxieties about TV-induced brain rot, General Foods publicized its investment as "one of the best things we've done . . . you can't sell packaged goods in a sick society." The comment was directed in part at suburban moms, some of whom, according to news accounts, had organized neighborhood block parties promoting *Sesame Street* as an alternative to unproductive hours spent vegetating in front of the TV set. When commentators touted the benefits of *Sesame Street* for middle-class children, the poor quality of children's television—not the culture of poverty—was the rationale. At the same time that *Sesame Street* promised to uplift the poor, experts told middle-class parents, "Here's TV Your Child Can Watch" and "Kids Glued to the Tube? Don't fret. TV learning show makes it scholarly."[31]

Sesame Street appealed to parents across race and class differences precisely because it soothed anxieties about television while simultaneously renewing faith in the American Dream. The radical egalitarianism that troubled thinkers like Gardner was contained by competitive individualism, as epitomized by one *Sesame Street* "success story" chronicled by WNET's *Image*. The 1971 article credits the program with nurturing the natural talent of Darrett, an elementary-school student who lived with his blue-collar black parents in the Bronx. A Head Start graduate and avid *Sesame Street* viewer, Darrett aced kindergarten, after which a guidance counselor suggested he apply to a private school so that his "extraordinary intelligence could be developed to its fullest." Accepted on full scholarship to one of the "finest private schools in New York," he was presented to the predominantly white professional middle-class *Image* readership as a living symbol of public TV's cultivating potential.[32] As this portrait demonstrates, the promise of equality of opportunity that surrounded *Sesame Street* was perfectly compatible with the discourse of meritocracy. The claim that *Sesame Street* would level the playing field for children coexisted with the underlying presumption that only the most intelligent, talented, and ambitious among them would reach the peak of the pyramid. The *Image* article made this qualification clear, implying that *Sesame Street*'s universal benefits had facilitated Darrett's exceptional potential for social mobility. A similar pattern was continually evoked to explain public television's close relationship with well-placed adults. In a curious way, *Sesame Street*'s ability to attract a broad and diverse child audience helped legitimate the high dropout rate for prime-time PBS.

Get Yourself Together

In the late 1960s and early 1970s, public television produced variations of *Sesame Street* geared to disadvantaged adults. Unlike formal ETV literacy programs like *Operation Alphabet* and *Learn to Read*, this "personal and social development" genre coupled popular entertainment with self-help strategies. Combining behaviorist psychology with TV technology, the programs promised to help poor minorities overcome their disadvantaged situations. Developed and broadcast by local public TV stations, these programs were another manifestation of the quest to cultivate that was explicitly tied to solving social problems, from chronic unemployment to disobedience and drug use. Although the programs have not been preserved, documents that circulated among stations, researchers, and funders provide detailed information about their content and institutional aims. The public broadcasting archives include scholarly reports with titles like "Television: A Viable Channel for Educating Adults in Culturally Different Poverty Groups," a 1971 document that draws heavily from the "culture of poverty" thesis. According to the report's author, the poor (defined as ghetto dwellers, Mexican Americans, rural Appalachians, and Native Americans on reservations) shared "attitudinal differences" that were transmitted generationally, keeping people trapped in poverty. How might educators "communicate with these groups" via television? The document proposed that they provide practical information and guidance designed to assist "maladjusted" populations.[33] This reasoning and the television programs it spawned demonstrates Ien Ang's argument that noncommercial public-service programs designed to "transfer meaningful messages" to audiences can be just as controlling—albeit in different ways—as programs used as "vehicles to deliver audiences to advertisers."[34]

Civil unrest, race rebellions, and the anxieties that these events caused among the white upper-middle-class power structure permeated the "personal and social development" genre with progressive intentions and disciplinary logics. When the 1968 *Report of the National Advisory Commission on*

Civil Disorders revealed that the average ghetto rioter was an unemployed high-school dropout, public television was called on to address the "poverty of hopelessness and despair." For U.S. Commissioner of Education Harold Howe, it was the "only hope for providing the continuing education that can prevent our marketplaces from becoming riot places." Vice-President Hubert Humphrey also called on public television to provide education and guidance to the disenfranchised urban poor. However humanitarian, this cultural manifestation of the quest to cultivate was rooted in a governmental attempt to reform the morals and behaviors of the economically and racially oppressed. Summing up the rationale that oriented public television's early programs for adult "have-nots," Humphrey suggested that

> the most serious kind of poverty that faces America today is the poverty of illiteracy; the poverty of despair; the poverty of helplessness; the poverty of not finding one's place in this society. That kind of poverty cannot be answered by just another federal grant of money or just another loan. It is the kind of poverty that has to be answered by communication. . . . It just boils down to reaching into the minds and hearts of people through communication and through ideas, through the spoken word, through the visual aid, through the photograph, through the dramatic event, through constant, patient counseling, advice and indicating that there is a place for people, that these people can be moved into the mainstream of American life.[35]

The Corporation for Public Broadcasting responded to this mandate by inviting Harold Mendelsohn, a social psychologist specializing in the media and the poor, to deliver the keynote address at its 1970 programming and promotion conference. Demonstrating what Stuart Hall terms inferential or unconscious, taken-for-granted racism, by ascribing the "problem" of race rioting to urban blacks, Mendelsohn labeled commercial television a virtual "socialization failure" when it came to addressing impoverished minority groups. Public broadcasters, he said, could do better with programs that (1) transmitted particular values and skills, (2) promoted institutionalized social service agencies, and (3) offered sufficient "entertainment relief" to attract the target audience to these deeper educational messages. In this way, public television could channel "dysfunctional" attitudes and behaviors toward a professionally managed "consensus" approach to social change.[36]

Mendelsohn's "Operation Gap-Stop," an experimental television program "for and about" public-housing residents in Denver, embodied his behavioral approach to cultural uplift. After obtaining "knowledge about the urban poor," Mendelsohn and a team of social scientists created a program template called *Our Kind of World*, an educational soap opera about two urban families living in subsidized housing, one black and the other of Spanish-speaking descent (their ethnicity was not specified). According to a 1968 institutional survey entitled "ETV in the Ghetto" prepared by educational broadcasters for Hubert Humphrey, the scripts were written "*about* the poor and *for* the poor" (emphasis mine), designed to "appeal to this particular target audience" with the larger purpose of conveying informational and behavioral goals established by "preexposure" tests. The merger of television and socialization, which was carried out with the support of the Denver Housing Authority, was taken as proof that television could be harnessed to provide guidance in a variety of areas in which the poor were found lacking. Along similar lines, *Cancion de la Raza*, a soap opera produced by public station KCET-Los Angeles in collaboration with social service agencies, presented "messages of social adjustment in the context of a barrio family." Funded by the Ford Foundation and produced mainly by Anglos, this short-lived program about a Mexican American family in east Los Angeles also coupled entertainment with educational messages carefully designed by professionals to change "complacent" attitudes.[37]

One of the most documented experiments in the personal and social development genre was conducted by WETA-Washington, D.C., with partial funding from the U.S. Department of Health, Education and Welfare's Social and Rehabilitation Service. The grant included a postproduction evaluation that cited Oscar Lewis's culture of poverty thesis to assess the success of three programs designed to transmit the skills, attitudes, and behaviors needed to "find and keep a job." The project's goal, established in consultation with social service agencies, local business leaders, and Vice-President Hubert Humphrey's national Task Force on Urban Problems, was "self-help through rehabilitation." In academic terms, the producers developed "new and effective ways of reaching a neglected and dispirited segment of the population" with help that would lead to a "commitment of change in attitude and behavior." In other words, television technology was used to "motivate" and train unemployed people to find and keep a job. The producers believed that even the most "resistant and incredulous could be helped—to help themselves."[38]

TV Job Center, the first program in the series, was created in 1967 with the stated goal of providing "jobs, training, educational opportunities and community services." The first TV show in the Washington, D.C., metropolitan area specifically addressing black viewers, it was guided by a "program psychology" that attributed both poverty and unemployment to the culture of poverty, particularly low motivation, substandard social skills, and underdeveloped work ethics. The assumptions that gave rise to the initiative envisioned poor people of color as deficient beneficiaries of expert white middle-class guidance. Believing that television was "one of the most important influences on attitudes and behaviors," the producers tried to enlist its power to adjust behaviors and attitudes.

TV Job Center also presented interviews with professionals at social service agencies and employers as well as local job listings and advice on subjects from applying for work to "making a good impression." According to the WETA evaluation, although it was broadcast during the coveted prime-time hours four nights a week, the program failed to attract the "jobless audience." The lesson learned was that a "reasonable entertainment element must exist if any sizable audience is to be generated." Producers therefore modified the program by borrowing a popular aesthetic to broaden its appeal to its target audience. The new program, *Jobs 26*, was already in development in April 1968 when Martin Luther King Jr. was assassinated and riots broke out in Washington, D.C. Station personnel referred to the mounting tensions in poor black neighborhoods in their funding pitch to the U.S. Department of Health, Education and Welfare. WETA noted that many urban dwellers had acquired brand-new TV sets through direct or secondhand "participation in looting." For producers, though, the thefts had a silver lining: the saturation of reception hardware enabled them to reach many more jobless residents with public television programming designed to combat "employment inadequacy." The new program embraced popular multiethnic entertainment not as an end in itself but as a necessary means to attract deviant viewers to socialization messages. Appropriately, the promotional vignettes advocating participation in the city's job-training programs were accompanied by soul and blues music. According to the evaluation of *Jobs 26*, "attractive" black female hostesses were employed as another lure, employed to hold the oversized pages of job listings presented weekly over the air. WETA also hired black cinematographers to create short films about local ghetto life (food, culture, music). Assuming that the target audience would appreciate the films more than the job-related advice, producers interspersed them between instructional messages.

Like *TV Job Center*, *Jobs 26* also was broadcast four nights a week during prime time. This unprecedented use of prime hours for programming aimed at urban minorities spoke to the racial unrest. The concentrated "strip" scheduling did not represent an attempt to diversify public television and its audience in regard to race and class. Rather, the rationale was to solve a racial "problem" conceptualized by white middle-class professionals and ascribed to impoverished blacks. From a white vantage point, the goal was to motivate the poor to seek productive employment and, once found, to "adjust" to working life. In this regard, *Jobs 26* exemplified the critique by Charlie Cobb, a member of the Student National Coordinating Committee, of the patronizing logocentrism that underlay many Great Society poverty programs, however well meaning they may have been. "The new consensus is that the poor must be changed," Cobbs wrote about this logocentrism. "The assumption is that the rest of us are OK, so we know what the poor need: they need what we have. The arrogance may be wrapped in good intentions, but it is there nonetheless."[39]

Because *TV Job Center* had made the "mistake" of publicizing jobs that required education and skills the disenfranchised urban poor did not have, *Jobs 26* emphasized low-paying positions like clerical workers, kitchen helpers, and hospital aides. The WETA evaluation gives little indication that producers or funders recognized the structural biases that kept poor blacks either unemployed or relegated to these minimum-wage positions. Chronic unemployment was defined as a shared character flaw, not a symptom of a racist capitalist society. *Jobs 26* believed that it could resolve this problem with motivational improvements, such as prompting viewers to place a telephone call and travel "some distance to be interviewed via city bus, or fill out an application." WETA's promotion of the male hosts—one white and college educated, the other a "black, ex-drug addict, ghetto-reared, school drop out" who was said to be active in a self-rehabilitation program for former convicts—reinforced this individual, motivational explanation for success. Petey Greene, the black host, was portrayed as a man who had taken a few wrong turns in life, but not as a representative victim of racial and economic injustices. According to WETA's publicity, Greene experienced hardship because he "idealized the wrong models as a youngster" and turned to drugs and alcohol, which ultimately led to his incarceration. Eventually he made a "conscious decision for change." Racism and classism apparently had no place in this American Dream story. According to the WETA evaluation, Greene's biography perfectly symbolized *Job 26*'s message that "you can do it, too!" And once you've made it, it's not enough to stand still. You reach out and help the next person . . . and the next. That's rehabilitation with style, man!"[40]

Where It's At, the final program in the WETA series, first aired in 1969 with the goal of attracting youth, in particular, to the audience. Introduced by Hubert Humphrey, this program was the one most explicitly focused on popular entertainment, showcasing a house band that played rock, blues, gospel, and soul; comedy skits; and a studio audience that participated in discussions. Once again, however, black popular culture was envisioned as a means to a greater end, conveying the message that "it's more hip to get yourself together." According to the producers, the "format was planned to entertain and attract the audience first, and then to follow with rehabilitation content." The "hidden" rehabilitative lessons were carefully designed to cultivate appropriate work habits, encourage enrollment in job-training programs, and instill "cooperation" in the context of mounting racial tensions. Since the summer heat was thought to incite "irritability and wanton provocation" among the target audience, *Where It's At* was broadcast after sundown to encourage young blacks to stay at home, away from misbehaviors and conflicts percolating in the streets.

WETA was praised by government officials, journalists, and business leaders. The publicity legitimated the disciplinary precedent it established for public television's relationship with "have-nots." Despite their humanitarian components, TV job programs cast the black poor as unruly pupils who could be motivated by experts to pull themselves up by their bootstraps and internalize white, educated, middle-class norms. The postproduction evaluation defined their proclaimed success in similar terms. According to one viewer quoted in the report, "*Where It's At* . . . helped me to see that I had no excuses as to why I couldn't get it together just like anyone else." Job-training programs epitomized the extent to which public television was *for* the people—especially oppressed people—not *by* them. It would cultivate disadvantaged minorities in white middle-class terms, but it would not be governed by such people. Programs like *Where It's At* conflated public service to "have-nots" with top-down socialization strategies and technological cures for structural inequalities and problems. As the 1968 report "ETV and the Ghetto" proclaimed, "Costs for television in the ghetto are minuscule compared with the potential. It is impossible to predict the new sense of pride, the grasp of basic facts and the discovery of American ideals which the poor may acquire from this electronic medium."[41]

WETA was not the only public television station to join "social and personal development" with job training. The impetus cut across geographical lines but materialized mainly in locales with sizable black populations. *Job Man Caravan*, produced by the South Carolina Educational Television Network with funding from the Ford Foundation, was broadcast in August 1968 with the stated goal of combating unemployment among "minority groups." According to an evaluation in *Educational Broadcasting Review*, a trade publication for public broadcasters, it shared with the WETA programs an attempt to attract the "target audience" by means of popular entertainment, particularly live and taped musical performances and occasional appearances by black celebrities like Stevie Wonder or Dionne Warwick. The host, a black disk jockey named Bill Terrell, profiled different jobs each week on the show while the female "Jobettes" held up oversized cards containing handwritten information promoting job openings and employment centers. Instruction on subjects ranging from successful interviews to "good work attitudes" were interspersed throughout these segments, and the program—true to its name—occasionally went "mobile" across South Carolina.

Job Man Caravan is believed to have generated a sizable black following. According to *Educational Broadcasting Review*'s estimate, it drew as many as 45 percent of households in black neighborhoods. While the program presented a rare opportunity to see black people and black culture on television, its presence on public television was not rooted in representational equality. As with WETA's job-training programs, the underlying aim was to curb societal unrest by facilitating the personal and social development of "employable" individuals. Accordingly, success was measured in behaviorist terms, according to the number of people who applied for jobs after viewing *Job Man Caravan*. The *Review* article deemed the program a moderate success because "at least 150 people" had inquired about jobs publicized by the TV show within a six-month time span. However well intentioned it may have been, the cultural policy epitomized by *Job Man Caravan* was narrowly conceived and inferentially racist. Attempting to bring minorities out of the culture of poverty by disseminating approved attitudes and behaviors, it legitimated top-down, white control over public television's priorities and resources. These power dynamics were accompanied by the promise of democratizing the American Dream through the electronic provision of valuable information and income-generating skills. The upward mobility promised by *Job Man Caravan* and other programs like it was limited, however, to the meritocratic terms of a capitalist society. *Educational Broadcasting Review* illustrated an ideological contradiction at the very heart of the "personal and social development" genre when it implied that public television could eliminate widespread poverty in terms that glorified the efforts and achievements of exceptional individuals. Erasing structural barriers, its evaluation credited *Job Man Caravan* with the "case history" of a formally unemployed black man. The biography it presented cast the man as a representative symbol of the program's success and, simultaneously, as an exception to the rule among the chronically unemployed black viewers it addressed. After obtaining employment after watching *Job Man Caravan,* the man became a "productive" member of society. Eventually he was even able to purchase a modest home in a "suburban area." In an era marked by deep inequalities and racial unrest, *Job Man Caravan*'s capacity to translate hardships and discontents into American Dreams like this one was praised as a "remarkable sociological force."[42]

Public television's address to disadvantaged adults has historically hinged on its presumed capacity to improve them according to educated white middle-class norms. This approach to cultural policy "others" the people it claims to serve and represent. It also tends to fade when political winds shift and rebellions dissipate. By the mid-1970s, the tensions that gave rise to the "personal and social development" genre and the TV job programs it generated had subsided, and both funders and stations lost interest in programs specifically designed for poor people of color. Yet the reasoning that produced this programming lingers in policy contexts, shaping the way that public television's relationship with "have-nots" is conceptualized and defended. Liberal supporters continue to insist that public television is "democratic" because it has the potential to uplift the disadvantaged or combat problems like juvenile delinquency. This rationale is not always progressive, though, and it hampers other possibilities for public television that are not based on acculturation and the one-way flow of wisdom and expertise.

Civilizing Prime-Time Television

While *Sesame Street* mimicked mass culture and *Job Man Caravan* infused the popular aesthetic with behaviorist self-help, prime-time PBS was expected to raise the cultural level of television by avoiding programming that lowered "average tastes instead of trying to develop capacities."[43] The quest to cultivate prime-time television unfolded against a negative image of the vast wasteland and its mass audience. Public television would help solve the "TV problem" with quality programs that enlightened people culturally and intellectually. The rewards for "have-nots" would not be handed out in the classroom or the job sector, but in the less tangible realm of thinking and taste. Theoretically, public television would dismantle the exclusivity ascribed to high culture, along the lines of philosopher Walter Benjamin's argument that mass reproduction would subvert the high-class aura of artistic "masterpieces" like the Mona Lisa. At the same time, supporters like Garner believed that public television could enhance people's capacity to appreciate excellence. In Great Society lingo, public television would cure "cultural poverty" by disseminating culture and knowledge into potentially every home.[44]

In 1969, the prime-time equivalent of *Sesame Street* was said to be *Civilisation,* a prestigious thirteen-part documentary imported from the British Broadcasting Corporation. *Civilisation* warrants critical consideration for two reasons. First, it typifies the kind of prime-time programming that quickly established public television's cultivating relationship with adults. Second, its presentation on U.S. public television was the most publicized event of PBS's first season. Still billed as the "greatest culture program of all time" by public television's video-marketing arm, the program chronicled sixteen hundred years of Western culture, history, and ideas through the learned eyes of art historian Kenneth Clark. Coupling footage from museums, galleries, libraries, and architectural landmarks with Clark's upper-class, British-accented tutorial, *Civilisation* symbolized public television's distinction from mass culture and its promise to cultivate learnedness and taste. At the same time, the program established public television's mode of address to adults closest to the "peak of the pyramid." Just as Gardner warned that "excellence for all" would be tempered by competitive individualism, the PBS broadcast of *Civilisation* became a means of classifying television viewers according to hierarchies of intelligence, influence, character, and ambition.[45]

Like many of public television's more expensive prime-time programs, *Civilisation* was made possible by a "silent sponsor." In exchange for a discreet on-air credit and repeated mentions in newspapers and magazines, the Xerox Corporation picked up the tab to publicize and broadcast the BBC series in the United States. Corporations like Xerox did not subvert the course of U.S. public television as much as they seized on the chance to associate themselves with the distinctive cultural milieu it promised to provide. In no golden age have ideals like edification, quality, and service not been bound to commerce. Public television was not formed in opposition to commercial ownership and control; it was created to remedy the cultural condition of the wasteland. Sponsors who were willing to fund programs that were "good for society" were solicited from the earliest days of educational television. ETV's many corporate-sponsored prime-time programs include "Men of the Philharmonic" (Bristol Meyers Company), "The Age of Kings," a series of Shakespeare's plays also imported from the BBC (Humble Oil), and "Industry on Parade" (National Association of Manufacturers). Just as the Great Society depended on alliances between public and private, broadcast reformers anticipated private support for public broadcasting, including corporate funding as well as viewer donations and start-up gifts from the commercial networks. Public television's first executives sought underwriters for idealized programs like *Civilisation*, which were otherwise outside their scope and budget. The legacy of this arrangement is more complex than the exchange of corporate dollars for the increasingly elaborate credits protested by leftist media watchers. Motivated by the desire to know and impress "influentials," corporations like Xerox drew from the meanings, images, and distinctions that already surrounded public television to reconstitute the "selective" viewer in corporate terms.[46]

The corporations' strategies emerged from a particular historical context. While broadcast reformers were pitching public broadcasting as the solution to the "TV problem," marketers were desperately looking for new ways to target upscale audiences with a critically condemned medium geared to the "lowest common denominator." As the economist John Kenneth Galbraith observed, the postwar mushrooming of consumer culture created a subtle but discernible backlash against advertising, especially among the professional middle class. Herb Schmertz, a public relations guru who orchestrated Mobil Oil's sponsorship of PBS's *Masterpiece Theatre*, recalls this backlash as a "struggle" to impress the "growing number of consumers" who think that advertising is "infantile, shallow and misleading." To escape the crass and "cajoling" sales environment protested by critics like Newton Minow and increasingly shunned by educated and affluent consumers, marketing experts recommended "inventing" cultural and intellectual associations. According to Galbraith, corporations were advised to "reengineer" their public images, a process that entailed presenting themselves less as "hucksters" and more as benevolent sponsors of art and education. But the indirect "culture sell," a staple of radio as well as early television, gained currency in the corporate sector once the invitation to underwrite prestige programs had disappeared. Competition for maximum audiences, coupled with the shift from single-sponsored programs to network-controlled spot advertising, ran counter to the prestige approach. At a time when demographic-based ratings had not yet been implemented and upscale cable channels like Arts & Entertainment, Bravo, and the Discovery Channel did not exist, commercial television was considered a "very poor instrument" for discreet upscale marketing.[47]

The challenge facing marketers coincided with what cultural critic Russell Lynes in *The Tastemakers* called the growing importance of "taste and high thinking" as signifiers of class difference. According to Barbara Ehrenreich, the boon in postwar consumption led many commentators to declare the United States a classless society, with the key exception of the newly "discovered" poor. While the income differential of executives, bus drivers, and secretaries "did not change much," established status distinctions became blurred in a "world where so many people had access to the same vast display of consumer goods." As Vance Packard explained in *The Status Seekers*, substantial differences in wealth, education, and occupational prestige became less immediately apparent, concealed by the "mass-selling of standardized goods and services once available only to the better off." Some critics simultaneously lauded and feared the seeming collapse of traditional class hierarchies. "What happens to class distinctions," pondered Packard, "when most people are able to dine on mass-merchandised vichyssoise?"[48]

Competitive individualism persevered with cultural and intellectual markers of class that could not be bought. "Most of us surround ourselves, wittingly or unwittingly, with status symbols we hope will help influence the raters appraising us, and which we hope will help establish some social stance between ourselves and those we consider below us," wrote Packard about the desire for distinction that could no longer be filled by consumer products alone. Market researchers reported that society's "better-educated" groups were increasingly turning away from a mode of conspicuous consumption that was so "easy as to be pointless." Instead, the most desired consumers of all were adopting "intellectual" and cultural pursuits as the means to express their social differences. This phenomenon was spread by advertisers who incorporated high cultural references into sales pitches directed at the upwardly mobile, such as the housing developer cited by Packard who liberally used French phrases to pitch "une maison ranch" to consumers seeking a place above the mass-produced crowd. However opportunistic, the phenomenon supports John Fiske's argument that when "money loses its ability to signify class difference[,] . . . culture moves in to fill the gap." Fiske rejects reductionist Marxism, particularly its presumption that capitalist production determines everything about class identities, differences, and inequalities. Culture and the "knowledge that is integral to it . . . [are] just important as a means of differentiating classes," he asserts. Corporate America banked on this possibility, seeing in the PBS logo a lucrative symbol of sophistication and prestige.[49]

Xerox's relationship with *Civilisation* illuminates public television's broader corporate appeal. According to the trade newsletter *Xerox World*, the office equipment manufacturer found the commercial television of the 1960s unsuitable to its niche-marketing goals. To impress professionals and managers in a position to make purchasing decisions about its patented new office copier, Xerox wanted its corporate name associated with television programs that "stretch the mind, inspire, stir the conscious and require thought." Xerox-sponsored shows should also "advance" the quality of the medium and associate the company with a posture of "social responsibility." These priorities sounded exactly like the broadcast reform discourse that gave shape to public television. The similarity makes sense, for the Xerox mission was to reach the influential people who "approved of and watched such programs." By sponsoring "outstanding" television programs that were respected by people unhappy with commercial entertainment, Xerox executives felt the corporation was certain to reach selective audiences filled with "current and prospective customers."

For Xerox, the principal problem was distribution. In the early 1960s, Xerox tried to bypass the commercial TV networks by pitching educational and cultural specials directly to local stations. When that plan failed, the corporation saw a better alternative in the newly created Public Broadcasting Service. Public television was more visible and more convenient to corporations than ETV was, since sponsors no longer had to deal with a "maze" of local entities that relied on tapes distributed through the mail to arrange national coverage. Xerox saw public television as the new frontier of tasteful image advertising, and it jumped at the chance to fund programs that coupled the aura of cultural and intellectual prestige with bona fide opportunities for self-cultivation that public television was said to represent. Among the recipients was *Film Odyssey*, a showcase for art-house cinema that combined screenings with scholarly commentary. *Civilisation*, which had been rejected by all three commercial networks, was considered a particularly important coup. Xerox was delighted to sponsor a program with little "mass appeal," for the simple reason that the "in" people had been raving about the BBC series for some time and were reportedly waiting in "long lines" to catch museum showings of the documentary at the National Gallery. Characterizing the desire to identify and impress a "selective" audience that drew companies like Xerox to public television, one official explained, "There is a certain amount of prestige to be attached to *Civilisation*. It won't get a big audience, but we will reach the kind of audience we're looking for."[50]

The idealized public television audience imagined here was exploited but not entirely invented by corporate America. Xerox based its prediction on the social scientific construction of the ETV audience and the sophisticated cultural "minority" constructed by broadcast reform discourse. Drawing from Schramm's studies, ETV's marketing had pitched a viewership that was well educated, professional or managerially employed, and interested in culture, learning, and self-improvement. The public television audience was similarly characterized. According to one 1970 fund-raising report, public television's affluent and intellectually oriented viewers comprised an "attractive market" for upscale advertisers. In another marketing brochure, the broadcast of *Civilisation* was presented as an example of public television's ability to attract exceptionally "selective" and hard-to-reach television viewers. Negotiating the implications of this highly "selective" audience with public television's broader Great Society goals, the brochure claimed that the broadcast of *Civilisation* also served the public interest by bringing quality to the vast wasteland. Even though 2 percent was "not a very good rating on a comparative basis," it was more important that interested viewers "see this program than to win a third or even a fourth of the total audience by showing another Western." The underwriting guidelines formalized by the Corporation for Public Broadcasting in 1972 described public television viewers as "selective, decision-making, affluent, well-educated, and loyal" persons of influence in an "uncluttered" medium. As these characterizations attest, sponsors like Xerox seized on and magnified an image of public television and its audience that circulated within and across institutional venues, in marked tension with its cultivating promises.[51]

Corporations helped mold public television in much the same way that the department stores that Packard analyzed developed a "clear cut image conveying their socio-economic status." Packard's study of lingering class behaviors in the reportedly "classless" society noted that some shoppers experienced enormous "prestige, pride and pleasure" when patronizing upscale stores. The refined atmosphere of these stores—coupled with the distinctions and idealized shopper identities constructed by their advertising campaigns—encouraged patrons to envision themselves as "respectable, proper, cultured and socially above the working masses." The exclusive image associated with upscale department stores "worked" because it ensured that consumers who ventured "beyond their status" would feel unwelcome and uncomfortable, much like a WalMart shopper who accidentally wandered into Saks Fifth Avenue.[52] Corporations wishing to reach and flatter the "right" consumers via public television adopted similar strategies. Although corporations did not manufacture public broadcasting's contradictions, they did support programs and promotional strategies that constructed upscale images distinct from those of commercial television and its audience.

Civilisation and the fanfare surrounding it illustrate this positioning. More like an illustrated lecture than television, the documentary revolved around Clark, an embodiment of gentility and expertise with his English title, sophisticated vocabulary, classic tweeds, and bowler hat. Stylistically, its slow-moving and staid camera movements, fetishized close-ups, loving pans of great works of art, and dulcet tones of chamber music conveyed an aura of serious contemplation. In ideological terms, the program conflated crass commercialism with cultural decline, much as the discourse of the vast wasteland had done. Clark's dispute with modernity may have been anti-industrialist, but it was hardly anticapitalist. In the final episode, "Heroic Materialism," he expressed sympathy with the enduring problem of poverty but rejected Marx and his socialist comrades as dangerous radicals. Clark valued artistic purity and scoffed at political art, which he condemned as mediocre propagandizing. Despite his distaste for mass society, Clark found hope amid the cultural wreckage in the "ideal of corporate humanism." For many TV critics, this ideal was embodied by the corporate sponsors who were finding they could "perform a public service and at the same time reach an influential audience." For press critics, corporate underwriting was perfectly in tune with public television's cultural priorities as they understood them. *Reader's Digest* praised the "valuable role" played by corporate underwriters and agreed that for the "selective viewer, this type of notice probably constitutes the most effective commercial of all." In addition to legitimating the role of sponsors, TV critics magnified their investment, as typified by a newspaper that concluded its favorable review of *Civilisation* with the statement "God bless Xerox." Another newspaper thanked PBS and Xerox for specifically catering to "sophisticated" viewers. Such commentary reconstituted the "influentials" so desperately sought by Xerox as the "natural" audience for public television. Viewers who saw themselves in this image were encouraged to accept the sponsor as an integral component of "quality" television, as typified in the following letter sent to New York's public television station. Associating the Xerox name with artistry and good will, the viewer proclaimed,

> Having just seen the final program of the wonderful *Civilisation* series with Sir Kenneth Clark, I must write this letter. Never have I seen television that could compare with this; the series is truly a landmark in the march of civilization itself! Lord Clark is obviously a compassionate, enlightened human being. To know that such a person exists, and that television of this caliber can be produced, is a revelation to me. That an industrial giant like Xerox Corporation was moved to underwrite this production indicates to me that we can have hope that our own civilization may be able to survive.[53]

Big Bird and Lord Clark?

In his memoirs, CPB President John Macy recalls that if *Sesame Street* was public television's most beloved program for children, Clark's tour of Western civilization was considered the "ideal for the new national schedule on PBS." Macy did not mention that the zippy, educational program for kids could not have been less like the slow-moving documentary for adults. The mismatch between these iconographic programs speaks volumes about the difference between children's programming and prime-time public television. Whereas

Sesame Street addressed social equality and multiculturalism, *Civilisation* glorified the cultural heritage and expertise of the European bourgeoisie. Clark's summation of extraordinary achievements presents each instance of artistic and intellectual genius as another step in the steady march of progress. His tour of the greatest music, literature, art, architecture, poetry, science, politics, and philosophy places the Western European high society at the undisputed center of "man's common heritage." A recurring issue in both the series and its cultural reception was the "near collapse" of this common heritage at the hands of barbarians. In a PBS press release, Clark explained that "civilisation was better than barbarism and I fancied it was the moment to say so," while a press commentator surmised that *Civilisation* is "issuing a warning that we could lose what we have so painfully gained." The great culture of the past was juxtaposed with the "squalid disorder" of the modern epoch, which by the late 1960s was epitomized by commercialized U.S. pop culture, particularly television. This analogy was not lost on TV critics, who often substituted the fictionalized mass audience deemed responsible for the vast wasteland for Clark's barbarians. Wondering whether American television could be a "civilizing force" instead of a "distraction for mass man," the *Washington Post* found tentative hope in PBS's presentation of Clark's masterpiece.[54]

The huge difference between *Sesame Street* and *Civilisation* was apparent stylistically as well. *Sesame Street* looked and sounded like upbeat, fast-paced, amusing, popular television. *Civilisation* moves at the pace of molasses, relies on static shots of Clark pontificating, and requires a dictionary to follow. These aesthetic contrasts speak to the different imagined audiences for child and prime-time cultivation. According to *TV Guide*, while *Sesame Street* reached across differences of class and race, *Civilisation* was expected to appeal to "discriminating viewers." Whereas PBS left the negative image of mass culture and its fictionalized audience implied rather than stated, commentators filled in the blanks. One critic opened her review with the observation, "There are two groups of people in this country—those who have a TV and those who don't." For those who shunned the medium because they feared addiction or preferred "productive" leisure activities like reading, "*Sesame Street* for the youngsters and *Civilisation* for the adults" would finally get television into the house. Articulating anxieties that revealed her to be the type of person Xerox wished to impress, she ended her review with this qualification: "Of course, it will only be used for selected watching, we'll still read and talk."[55]

Whereas *Sesame Street* presented universally intelligible narratives, *Civilisation*'s educational format presumed that its viewers possessed a certain kind of cultural capital to begin with, as indicated by *TV Guide*'s observation that the program "overrates us."[56] As in other prime-time public television programs, Clark pushed the boundaries of upper-middlebrow culture, dropping complex references to painters, thinkers, and composers of "great works" with little introductory background. Although PBS's publicity quoted him as promising to use the "power of the telly" to make culture accessible, he makes no attempt to "sugarcoat" the difficult and often tedious material, and he speaks as if the viewer-pupil at home is a note-scribbling graduate student with reference books on hand. The broadcast of *Civilisation* flattered intellectuals who felt that the program spoke to them, offering an opportunity to pursue self-cultivation and acquire the markers of European high cultural traditions to the upwardly mobile middle class.[57] Certainly, not everyone would have read the show in this way, but the public discourse surrounding it encouraged such associations. Referring to the biography provided by PBS, one impressed TV critic reported that Clark was a "civilized man" because his castle had been a summer residence for the archbishops of Canterbury and Queen Elizabeth I had stayed there as an overnight guest.[58] Like other high-end BBC programs imported for PBS, it conveyed classiness via the sign of aristocratic Europeanness, enabling people seeking an escape from the consumer crowd to take part in aristocratic traditions. If *Civilisation* embodied public television's promise to close the culture gap, it was also a venue for constituting the difference and alleged superiority of its adult audience.

There was no guarantee that it would work this way. As Benjamin theorized, the mass reproduction of high culture can subvert its restrictiveness by making images behind glass in galleries, museums, and private homes available for all to see—and perhaps perceive as they will. The scholarly text that framed *Civilisation*, coupled with the meanings circulated by publicity and press coverage, closed down the ambiguity by fusing particular meanings and connotations with the program. Xerox constructed a symbolic fence around *Civilisation* with campaigns that pitted suitable viewers against a fictionalized mass audience. In an example that played on the relationship between culture and status in an era of mass-produced consumer splendor, Michelangelo's statue of David was superimposed over a Xerox copy machine, with the caption "Xerox Brings Back Civilisation." The promotions so effectively ascribed sophistication to the program that other corporations capitalized on the cachet. *Newsweek* courted subscribers with an advertisement featuring Lord Clark inside a TV set, with the caption "Be Civilized. Quote *Newsweek*."[59]

The Culture of Meritocracy

Claims of *earned* privilege were pivotal to the complex class coding of public television. The aura of inbred taste and sophistication that surrounded public television was tempered by a particularly American rejection of aristocratic (and therefore undemocratic) class privileges. Across policy, social scientific, and press discourse, the public television audience was often characterized as a self-made elite, a claim that connected its prime-time cultural priorities to the promise of equal opportunity represented by *Sesame Street*. Such claims of meritocratic fairness were necessary to justify tax funding for a public service that was widely reported to attract an educated and upscale slice of the adult population. Thus, while Xerox aggressively played up *Civilisation*'s cultural cachet, PBS publicity consistently toned down the arrogance. In a PBS press release, Clark summarized its value to the upwardly mobile middle class with the credo: "man can improve himself." Likewise, many local stations promoted *Civilisation* as an opportunity for self-cultivation that was theoretically available to everyone. The program guide of WQED-Pittsburgh advised anyone with "an interest in enlarging his own knowledge" not to miss a single episode.[60] The advice was not confined to this particular BBC import. Public television was often promoted by both program guides and TV critics as a productive alternative to the passive consumption of commercial entertainment, a distinction that hinged on deeper concerns about one's character, discipline, and work ethic. KOCE-Huntington Beach, California, explicated public television's residual link to genteel middle-class self-culture with a membership pitch based on self-improvement:

> Ol' Buck used to be the life of the party. . . . But if you've heard his stories once, you've heard them a hundred times. His trouble is that he has given up on self-improvement. If he would just watch Channel 50 he could learn about music, art, science, history and probably a whole lot more about himself. Then maybe he would be more interesting to talk to. If you know someone like Buck, why not give him a membership subscription in the "Friends of Channel 50?"[61]

Self-cultivation proposed that any sufficiently ambitious and disciplined viewer could reap the rewards of prime-time public television. The promise was kept in check by the discourse of meritocracy, or the tendency to view capitalist society as a pyramid with limited space at the top, earned through competitive talents and achievements. Despite his nobility, Clark also symbolized meritocratic theories. PBS publicity marveled at Clark's exceptional talent and intelligence, as did press critics. Claims of hard work and advanced intelligence were also attributed to the public television audience by critics, who themselves found its programs more sophisticated and demanding. When PBS announced a plan to measure its national viewership, some commentators worried that low numbers might lead to programming changes that would undermine public television's "dignity." Quoting a PBS executive off the record, one TV critic recommended that researchers instead tally "viewers' scores on elementary school tests." The marks earned by the public television audience, he speculated, would produce a "truer" measure of its value and importance. Another alternative, said the TV critic, would be to "add up how many doctors, lawyers, biophysicists watch public television versus the opposition," as a "Ph.D. obviously carries more weight than a diploma from a vocational school."[62] Although these suggestions were never implemented, they exemplify characteristics ascribed to the "self-made" public television audience.

Quoting the literary critic Lionel Trilling, Gardner's blueprint for the Great Society deemed radical democracy corrosive to the "superbness and arbitrariness which often mark great spirits." Likewise, in *Civilisation*, Clark promoted the "God given genius of certain individuals" and societies that "made their existence possible." His view of culture was in perfect sync with the meanings and assumptions circulating about public television, which is why the program was so useful to Xerox. It was not just that *Civilisation* showed up the vast wasteland: it also promoted Western high culture as an instrument of traditional, middle-class character building, which was considered especially important in light of the social and political turbulence of that time. Many observers of the day blamed a cultural climate that condoned "permissiveness and play" for middle-class student rebellions, which were doubly threatening to elites because they assaulted the university. "The kids . . . were tearing down the elaborate machinery of culture which had been built up in the West since Aristotle," said one historian of the anxieties provoked by youth counterculture, New Left activism, antiwar protests, and other manifestations of discontent.[63] Clark treated these uprisings and the cultural uncertainty they produced as misguided attacks on society's institutions. While he expressed sympathy for the students, he equated their disruptive activities with those of the barbarians. Fondling sculptures, quoting philosophers, and gazing at Renoirs, Clark affirmed the comforting appeal of the Western high cultural tradition at a time when anarchy was "loose upon the world." Near the end of the documentary series, Clark reiterated the lesson to be learned by *Civilisation*. He sounded a lot like the early radio reformer Joy Elmer Morgan when he explained that he—and, by extension, the culture he represented—preferred order to chaos, sympathy to ideology, and knowledge to ignorance. In the process, Clark delineated the very priorities ascribed to prime-time public television.

Sesame Street and *Civilisation* spawned two strands of "cultivating" programming that are still seen on public television, each operating with its own priorities, aesthetics, and assumptions about the imagined audience. The difference between the large and diverse audience cultivated by *Sesame Street* and other daytime children's programs and the considerably smaller, more "selective" audience associated with prime-time public television was implicitly and sometimes overtly rationalized as the outcome of competitive individualism. This meritocratic explanation—so evident in mediated cultural responses to early signature PBS programs—was quickly institutionalized by social science. If the extraordinary intelligence, character, ambition, and taste ascribed to the tiny ETV audience by prominent researchers like Wilbur Schramm had a demonstrable impact on the cultural construction of public television, such claims eventually came full circle. In 1974, the Corporation for Public Broadcasting mined the earlier studies and their ideological answers in an attempt to explain the first comprehensive report on the public television audience.

The 1974 report documented a pattern that continues to this day, in marked tension with public television's claim to benefit all Americans equally. On the one hand, children's programs were found to cut across social differences and reach large numbers of working-class and minority families. On the other hand, the prime-time audience tended to share "education and high status occupations," a finding that confirmed the claims of distinction ascribed to adults in public television-marketing discourse. The research was supervised by Jack Lyle, a one-time graduate student of Schramm's who had worked on *The People Look at Educational Television*. Lyle wrote the narrative explanation for the CPB study, in which he lamented that bringing the parents of disadvantaged children "into the adult audience" did not seem likely. According to the interviews gathered by researchers, "It is not the traditional TV fan, drawn from the group of less-educated Americans, who is pleased with what has been happening. It is the college-educated man or woman, the critic of the medium, who seems happiest with television's altered condition."[64] While Lyle acknowledged the apparent tension between excellence and equality, the very terms of the dilemma—how to bring "others" into the natural (i.e., white, educated, middle-class) prime-time audience—prohibited questions about public television's purpose. If this idealized audience had grown "somewhat" larger and more diverse partly because of public television's popular children's programming, Lyle accepted as inevitable the extent to which "the basic description" supplied by *The People Look at Educational Television* "remained the same." As did the earlier study, Lyle presumed that prime-time public television could never be popular because its mission appealed to only a limited number of individuals. Quoting Schramm, the CPB report concluded that

> this is a remarkable audience, strongly representing the best educated people in the community, the people with the professional and managerial jobs, the people who are most active in civic and cultural affairs, the people who are the most serious and purposeful users of the mass media. It is an audience that any television broadcaster should be happy to have, and that any community organization, educational institution, or state commission should be proud to serve. Yet we must note what this audience is NOT. For one thing, it is not large, by commercial standards; it is a selective rather than a mass audience. Second, it does not represent equally all levels of society.[65]

Legacies and Gaps

Public television's quest to cultivate encompassed multiple ideals, tensions, and disciplinary logics. Uplifting priorities took different forms for different imagined audiences, underscoring the ideological contradictions inherent in the "democratization of culture" in unequal societies. Although the promises of social and cultural mobility that surrounded PBS in the beginning are not as explicit today, policymakers and supporters revive these claims whenever public television's future is called into question. During the controversy of 1995, those who opposed Gingrich's plan to "zero out" public broadcasting defined its importance to "have-nots" in precisely such terms. Basing their arguments on the discourses examined here, they claimed that *Sesame Street* could help elevate children out of disadvantaged situations, whereas prime-time PBS could provide wisdom and taste to lower-income families unable to afford the many cable channels that now duplicate public television's once exclusive "high-culture" focus. Some claimed that public television programming could combat deviant behaviors ascribed to gangs, juvenile delinquents, and other class- and race-coded "troubled populations." Supporters framed public television's cultivating relationship with "have-nots" in logocentric terms that justified its existing cultural priorities. In so doing, they assumed that cultural service for "others" inevitably meant improving them.

Promises of televised uplift cannot erase structural inequalities in the social world. Humanitarian efforts to combat poverty and other symptoms of these structural inequalities should not conflate help with the imposition of idealized cultural tastes, behaviors, attitudes, and norms. At their worst, such conflations are prone to the deep-seated racial and class biases that produced public television's experiments in personal and social development. The liberal and progressive discourses that position public television as a cultural path to upward mobility need to be addressed, for the programming choices they continue to legitimate are neither practical nor democratic. TV viewers cannot be "excellent and equal, too," when those terms are narrowly defined and mutually exclusive. Public television may have the potential to bring socially legitimated culture and knowledge into every living room, but it also has embraced elitism and marginalization by doing so. With the exception of the children's programs allowed to pursue mass appeal in the residual name of equality of opportunity, public television cannot be democratic and maintain its cultural superlatives. It cannot reach beyond the idealized characteristics ascribed to a small and "selective" audience without adopting new ways of defining and measuring excellence.

Most people do not benefit when broadcasting is structured like a pyramid, with commercial channels monopolizing the base and public television perched on the top. More inclusive ways to conceptualize cultural policy can be seen in the popular noncommercial programs offered by public broadcasting systems in Europe. Defensive responses to the public television culture wars discourage societal debate about such possibilities by clinging to a narrow interpretation of the public interest as it pertains to "other" people. By conflating cultivation with cultural democracy, such responses idealize the white, educated middle class and its unexamined place at the center of public television's normative goals. Any attempt to reimagine public television in more democratic terms will require dismantling this centrality and the intersecting discourses that keep it in place.

Don't be just a spectator—be a participant.
—PBS promotion, 1969

CHAPTER THREE

TV VIEWING AS GOOD CITIZENSHIP

In 1992, conservative media watchers affiliated with the Committee on Media Integrity spearheaded a campaign against public television, claiming that it drained tax dollars to propagate liberal ideology. PBS public affairs programs have a chronic bent to the left, said the critics, whereas "conservative opinions remain much less common on public TV than in the nation that helps pay for them." As sparks flew in Washington and the editorial pages of national newspapers, the media watch group Fairness and Accuracy in Reporting (FAIR) weighed in from the Left with a political cartoon. An image of suit- and tie-clad men gathered around a conference table graced the cover of its magazine *Extra!* with the caption "Coming up next: a gathering of public TV hosts discuss the invisibility of conservatives on PBS stations." The satire hinged on the fact that the six males were the real-life hosts of *The MacNeil/Lehrer Report* (now *The NewsHour*), *Washington Week in Review*, and other public affairs shows underwritten by corporate sponsors. FAIR's point was that public television "tilts toward Conservatives, not the Left," because over the years it has been forced to rely more on corporate funding. Although supported by meticulous charts and graphs documenting the corporate affiliations of public television's experts and roundtable guests, this response to the public television culture wars misses the forest for the trees. FAIR did not question public television's print-derivative, expertise-oriented approach to news and public affairs, a choice that reproduces the cultural habitus of well-educated, white male opinion leaders. From a critical cultural studies perspective, the fundamental issue is not a balance among the talking heads but public television's trickle-down approach to democracy as a whole.[1]

This chapter situates public television in a genealogy of reformist thinking about the media and democracy and shows how diffuse anxieties about the mass audience and unruly protesters shaped a public affairs philosophy that survives in residual form. Conceived in contrast to Newton Minow's vast wasteland, public television debuted in a tumultuous era defined by the Vietnam War, student activism, black power, labor strikes, and the emergence of the women's movement. Consequently, demands for equal rights, countercultures, and civil disobedience, coupled with the elite's fears that society was breaking down because of these developments, came to bear on its "political rationality." Beyond combating the mediocrity and hedonism ascribed to commercial television's "majority-ruled" cultural democracy, public television's capacity to address angry and disenfranchised populations, mediate bitter conflicts, and restore social order became concerns for foundations, policymakers, and bureaucrats. PBS devoted 30 percent of its prime-time schedule to news and analysis, debates, government affairs, and electronic town halls designed to extend participation in the political process.

At a time when the commercial networks devoted only 2 percent of their prime-time hours to such fare and specialized cable channels such as CNN and C-SPAN did not exist, public television addressed the viewer at home as a citizen.[2] The paradox was that the expansion of democracy was presumed to require professional experts who could guide decision making and orchestrate consensus. Public television extended the visibility of these processes, but the citizen subjectivities it offered were loyal to requirements of professionalism, civility, and detached objectivity, so that becoming a "good citizen" also meant acquiescing to the expertise, cultural capital, and behavioral proscriptions of a higher authority.

Public television's campaign to transform TV viewers into active citizens has not been critically analyzed, partly because the impressive programming lineup it spawned was scaled down in the mid-1970s. As scholar Michael Tracey argues, progressives tend to cling to what passes as public broadcasting in the United States precisely because conservatives claim that its programs promote liberal social change. Because early public television was less corporatized at that time than it is now and was bullied by the Nixon White House, it enjoys an idealistic reputation against which commercial television's faults are held up. Critics often protest the political meddling and corporate underwriting but defend the concept of public television (glimpsed during its early years) as a democratic alternative to the commercialized marketplace of ideas. Likewise, the idea of addressing citizens who "require information to participate fully in the nation's political and cultural life" is advocated against the consumer sovereignty claimed by commercial broadcasters. Political economist Graham Murdock summed up this stance when he stated that a public communications system was "indispensable to the development of full citizenship in complex societies." This may be true in theory, but as cultural studies scholar Ien Ang argues, public broadcasting's attempt to educate, guide, and reform citizens can be disciplinary and controlling in practice. To move beyond a narrow debate over "political balance," we need to consider how public television's broader relationship to democracy was conceptualized during its formative years.[3]

Public Television and the Crisis of Democracy

In 1972, the TV critic for the Washington, D.C., *Evening Star* declared that "these are wonderful days for citizens who own television sets." As was typical, his praise was confined to the new Public Broadcasting Service. While myriad factors created a historical moment ripe for the creation of public television, the push for participatory democracy that referenced the twin problems of mass apathy and minority deviance was often evoked to explain the new service. The progressive elements of this discourse meant that public television was introduced under different terms than those of the unambiguously paternal European public broadcasting systems critiqued by Raymond Williams. Tony Bennett's approach to cultural policy accounts for the impetus to activate *and* reform the citizenry, inform *and* differentiate TV viewers in accordance with knowledge and power relations. Bennett bases his approach on that of social theorist Michel Foucault, who traces disciplinary "technologies of power" like prisons and mental asylums to the emergence of modern forms of government.[4] For Foucaultian theorists, these technologies construct a rationality, or a "system of thinking about the nature of the practice of government (who can govern; what governing is; what or who is governed)" that makes democracy "thinkable and practicable."[5] Governmentality refers to efforts to shape, guide, and reform the conduct of others—and to the way that we regulate ourselves according to such norms—in order to accommodate certain "principles and goals" that often intersect with democratic ideals.[6] The crucial point is that citizenship is a social construct, that citizens are not born but made. As an introductory college textbook explains,

> Each and every individual must be capable of governing himself or herself. . . . Some have called it "the making of citizens," or citizen training, or civic education. More recently, we have come to call it political socialization, which implies a long process of introducing each individual into the political culture, learning how to accept social authority, and learning what is legitimate and what is not. Still others describe the process in more conventional terms, such as "learning good behavior," "learning the rules of the game," "learning the American way of life."[7]

Extending this citizen training process to cultural technologies, Bennett charts a diffuse mode of social control that emerged in the late 1800s, as institutions like museums opened their doors to the mass public. While hegemony theory is often consulted to address the struggle over dominance and consent waged through commercial popular culture, Bennett proposes that public museums are "governmental" apparatuses with different (but often complementary) power dynamics. Museums were enlisted in the production of human subjects, called upon to "form and shape the moral, mental and behavioral characteristics of the population," which included uplifting tastes and curbing degenerative effects (hedonism, crowd mentality, the decline of standards) attributed to commercialized mass amusements. The "look and learn" pedagogic orientation of the public museum sought to instill "capacity for self-improvement culture was said to embody." Because the museum also symbolizes the democratization of restricted culture and knowledge, its contradictory "political rationality" was not fully recognized. By incorporating the citizenry into "power-knowledge" hierarchies, it became an instrument for the "self-display of bourgeois-democratic society."[8]

Although public television operates with its own multilayered and contradictory "political rationality," it is also best analyzed as a governmental apparatus with an institutional logic that is historically bound. Public television appeared at a moment when cultural and democratic ideals were in crisis, partly because commercial television represented the symbolic encroachment of mass tastes and desires. The medium's avoidance of serious public affairs was explained by commercial broadcasters and many TV critics as "giving the people what they wanted," conjuring up an image of an apathetic and hedonistic public that refused to act as responsible citizens and, through its choices, prevented opinion leaders from doing likewise. When urban rioting and antiwar protesting erupted later in the decade, the visibility of unruly, disobedient activities on the evening news presented another perceived threat to democracy. These overlapping dilemmas warranted a new cultural technology capable of guiding and affirming good citizenship, and it is in this context that we can see the governmental logic orienting public television.

As cultural theorist Toby Miller argues, the often conflicting demands of the consumer economy (which wants citizens to be selfish, indulgent, and hedonistic) and the political order (which wants citizens to be moral, disciplined, and responsible) may present a predicament for the liberal corporate capitalist state. Much cultural policy, he contends, pertains to the administrative training of "citizen subjects" to meet these opposing duties. The belated formation of U.S. public broadcasting is an example that supports his thesis. When "television forwards image and emotion as opposed to sound and rationality," says Miller, "the next move is often for television to become the source of power and the warrant/technology for training publics into a citizenry loyal both to the state and to a particular model of dialogue." Commercial television stimulated the consumer economy but was charged with pandering to mass wants over national needs and, later, with sensationalizing disruptive behaviors to attract maximum audiences. Since reformers like Minow had failed to regulate the wasteland, public television was assigned the corrective "training" role discussed by Miller. Like the relationship between mass culture and the museum, commercial and public broadcasting operated with distinct but complementary logics or aims. With the arrival of public television, people could be hailed as consumers and also, in Ang's words, as "citizens who must be reformed, educated, informed" so that they might "better perform their democratic rights and duties."[9]

We can see this corrective, governmental purpose being negotiated in policy discourse. The congressman who introduced the 1967 Public Broadcasting Act in the House did so because "for a government by the people, a successful democracy depends on enlightened and well-informed citizens . . . public TV can contribute to this end." The Senate Commerce Committee's Report agreed that "particularly in the area of public affairs . . . noncommercial broadcasting is uniquely fitted to offer in-depth coverage and analysis which will lead to a better and enlightened public." In his State of the Union address announcing public broadcasting, President Lyndon Johnson proposed that it would "make our nation a replica of the old Greek marketplace, where public affairs took place in view of all the citizens." These statements spoke to a decline of citizenship ascribed to television entertainment, while claims of expanded participation in democracy spoke to rioting, marches against the war, and clashes with the police. Equating the "demonstrations, disorders, retaliatory blows and other extreme measures" with the breakdown of America's "neural system," one supporter promoted public television as a way to restore an "affirmative relationship between the government and the people."[10]

If the "TV problem" could be explained as "giving the people what they wanted" and political unrest could be deemed a crisis of citizenship, it would follow that public television had to be protected from the mass audience. Public television was *for* the people, not *by* the people, because its political rationality as the bearer of the public interest derived from their failed performance as citizen subjects. It required careful management, said Johnson, because "in weak or even irresponsible hands, it could generate controversy without understanding; it could mislead as well as teach; it could appeal to passions rather than reason."[11] Of course, the people could not be forced to watch public television instead of commercial channels—but those who did watch were characterized as good citizens as well as "primary influentials." The idealized public television viewer was a well-educated white male, but the upward educational skew of the audience was seen as identifying society's "natural" opinion leaders, not the enlightened democracy constructed by its public affairs programs. To see how this occurred, we shall make a brief detour through the media and democracy debate.

The Media and Democracy Debate

Joan Shelley Rubin traces attempts to elevate the common person to the genteel liberalism of the Victorian era, particularly the warnings by thinkers like John Stuart Mill and Matthew Arnold against the "leveling down" of public discourse. As Stanley Aronowitz argues, U.S. democratic ideals are also rooted in the contradictory ideas of Thomas Jefferson and John Dewey. Jefferson advocated universal education to prepare the franchised populace for self-government. Dewey insisted that democracy was rooted in the face-to-face deliberations of the agrarian town hall.[12] Both ideals were thought to be seriously undermined by industrialism, population growth, urbanization, and mass culture, prompting the "careful and logical application of scientific principles to the management of government." Hoping to lift up the immigrant working class, maintain order, and create a "progressive version of the old community ideal" of gemeinschaft, professional reformers of the early twentieth century deployed the "show and tell" governmentality that Bennett describes. The creation of public alternatives to popular amusements attached affirmative citizenship to self-shaping strategies. As John Kasson argues, rational recreations were based on the premise that expert supervision and "enlightened municipal auspices" could develop culture as a "constructive force in social integration and moral development." While considered as a progressive alternative to commercialized amusements, the aim was not to equalize cultural resources. It was to instill tastes, knowledge, and behavioral norms in the people, crafting a cohesive public in sync with the American Way. In the eyes of authorities, "safe and sane Fourth of July celebrations would rekindle a sense of common faith"; public parks would instill "habits of discipline and cooperation" in the poor; and community centers would "supplant poolrooms and saloons as agents in the acculturation of recent immigrants," according to Kasson.[13]

By the early 1920s, social critics such as Walter Lippmann were questioning whether popular democracy was possible. Progressive reforms, he believed, were no match for the banalities, fragmentations, and distortions he attributed to the mass media and modern life. Lippmann's treatise *Public Opinion* called for university-trained objective experts to restore reason to politics, relieving the mass public from the "impossible" task of forming a competent opinion.[14] In the 1950s, Paul Lazarsfeld and his associates at the Bureau of Applied Social Research tempered Lippmann's call for a two-tiered democracy with a theory that was pivotal to broadcast reform discourse. Since the 1940s, the social scientists had named college-educated professionals as the primary audience for serious public affairs. In their *Personal Influence* study, Elihu Katz and Paul Lazarsfeld explain this finding with the "two-step flow," the theory that information trickles down from "experts who can be trusted to know what is really going on" to the "less active sections of the population." They labeled males with college diplomas the primary "opinion leaders" and asserted that leadership among women rose "with each step up the status ladder." Whereas wage earners often turned to their peers for political advice, business executives and professionals rarely consulted those "below them" in the socioeconomic hierarchy, a pattern attributed to "vertical influence." Ideas flowed from well-placed "primary influentials" to wage-earning opinion leaders, who passed the information and advice to other working-class citizens. Affirming and naturalizing power differentials, the study attributed enormous influence to men of the "higher strata" who read more newspapers and magazines and "possessed education and social prestige." According to the two-step flow, the information needs of these well-placed opinion leaders were the priority of democracy.[15]

As TV sets saturated living rooms and the cold war escalated, the problem of mass democracy resurfaced. While some critics scorned experiments in televised debates and panel discussions on the grounds that television catered to "popularity and emotion" over "intelligence and reason," others saw in the medium a chance to cultivate "first-class educational citizenship." The Ford Foundation nurtured educational television (ETV) partly because it believed that the medium could be used to combat the public's political apathy and lack of "realistic and meaningful" values. Noting that the Russians and Chinese were using television to "educate as well as propagandize," Newton Minow pitched educational channels as a device to bring the "knowledge needed to keep our society growing, the cultural heritage to keep our society rich, and the information needed by our citizens to keep our society free." The manager of one local ETV station took Minow's stance one step further. Quoting Aristotle, he argued that in a democracy it was "particularly necessary for people to be educated and informed," because if they were not, "their bad judgments would plunge the state into disaster."[16]

Within broadcast reform discourse, the pedagogic promise of citizenship for all and the special urgency assigned to opinion leaders existed in constant tension. Some reformers boldly maintained that public broadcasting must focus on getting "vital information" to influential people. Political scientist Harold Lasswell, who had advised National Educational Television as a board member, called for a higher level of "civil enlightenment" from noncommercial channels. Better news and public affairs should provide superior "information and interpretive detail" to people who already possessed a well-developed "framework of knowledge." The knowledgeable opinion leaders singled out by Lasswell were similar to Wilbur Schramm's characterization of the ETV audience. Schramm believed that people who chose ETV over commercial television were more apt to read the "better" newspapers, "talk and think about the news more," and participate in political, civic, and PTA organizations. His studies ascribed good citizenship, like good TV viewing, to the educated middle class that watched ETV. Still, the results of a current events quiz cast doubt on the fledgling system's capacity to adequately inform the opinion leaders it attracted. Among the "shocking" lapses of knowledge that Schramm discovered was that "two-thirds of our WGBH viewers had forgotten who [scientist] Robert Oppenheimer was, if they ever knew."[17]

Fred Friendly, who shaped the formation of public broadcasting as the television consultant to the Ford Foundation, pushed the expansion of ETV to combat this problem. In his 1967 memoir, Friendly, who had resigned from his post as the president of CBS News in 1966 when network higher-ups broadcast an *I Love Lucy* rerun instead of Senate hearings on the Vietnam War, did not protest private ownership and control of broadcasting. Rather, his dispute with advertising was that the quest for high ratings had killed "first-rate" news and public affairs. Taking this as a sign that quantity was incompatible with quality, Friendly advocated a Lippmannesque public-service alternative that could show not what was popular but what was "good." By this point, however, race rebellions, antiwar protests, and generational conflicts were influencing discussions of television journalism and forcing public television's supporters to reach beyond the expected audience for "quality" programs. Equating the turmoil with a crisis of democracy, U.S. Commissioner of Education Howard Howe, who had once been on the Ford Foundation's payroll, called on public television to address the "urgent ills of the community."[18]

The "TV problem," the turbulence of the late 1960s, and a widespread perception that "American achievements in community-building had been overrun by the automobile" positioned public television as a device capable of solving problems, resolving conflicts, and reconstituting TV viewers as citizens instead of consumers of washing machines and potato chips. Public television's concerted attention to public affairs promised to revitalize democracy, and yet as Patricia Aufderheide argues, the institution's quasi-corporate structure was ultimately no more "public" than was commercial broadcasting. Public television's subdued, writerly, expertise-oriented look and sound also constricted its claim to representative publicness while undermining the radical democracy promoted by activists like Stokely Carmichael, who refused to accept that only educated, well-spoken people were "qualified" to participate in democracy. PBS's concentration on public affairs hinged on the restricted participation that Carmichael questioned. Consider the views of Ford Foundation President McGeorge Bundy, whose checks helped make possible public television's public affairs heyday. In his 1968 book *The Strength of Government,* Bundy confessed to an affinity with university professors over "practical people." He also opposed "left-wing revolutionary sentiment," believing that some forms of protesting symbolized an "infantile" tantrum that often does more harm than good. Douglass Cater, who, as an assistant to Lyndon Johnson, helped draft the 1967 Public Broadcasting Act, also promoted "enlightened leadership." Cater's book *Power in Washington* took issue with leftist sociologist C. Wright Mills's critique of *The Power Elite.* Unlike Mills, Cater believed that democracy required "the existence of a power elite" that could offer "genius" and "self-restraint" to the practice of governing.[19] Such thinking was everywhere apparent in public television, whose citizenry-building programs modeled the enlightened leadership that reformers like Bundy and Cater espoused.

Public television was not conceived as a speaker's corner or popular assembly. According to the Carnegie Commission, its purpose was to provide a "civilized voice in a civilized community." Ford Foundation consultant Robert Blakley summed up why in *The People's Instrument*, a "programming philosophy" inspired by a 1969 programming conference held in Racine, Wisconsin. According to these programming guidelines, public television was not created to turn over the airwaves to a cacophony of angry voices demanding equal access to television. On the contrary, by transforming "discontents into proposals," "high-decibel talk into high level discourse" and "problems and issues into orderly procedures," public television would "mediate" conflicts and restore "reason" to democracy, tasks requiring objectivity and expertise. In this way, it would make sure that those who govern "respond to fair and reasonable arguments" and that those who are governed respect authority by limiting their "protests to ways that do not wreck society."[20] Such perceptions were widely shared by public television's leadership. Harvard Law School graduate Frank Pace, the Democratic chairman of the board of the Corporation for Public Broadcasting, even called public television the "Marshall Plan of America." In 1970, Pace told a group of supporters that

> all of us in public broadcasting have a clear and unqualified sense that this is the answer to the transition that America must undergo as it moves from a great nation to a great civilization. In its essence, it is the kind of education—preschool and adult—that can make a nation great and cause it to realize its heritage. As I look at the variety of problems that face this nation—as I look at the inadequacy of most of the solutions, I can see in every one of them a constructive role to be played by public broadcasting. Drugs, law and order, education, growth of the individual, breadth of the democratic process . . . we are the sole instrument that can provide the answer.[21]

Experts, Opinion Leaders, and Deviants

Public television's close relationship with experts and opinion leaders was anticipated by *Public Broadcast Laboratory* (PBL, 1967-1968). Initiated by Fred Friendly with a large Ford Foundation subsidy, this Sunday evening "interconnected" experiment was prominently billed as the pilot for public broadcasting. As the nation grew increasingly divided and network journalism more contested, this magazine-style program promised to shed "new light on the most confused and troubled dark areas in contemporary life" by introducing scholars to television technology. It would put "meaning into a test tube" said one newspaper. Originally called *University Broadcast Laboratory*, *PBL* was overseen by an academic board chaired by the dean of Columbia University's Graduate School of Journalism. During the first season—which included a live bicoastal discussion among political scientists and historians in studios in New York, Boston, and San Francisco and a guest appearance by Walter Lippmann—academics were paired with producers on every story, from start to finish. The Russell Sage Foundation contributed "specialty in the behavioral sciences" through a formal partnership with *PBL*, providing academics and other consultants with "credentials" to participate both behind the scenes and before the camera. Our approach starts "with the expert and then develops the story," said executive producer Av Westin, Friendly's one-time protégé at CBS, referring to the program's expertise-oriented approach to television journalism. "Our reporter's job is to . . . come up with story ideas, find the [credentialed] experts who know something about it and 'print' in television terms their findings."[22]

An episode entitled "The Whole World Is Watching," in reference to the slogan chanted by protesters outside the 1968 Democratic Convention, took a hard look at TV journalism. Hosted by an earnest young correspondent named Robert MacNeil, the program opened by noting that two-thirds of adult Americans "now depend on television as their major source of news." Commentators then blamed the commercial networks' quest for high ratings for the demise of the quality of television news, as evidenced by the proliferation of human-interest fillers, gossipy tidbits, and the increased use of "dramatic pictures over reasoned statements." While conservatives of the era accused the TV networks of colluding with radicals in broadcasts showing police beating protesters and U.S. soldiers massacring Vietnamese, the liberal critics interviewed by *PBL* protested the very same news coverage. For them, the problem had nothing to with ideology; it was that broadcasters pandered to mass demands for sensationalism and excitement.[23] What, then, was the alternative? This *PBL* episode's own scholarly aesthetic, heavy on expert commentary and light on visuals, was clearly the approved template for serious television news. When *PBL* strayed from this format, controversy erupted.

In a 1970 speech to the National Press Club, CPB President John Macy defined public broadcasting's approach to public affairs in similar terms. Referring to perceptions of declining news standards and a growing "credibility" gap among the people, the networks, and political authorities, he identified three priorities: (1) providing an alternative to "sensationalist" and "distorted" television news, (2) demonstrating that "reasonable men could work to solve public issues" through rational debate, and (3) using broadcasting to enable citizens to make known their opinions and judgments. Macy attributed the TV problem to the mass audience. But "none of this should be interpreted as criticism of the commercial networks," he insisted. "By and large, they are doing—and doing very well indeed—what they must do under a system which measures survival and success in terms of mass-audience ratings that respond more to the stimulus of entertainment and excitement than to information."[24]

Public television's purpose was to combat audience demands for emotion, triviality, distortion, and conflict. Accordingly, its public affairs tended to emphasize reason over passion, tedium over drama, expert over personality, civility over rudeness, seriousness over human interest, and officialdom over dramatic events. The assumption that "too zealous an intent to entertain can lead to the falsification of what should be presented as unadorned as possible" led to "cross talk" based on locally produced experiments like *Newspaper of the Air*, later called *Newsroom*. Dubbed "TV's first real paper," *Newsroom* was conceived as a counterpoint to "trivial and meaningless" news stories presented by "plastic, deep-voiced readers of another's copy." Featuring long reports read by newspaper journalists and little visual or human interest material, the program was "an oasis of news in a television desert" distinguished by the adjectives *authoritative*, *serious*, and *professional*. Although it was intended to "provide the kind of coverage not available elsewhere" on television, the program addressed a "readership, not a viewership." It was a televised version of the quality press, not the tabloids, situated in the legitimated masculine habitus and devoid of the everyday connections and universally accessible elements (pictures, person-on-the-street perspectives, narratives) that make journalism popular. An audience analysis sponsored by the Ford Foundation, which helped underwrite the *Newsroom* programs, contended that less than 1 percent of the TV-viewing audience actually watched them, regardless of locale. The study confirmed the program's distinction from commercial television's journalism, but it also raised questions about *Newsroom*'s capacity to serve the public interest when the programs were so widely ignored. As the researchers concluded, *Newsroom* was "too written and too demanding for the average person to follow."[25]

When the National Public Affairs Center for Television (NPACT) was created in 1971 to produce public affairs programming for PBS, it nonetheless favored the very same print-derived formats found on *Newsroom*. NPACT's programs were not intended to surpass the much-contested nightly newscasts provided by commercial broadcasters or provide a similar service minus commercial constraints. Instead, the intention was to develop televised equivalents of serious national newspapers like the *New York Times,* the *Washington Post,* and the *Wall Street Journal.* That is, public television's priority was to squelch what John Hartley calls the merger of journalism and "popular reality" and Daniel Hallin terms the decline of TV journalism's "high modernist" period.[26] When commercial broadcasters realized that newscasts formerly envisioned as a public-service obligation could be profitable, they incorporated popular appeals intended to attract the largest audience possible. It was at this point that TV news began to rely more heavily on human-interest material, everyday spins, and anchor personalities. An 1971 advertisement in *TV Guide* illustrates this attempt to recast news as popular culture. The headline asked, "What makes the Eyewitness News team so popular?" Answering the question, the copy promised: "In short, a more human news program." Public television might have taken popular news in less commercialized directions. Instead, it bucked the trend with what NPACT President Jim Karayn called serious, selective, and focused journalism. Extending to television the established hierarchy between major national newspapers and the tabloid press, correspondent Robert MacNeil explained public television's priorities with the statement "In a democracy, the "quality of information you consume" is as important as the "quality of the automobile you buy."[27]

The journalistic hierarchies presumed by MacNeil are related to social hierarchies, as Bourdieu has shown. Tabloid journalism may be commercialized and exploitative, but it also coordinates with popular aesthetics and the immediacy of everyday life in ways that serious newspapers, with their unadorned style and focus on official doings, do not. The cultural opposition between tabloid journalism and legitimate news is also based on the different citizen subject positions of the imagined readers, with people who read papers like the *New York Times* granted more "dignity as a political subject capable of being, if not a subject of history, then at least the subject of a discourse on history." For Bourdieu, legitimated practices like reading the *Times* should not be interpreted as inbred capacity for enlightened citizenship, for they are closely connected to the possession of education and cultural capital, as well as the sexual division of labor. White men with degrees, he points out, are more apt to be offered "full membership in the universe of legitimate politics and culture," including the "sense of the right and duty to read a legitimate newspaper."[28] The criteria used to categorize high and low journalism conflate substance with form, overlooking the fact that popular news can be just as informative and relevant to its audience. Freed from market constraints, it might fuse popular culture with investigative reporting on public life. Rather than developing popular news, however, NPACT translated the written conventions of the quality press for an imagined audience of opinion leaders.

A Public Affair (1972), an election-year NPACT program that promised to improve on commercial television, was "long on interviews, filled with visiting experts, marked by discussions," establishing the aesthetic template for today's PBS *NewsHour*. Praised for "outclassing" the commercial networks, its scholarly approach was so admired that it was distributed overseas by the United States Information Agency. "Cross talk" programs like *Washington Week in Review* (1967-present) and *Wall Street Week* (1970-present), picked up for national distribution from the largest public stations, also were modeled after the supplementary journalism provided by "better" national newspapers. A more somber, intellectual version of commercial television's *Meet the Press*, *Washington Week* presented a static camera shot of print journalists discussing the machinations of inside-the-Beltway occurrences. Visuals were so unimportant that its staff boasted that one could "listen to the show." Another NPACT program called *This Week with Bill Moyers* pioneered the TV news "essay," a narrative and thus potentially popular format. This too, however, was pegged as high-quality and thus scholarly journalism. The program minimized visuals and, gearing itself to opinion leaders, presumed a prior knowledge of its often complex subject matter. Describing the note-shuffling Moyers as a "scholarly" newsman, a reviewer who lavished enormous praise on *This Week* was nonetheless compelled to caution: "Not everyone may appreciate this type of program, for some people would rather read detail than view it."[29]

The Nixon administration, which was already battling the news media, was outraged to discover what it perceived as a "liberal bias" on public television. The White House criticized NPACT programs for tolerating anti-establishment perspectives and labeled correspondents as overpaid limousine liberals and "known Kennedy supporters." The ruckus set into motion the conservative criticism ridiculed by FAIR's cartoon. In 1972, PBS tried to debunk these charges with a statistics-laden document called "PBS on Record," which meticulously tabulated the party affiliations of every expert who had appeared on NPACT's public affairs shows. The findings showed an even split among Democrats and Republicans, neglecting—as did the programs—all other political beliefs outside this binary. While the quest to "prove" bipartisanship was meant to quiet the Nixon White House, it ignored another complaint having to do with public television's narrow appeal to opinion leaders. Long before Nixon's advisers joined political complaints to broader accusations of cultural elitism, reformers were conflating the ideal public television audience with constituencies who might "provide financial, political, social, intellectual and moral support."[30] While such constituencies were concentrated among the white professional middle class, public television's promise to revitalize democracy created an institutional imperative to bring "others" into the audience for quality public affairs. But the political rationality that gave rise to public television meant that its focus on serious, print-oriented, expertise-heavy cultural formats could not be questioned. The promise of universal enlightenment existed in perpetual tension with an address to "influentials" in sync with the tiered democracy envisioned by the theory of the two-step flow. While officials promised benefits to all Americans, an unpublished 1973 audience profile describes a different institutional sentiment. According to the report, which was commissioned for the Corporation for Public Broadcasting by the Ford Foundation,

> the commercial networks aim primarily for the blue-collar class, and are grateful for white-collar viewers. Blue-collar households prefer the sitcoms and action series that are the staple of commercial television. The skew toward the better educated is a strength, not a weakness . . . if the skews were toward middle and lower income[people], public broadcasting would be competing directly with the three large networks, who are already adequately serving those groups. Public television has to be an effective way to reach opinion leaders.[31]

The public affairs philosophy spelled out by the president of the CPB, John Macy, also made expanded opportunities for active citizen participation in democracy a priority. Public television delivered, but the gains were contingent on unstated discursive requirements and behavioral rules. Public television was called on to manage the contradictory requirements of the consumer culture and the liberal corporate state theorized by Miller, which meant constituting citizen-subjects loyal to a "reasonable" form of dialogue. The desire to impress on TV viewers the importance of the rational debate was based on Enlightenment ideals and biases. While reason has historically been associated with educated white European men and the written word, traits judged as irrational (such as emotion) have been tied to mass culture and are often implicitly associated with women, people of color, and the uneducated, subordinated, working classes. The legitimation of objectivity as the solution to the late 1960s' demands for "group access" to television came from the related presumption that only experts are suitably equipped to distinguish objective reality from the modern distortions and everyday distractions that troubled critics like Lippmann. But objectivity is not just a conceptual framework for evaluating what kind of knowledge is trustworthy and reliable, maintains Michael Schudson. It is also "a moral philosophy, a declaration of what kind of thinking one should engage in" and a subtle form of gate keeping that insulates and valorizes professional authority over experiential knowledge.[32]

Likewise, the cultural construction of "rational thinking" on public television was more than a humanitarian effort to enlist viewers in the productive and nonviolent resolution of conflicts. It was also a template for enlightened citizenship that excluded emotionally and bodily invested forms of political expression and participation, like women's consciousness-raising groups, union meetings, strikes, consumer boycotts, and mass protests. The emphasis on "civility," though certainly progressive in some regards, can be construed in ways that undermine popular participation. As John Kasson argues, the "established codes of behavior" often ascribed to civility have historically functioned as a social classification system "against a fully democratic order and in support of special interests, institutions of privilege, and structures of domination." Critics who idealize public television as a truly democratic public sphere, similar to the theories of philosopher Jürgen Habermas, ignore a cultural limitation that cannot be blamed squarely or exclusively on corporate funding. In its basic form, public-sphere theory calls for spaces separate from the commercial marketplace and the political state, where people can either physically or virtually meet and act as citizens, discussing issues, advocating positions, and forming "publics" with collective stakes. Public television's capacity to serve as a public sphere was limited by the discursive and behavioral rules ascribed to it when the mass television audience and irrational protesters were, for different reasons, perceived as threats encroaching on democracy.[33]

In some ways, early public television did craft the electronic "public sphere" advocated by Aufderheide, as programs sought to "establish relationships between people whose differences are deep, with the goal of finding some common ground to articulate and address issues that pertain to the common good." Yet public television's raison d'être was to create a "better" public, as she also acknowledges, a mandate that justified its narrow and ultimately constraining cultural boundaries. The public affairs philosophy articulated by Macy differentiated good citizenship—cerebral discussions of state affairs, calm and guided deliberation, ritualized voting—from disorderly conduct. The ability to participate in televised democracy hinged on education, social clout, and approved decorum—not just in terms of who was "qualified" to appear on the programs, but also how they addressed imagined viewers at home. Borrowing from Peter Stallybrass and Allon

White, Bennett traces these proscriptions to the "enlightened" democracy of the Parisian cafés idealized by Habermas:

> No swearing, no spitting, no brawling, no eating or drinking, no dirty footwear, no gambling: These rules which, with variations, characterized literary and debating societies, museums and coffee houses, also, as Stallybrass and White put it, "formed part of an over-all strategy of expulsion which clears a space for polite, cosmopolitan discourses by the construction of popular culture as the 'low-Other,' the dirty and crude outside to the emergent public sphere."[34]

For most television viewers, adopting the subject position of a good citizen as constructed by public television meant accepting an aesthetic order governed by a higher authority. It required access or acquiescence to communicative "codes" rooted in the specialized habitus of legitimated opinion leaders.[35] This requirement undermined democracy by insisting, in accordance with Blakely's programming philosophy, that action without such "knowledge and understanding" is the "wrong action." Live coverage of congressional activities was introduced as a form of citizen education that might quell misguided protesting. The purpose, said Macy, was to show that "laws are not made in a vacuum" and that those "responsible for making them must consider many factors before recording a vote." The purpose of live, "gavel-to-gavel" coverage of the 1972 Republican National Convention was to counter ratings-driven sensationalism by "focusing exclusively on official business." This also meant ignoring popular dissent of the sort that materialized outside the 1968 conventions. As Todd Gitlin shows in *The Whole World Is Watching*, the commercial television networks publicized the bitter conflicts of the era and portrayed the protesters as deviants. But public television could not display and promptly recuperate dissent in a similar way. The mandate to produce a "better," more enlightened public could not justify dwelling on civil disobedience or shocking images of police brutality. Conceding that "nobody pretends this will be the most exciting program" on television, a PBS spokesperson explained that if "Jerry Ford is giving a very dull speech and a riot is going on outside, we will stay with Jerry Ford."[36]

The electronic simulation of the New England-style town hall was rooted in the democratic ideals that Dewey championed. According to Mobil, which sponsored several PBS "town meetings," the idea was to "revive public discussion" and recapture the "discourse between governed and governor that was possible in the village town meetings of our country's formative years" in the context of "today's causes and controversies." The format would "fill a void in communication," but it was also perceived by some as a technology integral to democratic uplift and social control. While progressive in their attempt to re-store community cooperation lost in the massification of society, these formats reflected institutional concerns about the "kind of training" necessary to pre-pare ordinary television viewers for larger roles in democracy. To ensure the quality of the town halls and their outcomes, one programming consultant proposed balancing the invitation for all "citizens to exercise intelligent deci-sion making" with an emphasis on "the leadership segment of society."[37]

That trained professionals would mediate the discussions and conflicts went without saying. Remembering a sticky situation at WJCT-TV in Jack-sonville, Mississippi, where the public station avoided trouble by placing some citizens in an expensive club and others in a community hall on the poor side of town while the "experts held forth in the studio," Macy ex-plained that disputes alone do not "lead to action."[38] His remark was refer-ring to public television's experiments in live "confrontations," a short-lived format that pitted representatives of conflicting social groups against one an-other in the hopes that the "expected" dispute would burst out, deflating pent-up tensions.[39] In a departure from the scholarly approach advocated by its editorial board, *PBL* staged such an argument between black revolution-aries and middle-class whites. While eventually "put into context" by a Har-vard professor, the uncivilized "spectacle" of a black power advocate arguing "heatedly and at length" with a white housewife, a staged conflict that antic-ipated in some ways today's afternoon talk shows, was condemned by the guardians of journalism. The problem was decorum, explained *New York Times* TV critic Jack Gould, who called the segment a "screaming match" that sacrificed rational debate to unmanaged emotions.[40]

National town halls also spoke to the tension between participatory democracy and social control. Cofunded by the Corporation for Public Broadcasting, government agencies, and private corporations, these initia-tives coupled "problem-solving" programming with interactive opportuni-ties to seek further assistance and advice, including telephone hot lines, community outreach, and supplemental study guides. Promising advice from "countless authorities," the ventures addressed deviant and disenfran-chised citizens—particularly the student counterculture and the urban poor—from the perspective of educated, white, middle-aged opinion lead-ers. While progressive in some respects, they also fused expertise and self-rehabilitation strategies. Like the mass audience, "others" requiring civic at-tention tended to be conceptualized as hedonistic, irrational, and/or childlike. *The Turned-on Crisis* (1971), an attempt to "detect, educate and re-habilitate drug users" funded by the CPB, the National Institute of Mental

Health, and pharmaceutical companies, was hailed as the "first massive use of primetime television to attack a specific social problem." To attract counter-cultural youth more inclined to appreciate the aesthetics of *Sesame Street* than *Washington Week in Review*, it featured televised drug therapy and social-problem docudramas like "Stopped Running," a program that reenacted "creative alternatives to the drop-out-turn-on lifestyle." Despite this concert-ed attempt to create popularity, the month-long event was filled with author-itative talking heads, leading one wisecracking TV critic to lament that *The Turned-on Crisis* "had all the effect of a sleeping pill."[41]

The Turned-on Crisis illustrated the "appropriate" democratic tech-niques for handling conflicts over recreational drugs. While ostensibly a public service for troubled drug users, it also showed that officials, profes-sionals, and parents could resolve disputes, provided that they followed ra-tional procedures (learned from watching the program). In one episode, the self-described white-collar town of Wayne, Pennsylvania, addresses the problem of drug use among high-school students.[42] In this program, adults were the unquestioned authorities, as revealed through content, camera movements, and editing. An orderly discussion among professionally dressed grown-ups at the high-school gymnasium is juxtaposed with shaky camera footage of unkempt youth, including a long-haired hippie wearing a psychedelic T-shirt who disdains the "establishment" and defends pot smok-ing because it makes him "feel good." Interspersed are reenacted encounter sessions among students and their parents (mother and daughter argue over the daughter's sloppy clothes) and parents and school personnel (a teacher advises a father that discussion is more effective than the "paddle"; a guid-ance counselor explains the need for hall monitors in the bathroom).

In one reenactment, the mayor threatens to close down the town's youth center because adults have complained about loud music, shouting, drug dealing, and rowdy teenagers "peeling out of the parking lot." The incident is presented as proof positive that citizens who play by the rules have oppor-tunities for legitimate participation in the political process. Students who prefer innocent activities like Ping-Pong over deviant ones like partying are shown meeting with the mayor at city hall to discuss the behaviors of their disruptive peers. When they promise to take it upon themselves to monitor their peers and enforce the rules at the center, the mayor reverses his deci-sion. Lecturing from a book-filled library, a fortysomething male narrator later explains that law enforcement and medical authorities cannot manage the "turned-on crisis" without citizen participation. Like many PBS public affairs programs, he concludes by stressing the importance of "objective and unbiased information" as the path to conflict resolution and consensus.

VD Blues (1972), declared "one of the most significant events in the history of television as a medium for education, enlightenment, and raised consciousness," rejected stodgy public television formats in an aggressive attempt to popularize public affairs. The innovative format spoke to a perception in public broadcasting that youth had "rebelled" against the conventional media. Aimed at teenagers and young adults, *VD Blues* addressed the medical consequences of the sexual revolution with slang, skits, and folk songs. Like other forays into the popular aesthetic, the format was justified only by a higher purpose: publicizing a national epidemic said to be caused by "young people loving young people." Breaking prime-time barriers by blending medical information, humor, and frank talk about the clap and love bugs, it promised to solve a problem defined largely by adult male experts. Much of the program unfolds from the vantage point of medical professionals who put the kibosh on free love with stern warnings about "dosed" partners. The viewer at home is suspected of having an undetected venereal (sexually transmitted) disease and throughout the presentation is urged continually to seek medical attention. While undoubtedly rooted in helpful intentions, *VD Blues* makes sexually active citizens—particularly females—seem like sexual deviants.

PBS declared the broadcast a success in behaviorist terms, citing the fact that VD clinics around the nation reported a surge of calls and visits following its presentation. In Chicago, clinics were reported to have closed for several hours, literally swamped by the crowds of young people seeking blood tests. While the purpose was to enlist "voluntary cooperation" to resolve a national social problem, *VD Blues* did more than prompt some young people to seek testing. More broadly, it attempted to shape, guide, and reform sexual mores. Like the excerpts of the World War II army training films warning GIs about "loose" women that it showed, the program's lessons were steeped in judgments about active female sexuality. In every scenario, young unmarried women (or homosexual men) were tellingly cast as the victims of venereal disease. In one skit, the jokes revolved around a middle-aged male doctor who scolded a "nice middle-class girl" for contracting VD; in another, syphilis and gonorrhea do battle in an oversized uterus. A young black couple is shown making love in another dramatization, but only the woman turns up at the hospital with a sexually transmitted disease.[43]

The *Just Generation* (1972) also incorporated popular cultural elements in its attempt to legitimate the legal system as a "positive, civilizing force in society." Educational segments about criminal offenses and the "penalties assigned to them" were accompanied by performances by a comedy troupe. The goal, acknowledged by the producers, was to mitigate youthful disrespect for authority. According to PBS publicity, the program was intended to help curb youth rebellions such as a case in New York, where an "unauthorized rally called by students to protest school policy turned into a rampage with desks overturned, papers scattered, and windows broken." Believing that "law has deteriorated, especially among young people," the show sought to combat the "quantum leap in the intensity of illegal, disruptive and violent action." Humorous skits were interspersed with discussions of drug and Secret Service violations, among other crimes, and remote visits to courtrooms, jails, and state legislatures. Here again, the fusion of popularity with active citizenship was tied to an ulterior attempt to shape the attitudes and behaviors of rebellious and discontented youth.[44]

TV Viewing as Good Citizenship

The flagship PBS public affairs program, and the clearest example of public television's approach to "enlightened democracy," was *The Advocates* (1969-1974), whose stated purpose was recasting "the passive TV viewer in an active role, working and voting to make democracy a reality."[45] Conceptualized by a law professor at Harvard University, the weekly show epitomized the move to bring reason to America's living rooms by "combining the vivid communication of television with the cool analytical power of experts." Each week, two professional male "advocates" argued liberal and conservative positions on pending (or potential) legislative issues in a courtroom setting. The advocates, who were lawyers in real life, made their cases by calling witnesses and advancing arguments in a "logical, orderly fashion," culminating in a studio audience vote and the judgment of a "decision maker," usually a public official. Later episodes extended the final decision to viewers at home, whose mailed-in responses to the vote were tallied by producers and forwarded to Congress, the White House, government agencies, and the news media. For this service to democracy, *The Advocates* drew bipartisan praise from scores of TV critics, politicians, and the *Congressional Record*.

The Advocates, which was cofounded by the Ford Foundation and the Corporation for Public Broadcasting, took up timely and often controversial issues, ranging from the withdrawal of troops in Vietnam to school desegregation to whether to impeach Richard Nixon. Ostensibly aimed at informing and activating citizens, it also demonstrated legitimate ways to express and resolve conflicts. The program's guiding reform logic is best understood as governmental, not ideological, in the sense theorized by Bennett. As PBS publicity explained, the purpose was not to "wade through the muck and mire of the past . . . to understand the social, political and economic forces that contributed to the mess." It was to empower citizens to "do something," an invitation that was, however, constrained by the model of democracy constructed by the program. *The Advocates* offered only two positions on any given issue: liberal and conservative. Experts were best equipped to define these issues, and both sides were presumed to be equally defensible within the rational-debate format. Most of all, the program presumed that consensus on any issue, however contested, could be achieved within the existing structures and institutions.

Though described as the closest that television had come to "participatory democracy," the opportunity to vote for one of the two "sides," as construed by professional advocates, was the only participation offered to the TV viewer. The male moderator established the atmosphere with an authoritative call to order. As camera zoomed in on a pounding gavel, the "ladies and gentlemen" of the studio audience (and, by extension, viewers at home) were addressed in the manner of a judge presiding over a courtroom. From there on, the television courtroom was an ordered sanctuary where the people spoke only when spoken to by authorities. As the trial progressed, two television screens displayed in a concise sentence the question being debated, followed by the two choices, yes or no. When the experts had finished, the announcer confirmed that "now is the time for you at home to act." Within these highly controlled symbolic boundaries, viewers at home were urged not to be "just a spectator—be a participant."

Broadcast live from authentic courtrooms in Boston and Los Angeles, *The Advocates* was unadorned, harshly lit, and slow moving. Staged for the camera, the mock debates were carefully composed and thus predictable. Visuals were sparse, confined to occasional charts or filmed interviews with witnesses who could not appear in person. Still medium-to-long shots, minimal editing, shuffling papers, long-winded replies, and the absence of dramatizing effects (such as music) constructed an educational aesthetic, a civics lesson that drove home the idea that the actual practice of democracy was a solemn affair indeed. A self-conscious emphasis on the rational-debate format conveyed something similar. The fairness of the reasoned debate was fetishized over the importance of any issue, and the professional orchestration of "balance" took precedence over the rightness or wrongness of any position articulated on the program. The "two committed halves equal one balanced whole," promised PBS publicity, a message emblematized by *The Advocates* logo, which featured two arrows pointed in opposite directions coming together as a unified symbol. On one hand, a debate among amiable opponents was an ingenious way to please Congress, which wanted public television to achieve objectivity and balance. Whether consciously or not, the choice of format screened out "unenlightened" participation, a pattern that Bennett also ascribes to museums. *The Advocates* epitomized Blakely's argument that public television must balance the "understanding and skills" of objective experts with the upsurge of angry citizens demanding a "piece of the action," the "right to have a say," a share of the "power."[46]

PBS simply assumed that everyone who appeared on such a program would have sufficiently impressive credentials to articulate a sound position. According to PBS, professional advocates were indispensable, because "commitment alone may lead to gross errors of judgment." Socially legitimated dispositions, or ways of conversing and behaving, concentrated in the dominant social groups were presented as supremely democratic. The most important qualification for being an advocate was the disposition to avoid "the temptation of making a highly emotional but fallacious argument." On every episode, the advocates were instructed by the narrator to argue "not his personal opinion but responsible arguments for each side of the case." During the first season, the men randomly took a side on the issue being debated, and liberals sometimes played conservatives in the mock trials. Later, advocates were presumed to be committed to a particular side while still adhering to professionalism and decorum. The two who appeared most were Howard Miller, a University of Chicago Law School graduate who, according to PBS publicity, balanced his arguments with "lessons in philosophy, history, and the morality of Western man," and Harvard Law School graduate William Rusher, a former Wall Street lawyer and publisher of the conservative *National Review*. Although they "disagreed about the issues," the men described themselves as personal friends, equally committed to a "reasonable" process of dealing with conflicts. It was the televised display of this *process*—not the content of the debates or the party affiliations of the experts—that defined the public interest logic of *The Advocates*. As Rushner explained,

> I think our common ground comes mostly in having the same kind of job to do and the same kind of attitude towards it. I've said to people who've asked whether I get along with Howard, that I do. The reason is, we have a great many more things in common, in terms of the problems we face, than we have separating us . . For two men, speaking calmly and intelligently, to disagree profoundly about an issue may be polarization; but to have people yelling "pig!" at each other, or shouting "burn, baby, burn!" is a different kind of polarization—it is non-communicative polarization. I don't think *The Advocates* contributes to it; I think quite the reverse.[47]

Suggesting how the program's lessons may have been perceived by some viewers, one man wrote: "This is the best one I have ever seen and it was so fair and dignified that at the end I liked the lawyers and witnesses for both sides equally well and could have voted either way."

The people who "put such a show together" included an impressive team of journalists, lawyers, political scientists, and other experts that would have pleased Lippmann. The people who appeared as moderators, decision makers, and witnesses formed a "guest list that reads like Who's Who," promised PBS publicity. The usual moderator, Victor Palmieri, was the CEO of an investment company and had served as deputy executive director of Lyndon Johnson's National Advisory Commission on Urban Problems, commonly known as the Riot Commission. Nearly everyone called to testify on *The Advocates* was college or graduate-school educated, usually male, and frequently employed as a government official, politician, writer, professor, or professional ("top men, well informed," said *Daily Variety*). The members of the studio audience conformed to the professional middle-class dress and behavioral codes of conduct established by the program's producers, such as keeping quiet, "behaving with reasonable calm," and not heckling the experts. When people who were not college-educated professionals were invited to appear, they were "othered" by the logic of the program in ways that undermined their knowledge and credibility. For example, during a debate about whether students should receive time off from college to volunteer for electoral campaigns, a construction worker was called to testify as a "hard hat" with "no particular purpose except he was against special favors to college kids."

People without education and professional status were also fodder for ridicule in the press. On an episode dealing with a welfare reform bill, a minimum-wage worker was called to testify that he earned less from his job than mothers on welfare received, and he took the opportunity to elaborate on his views beyond the prescribed line of questioning. Later, a welfare mother in the studio audience broke the rules by shouting out her opinions and eventually storming out of the courtroom as a gesture of protest. Contrary to the praise usually bestowed on *The Advocates*, the TV critic for the *Boston Globe* reported that this episode was "not particularly illuminating." It provided "some laughs," he conceded, when a "belligerent witness told how he felt in earthy terms, including a swear word here and there," and an unruly woman "shouted epithets that reached the microphone." Unfortunately, he reported, the "cause of enlightenment wasn't served much until an assistant secretary of labor . . . showed up near the end and explained the provisions and implications of the measure in voluminous detail."[48]

This episode of *The Advocates* epitomized Michael Harrington's criticism of Great Society antipoverty rhetoric. Just because the United States had declared a war on poverty, Harrington argued, did not mean that the "well-bred citizenry" intended to "have field hands and janitors speaking up for themselves."[49] While the testimony of people with life experiences relevant to welfare legislation was discredited, the congressman who served as the credentialed decision maker was praised for "simulating" the poor lifestyle of welfare recipients to see whether reform was necessary. Quoting PBS publicity, many TV critics reported that the Democrat and his wife "ate for a week on foods available for the welfare-budget of 66 cents per day and found that with ingenuity a healthful menu was possible." Qualifying the evidence with another PBS quotation confirming the superiority of expertise over experiential knowledge, many also explained that of course, "Mrs. Bingham is a nutrition expert with knowledge unknown to the majority of the welfare recipients." *The Advocates* and the discursive formation around it divorced politics from the everyday lives and emotions of ordinary people, casting democracy as an affair managed by professionals.

As Barbara and John Ehrenreich have argued, student radicalism in the late 1960s and early 1970s was perceived as a grave threat to idealized notions of reason and expertise. Such traits have historically been closely bound to the professional middle class, yet the offspring of this class were protesting, breaking the law, rejecting dominant institutions, and otherwise refusing to act within the accepted boundaries of the bourgeois public sphere.[50] *The Advocates* spoke to anxieties provoked by student radicalism when it attempted to return campus activists to legitimate dispositions and rational debate as the best way to handle disputes. PBS encouraged stations to promote the program on college campuses by seeking out "student representatives" who could help gather a youthful audience by word of mouth. Debates were held on issues that mattered to student activists, including amnesty for draft resisters and FBI surveillance of the New Left, and on these episodes, college students were called to testify. Among the debates were the legalization of illegal recreations like marijuana smoking and the institutionalization of legitimate outlets for political participation, like receiving college credit for volunteering to work for elected officials. These episodes provided space for dissenting views, and their outcomes sometimes challenged existing laws and policies. Within the overall logic of *The Advocates*, however, they also channeled the realities of grassroots activism into the display of professional reform logic. A debate on the Vietnam War that culminated in a vote to withdraw U.S. troops illustrates this process. On the one hand, this episode suggested that the people can challenge government decisions. Yet both the episode and the PBS publicity surrounding it also suggested that public opinion produced in an orderly way on *The Advocates* was credible—whereas the activities of unruly antiwar protests were not.

The Advocates also discussed a number of issues that mattered to feminist activists, including the equal rights amendment, work schedules to accommodate parenting, no-fault divorce, and access to birth control. Such episodes offered a higher profile for female experts, and one pre–*Roe v. Wade* debate over the legalization of abortion even featured as the guest advocate a female lawyer described as a "women's liberation activist." These episodes were unusual in that they invited women into the male-coded public sphere, but as with student-related issues, democracy was still dependent on legitimated codes of thinking, behaving, and governing. Modes of political expression associated with the women's movement, such as sharing personal, often painful and emotional, experiences, had to be incorporated in the dominant logic of the "rational debate." Nonhierarchical decision-making practices idealized by feminist activists gave way to a formal institution presided over by a male judge. If social change emerged from expert debate followed by a vote and an official procedure, grassroots struggles could be downplayed as well, as shown by PBS publicity crediting *The Advocates* with liberalized abortion legislation in several states, though without mentioning the women's movement.

The Advocates made some effort to reach a potentially broad (but still male) audience by using popular athletes and sports-related metaphors in promotions pitching *The Advocates* as "the PBS fight of the week." Researchers soon found that the program appealed to mainly to educated opinion leaders, as *TV Guide* also pointed out with the headline "The Thinking Man's Fight of the Week."[51] PBS courted this audience by situating the "fight" in a scholarly habitus, telling viewers, "In a medium that has bred the sixty-second attention span, *The Advocates* requires thoughtful attention for an entire hour. And it's getting it." In statements like these, PBS placed the responsibility for resisting commercial television—and becoming a good citizen—solely on individuals. Such thinking was reproduced in the press, in which reviewers constructed hierarchies of citizenship between the responsible television viewers who watched *The Advocates* and the less responsible masses who preferred "the movies on ABC and the second half of *Hee Haw*."[52] Viewers' letters excerpted from tallies sent to Congress often drew from the discourse of the wasteland to connect good citizenship with social and cultural distinctions. *The Advocates* provided the symbolic material for some educated viewers to differentiate their own rational thinking, self-discipline, and good taste from that of the mass audience, as suggested by the following letters:

Friends—and you are my friends when you present such thought-provoking programs, implying that some of us out here in the Vast Wasteland can and do think. Not many TV programs pay us this compliment.

A truly splendid program. Of all the myriad and generally spiritual-ly demeaning offerings on television only your broadcasts are con-sistently interesting and civilized. Keep up the good work.

This construction of good citizenship complemented the scientific logic of the two-step flow. According to *TV Guide*, *The Advocates* was no success by mass standards, but it attracted the most "influential people" and thus had "an impact where it counts."[53] While participation did not extend beyond the ritual of voting, the more than 22,000 votes received after each debate were taken as public opinion that "mattered." Neither the sociodemographic pro-file of the public television audience nor the fact that preaddressed postcard ballots were available only to people who made financial contributions to their public television stations were seen as a reason to qualify the results of the debates. Instead, the bipartisan voting audience was evoked to confirm public television's ability to orchestrate balance and consensus. The "vote swings heavily from conservative to liberal and occasionally perches in the middle of the fence," while the "majority of liberal positions on social issues" are balanced by some "very conservative thinking on the subjects of law and order and the economy." However well intended, this affirmation of demo-cratic processes legitimated the leadership abilities of the experts who ap-peared on the show and the "primary influentials" who tuned in. People who chose entertainment over this particular brand of televised democracy were positioned as hedonistic and apathetic citizens, and those who refused to play by the programs' rules were deviants, as illustrated by an incident, much pub-licized by PBS, in which the "pot cigarettes" sent in after a debate over mari-juana were "promptly turned over to the police because under existing feder-al and most state laws, the possession of marijuana is a crime."

Race, Class, and Radical Democracy

Not all early PBS programs were born of an "enlightened" public affairs philosophy. Muckraking and experimental documentaries also appeared amid enormous controversy, as we will see in the next chapter. *Woman Alive!* (1974) lasted for a single season, coupling women's folk music with female experts and personal documentaries about women's everyday lives. The struggle for black empowerment also created some space for PBS public affairs programming by and for blacks. Popular uprisings in Watts (Los Angeles), Detroit, Washington, D.C., and other cities made race relations an issue for benefactors at the Ford Foundation and for the Corporation for Public Broadcasting. The 1968 report "ETV and the Ghetto," prepared for Vice-President Hubert Humphrey, indicates that government officials also looked to public television to resolve the "racial crisis." Citing the Kerner Commission's indictment of the media for failing to report on the "causes and consequences of civil disorders," the 1968 report called for enhanced "two-way communication" between the inner city and the white power structure. As we have seen, the earliest black programs were produced by whites and offered "personal and social development," particularly job training. Demonstrating the white anxiety and inferential racism that accompanied these programs, the *New Republic* praised the increased attention to blacks on the grounds that only television, the "great addiction of the ghetto, far more extensive than booze or heroin or cocaine, can reach the ghetto this summer."[54]

Programs by and for blacks, however, spoke to the burgeoning demands for a diversified television culture and typically addressed social and political injustices, including racism and economic disenfranchisement. Shoestring budgets forced most local black public affairs programs into the unadorned studio talk show format. *Black Journal* (1968-1976), a hybrid cultural/public affairs show distributed by PBS, was an exception. Blending performance, entertainment, documentary, popular education, and discussion, *Black Journal* deliberately collapsed boundaries between high and low in what producers saw as an attempt to "bring television back to the people." Black journalists, professors, celebrities, musicians, sports figures, and activists—including members of the Black Panthers and the All-African People's Revolutionary Party—appeared regularly on the show. Rejecting the premise of detached objectivity (and its alleged existence in white journalism), *Black Journal* adopted the crusading role of the black press. "Experts" were presented as representatives of the black struggle who were invested in its outcome. Collapsing the artificial boundary between reason and emotion, *Black Journal* constructed a black counterpublic sphere in which serious topics, popular pleasure, multiple modes of expression, and everyday black experiences were compatible with one another. The show also cast a wide net around legitimate knowledge, pioneering call-in opportunities for viewers at home and taking seriously spirituality, black astrologers, and clairvoyants, one of whom predicted Nixon's resignation.[55]

Black Journal began as a monthly program conceived and overseen by a white producer as a response to the assassination of Martin Luther King Jr. Created under the auspices of National Educational Television's weekly *NET Journal*, the premier episode opened with a black man covering an oversized window with black paint. Refusing to distinguish between so-called hard and soft news, black hosts William Greaves and Lou House interspersed live skits, studio reports, political commentary, gossip, documentary films, and segments on music and fashion. The newscast did not forbid human-interest material (like the news that Stokely Carmichael and his wife had purchased a home), provided it was relevant to a black audience. The white producers were evident, however, especially in a long segment on jailed Black Panther Huey Newton that went to extraordinary lengths to avoid offending white viewers. The filmed interview with Newton was juxtaposed with police rebuttals and an "objective" analysis to put the whole segment "in perspective." When the crew fought for a black producer to make good *Black Journal*'s claim to be a show "by, for, and about blacks," the new opening projected Africa on a red globe alongside black leaders, public figures, revolutionaries, professionals, and workers. Black control behind the camera was both a political and an aesthetic issue, observed *Ebony* magazine in an article that questioned white-defined standards of objectivity and quality. From a black perspective, the "selective focusing of the cameraman, the process of filming each part of a show, the background music . . . the way a host is made to talk and gesture and the minute editing of a script so that it may conform to the conventional standards of 'professional excellence' all communicate with the viewer and tailor the intended message."[56]

Addressing the imagined audience as black "brothers and sisters," *Black Journal* strove to raise political consciousness and forge affirmative cultural identities. When Greaves was appointed executive producer, *Black Journal* implemented a policy to ensure that the "people in news reports and films "speak for themselves as much as possible and, if narration was used, the narrator assumed a tone of advocacy."[57] In an episode that featured performances by blues musician John Lee Hooker, a characteristic news report on the Transport Workers' Union eschewed "balance" and instead presented the story from the perspective of black workers. Interviews and footage of rank-and-file transit workers being thrown out of the New York City subway for protesting on "company turf" dramatized the explanation for their discontent offered by the narrator. In the same episode, a black professor analyzed the political uprisings of the 1960s on a spotlighted stage, seated in an armchair. Unlike PBS public affairs programs that ignored racial minorities, however, this ultrascholarly presentation did not define *Black Journal* but was part of an editorial mix that continually bridged popular culture, advocacy, and politically invested expertise.

Contrary to the stereotypical image of the mass audience circulated by policy and cultural discourse, the relationship between black intellectuals and uneducated viewers as constructed by *Black Journal* was respectful and reciprocal. The program's purpose of educating viewers was not conceptualized as cultural uplift or social control. Rather, it was defined as a "force" in the sense of "elevating the black consciousness—culturally, politically and socially."[58] According to Jannette Dates, *Black Journal*'s aesthetics were conceived and debated in relation to racial identity, not cultural hierarchy. Greaves wore a dashiki and African music was used to signify the program's commitment to black heritage and pride. Greaves's goal as executive producer and host was to develop television as a black cultural form by creating a visual equivalent of jazz. In the process, *Black Journal* would "liberate the African American spirit."[59]

Black Journal aired weekly on PBS until its funding was sacrificed in the institutional downscaling of minority programs and public affairs. As resources dwindled, Tony Brown, dean of communications at Howard University, took over as the program's executive producer and host. *Black Journal* was forced to curtail its use of cultural segments and field reports and rely more on the low-budget panel discussion format to which local black shows were relegated. Brown continued to combine information, politics, and entertainment, however, avoiding the staid talking-head format with panels on racism in sports featuring popular black athletes and blaxploitation films with black actors and directors. Even the most scholarly episodes of *Black Journal* unmasked their own role in the production of knowledge. On one panel, revolutionary Kathleen Cleaver acknowledged her purpose on the program, telling viewers she wanted to provide political education and consciousness-raising. Another guest told his fellow experts, "We have a responsibility to be very clear to black people on shows like this."

Some critics felt that *Black Journal* was a token "safety valve" in which mostly middle-class blacks could "blow off steam" while public broadcasting as a whole marginalized people of color, both on camera and behind the scenes. Others said that its very appearance on PBS—the "educational" channel—was a symbolic barrier to building a cross-class black constituency. PBS publicity, meanwhile, positioned *Black Journal* as evidence of racial pluralism, not as a universal template for good citizenship. A typical press release normalized the unstated white orientation of the vast majority of PBS public affairs programs by "othering" *Black Journal*, explaining to the imagined white reader that "today's black communities have their own special needs, problems and issues." Another PBS press release implied that the program's purpose was to cure black delinquency, pitching it as a "weapon of survival" for the black man in his "dark and vice-ridden milieu." Despite this inferentially racist framework, *Black Journal*'s subversion of the approved public affairs format was duly noted, defined less as ideological deviance than as stylistic inadequacies. *New York Times* TV critic Jack Gould faulted the program for opting for fast-paced "bridges of song" over legitimated journalistic conventions. Critics like Gould simply could not accept this approach to black public affairs. As Brown put it in a furious response to the newspaper of record, "It is imperative that black programs contain as much emotionalism as possible . . . what your critic saw as 'bridges of song,' we understood as messages to explain ourselves."[60]

In 1974, facing cancellation, Tony Brown obtained modest corporate underwriting from Pepsi Cola and announced that *Black Journal* would adopt a popular variety format. While continuing to probe serious issues and convey the message that "black is beautiful, proud and an important part of our society," the new format would combine entertainment, discussion, music, fashion, celebrities, and a popular game show called *Can You Dig It*. The debut, which was cohosted by actress Diahann Carroll, featured a short film about abolitionist Frederick Douglass and an appearance by Jesse Jackson as well as performances and a quiz segment, modeled after commercial game shows, in which contestants answered questions about black history and culture. While the show was "definitely more entertaining" than the formal studio format into which the program had been forced, the *Washington Post* skewered the game show segment and questioned the program's news value "to a black audience already inundated with entertainment programming on the commercial channels." The critic rejected the idea that popular black programs free of commercials *and* aimed at large audiences had a place on public television.[61] He need not have worried: The new *Black Journal* failed to generate sufficient station support to keep it on public television, forcing the show to migrate to commercial syndication. The paradox was clear: As the civil uprisings that gave rise to *Black Journal* began to subside, its attempt to fuse popular culture, news, and politics became less attractive to public broadcasting. When the program proved it could couple mass culture with black public affairs, it was relegated to commercial television. When it became commercially viable, it lost public support and the chance to develop black television in a noncommercial context. The very binary oppositions that *Black Journal* sought to avoid ultimately undermined its ability to survive on public television.[62]

Also created in response to the Kerner Commission, *Black Perspective on the News* got its start on WHYY-Philadelphia and was picked up for a short national run on PBS (1975). Envisioned as a cross between black newspapers and *Meet the Press*, this public affairs show was more conventional in appearance. Although *Black Perspective* emulated the talking-heads format, it also rejected the premise of objectivity by exposing racist news frames and "correcting the record" on issues related to the struggle for black empowerment. Producer Jimmy McDonald defined *Black Perspective*'s mission against a white-controlled commercial broadcasting system criticized for its narrowness of mind as well as its blatantly commercial priorities and disrespectful treatment of black citizens. "In America today there are more than two sides to every story. It is no longer adequate to read all the news that's fit to print, nor is it enough to watch topless, bottomless, laugh-a-minute quickie evening news," said McDonald of the need for black commentary and analysis.[63]

McDonald critiqued the vast wasteland from a politicized perspective, stressing the failure of commercialized entertainment programs to inform and represent black people. So did many letters protesting its cancellation when the CPB phased out support for local and national public affairs in 1973 (around the same time that the Ford Foundation moved on to other projects, and reforms set in motion by the Nixon White House were implemented). Several targeted programs generated letter-writing campaigns, but based on the preserved responses, blacks and whites protested on quite different grounds. People who wrote to "save" *Washington Week* and other white-oriented public affairs programs were more apt to describe themselves as selective television viewers distinct from the unintelligent and hedonistic mass audience. While clearly grateful to be treated respectfully as citizens by public television, many could not express their appreciation without evoking a negative image of the people held responsible for the vast wasteland:

> My wife and I are not addicted TV watchers, but we regularly view *Wall Street Week*, *Washington Week in Review*, and *World Press*.

> We contribute to [public TV] because we find it hard to believe that the American people have degenerated to the level of most of the programming on commercial TV, but will find this support difficult if its better programs cease.

Those people who wrote protesting the cancellation of *Black Perspective* in Philadelphia were more apt to define the public affairs program as a venue for political enlightenment and social change. They, too, compared *Black Per-*

spective with commercialized entertainment, but their comments emphasized TV's racism, not its low cultural quality or appeal to masses with low taste:

> The Black community is starving for a means of communication to which *Black Perspective* has forfilled [*sic*] and serves as an enlightenment means for those who are concerned about their conditions . . . stopping the production of *Black Perspective* would be like denial of a transfusion to one who needs it.

> Certainly we pay taxes and have to fight your wars. . . . We would like to know why *Black Perspective* is being forced off the air when the *Beverly Hillbillies*, *I Dream of Jeannie*, and hours and hours full of white-oriented garbage is left to try to pervert our lives?[64]

Black Journal and *Black Perspective* were two exceptions to a public affairs philosophy that normalized the white, educated, male center of U.S. democracy. By the mid-1970s, when the political turbulence that gave rise to them had subsided, the "minority" programs were gone as well. NPACT was also substantially downsized and forced to merge with WETA-Washington, and *The Advocates*, public television's most acclaimed public affairs program, was canceled in 1974. By this time, the nation had stabilized and cable was being developed to serve niche audiences, alleviating the pressure to address "news junkies" and find opinion leaders with a "mass appeal" medium. PBS's gavel-to-gavel coverage of the Watergate hearings was the last hurrah of its campaign to transform TV viewers into active citizens. The people who watched the event on public television—versus those who watched highlights on commercial television or not at all—were discovered by researchers to be "influential opinion leaders" more apt to be college graduates, to have voted in the last election, and to have made a public speech in their lifetime. The findings were used to justify funding for public affairs: "Considering the very important role of politically active citizens in a democratic society," said one study, "the occasional state subsidy of their efforts to get additional and detailed information about public events of high political salience seems appropriate."[65] Constructing a portrait of the public television audience from viewers' letters sent in response to the hearings, a former NPACT producer concurred that even more precious than the "selective and better educated segment of the population," represented by this burst of support, was the loyalty conveyed by public television viewers who felt they belonged to a privileged fraternity."[66] And indeed they did.

Public Television and Citizenship Today

In 1993, the Corporation for Public Broadcasting attempted to combat claims of "liberal bias" emanating from the Right with a study entitled "Perceptions of Balance and Objectivity in Public Broadcasting."[67] Like the quantitative response amassed by PBS to mollify Nixon's attack, the report documented "very small percentages" of people who believe that "public TV is biased toward liberals or conservatives." While the statistical evidence was impressive, the report ignored the fact that most people do not benefit from the information and analysis found on public television because they do not watch its programs. This dilemma speaks less to the narrowly defined partisan "bias" rejected by the report than to the social and cultural hierarchies at the very heart of public television's address to citizens. Although the public affairs lineup on PBS is much smaller today, traces of "enlightened democracy" can be seen in the subdued officialdom of *The NewsHour* and *Washington Week in Review*, in attempts to educate citizens with electoral campaign specials, and in the imagined audience of educated male opinion leaders associated with these programs. Public television no longer has a cultural monopoly on such viewers, however, which makes it easier for free-market conservatives like Newt Gingrich to label such programs as a "dated" service in the age of CNN, MSNBC, and C-SPAN. At a time when policy debates are dominated by such arguments, cultural studies can help denaturalize the "rationality" that shaped public television's enlightened democracy, so that democratic alternatives can be developed.

Public television also justifies its existence on the basis that it transforms passive TV viewers into active citizens. Recently, it embraced the credo "social capital" as a new phrase for "good citizenship." Taking cues from Robert Putnam's influential book *Bowling Alone: The Collapse and Renewal of American Community*, it has committed its resources to combating the troubling "erosion of civic life," a problem that is said to be caused in part by commercial television's distracting "infotainment." Among the goals stated in public television's 2001 "strategic plan" are "building trust," creating "connections," and encouraging "citizens to take action, become involved, and build the social capital that characterizes healthy communities." Unfortunately, while these priorities have potentially progressive dimensions, they also reproduce public television's tendency to favor well-placed "opinion leaders." The report defines "social capitalists" as people who "vote, attend PTA meetings, visit museums or engage in some range of civic or cultural activities," in short, precisely the people who can be expected to benefit from—and contribute financially to—the "public television experience" as it currently exists.

Under the rubric of "social capital," public television has promised to provide televised town halls and other programs that promote community-based problem solving. Yet it continues to idealize the enlightened leadership of educated "influentials" in a society in which "neighborhoods work, people are safe to walk the streets, the schools educate and enlighten our children, and happiness is possible." In so doing, it continues to overlook the inequalities that undermine U.S. democracy by fetishizing technological solutions that place "social capital" in the hands of powerful citizens who, according to the tenants of "enlightened democracy," have earned their place in the small public television audience because they are capable of making rational decisions, resolving conflicts, and producing consensus. Instead of expanding the parameters of this circle of "people who participate in community affairs," as Putnam advocates, public television's renewed commitment to citizenship is poised to reinscribe the two-tier democracy it has historically espoused.[68]

As Stanley Aronowitz notes,

> the ultimate referent of mass society is the historical moment when the masses make the (still) contested demand for the full privileges of citizenship, despite the fact that they are obliged to work at mundane tasks, are typically untrained for the specific functions of governance, and are ensconced in the routines of everyday life.[69]

Public television's ambivalent view of the "masses" needs to be challenged, for it has created a cultural template for democracy that legitimates some citizens and ignores or "governs" others. Presuming that the people are inherently apathetic or disorderly, public television has valorized the aesthetic and behavioral norms of an empowered slice of the population. It has tolerated broader interpretations of "radical" democracy accountable to race and class difference only during times of crisis. It has used popular culture as bait to lure "deviant" citizens but has relegated potentially popular democratic forums, from women's daytime talk shows to Rock the Vote, to the commercial market. Buzzwords like *social capital* cannot correct these biases. Until the underlying construction of democracy that orients public television is questioned, it will be prone to marginalization and conservative culture wars. Reforms that subvert the binary between mass culture and democracy and that refuse to universalize "approved" (i.e., educated, masculine, Eurocentric) ways of thinking and behaving are necessary to move beyond a marketplace construction of the people and a liberal ideal rooted in enlightenment and social control.

The public television system we visualize is not for the elite, but for a broad cross section of the population. We are talking about a lot of specialized, diversified interests. When you put them all together . . . you get a representative group of Americans.

—James Killian, chairman of the Carnegie Commission

CHAPTER FOUR

SOMETHING FOR EVERYONE

In 1994, PBS president Ervin Duggan raised eyebrows during a national press conference when he claimed that "we are all Anglophiles." Given the ethnic diversity of the United States, the journalists who attended the event wanted to know how this logocentric presumption correlated with the promise that "PBS should reflect America." Duggan denied having made a "sweeping statement" and redirected the remark to PBS's iconographic British imports, a "strain of programming . . . that says something about the taste and enthusiasm of our audience."[1] While dismissed as a curious misstatement, the incident points to a cultural contradiction at the heart of U.S. public broadcasting: Since the Carnegie Commission coined the motto "excellence and diversity," public television has promised "something for everyone," from people with specialized cultural palates to members of racial groups. For just as long, critics have protested tokenized attention to people of color and other marginalized segments of society, including the working classes. This chapter traces the contradiction in public television's founding conception of cultural pluralism and shows how multicultural promises intersected with the normalization of whiteness and class privilege. Drawing from institutional records, policy debates, media commentary, and signature PBS programs, the chapter charts the social construction of public television's taken-for-granted cultural "center."

Public broadcasting's approach to cultural diversity drew from pluralist ideology the presumption that power is shared among special-interest groups.[2] Such thinking gained currency during the cold war, notes Andrew Ross, as intellectuals embraced an idealized image of "America not as a uniform society, but as a various and pluralistic society, made up of many groups with diverse interests" to differentiate the United States from statist communist enemies. Intellectuals also offered pluralism as the answer to America's mass culture problem, as did reformers who protested the "vast wasteland" of commercial television.[3] According to Stuart Hall, while cultural diversity sounds like a logical solution to "mass appeal" homogeneity, pluralist conceptions of the American melting pot tend to obscure inequalities between groups and to deny class formations and the differentiated knowledge/power relations on which they depend.[4] Templates for better television revealed these blind spots, casting white, educated-taste minorities with high-culture tastes as the "special-interest" group least served by a mass medium whose profits had come to depend on lowbrow amusement. Class difference was "repressed" by pluralist discourse, to use John Guillroy's terminology,[5] and only with the social and political upheavals of the late 1960s did subordinated nonwhites accrue the power to enforce, to some extent, public television's decree to restore diversity. The limited gains offered to specially designated racial "minorities" were conflated with programs for a plurality of specialized taste cultures whose very constitution was steeped in *unacknowledged* racial and class differences. Service to the unstated center and the designated margins was introduced under the common sign of pluralist progress.

Masses and Minorities

The Carnegie Commission took from postwar pluralist ideology an unwavering commitment to public broadcasting's capacity to combat "increased pressure toward uniformity" in television culture. During the congressional hearings on the 1967 Public Broadcasting Act, the commission president, James Killian, advocated target programs for myriad subgroups, excluding no one: Public television is "not for the elite . . . we are talking about a lot of specialized, diversified interests," he told policymakers.[6] The homogenous mass audience would be reconstituted as many "different audiences" served at separate times, reiterated commission staffer Hymin Goldin.[7] Despite this pledge of inclusiveness, sophisticated people who sought programs of "cultural worth" were the implied beneficiaries of television's proposed diversification. The absence of socially legitimated culture on commercial television was the grounds for a pluralist solution that advocated cultural "difference" but obscured differences in cultural power. However unconsciously, supporters placed the cultural needs of the well-educated white power structure at the center of public television's ostensibly fragmented mission. Erasing whiteness and class privilege from the demarcation of such "selective" tastes, supporters told Congress that "there are many areas of interest to minority 'publics,' especially in the fields of art, drama and music, that cannot be economically profitable. . . . It is these areas that are in need of public support."[8]

Race rebellions and student activism stretched the ideological seams of cultural pluralism just as the burgeoning dissent challenged the official proposition that power was "shared" and decision making was consensual. Public television's still-forming mission was no exception. In 1969, the private Kettering Foundation and the Corporation for Public Broadcasting sponsored a conference in Racine, Wisconsin, to chart its "programming philosophy." Unlike the men who debated the Public Broadcasting Act, the consultants, public television executives, and producers assembled for this task paid some attention to "other" potential subaudiences, particularly blacks and youth, populations closely associated with the era's movements for societal change. Some called on public television to foster "cohesion" between the presumably conservative mass audience and the "dissenting" elements of a society whose pluralist differences had grown into deeply politicized divides. Officials rejected the suggestion outright, for the simple reason that it carried with it the assumption of reaching a large viewing public. Public television's raison d'être, as reiterated by CPB President John Macy, was to avoid the "common denominator" in all circumstances. Its purpose was to serve "all of the American people," including racial minorities and perhaps even dissenting subcultures, "but not in massive and simultaneous terms."[9]

The limits to inclusion in the infinitesimal subgroups to be served by public television were clarified when the issue of class difference was unexpectedly raised during the 1969 meeting by some conference participants. The topic surprised those in attendance, who were clearly unaccustomed to thinking about class in direct and therefore political terms, as a social "difference" that public television should account for. Executives who failed to acknowledge any correlation between high culture and class privilege were equally unprepared to define public television's anticipated service to the working classes. CPB Vice-President Ward Chamberlin frankly admitted that programming for such people "hadn't occurred to him." For Chamberlin and other bureaucrats, cultural pluralism was incompatible with the class-coded stereotype of the uneducated and uncultured "masses." This institutionalized assumption made it impossible to conceptualize unprivileged whites as deserving "taste groups" and equally difficult to account for intersections of race and class obscured by singular "minority" labels.[10] Above all, it meant that public television could not facilitate difference within mass culture, for to do so would be incompatible with the pluralist logic that planners like Chamberlin and Macy espoused.

When PBS debuted, television viewers were promised a "mosaic of programs designed to reach all the American people."[11] The pluralist smorgasbord that materialized, however, was more like a gourmet buffet, full of European-influenced delicacies, but with only a few ethnic and countercultural side dishes. Regularly on the menu between 1969 and 1973 were "distinguished" classic and modern plays for theater lovers; *Book Beat*, filling a "niche with taste" for readers of serious literature and nonfiction; mostly European art-house films for cinephiles; filmed Shakespearean plays performed by British actors; literary costume dramas imported from the BBC for those who enjoyed masterpieces; documentaries, panel discussions and debates for "news junkies"; educational programs like *Civilisation* for lovers of fine art, science, history, and culture; ballet, opera, jazz, symphony orchestras, and occasional folk and rock concerts for performing-arts aficionados; *The French Chef* for gourmands; and "special programs" for blacks and—in very rare instances—Latinos and Native Americans.[12] By failing to acknowledge that educated whites were most apt to sample such gourmet delights, public television normalized whiteness—however unconsciously—in pluralist terms. Indeed, so invisible was the racial coding that the TV critic for the *San Francisco Examiner* pointed to the "boost for black pride" offered by the specially designated PBS "minority" program *Black Journal* and demanded a similar "white journal boosting white pride."[13]

Public television's facilitation of cultural pluralism paralleled the fragmentation of commercial magazines during the 1960s. David Abrahamson attributes the decline of mass-circulation icons like *Life* magazine and the proliferation of specialized niche magazines partly to changing class formations. While television's luring away of the general magazine-reading audience and the refinement of advertising goals within the magazine industry were certainly factors, the upscale nature of cultural fragmentation also contributed to the expansion of the mostly white and increasingly well-educated professional middle class. Postwar college enrollments facilitated upward educational mobility for more Americans than before, Abrahamson observed, and prompted a surge in cultural activities that could signify individuality as well as social distinction. High culture proper was not the only way to escape the mass audience. Leisure pursuits that required specialized knowledges and carried prestigious "cultural, symbolic and historical associations" (e.g., gourmet cooking, antique collecting, sailing) also gained enormous currency as signifiers of "difference."[14] Light programming on PBS tended to feature these distinctions, which—along with differences in cost—contrast upscale leisure practices (tennis, chess, classic guitar, yoga, fine-home restoration) with downscale counterparts (bowling, bingo, garage bands, shooting hoops, remodeling the ranch-house basement). Here again, the pluralist "subgroups" to which public television catered most were closely tied to class distinctions rooted in education and culture as much as in economics. The important difference was this: The fragmenting commercial magazine industry acknowledged its pursuit of upscale audiences, as did the commercial cable television industry that developed in 1970s and the commercial networks once they turned to demographic-based ratings that could identify and target the "right" people sought by advertisers. Public television, however, did not recognize—or admit—that race and class had anything to do with its "quality" programming.

Public television's pluralist mission was not created by corporate sponsors, but it *was* promoted, from the very outset, as an ideal way for corporations to skim off the cream of the consumer crop. A 1970 Ford Foundation study of "profit-making ventures" in public television declared its uncommonly discriminating, and therefore difficult to reach, viewers to be an "attractive market" for certain types of advertisers because they consumed "good food and good wine"; bought more books, automobiles, and water beds; saved and invested; and traveled. By 1972, the CPB was pitching public television to corporate underwriters as a fragmented institution "closely resembling a group of specialty magazines." The magazines cited were, coincidentally, mainly prestigious magazines with strong intellectual associations. "Like *Harper's*, we have programs that attract very literate people. Just as *Scientific American* boasts that audiences seek it out, public TV programs are found by very selective audiences," promised the brochure. Race was absent from the description of every "specialty" audience except blacks, served by the equivalent of *Ebony* on public television's unacknowledged—and thus normalized—white newsstand. Behind the scenes in public broadcasting, class differences obscured by the promise of "something for everyone" were emphasized to pitch the shared characteristics of public television's pluralistic audiences to prospective corporate sponsors. Within this marketing discourse, public television viewers as a whole were said to have higher-than-average incomes; most had a college education; and an astounding number—41 percent—also had graduate degrees.[15] The corporate sponsors who used public television as a cultural vehicle to reach such people did not exploit its mission as much as they accentuated its inherent contradictions. The confluence of upscale niche marketing and public television was invited—and legitimated—by the blind spots of pluralism itself.

Black Is Beautiful

Until the late 1960s, the term *minority* was used in broadcast reform discourse primarily as a euphemism for educated white people with uncommonly sophisticated cultural tastes. In 1970, the *Washington Post* drew from this semantic legacy to promote public television as the television "channel for the minority," by which the newspaper meant tastemakers and opinion leaders unhappy with the television programs targeted to the lowest common denominator.[16] The National Commission on Civil Disorders, whose influential report cited inadequate media attention to blacks as a cause of urban rebellion, prompted public broadcasting to reach beyond this niche.[17] Public stations were, by the time that PBS appeared, already recognizing racial minorities in several ways. Educational documentaries like *The Black Frontier* (1969), produced by Nebraska Public Television for national distribution, presented the untold history of African Americans without addressing conflicts or acknowledging structural racism. This four-hour series, which was characteristically promoted as an edifying alternative to fictionalized TV Westerns, studied the "forgotten" role played by black pioneers in settling the nation's grasslands. *The Black Frontier* brought African Americans into the pluralist melting pot without questioning the white center, establishing a template for periodic specials that recognized the experiences and accomplishments of Mexican Americans, Native Americans, and other ethnic groups.

Staged confrontations, TV job programs, and documentaries about victimized minorities also reflected the impact of the Civil Disorders report. While cognizant of racial tensions, these gestures were routinely influenced by the sensibilities of white creators and imagined white audiences. Programs *by* and *for* people of color, in contrast, provided important venues for cultural representation and community building that were not framed by a white lens. Most of these programs addressed blacks, the most organized nonwhite population of that time. Between 1968 and 1973, when funding for minority programming began to dry up, public television supported programs "by, for, and about" blacks that explicitly rejected what scholar Herman Gray calls the white "imaginary middle" constituted by most TV programming. Local productions like *Say Brother* (WGBH-Boston) and *Black Horizons* (WQED-Pittsburgh) appeared in numerous cities, and some gained national exposure on PBS. A 1969 *Ebony* report, "New Black TV," detected the common thread among them. Instead of "dramatizing a white writer's concept of black people," black television attempted to "de-honkify" minds by addressing racism and affirming black knowledges, cultures, and social realities. It addressed viewers who were presumed to be black and therefore to share certain experiences, meanings, and identities. When we "don't stop to translate what we've said," that is black programming, said one of the producers quoted in the story.[18] Black television also attempted to cultivate black pride by stressing cultural signifiers of "blackness." Historian Jacqueline Bobo summed up the historical moment in which the programs emerged as one in which

> black people had emerged from a time of nonviolent resistance in the face of social and economic oppression into an active and vocal stance—black, proud, and visible. Even the politically charged designation of the racial group had gained widespread acceptance: Black people had advanced from being "colored" to "Negro" to "Black." Other manifestations of this change were the clothes that displayed African origins, the "natural" hairstyles, and the conspicuous use of black "folk" language.[19]

The PBS program *Black Journal* (1969-1974) combined documentary segments, political discussion, cultural performances, and popular entertainment to achieve these goals. According to its black producers, the purpose of *Black Journal* was closely bound to the construction and affirmation of black cultural identity.[20] Early episodes profiled African American and Pan-African cultural traditions in an attempt to combat white bias in venues from television to history books while also encouraging black pride. "Because many scholars have concentrated on Egypt as the original Western civilization almost to the exclusion of the more ancient civilizations in Africa, south of the Sahara desert," a *Black Journal* film crew traveled to archaeological sites in Ethiopia to uncover the origins of black civilization. Another profiled the African American painter Jon Locard, who reworked the commercially exploited character of Aunt Jemima into an "angry woman raising a clenched fist and donning a bandanna with the tri-colors of the black liberation flag."

Still another episode visited Trinidad to film "Ti-Jean and His Brothers," a story about a Caribbean boy's struggle with the "white man, the devil."[21]

Black Journal was evidence of *Ebony*'s observation that black television refused to draw traditional boundaries between culture, education, politics, and entertainment. *Soul!* (1968-1972) combined activism, music, performing arts, and popular culture under the slogan "Black Is Beautiful." Carried by PBS for three years, this New York-based variety program was filmed on a vibrantly lit, multicolored stage in front of a predominantly black studio audience. Boasting "*Tonight Show* undertones and Apollo Theater overtones," it too provided the cultural and symbolic material to craft affirmative black identities. "We hope that our expression of *Soul!*, which is a part of all black people, will sustain and perpetuate this strategic part of our culture," stated producer Ellis Haizlip, a former theatrical director. Rejecting the patronizing promise of cultural uplift that surrounded public television, *Soul!*'s purpose was "neither to educate nor entertain but to give people the chance to share the black experience." As one promotion explained, "*Soul!* is Black America. . . . "*Soul!* is dynamite. . . . *Soul!* is you. . . .Watch *Soul!*"[22]

Although most episodes of *Soul!* were built around popular musical performances, political and practical schooling also were part of the mix. Producers did not seek to improve the audience, nor did they conceptualize disadvantaged blacks as "others." Rather, the program tried to educate, politicize, and inspire the broadly defined black community from inside that community. In one episode, an actor fused biography with black oral traditions to dramatized the story of abolitionist Frederick Douglass; another featured a black dentist who, because many black people could not afford regular dental care, demonstrated effective brushing techniques and discussed preventive dentistry. Black leaders of multiple political stripes shared the *Soul!* spotlight, including Nation of Islam leader Elijah Muhammad, representatives from the NAACP and revolutionaries like Kathleen Cleaver, wife of exiled Black Panther Eldridge Cleaver. On one episode, Cleaver discussed her recent visit to the People's Republic of Congo, the U.S. government's ongoing harassment of black activists, and the need for alternative media to convey news of political movements. In an attempt to enliven the studio-based stage interview, the producers projected a second head shot of Cleaver shot from another camera angle onto the screen, literally doubling her visual presence. Similar low-budget innovations distinguished *Soul!* from the staid prime-time PBS look. However appreciated by the program's viewers, the experimental techniques drew some complaints from white critics who preferred public television's somber style, including one who equated *Soul!*'s experimental approach with marring "by McLuhanites in the control room who used their special effects generator with the savvy of a con artist editing a deodorant commercial."[23]

Soul! celebrated black fine arts, African-inspired folk culture, and commercially successful black popular culture and refused to construct either aesthetic or political hierarchies between them. The series anticipated social critic Michael Eric Dyson's nonessentialist, nonhierarchical approach to the definition of "black culture." While he recognizes that corporate control of culture brings inherent constraints, Dyson values all black expression—from literature to gangsta rap—for the *social experience* it articulates.[24] Likewise, on *Soul!* poetry readings by artists like Amiri Baraka (LeRoi Jones) and Nikki Giovanni were stripped of high-culture connotations and contextualized in black identity politics. Cultural forms like poetry were, moreover, programmed alongside performances by famous musicians like B. B. King and Miles Davis and pop singers like the Delfonics, Gladys Knight and the Pips, and the Dells, best known for their chart topper "Oh, What a Night." Over the course of its short history, *Soul!* interviewed novelist Toni Morrison, who read from her acclaimed novel *The Bluest Eye*, appeared live from Lincoln Center with a choir performance, and presented Stevie Wonder in concert. Over the course of its run, South African folk singers performed tribal songs and dances; the black magician Presto the Great performed tricks; and "narrative jazz operas" explored the lives of jazz musicians in the United States.

On one episode, the National Black Theater, a small, independent theater company funded from the sale of African American crafts and clothing, presented *The Ritual*, a play publicized as an experiment in black identity. "Because theater is based on European concepts we, as Afro-Americans, want to create a concept of theater out of our own lifestyles," the director explained. Refusing to glorify the artist as creator, the troupe visited bars and churches, talking to ordinary people about their concept of black theater and learning that whites have the leading man but "we don't have that in life, so it should not be in our performances." Programs that explained potentially unfamiliar forms of artistic expression were not pedantic for art's sake. The goal was not to "uplift" cultural taste but, rather, to situate cultural works in the broader struggle for black liberation. For example, scenes from Melvin Van Peeble's Broadway musical *Ain't Supposed to Die a Natural Death* were enacted on *Soul!* against a jazz background, followed by an interview with the director. Subtitled *Tunes from Blackness*, the play revolves around everyday life in the urban ghetto, with blacks playing whites in whiteface. In one of the scenes, a man charged with loitering fantasizes about black revolution; in another, a woman accosted by a white police officer breaks into an affirmative song about Martin Luther King Jr. and Malcolm X. After the performances,

Van Peebles touted the players' capacity to "feel the nitty gritty of the piece" over their ability to interpret it in "university" terms. His conversation with *Soul!*'s Ellis Haizlip downplayed detached formal analysis and focused on the subjective "black ethos," prompting the playwright to share his frustration with white drama critics who panned the dialogue because they did not understand the "nuances and meanings" of black speech. *Soul!* valued cultural expression as social experience, fostering what one supporter called an "operation dig yourself."[25]

On Being Black (1969), a series of ten stage dramas written, produced, and performed by blacks, also probed the intersections of culture, politics, and racial identity. The plays addressed a broad range of topics, each probing the complexities of everyday black life, from a black boxer's struggle to reclaim his title to a cross-class romance between a black male social worker and a woman on welfare. *On Being Black* was defined by its producer station, WGBH-Boston, as esteemed black drama, not popular narrative. With this framing, the station cloaked the series in refinement and obscured the pleasures and recognitions it offered to black viewers across class backgrounds. Epitomizing a pervasive pattern in public broadcasting, the station also ascribed a deeper sociological purpose to *On Being Black*. While white stage plays appeared regularly on public television with no required agenda other than serving serious "theater lovers, " this series owed its existence to its presumed capacity to help solve a "crisis" that was implicitly ascribed to black people. Demonstrating how the goals of black television shifted when characterized by whites, executives claimed that *On Being Black* would resolve racial tensions by illuminating "experience in ways that cannot be realized by documentaries, by coverage of demonstrations or by the airing of grievances."[26]

Bird of the Iron Feather (1971), a black soap opera produced by WTTW-Chicago, was granted space on public television under the premise that it, too, could address the "racial crisis." The program was named after Frederick Douglass's analogy of African Americans and a "bird of iron feathers, unable to fly to freedom." Shown on PBS for one season, it defied commonsense expectations for public television, not just because it was by and for blacks, but because it was obviously and unapologetically a soap opera. According to its black producers, *Bird*'s mission was to counter popular commercial television programming like *Julia*, a "white show played in blackface," by exploring the everyday lives of a poor black family living in a Chicago housing project. The main story focuses on a black male police officer who is killed in a riot during the first episode. To build suspense while also contextualizing the murder, the narrative evolves in reverse, tracing in flashbacks the character's migration from the South to Chicago and his subsequent encounters with unscrupulous whites and black middle-class "sell-outs." Story lines revolving around young blacks dressed in dashikis, living in ghetto apartments, and victimized by unauthorized police raids combine social realism with soap opera conventions. In the process, the program fuses politics with pleasure, public issues with everyday life. Endorsed by sixty-one black organizations, *Bird* was said to be popular with black audiences, but it was not just a serialized drama teeming with black characters, tensions, emotions, suspense, and cliffhangers. It was also, asserted the black creators, a "sustained attempt to depict life in the ghetto as it is really lived." Indeed, one fictional segment about a Chicago police raid on local Black Panthers may have been too close to real life, for it was rejected by the producer Chicago station.

Bird of the Iron Feather coupled cultural service to blacks with the popular aesthetic, joining noncommercial black social and political interests with the derided conventions of a "mass appeal" television form. Because it was not compelled to court a white audience or appease advertisers, *Bird* could avoid the racist stereotypes and pat resolutions that constrained commercial "ghetto sitcoms" like *Good Times*, which also dealt with the struggles of everyday black life in housing projects.[27] If racial unrest made *Bird* a notable exception to the established binary that distinguished public television from mass culture, critical white responses anticipated its demise. The soap opera was duly skewered by some white TV critics and was called "simplistic" and "amateurish" by *Time* magazine. *Time* perhaps felt threatened by the show as well. The article's aesthetic snobbery was accompanied by a scathing rendition of *Bird's* "bitter black perspective," as evidenced by "recurrent talk of revolution," parodies of white employers, and profanity-laced lines like "Wait 'till the slave maids and housekeepers take to the streets—and them bitches have to do their own dishes," delivered by a disgruntled black domestic. Before the magazine's ink was dry, the innovative black soap opera was history. *Bird of the Iron Feather* was canceled after just twenty-one episodes, when its Ford Foundation grant expired, and public broadcasting failed to keep the show alive.[28]

While *Bird* provoked controversy, most black programs were completely ignored by the media blitz generated by the appearance of PBS. In 1970, in a feature story that omitted all reference to black programs, *Parade* magazine informed its huge readership that public television was "going places." The *Milwaukee Journal* typified local newspaper coverage by printing five large stills from PBS programs under the inviting bold headline, "Public Television Wants You." Not one of them was a black program. The black press was the only venue to review episodes of *Black Journal* and *Soul!* on a regular basis.

Unlike the white media, the black newspapers papers also covered an ongoing struggle to obtain equitable black access to public television. The *Amsterdam News* concluded a review of *Soul!* with a "word from the program's producers," who predicted that "the program will continue as long as there is no obstruction from the racist establishment regarding some angry outcry from several leading black entertainers on the program." PBS publicity omitted any notion of a racial struggle and promoted black programs as pluralistic problem solvers, an agenda seen from a white lens and not likewise ascribed to its cultural fare for music lovers or drama aficionados. Besides serving black audiences; the play *On Being Black* promoted "racial understanding" by probing "psychological" problems and the circumstances through which blacks might "escape ghetto life." Along similar lines, *Soul!* was publicized by PBS as "national television's only black variety program applies the arts to the problem of dope addiction."[29] According to this definition, the justification for public television's "minority" programs was to restore harmony as defined by the white power structure. Tellingly, once the race rebellions subsided, minority programming on public television nearly disappeared.

According to Jeanette Dates, while public television attended to the well educated, most racial minorities were concentrated "among the less educated groups" least likely to tune in. This presented an obstacle for black programs like *Soul!* no matter how hard they tried to communicate beyond the educated middle class.[30] The shows lost ground before their eclectic programming strategies could be fully tested: As the nation stabilized, public television stations, the CPB, and private foundations like Ford proved less willing to foot the bill for regularly scheduled black programs. As revolutionary sentiments were stirred into the melting pot, the pluralist promises that created space for black programs also legitimated their relegation to specials and historical documentaries. *Black Journal*'s William Greaves pinpointed the problem at the 1969 Racine, Wisconsin, programming conference where he protested that blacks, Puerto Ricans, and Mexican Americans had been supremely tokenized, brought only to "discuss their thing, their problem."[31]

In 1973, *Soul!* was axed and *Black Journal* soon migrated to commercial syndication. Local black shows were phased out, too. By 1977, the Task Force on Minorities in Public Broadcasting had confirmed that programming "by and about" minorities was seriously underrepresented on public television. The same year, audience research commissioned by the CPB contended that blacks were nearly five times as likely to watch commercial fare like *Good Times*, *The Jeffersons*, and *Redd Foxx* than to watch PBS's more heady *Black Perspective on the News*—the sole survivor of its pluralist heyday and the least entertaining of the black programs that PBS once featured. The study constructed the black mass audience as "other" to public television viewers, defining the problem from an institutionalized perspective as one of habitual black television viewers' neglecting to watch the more respectable and edifying alternatives shown on PBS. At no point was public television's disinterest in black popular culture mentioned or problematized as the "social problem" rationale for it waned. Nor were questions considered having to do with racial representation or equal racial access to public television's resources. The thinking represented by the audience study was pervasive, but certainly other discourses, even in public broadcasting, called race into question. The public broadcasting archives include a mock teleplay called *Mr. Minority*, an unpublished commentary written by anonymous PBS staffers about the rise and fall of black television, that suggests that some people in public broadcasting were critical of this situation. In the mock play, the year is 1975, and the lead character, Mr. Minority, approaches his public television station with an idea for a program. He finds instead a bureaucratic nightmare, eventually learning that no one cares about his idea and that the onus is on him to find a corporate sponsor or to hold a fund-raising "bake sale." As the problem-solving justification for minority programming faded, so did noncommercial support for "minority" television. Cultural pluralism went only so far.[32]

The British Are Coming

"When you talk about black power, you talk of building a movement that will smash everything Western civilization has created," said Stokely Carmichael about the black revolutionary movements of the late 1960s.[33] Such sentiments did more than make the white power structure uneasy. They also prompted a racial identity crisis that came to bear, in myriad ways, on public television's cultural priorities. Stuart Hall described the backlash as "aggressive resistance to difference, the attempt to restore the canon of Western civilization, the assault, direct and indirect, on multiculturalism," and the return to "grand narratives" prompted the decentering of Western culture in the late 1960s.[34] To understand U.S. public television's pluralist logic, we need to address its construction of whiteness as well as its simultaneous obsession with, and disavowal of, the cultural signifiers of social class. Class, Pierre Bourdieu observed, is rendered invisible when the particular tastes, experiences, and interests of particular class formations (typically the upper-middle class) are conflated with universal ones, or the "general interest."[35] Similarly, as Richard Dyer argues, whiteness is presented as the invisible, unquestioned center of the pluralist melting pot, as opposed to a racial "difference."

Dyer's critique of racial representation applies to cultural policy as well: Black, he says, "is always marked as a color . . . and is always particularizing; whereas white is not anything really, not an identity, not a particular quality, because it is everything—white is no color because it is all colors." The normalization of whiteness is reproduced by its erasure, for "the colorless multicoloredness of whiteness secures white power by making it hard, especially for white people and their media, to 'see' whiteness."[36] Such was the case with the cultural formation of public television. While public television was legitimated as pluralist by its tokenized attention to black culture, it also served as a site where whiteness was celebrated and imbued with culture, lineage, and prestige borrowed from the European aristocracy. These programs were the most prevalent and publicized of PBS's prime-time offerings, which meant that public television's cultural identity could not escape them. *The French Chef, Civilisation, The Forsyte Saga,* and *Masterpiece Theatre* were not just niche programs for French gourmet food lovers, cultural history buffs, or the literati; they militated against the multiculturalism evoked by Carmichael and the diversity promised by public television. They also circulated symbolic material that encouraged viewers to assert—or aspire to—upper-middle-class white identities.

Sponsored by Polaroid, Julia Child's *The French Chef* (1963-1973) first appeared on WGBH-Boston just as the civil rights movement was getting started. In 1970, would-be gourmands were invited to feast on the first new *French Chef* programs in three years, this time on PBS. Child's heavily promoted "cooking school of the air" was authenticated by scenes of her visiting France, dropping in on fellow chefs, going to markets, and dining at French restaurants. The show was more than practical instruction on haute cuisine: it was a lesson in how to be cultured, which was defined as European, specifically French. With her cooking school badge, Child addressed the imagined viewer as a pupil hungry for cultural sophistication, instructing not only how to prepare sumptuous dishes such as the perfect mousse au chocolat or bouillabaisse à la marseillaise, but on the practicalities of the formal sit-down dinner, dissected course by course. At other times she discoursed on how to plan a wine-and-cheese party, concentrating on the ins and outs of Bordeaux and Chardonnays and the fine distinctions between Brie and Camembert. As PBS promised, "Julia shows how easy it is to cook in the French way." You can make what you thought could be found "only in chic French restaurants" or in France. *The French Chef* emphasized the cultural "difference" of French cooking, just as black programs drew from African traditions to affirm black pride. Whereas *Soul!* was a specially designated example of racial diversity, however, *The French Chef*'s weekly celebration of aristocratic European culture was simply normalized.[37]

The enormous fanfare surrounding PBS's presentation of the BBC documentary *Civilisation* (1969), described by CPB President John Macy as the "ideal" program for the prime-time PBS schedule, worked in a similar way. Lord Kenneth Clark's thirteen-episode chronicle of Western cultural history made no bones about legitimating Western Europe as the center of "man's common heritage" and reinforcing the de facto supremacy of white, Western culture as the world's dominant ethos. Nothing could have been more comforting to the white power structure at time when "interest and minority groups" were demanding visibility. "All of a sudden these pre-Columbian and African creations are in competition with masterpieces of the West. What could be more confusing? Who knows what is a value under these circumstances?" wrote one historian of the social context during which public television developed culturally.[38] The imported *Civilisation* appeased these anxieties, proposing that "order is better than chaos, creation better than destruction." At the same time, Clark fed fears of civil unrest by harking back to near threats to Western civilization and quoting William Butler Yeats's insistence that when chaos leads to social disintegration, "things fall apart, the center cannot hold." TV critics picked up on this anxiety, drawing parallels between protesters and the "barbarians who roamed medieval Europe." According to one TV critic, the "barbarians" of contemporary America were underground radical groups like the Black Panthers, the Weathermen, and antiwar activists who—in the same year that PBS showed *Civilisation*—destroyed a national guard armory in San Francisco and a ROTC building at the University of Washington.[39]

British dramas were another site where the construction of race intersected with signifiers of European ancestry and legitimated taste, in both programming and policy discourse. Like *Civilisation*, these shows attracted private underwriters hoping to identify and impress "influentials" while infusing their corporate images with cultural sophistication and noblesse oblige.[40] The United States, Andrew Ross argues, has always depended for "authority, upon borrowed and accumulated" European traditions and "canons of judgment."[41] National Educational Television clearly recognized as much in 1962, when it imported the "prestigious" 1962 BBC series *An Age of Kings*, a collection of Shakespeare's plays underwritten for U.S. broadcast by Humble Oil. But the British invasion did not take U.S. public television by storm until 1969. That year, *The Forsyte Saga*, a serialized teledrama based on the novels of Nobel Prize-winning author John Galsworthy, was carried by PBS. *The Forsyte Saga* depicted the "lives and loves of several generations of an upper-class British family between 1879 and 1926." Well publicized, adored by TV critics, and considered important enough to warrant consideration by the *New York Times Magazine*, it became an instant cultural phenomenon. The imported BBC drama, televised each week over a period of months, inspired tea-and-crumpet parties among loyal viewers, catapulted Galsworthy's novels from recent obscurity to prominent display in bookstores, and became one of public television's most widely recognized programs. Its success in the United States had something to do with its emphasis on a well-to-do British family's dynasty. The opening credits showed the Forsyte family tree; the episodes traced the British clan over several generations; and PBS underscored the appeal with a promotional image of the actors posed for a family portrait.[42]

At a time when the white power structure was being challenged, the *Forsyte* phenomenon constructed race through the display of English lineage, high society, and history. The lavish period setting, combined with the focus on lineage, tapped into a search for white cultural heritage and identity sparked by the black power movement. "What a wonderful thing to do for this country, particularly at this unsettled time," wrote one grateful viewer to the New York public station.[43] Whereas *Soul!* was a "special" program for blacks, this was television for drama lovers, a pluralist conflation that normalized white culture and, more important, its centrality on prime-time PBS.

The Forsyte Saga crafted a space for upper-middlebrow culture in that it contained "references to legitimate culture" while also incorporating the more formulaic and therefore accessible genres, narratives, and pleasures usually associated with popular taste.[44] Precisely because of its Anglo-Saxon high-culture references, the BBC import was hoisted above the vast wasteland and seized as the prototype for the long-running public television series *Masterpiece Theatre* (1971-present). In contrast, *Bird of the Iron Feather*, described as a black soap opera, was hardly considered "great literature" and was tellingly short lived, a fate that speaks to the racial and class hierarchies governing public television. Although executives reportedly "gagged on its advanced billing as a British Victorian soap opera," *The Forsyte Saga* quickly became PBS's "signature" drama series, CPB President John Macy reported in his account of public television's formative years. Although "no competitor in the ratings," it attracted a larger audience than most public television programs. While public television normally avoided the "numbers game," this program's relative popularity was condoned by its British origins and prestigious literary associations.[45] Telecast on Sunday nights in one-hour installments, the series was said to bring "great literature" to the small screen, yet its publicity consistently emphasized melodramatic highlights and sexual intrigue. Viewers were promised an engrossing variety of domestic complications and emotional cliffhangers, teased with program descriptions like "Fleur seduces Jon but fails to win him back" and "Jo goes to live with his pregnant mistress, Helene, after Frances refuses to divorce him." Conveying the idea that the *Saga* was still legitimate culture, producers tacked on "Behind the Scenes," a talking-head program filmed in London, featuring conversations between NET President James Day and the actors, directors, and set designers associated with the show. Despite the regal, antique-filled parlor where the interviews took place, Day was clearly unsure about the purpose of this precursor to today's "infotainment." He worked hard to keep the conversation focused on literary and theatrical details, despite the crew's tendency to resist such framing (one British actor said Galsworthy had been a snob; when asked about the "apprehension" factor in putting great literature on TV, another guest claimed to love television).

The Forsyte Saga's high billing as a literary drama also made it acceptable for public television, when beneath the British accents, European cultural signifiers, and classic black-and-white cinematic style, the series anticipated prime-time soap operas like *Dallas*. As the *New Republic* pointed out, *The Forsyte Saga* was a good deal "more pleasurable" than the panel discussions, stock market reports, and stage dramas usually found on public television.[46] Like any soap opera, several subplots were always taking place at once, touching on love, heartbreak, illegitimate sons, adultery, workplace villainy, family black sheep, and sibling rivalry. The costumes were over-the-top, with the women cinched into corsets beneath ruffled blouses and wearing elaborate hats, and the men dandied up in Victorian finery. Interior settings conveyed opulence with overstuffed furniture, dark oil portraits, and candelabra, and the characters dined on lobster, visited art galleries, dropped French phrases into ordinary conversation, attended the opera, and gossiped at length about the "ill bred," even though they themselves were not nobility but self-made millionaires.

The program won an Emmy award, backing up Macy's assertion that the "excellent writing, acting and production justified its appeal to the largest adult audience attracted" to public television up to that time. To be sure, some media commentators noted the irony by calling *The Forsyte Saga* a "high-class *Peyton Place*." But most writers carefully distinguished the British drama from lowly, feminized forms of mass culture. Reminding the reader that the program was adapted from a literary novel about a wealthy English family, one critic opined that while "there is no mistaking that while *The Forsyte Saga* is soap opera," it was "several levels above its American counterparts" on daytime television because it featured some of "England's finest actors" and "captured the atmosphere of Victorian England handsomely." The legitimation of its popular elements was cinched when The Scribner Library published *Forsyte* study guides to emphasize the educational value of the series and therefore its deserving place on public television.[47]

Masterpiece Theatre, the offspring of *The Forsyte Saga*, also constructed white culture through a celebration of upper-crust European lineage, history, and culture. Created by WGBH-Boston and underwritten by Mobil Oil, the show started in 1971 with *The First Churchills*, a serialized drama about the first duke and duchess of Marlborough, ancestors of Sir Winston Churchill. Filled with the glamour of the aristocratic family's career at court, the program was publicized with a photograph of public television's first "sex symbol," Susan Hampshire, the actress who played Churchill's grandmother and who had starred in *The Forsyte Saga*, accompanied by the headline "Winston Churchill's Great-Great-Great-Great-Grandmother." The promotion tied the pleasure of the British soap to the prestige associated with Eurocentric high culture. According to Mobil public relations executive Herb Schmertz, millions of "culture-starved viewers" felt "enriched and ennobled, and hundreds of thousands soon became *Masterpiece Theatre* fanatics" following its presentation.[48] As Bourdieu notes, class and aristocratic "good breeding" are very closely linked in the cultural imaginary, and *Masterpiece Theatre* practically fetishized (blue) bloodlines. Emphasizing the Churchill family tree, the master of ceremonies, Alistair Cooke, informed viewers, "Don't be alarmed if you can't follow the court lineage—neither could the members of the court!" He then coddled the audience like a loving grandfather, saying,

> You may very well get puzzled at the start by some of the relationships and family relations. I hope it reassures you if I say you couldn't have got more puzzled than the original characters. Charles II really confused the bloodlines. He had various mistresses and twenty-nine illegitimate children.[49]

Mobil was interested in reaching influential opinion leaders, but it also wanted to sponsor program that would cut across cultural interests that were *too* fragmented and specialized. *Masterpiece Theatre* was a perfect vehicle to maximize the imagined audience for "quality" television because, like *The Forsyte Saga*, it coupled the pleasure of soap opera with literary cachet. Its respectability quotient increased with the inclusion of Cooke, the former host of the Ford Foundation's prestigious series *Omnibus,* and Mobil, which spent more money promoting *Masterpiece Theatre* than purchasing the rights to the programs and which cashed in on his reputation as an intellectual with a British accent. Advertisements promised viewers seeking legitimated culture that "Alistair Cooke (remember *Omnibus*?) will set the stage for you each week in his own quietly lucid way." Others traded on Cooke's intellect: "If you loved *The First Churchills*, that's wonderful. If you understood the plot easily, that's Alistair Cooke. His was the mind and the hand we held on to while galloping through the intricacies of seventeenth- and eighteenth-century British history." Acknowledging that there was also pleasure to be found in literary tomes for those who possessed or aspired to legitimated tastes, the same promotion noted that "when the scheming and the plotting and the loving and the mayhem get thick and heavy—that's when a viewer needs a friend."

In the 1980s Mobil underwrote several seminars at the Museum of Broadcasting (now the Museum of Television and Radio) to preserve *Masterpiece Theatre*'s reputation as high-quality television. Critic Les Brown nearly spoiled the tribute by calling the BBC imports boring and narrowly targeted to the cultural elite. Calling attention to the pro-aristocratic tenor of the series, the otherwise admiring critic for *Time* magazine acknowledged that literary sophistication had been ingeniously joined with the spectacle of "Lifestyles of the Rich and Famous." TV critics who commented on the new program also confused codes of high and low in their struggle to differentiate a series that was, essentially, high-class popular culture. The *Philadelphia Inquirer* solved the dilemma by situating *Masterpiece Theatre* in the "same class" as the BBC blockbuster *The Forsyte Saga,* calling it a distinguished but "sometimes confusing" drama series helpfully contextualized by the learned Alistair Cooke. Other TV critics warned that *Masterpiece Theatre* might prove "addictive" and noted the program's fondness for sexual promiscuity yet insisted that the program was "obviously" not mass culture because of its fine acting, magnificent sets and costumes, British origins, historical legitimacy, and literary associations. *Masterpiece Theatre* has "class," said a typical TV critic. "That was established even before the opening scene with the introduction by Alistair Cooke. We all know that our old friend from *Omnibus* moves only in the top circles."[50] The implication in all these reviews was that since *Masterpiece Theatre* was above ordinary television, so too was its audience.

Masterpiece Theatre's claim to be high culture was scoffed by the self-proclaimed "real" literati, prompting the same intellectual anxieties about "mid-cult" that surfaced around *Omnibus*. To put *The Forsyte Saga* in its place, the *New York Times Magazine* questioned Galsworthy's alleged status as a "great" writer, arguing that the novelist's overreliance on "rhythms and clichés" were appeals to the lesser tastes of "lending-library readers." According to the critic, such appeasements are now "so transparent that we feel little is lost when transference of the book is made to the small screen." But the *New Yorker*'s Michael Arlen did not deflate the reputation of the distinguished English novelists tapped by *Masterpiece Theatre*. His principal complaint was that the program traded on the "reputation and seriousness" of bona fide artists, only to undermine their genius by stooping to Hollywood-style simplicity and superficiality.[51] The problem for critics like Arlen was that television programs like *Masterpiece Theatre* sullied high culture. The same popular elements that he pilloried, however, Mobil exploited to attract the largest possible "quality" audience to the televised masterpieces. Teasers promised: "Mary Queen of Scots schemes to assassinate her cousin, the first Queen Elizabeth, in another exciting chapter of the *Elizabeth R* drama series." Another ad pitched the "most immoral court in English history." Sex, violence, and melodrama *were* commonplace on *Masterpiece Theatre*. *The First Churchills* opens with the duchess of Cleveland under the bedcovers and Charles almost catching his mistress with another man, who jumps out the window. Cooke's remarks accentuated the generic elements found in all soap operas, including heroes and villains. From his book-lined study, he declared: "We hope, as you did with *The Forsyte Saga*, that each week you'll see people you love to hate and whom you hate to love."

Popular appeals deemed "low" by the discourse of the vast wasteland were legitimated by the historical reputation of the figures dramatized, from the English actress Lillie Langtry (who in Cooke's series preview is shown putting ice down a scorned lover's back) to *I, Claudius*, adapted from author Robert Graves's novel of ancient Rome in a production so "sexually frank" it had to be edited for American television. Just as the British spelling of "Theatre" added cultural panache to the British flag, the regal theme music, and the credit appearance of the crown, Cooke's presence gave the show signifiers of educational value and masculine intellect. In the first episode, he greets the audience wearing a suit and tie as he sits on a Queen Anne chair next to a table with leather-bound books and a gilt-framed photograph of a man wearing a top hat: "We open tonight a new television theater which . . . will show you plays adapted from the works of Balzac, Henry James, Dostoyevsky," he promises while the visuals show English aristocrats and royalty. Mobil also produced study guides for many episodes, from *Jude the Obscure* to *The Six Wives of Henry VIII*, further legitimating *Masterpiece Theatre*'s difference from mass culture. The literature included oversized family trees, background information, and episode summaries that read like

Soap Opera Digest. PBS distributed Mobil-funded publicity on the "real life of Henry VIII," makeup artistry, and British stars, boosting the show with the equivalent of a white, Anglo-Saxon, high-class and thus culturally legiti-mated *Entertainment Tonight.*

Suddenly, an ability to follow intricate and overlapping domestic plots was declared respectable cultural capital—provided the families were white, costumed, English, and noble. At times, however, the fusion of popular en-tertainment with literary knowledge went too far in the minds of public tel-evision officials. One such case was *Upstairs Downstairs* (1974), a popular British soap about a wealthy family and its servants, recognized by Schmertz as an audience grabber but originally rejected by WGBH executives who did not agree that the series was "wonderful." *Upstairs, Downstairs,* billed as the "story of the inhabitants of a single house in the Belgravia section of London during the first three decades of the nineteenth century"—was not based on a novel, let alone a "masterpiece." Period costumes and British accents sig-nified "high culture" for U.S. viewers, but as British fans well knew, the show was a soap opera with no literary author to condone it. In the end, fifty-five episodes spanning four years solidified *Upstairs, Downstairs* in the *Master-piece Theatre* pantheon precisely because it displayed class and class differ-ences within European white culture and treated the subject with the "same gossipy feel as the Forsytes."[52]

Critics cite *Masterpiece Theatre* (now called *ExxonMobil Masterpiece Theatre*) as a textbook example of corporations using public television for their own ends, that is, of providing public television with the "safely splen-did" cultural programs with which they want to be associated. There is no disputing this point. But there are other, more complex reasons to explain why *Masterpiece Theatre* became a signature program.[53] Unlike the import-ed BBC series, with its weekly installments, cliffhangers, and soap opera ele-ments, domestic public television drama was modeled after the single stage plays broadcast during commercial television's "golden age." *Hollywood Television Theater* (1971-1978), funded by the Ford Foundation and the Cor-poration for Public Broadcasting, was public television's most notable at-tempt to bring live theater back to the tube on a regular basis. Its offerings were eclectic, ranging from literary classics to controversial off-Broadway plays like *Steambath* to the Civil War costume drama *The Andersonville Trial.* While respected by critics like Arlen, *Television Theater* remained outside the cultural imaginary and was eventually rejected by most PBS stations. Why was its fate so unlike *Masterpiece Theatre's*? For one thing, *Television The-ater's* plays were producer driven, selected, and publicized according to the intent of the author and the performance of the director and the actors, not according to the meanings to be made and the pleasures to be derived by viewers. The live performances tended to lack the popular elements that drew people to *Masterpiece Theatre*; certainly, they lacked the legitimating display of European culture and society and the pedagogical assistance in interpreting "great" television provided each week by Cooke and Mobil publicity. *Television Theater* self-consciously bypassed the middle ground between high culture and entertainment, speaking to intellectuals in complex terms that even some critics had trouble deciphering. Wrote the *Washington Post*'s TV critic, Tom Shales, about one *Hollywood Television Theater* play,

> A graduate-school literature professor might well be enraptured with the intricate theme dealing with dissent, character weaknesses and the instinct to survive at anyone's expensive . . . but for the more casual viewer, just figuring out who is who could take enough time and effort to exhaust you to where you haven't the energy left to concentrate.[54]

Favoring art over audience appeal, *Hollywood Television Theater* failed to connect in a sustained way with public television's core professional middle-class audience. The precursor of subsequent attempts to broadcast American prestige drama (*American Playhouse, Great Performances*) could not—or would not—straddle the cultural contradictions finessed week to week on *Masterpiece Theatre*.

Who watched *Masterpiece Theatre*? According to the Museum seminar, its demographics were "mostly elite" in terms of education and income. A commentator from *Time* magazine added more to this composite audience, claiming that unlike most TV viewers, *Masterpiece Theatre*'s audience had not been warped by commercial television's "eight-minute minidramas" and was willing to "see all the installments" and "pay attention." He could have been describing the audience for *Bird of the Iron Feather* or any daytime soap opera, for that matter, but he was pitting *Masterpiece Theatre* audience against the popular aesthetic. Downplaying its mass cultural elements, he claimed that *Masterpiece Theatre* "requires an intellectual aggression, not passive TV viewing," precisely because it contains overlapping plots and tends to be slow to unfold, a statement he would not have made about *Bird* followers or about the fans of any commercial soap opera. This frame situated *Masterpiece Theatre* within the legitimate culture, a categorization that was avidly disputed by a British guest on the panel, who claimed the "right advertising" and trendy music could draw larger audiences to the program. But this was not Mobil's intention, nor was it public television's anticipated role.

The discourse of cultural pluralism produced two strands of PBS programming that entertained elements of the popular aesthetic and affirmed racial pride, but only one was recognized as being about or targeted to a specific racial group. Because both public broadcasting officials and reviewers unquestioningly—and perhaps unconsciously—regarded white Western European culture as the dominant culture, race, like class, was simultaneously constituted and concealed by the fanfare surrounding *The Forsyte Saga* and *Masterpiece Theatre*. Black programs were conceived and publicized as counting toward problem solving and racial diversity, as are programs featuring ethnic minorities today, but the BBC imports were presented as serving specialized tastes seemingly unrelated to race. The serialized literary "masterpieces" were emotional, suspenseful, and much more popular than traditional experimental American stage plays broadcast on PBS. But they were accompanied by British accents, English references, and period costumes, as were the popular BBC mystery dramas sponsored by Mobil. *Masterpiece Theatre* was also imbued—through Cooke's discourse, the opening credits, and corporate publicity—with signifiers of cultural respectability and prestige. This frame constructed educated, upscale viewers as the natural audience and sent others the implicit message "This is not for you." Directed toward theater lovers, not soap opera fans, these programs fulfilled public television's pluralist mission to provide a "standard of excellence" in the legitimate drama niche. As cultural studies has shown, cultural hierarchies are arbitrarily constructed within social relations. The problem with *Masterpiece Theatre* is not that it "corrupts" public television but, rather, that its iconographic status reinforces the notion that popularity is acceptable only when high-culture references and white Europeanness are present.

Viewers Like You

The promise of "something for everyone" was also constrained by cultural and fund-raising appeals to the "viewers like you" who comprise public television's imagined audience. Its reliance on voluntary viewer funding is not simply an economic pressure that affects programming choices, as leftist critics have long argued. It is, just as important, a cultural phenomenon tied to symbolic meanings and cultural practices. From the outset, the "membership" culture has been the key site where public television's "community," a participatory constituency at the center of the imagined audience, is constructed. The cultural guardianship implied by making an annual donation or volunteering for one's local station grew out of the earliest attempts to

mobilize public support for public television. In 1967, the Carnegie Corporation and the Ford Foundation funded National Citizens Committee on
Public Broadcasting, a prestigious coalition of business and culture leaders,
to symbolize "grassroots" participation and give citizens a voice in the new
public institution. Chaired by the Princeton-educated director of the Metropolitan Museum of Art, the membership roster read like a "who's who," containing the likes of Newton Minow, orchestra conductor Leonard Bernstein,
architect I. M. Pei, editor Norman Podhoretz, artist Robert Rauschenberg,
and black novelist Ralph Ellison, whose token presence had also signified the
"pluralism" of the otherwise white Carnegie Commission. Even though national organizations from the PTA to the American Association of Retired
People were labeled public "advisers" on paper, they had little input—as was
clearly demonstrated in the mid-1970s, when the NAACP, the AFL-CIO, and
the National Organization for Women all protested what they saw as the
prevalence of British imports on public television, to no avail.[55]

Community input, however, was conflated with the mostly female volunteer culture that flourished around public television at the local level.
While the reformers and policymakers who developed public television at
the national level were men, the National Friends of Public Broadcasting was
composed of "high-power" women armed with experience from the Junior
League and charity drives. With a grant from the Carnegie Corporation,
local chapters of the Friends distributed promotional literature, provided
"citizen input," and helped local stations with fund-raising and clerical tasks.
In the late 1960s and early 1970s, the Friends also established a pattern that
continues to this day, by constructing themselves as the public "voice" of
public broadcasting. Many founding chapters organized letter-writing campaigns to establish local stations in their cities, to secure state funding, and
to make politicians continually aware of the "dire plight" of public television
at the national level. Others formed voluntary advisory committees, offering
input on program priorities and audience building. Mostly white and college
educated, the Friends were well situated in upper-middle-class professional
community of their particular locale. In this sense, they personified public
television's "cultural center" as construed by policy discourse. Archival
records show an earnest and humanitarian concern by the volunteers with
preserving "educational" television channels, fostering the well-being of
their communities, and developing broadcasting for a "higher purpose" that
extended commercial entertainment. Yet the same records reveal a tendency
to define a small and disproportionately privileged sector of the citizenry—
their own—as best equipped to define and mobilize the public interest.

What was required to be a Friend? "Taste, discretion and advanced knowledge of one's community," according to the typical guidelines followed by a San Francisco chapter. Former PBS employee and long-time public TV critic Willard Rowland observed as much, arguing that the

> general education, economic and social level of the volunteer leaders are suggested by the philosophical context within which they work. They may believe that leading citizen involvement in public broadcasting is best done by those whose position, background or training presumably makes them better prepared and more deserving than others.[56]

This unconscious strain of volunteer elitism was perpetuated by officials like CPB Vice-President Ward Chamberlin, who saw the Friends' mission as paramount to public television's survival. "We're in a very competitive business—the fight for people's minds, the fight to help them educate themselves, to widen their horizons," he told volunteers gathered at the Waldorf Astoria Hotel for a national conference. "Our opposition is powerful—in money and technique. And it has on its side a lineup that is menacing and very well entrenched. Their names are familiar to all of us: complacency, affluence, status quo, self-satisfaction, fear of change, habit." Chamberlin deemed women with the leisure time, economic means, cultural capital, and inclination to volunteer as Friends to be "people of substance" who could help realize public television's role in the "survival of American civilization."[57] The self-described "army of concerned citizen-volunteers" agreed that they were working for "something beyond any of the individuals involved, that will last beyond all our own lives and careers and commitment—and perhaps contribute to fundamental changes in the quality of lives of all Americans."[58]

Friends culture provided an unprecedented, and clearly welcome and exciting, opportunity for women to participate in television culture beyond their usual roles as viewers and consumers. The "community" the Friends culture represented however, was self-selective, concentrated among the white educated upper-middle class, and thus not representative of the people. For much the same reason that the National Citizens listed Ralph Ellison as a member, some local Friends chapters claimed one or two "distinguished" representatives of the black community among their ranks. People without means—white and black—are denied access to this grassroots component of public broadcasting, however unintentionally. Membership—and especially leadership—was contingent on unacknowledged social, cultural, and economic advantages. Just as pluralist discourse denies class formations and structural racism, the Friends culture denied its own racial and class privilege. "I would like to do something for Blacks. I would be a Friend . . . but I have no money," wrote a black teenager to the Corporation for Public Broadcasting upon the cancellation of minority programs. Excluded from institutionalized channels for public input supplied by the Friends, he asked, "Please tell me what I can do."[59]

The volunteer ethos posited no real distinction between fund-raising and audience building. The goal of creating a viewing constituency for local stations went hand in hand with the notion that those with the time and resources to pitch in would comprise the station's "grassroots" base.[60] According to Friends founder Mrs. William ("Frankie") Schuman, the organization's two goals were (1) to "develop an informed audience" and (2) to develop a "firm base for nationwide private financial support" from small donors.[61] Audience-building activities ranged from going door to door to obtain signatures and donations, to holding fund-raisers like concerts, plays, balls, art auctions, and chartered trips to Europe, to organizing children's activities around *Sesame Street* characters. All were geared to raising funds from people who might be inclined and equipped to pay for public broadcasting. Although minority shows like *Soul!* were promoted by Friends fundraising activities, they were implicitly "othered" and routinely outnumbered. The BBC imports that coupled popular pleasure with Europeanness and high culture were among the top income generators. In 1970, Boston volunteers shared the following success story with the National Friends:

> The success of the *Forsyte Saga* has inspired a money-raising idea at Channel 2 Boston. A red carpet party (champagne, black tie, expensive tickets) will be thrown in the studio to preview the last episodes. Guests may be invited to come in *Forsyte Saga* get-up. Hopefully this will appeal to *Saga* enthusiasts going away on winter vacations or just to those who like to be "in the know."[62]

One did not have to a volunteer to join the public television "community." Supporters and officials envisioned the core public television audience as the one that would help foot the bill by sending $25 or $50 or more each year as paying "members" of their stations.[63] Donating money was equated with "participating" in public television, and some stations allowed contributors to vote on station matters and program schedules. Mostly, however, the membership culture was a place where anonymous viewers were addressed, informed, and allowed to share their tastes, concerns, and identities. It was the place, in other words, where the public television audience was constructed as an imagined community. A series of 1971 "typical viewer profiles" in WNET's members-only program guide *Image* suggests the extent to which whiteness and class were normalized within this imagined community, often against the token inclusion of less economically privileged racial minorities. One viewer profiled Richard and Trish Stotz, "sophisticated, urban residents who bring highly selective viewing habits and exacting artistic standards to their television viewing." Trish, a Wellesley honors graduate and a Fulbright scholar, was an editor at a New York publishing house, and Richard was completing his doctoral dissertation at Columbia University. As selective TV viewers, they felt most shows were "intrinsically garbage," so they stuck to public television. "If we were paying by the program and there were a slot on top of the set, we'd drop money in to see a great many of Channel 13's shows," added Mrs. Stoltz.

Another profile described the Plummers, a family consisting of a Manhattan lawyer, his Vassar-graduate wife, and their two children. Ann, a homemaker, was more apt to pick up a book, whereas Hugh, "who spent a good deal of time reading for work," looked forward to watching television after dinner. The Plummers also were "highly selective" viewers who found public television's offerings more sophisticated and satisfying. They also appreciated public television because, as parents, they favored children's programs that were educational. The last viewer profile to appear in the *Image* series introduced the Pullins, a working-class black family living in the Bronx. Joe, a technician, and Gene, who stayed at home with their three young children, watched commercial and public television and were critical of both. They wanted to see more programs by, for, and about blacks, the bare bones of which they observed happening on public television. These portraits of viewers confirmed public television's commitment to cultural pluralism by including a black family, equating its selectivity—manifested as a tendency to seek out black programs and avoid racist ones—with the taste selectivity of the white families. The Pullins were defined *only* in relation to their blackness, whereas the white families were defined by their cultural sophistication, university educations, and leisure habits, their race unmentioned and apparent only in photographs. In a similar way, racial "others" were accentuated, and whiteness and class privilege were normalized by the taken-for-granted terms of public television's membership community.[64]

What did public television's membership culture mean to the participants who helped build it? By supporting public television financially, viewer-members were encouraged to feel as if they were shaping its direction.

They also were encouraged to see themselves as part of an uncommonly selective and refined in-group. *Image*, a deluxe membership magazine featuring articles, criticism, and advertisements as well as station news and program listings, epitomizes the social identity constructed, to varying degrees,
by many station publications. If the word *patron* connotes prestigious associations like "excellence, elegance, and tradition," as one critic suggested,
Image served as a constant reminder, even though most station members
contributed relatively small amounts compared with the traditional cultural
patrons—business tycoons and "old money" nobility—of yesteryear.[65] The
names and photographs of people who did give sizable gifts were published,
and the station's black tie fund-raising galas were covered as bona fide high-
society gatherings. In a typical month, station members were informed that
one such event had been held at the Waldorf Astoria, where tables were
"smartly decorated with centerpieces of perfumed candles and souvenir
scarves tucked into wine glasses." Guests dined on "artichauts vinaigrette
and coq au vin" and, between courses, danced to the "finest" orchestra
music.[66] While few station members actually participated in these events, the
associations they conveyed shaped the cultural identity of the imagined public television "community."

Even less upscale stations like WCET-Cincinnati drew from the cultural iconography of European high society to distinguish its imagined viewers,
as shown by a cartoon promotion featured in its program guide. The image
depicts the archetypical commercial television addict—an overweight, unkempt man in a hard hat—who affirms his uncultured nature with by "mis-
reading" public television's difference and proclaiming "Julia Child is a Real
Pussycat."[67] Within public television's evolving membership culture, reverence for French cooking and BBC costume dramas was often manifested as
chartered trips to England and France organized by station volunteers and
fund-raising activities (auctions, silent bids, events) built around the acqui-
sition of culture and antiques. Like *The Forsyte Saga,* gathering these perks
spoke to the search for white cultural heritage and inbred status that can be
conveyed only by the passage of time. As Bourdieu argues, the "taste for old
things," whether stately homes, paintings, vintage wines, or antique furniture, signifies inheritance—or years spent acquiring social distinctions that
cannot be bought en masse.[68]

Premiums offered to new members spoke to precisely these longings
and desires, cinching the cultural signifiers of upper-middle-class whiteness
that surrounded public television's imaginary "community." The biggest
draws during public television's formative years were Julia Child's *Mastering
the Art of French Cooking* and the companion book to *Civilisation,* offered as

holiday premiums with the slogan the "Gift That Honors the Giver."[69] Some TV critics acted as membership boosters, urging newspaper readers to give to their local public television stations and pitching the prestigious gifts that awaited them as an incentive: "The recipient seldom reads the book but places it on his coffee table as room decoration" was one explanation of the symbolic meanings conveyed by the cultural goods.[70] The sophisticated, upscale social image offered by premiums and program guides was seized by advertisers, too. Attempting to cash in on the image of the public television viewer constructed in part by this membership culture, one department store pitched high-end fashions to the "sort of gal who supports the superb programming of public television, who sits in the winners' circle, and who knows the best spot in town for a soufflé."[71]

Public broadcasting's architects regarded private viewer donations as an ideal revenue source and one that was cultivated from the beginning. Public television's contentious battle with the Nixon administration only emphasized the trend. In 1973, the Station Independence Project was created to coordinate fund-raising and market research on potential donors. A "National Pledge Week" functioned like commercial television's sweeps weeks to the extent that the goal was to maximize ratings, not by drawing new viewers, but by assembling at the same time the fragmented subgroups who already watched public television. During this week, public television stations offered programs believed to have a broad upscale appeal, including entertaining "blockbusters" such as tennis matches or old Hollywood films.[72] The special programs came with "breaks" during which local station announcers pleaded for donations and hawked membership premiums from lavish coffee-table books to tote bags bearing the station logo. The message was to flatter "viewers like you" for watching the quality programs on public television. Sometimes local celebrities and performers appeared to boost the cause. In the frenetic background, telephones rang, staffers and volunteers took pledges, and others tabulated the haul. Pledge Week was built around three purposes—filling the station's coffers, increasing its membership, and shoring up the loyalty of members who looked forward to the special programs. This activity has been blamed by the Left for subverting U.S. public television's noncommercialism and therefore its very authenticity; at the same time, it has been seized by the Right as evidence that public television can survive without public subsidies. Both arguments overlook the paradox of the development: Pledge drives provided new rationales through which public television could temporarily indulge popular rituals and uneducational pleasures, but only in upscale, consumerist terms.

Selling Class and Community

Like station program guides, pledge drives were an important site where public television's imagined community was constituted. Important too were the televised auctions, which gained iconographic status in the early 1970s, promoted by the Station Independence Project as a path to the stations' solvency. Also criticized by the Left as the antithesis of what noncommercial "public" television is supposed to look like, auctions were actually one of public television's most accessible, participatory, and, in some sense, carnivalesque programs. They undoubtedly traded on blatant class signifiers and pronounced materialism, yet public television's earliest auctions coupled old-fashioned hucksterism with the excitement of live on-air chaos. The auction studio was a hubbub of activity, with people milling in front of the camera and studio participants engaged in raucous countdowns and eruptions of cheers. WMHT-Schenectady even called its weeklong event the "auction game," saving the big-ticket items for the final round of competitive bidding and coupling the sales with singing and on-air banter. Combining consumerism, real people, and suspense, the auctions anticipated the broad appeal of today's *Antiques Roadshow*, in which people bring in family heirlooms and appraisers decide live before the camera whether or not they are actually valuable antiques. On a revealing episode of the sitcom *Frasier*, both the pretentious, art-collecting psychiatrist and his down-to-earth, humble blue-collar father enjoy *Antiques Roadshow*, the psychiatrist because it flatters his upscale identity and specialized knowledge of rare objects, and the father because he likes the thrill of popular game shows. In a similar way, the auctions permitted public television to join popular culture to upscale consumerism.

The auctions combined the conventions of commercial game shows with an early, prestigious brand of home shopping. Contrary to the working-class "taste culture" that Mimi White links to blatantly commercialized home shopping venues like the Home Shopping Network (HSN), public television's auctions connected an altruistic image of the viewing community to upscale consumer culture. Like HSN, the premiums offered for telephone bidding were fetishized by the camera and lovingly described and discussed by live announcers who blended salesmanship with community building. Unlike HSN, the imagined audience was addressed as both a distinguished community and a consumer niche. As selective "viewers like you" eager to pitch in and keep the station afloat and as people defined by gourmet goods, consumer values were legitimated by the "quality" of the items and the higher purpose behind the auction.[73] Viewers were urged to indulge and have fun, a lapse in their usual relationship with public television that was justified by the sense that one was doing her or his "part by bidding and buying." Claims like "it's your station, it's my station . . . here's your chance to support public television" fused participation, pleasure, and purchases.

The auctions were not much of a moneymaker, which is why they have been phased out by some stations, which now favor streamlined pledge drives. Yet, the auctions were a formative space where public television's core audience was defined socially, culturally, and economically. Part of the auctions' appeal was the fact that popular culture was used to draw sales, as evidenced by the inclusion in one auction of a scarf allegedly worn by Valerie Harper on *Rhoda*. More often, however, items had prestigious associations, from a signed museum artifact to an imported designer curio stand to vacations at an exclusive resort. Claims of status, good taste, and all-around sophistication—and, even more so, the desire for those traits—were apparent, as typified by WHRO-Norfolk's auction items: a gourmet picnic with caviar, french bread, gourmet cheeses, and imported champagne; a part in the chorus of an opera (minimum bid $100); season tickets to the theater; a charm course from a finishing school; and a signed print from a gallery. Once again, whiteness was completely normalized, whereas class difference was officially denied and everywhere present.

The search for class heritage coupled with the sort of status conveyed by the possession of antiques was joined by a focus on luxury goods in the bids, so that intellectual and cultural markers of class intersected with the flashier connotations of wealth. Both patterns spoke to the problem with the auctions: They contained the fun within the boundaries of a mostly white, presumably upscale private club. These tactics were rationalized with noble aims like fostering "community involvement" in public television, yet the cost and meanings ascribed to the goods made the auctions more like a gated community. A typical promotion for WTVS-Detroit's auction reasoned: "Since we are not allowed to have commercials, we depend almost entirely on the community. . . . Auction's fun, too! The whole community gets involved."[74] The station also boasted that viewers rushed to their phones to bid on antique cars, flying lessons, vacations to Spain, and an original painting by the artist Marc Chagall—all expensive items that cast the audience as upscale, sophisticated, and well-to-do, or aspiring to these traits. KERA-Dallas called its auction the "most talked about event" in north Texas and an "unusual chance" for viewers to take part in an actual television show. Participation here was confined to bidding on "everything dreams are made of," including vacations, luxury cars, air travel, and sailboats. Even though most of the goods presented for bidding were far less expensive, the meanings ascribed to them—and to the sorts of people who participated in public television as a whole—complemented the class subject implied by the big-ticket items.

Goods that were not sophisticated and upscale were noticeably out of place at the auctions. One tuxedoed master of ceremonies, for example, slyly smirked when he presented for bidding a "lovely white afghan handcrafted by the donor with acrylic yarn." For some stations—especially those in low-income, rural areas—the strategies promoted by the Station Independence Project were more like a nightmare. A West Virginia station that was not getting rich from offering items like skating passes, fuel oil, dance lessons at Arthur Murray, and a smoked ham attempted to auction off expensive, framed oil paintings of ponies, Canada geese, and ships. The live program got awkward when the phones remained silent for some time and the confused MC was forced to admit that "nobody's calling." The local high art might have appalled the urban cosmopolitans who bid on the Chagall, but it was more highbrow and costly than West Virginia viewers, however supportive of public television, could be easily coaxed into buying.[75] Critics ignored the contradictory cultural meanings conveyed by the televised auctions and attacked them as "one big commercial." The event "plunges the average mild-mannered PTV executive into the unseemly role of huckster," said one opponent, who also feared that the commercialized carnival drew a "whole new crowd" of bargain hunters to public television who returned to the vast wasteland when the fun was over.[76]

A similar conflation of commercialism with popularity underpins the argument that public television today, with its pledge drives, upscale BBC imports, mainstream blockbusters with "no clear public service rationale," and revenue-generating appearances by fading baby boom rock stars, has completely caved in to "market sensibilities." Critics fear what Ien Ang calls an "ellipse of the classic idea of public service" in favor of a "market-oriented approach" that addresses the audience as "consumers, at least at a general level." William Hoynes, author of *Public Television for Sale,* sees a shift from the "needs" of the citizenry toward the "wants" of the quality audience, an argument echoed by commentators who protest public television's willingness to broadcast high-class entertainment.[77] The argument knocks pleasure as much as the market forces that guide and shape public television, presuming that fun has no place on a channel whose only purpose is to educate, inform, and rally the troops. It dismisses entertainment, as the Left always has, presuming that public television must be serious as well as noncommercial. In my view, this approach to public culture is profoundly limiting. There is an irony, however, never addressed by conservatives who claim that complete privatization is the answer to public television's elitism. Reliance on viewer funding has forced U.S. public television to become more enjoyable and playful *and*, at the same time, has cinched its pervasive cultural address to the upper-middle-class and implicitly white center. From a cultural studies perspective, public television has not been corrupted by *Masterpiece Theatre*, classic Hollywood films, or even pledge drives. The problem is that popularity is pursued and legitimated only when it links up with the upscale consumers on which public television now depends.

The Cultural Contradictions of Pluralism

The cultural contradictions of pluralist discourse cut across public television programming strategies, publicity, journalistic commentary, and fund-raising appeals, constituting a white, upscale audience as the cultural center to which its "marketing strategies" are still directed. The tension between the promise of "something for everyone" and its failure to deliver has never gone unquestioned. In 1975 the Puerto Rican Media Action and Educational Council petitioned the FCC to revoke WNET-New York's broadcast license, on the grounds of discrimination against New York's Hispanic population, partly in terms of employment but mainly for its failure to provide "relevant" programming. The request was denied, but FCC Commissioner Benjamin Hooks, a black civil rights activist, issued a scathing dissent, accusing the station of "concentrating their efforts on cultured, white cosmopolitans to the neglect of the less fortunate minorities." The incident shows the limitations of attempts to make good on public television's pluralist logic, in that the demands sought inclusion without addressing an operational ethos that cannot account for difference because its focus on dominant groups is invisible and normalized. In its reply to the FCC, WNET renormalized whiteness, conflating racial minorities with taste cultures stripped of class and race and insisting it was "unwilling to accept the implication that the Puerto Rican community has no interest in classics, music, drama, anthropology, literature, art, cinema or history." John O'Conner, TV critic for the *New York Times*, revived the residual usage of the term *minority* as a reference to sophisticated people with uncommon tastes, disputing accusations of racism on the grounds that "WNET's programming is aimed at a minority effectively disenfranchised by the bulk of commercial television."[78]

While public television now has national consortia to ensure minority representation and avoid the charges issued by earlier media activists, programs like "The Mexican Americans," "The Chinese Americans," "The Puerto Ricans: Our American Story," "The Cuban Americans," and "The Greek

Americans" are relegated to occasional specials and documentaries that recognize the pluralist melting pot from the viewpoint of public television's unacknowledged center. There are no regularly scheduled PBS programs that provide popular information and entertainment by and for blacks, Latinos, Asians, or working-class white people, for that matter. This problem cannot be solved by simply by demanding a bigger piece of the pluralist pie for minority and disadvantaged groups. Nor can expanding the number of "fragmented" taste cultures served by public television address the power relations inherent to the ideological constitution of its idealized beneficiaries.[79] As cultural studies has shown, pluralist discourse is limited by a failure to acknowledge the extent to which social hierarchies undermine equality and, therefore, difference. We need to recognize how cultural policies that claim to promote pluralism can normalize dominant groups, presenting them as the universal "center" around which diversity is marked and conceptualized. Reconceiving public television as a popular and diverse cultural project will ultimately require dislodging its foundational assumption that race and class are for "other" people.

There is a universe going on that we forget about.
We must get to people who are not like us.
–Public television producer, 1970

CHAPTER FIVE

RADICALIZING MIDDLE AMERICA

Newt Gingrich was not the first conservative politician to protest against public broadcasting on behalf of the common people. The 1967 Public Broadcasting Act sailed through Congress on the wings of Lyndon Johnson's Great Society programs; PBS began broadcasting two turbulent years later under the watchful eyes of a new president, Richard Nixon. The White House's attacks on public broadcasting fused the president's perception of liberal bias with complaints about cultural elitism and the bruised dignity of Middle America. The dispute escalated in June 1972 when Nixon rejected an early funding bill on the grounds that public television had become a "centralized" fourth network with an umbilical cord to the liberal eastern establishment. The "veto to please Archie Bunker," as it was dubbed by one newspaper, sparked a congressional debate, institutional reforms, and an important rupture in public television's cultural image. In the extensive media commentary triggered by the turn of events, the oasis of the wasteland found itself charged with snootiness, East Coast attitude, and the dissemination of left-wing propaganda.

The Nixon saga is often credited with undermining public television's counterhegemonic potential. The "shadow of fear" set into motion by the White House during the early 1970s is said to have doomed unorthodox programming with leftist sympathies, which applied to only a small but important component of the early PBS schedule. Many critics believe that Nixon's insistence on downsizing large urban stations and production centers bolstered the noncontroversial "safely splendid" vision of public broadcasting preferred by smaller local stations and by corporate underwriters. Focusing on the fate of politicized programs that "challenged the status quo," this explanation ignores the cultural dimensions of the backlash against public broadcasting. Nixon's spokesmen also mobilized a number of percolating populist resentments against public television when they suggested rerouting federal money to the local stations to temper the impact of northeastern liberals and big-city radicals. Calls to end federal tax funding for a "socialistic" and "elitist" cultural service also arose during these years, prompted by similar tensions.

The conservative critique of public broadcasting set into motion by the Nixon administration constituted an "authoritarian-populist" discourse, as defined by Stuart Hall. As Hall notes in his cultural analysis of the New Right, authoritarian-populist discourses tend to gain currency by aligning reformers whose natural allies are the wealthy (e.g., conservatives) with the people against an arrogant power bloc (e.g., liberal cultural elites).[1] This chapter traces the "articulation" of populist criticism and conservative ideology to strategies developed by Nixon's policy advisers and supporters. Although the depoliticization and commercialization of public broadcasting brought on by the Nixon-era conflict have been thoroughly discussed, the meanings, the contradictions, and the tensions these reforms caused have evaded critical scrutiny.[2] With its attention to signifying practices and their place in media history, cultural studies can illuminate public television's vulnerability to conservative interventions carried out in the name of hard-working taxpayers. Drawing from declassified documents, mediated commentaries, local responses, and controversial PBS programs through the lens of cultural theory, I argue that the Nixon saga is important precisely because it legitimated the Right and disenfranchised the Left as the people's ally in the public television culture wars.

Public Television Versus Middle America

The White House's yoking together of cultural, political, and geographical complaints about public broadcasting mirrored the authoritarian-populist strategies used by the New Right to contest the social movements of the 1960s. As Michael Zazin observes in his political history of populism in the United States, Nixon-era conservatives deployed this strategy (which was later perfected by Ronald Reagan) to unite "Elm Street Republicans" with the white working- and lower-middle classes against a common adversary: upper-middle-class liberals accused of sympathizing with "the antiwar movement and the counterculture." Vice-President Spiro Agnew's crusades against the "effete intellectual snobs" who ran the eastern establishment, allegedly in cahoots with radical chic militants, were echoed in the *National Review*'s declaration of "class war" against "liberal establishment philanthropies" like the Ford Foundation for "social engineering" with its tax-exempt billions. Nixon's battle with the national news media also unfolded during these years, prompting the president, in a famous speech penned by far-right ideologue Pat Buchanan, to pitch his Vietnam War policy to the "great silent majority."[3] Nixon was especially irritated to see public subsidies pumped into public television programs that dared to question White House policies, and the fledgling public broadcasting system was more vulnerable to his influence than were the commercial media. Against this backdrop, the authoritarian-populist reform discourse that coalesced around public television aligned Nixon, conservatives, and the snubbed and maligned silent majority against an elitist East Coast bureaucracy with "pinko" sympathies.

Like the nations analyzed by political theorist Benedict Anderson, Middle America was constituted as an "imagined community" within this reform discourse, evoked to define and rally multiple oppositions (lower class versus upper class, conservative versus liberal, silent majority versus radical minority, local versus urban, regional versus coastal) against the national public broadcasting "establishment."[4] As Zazin shows, "Middle America" has always been as much a symbolic marker as an actual place. During the Nixon era, the term represented the "unstylish, traditional expanse" between the coasts, as well as large numbers of people situated between a "condescending elite above and scruffy demonstrators and welfare recipients below." Whereas Richard Nixon's imagined Middle America was as "wholesome" and patriotic as a "Norman Rockwell painting," for liberal intellectuals it was populated by uncultured provincials and narrow-minded blue collars. According to Zazin, when *Time* magazine declared Middle Americans the "Man and Woman of the Year" for 1970, it drew from both iconographies to construct another stereotypical portrait of the fictional masses. The article juxtaposed the presumably conservative social and political beliefs of middlers with their "presumed tastes in entertainment," which included baton twirling and John Wayne's 1968 pro-Vietnam War movie *The Green Berets*.

In so doing, magazines like *Time* stoked Nixon's appeal against the "slick cosmopolitans who mocked the patriotic, the un-hip, and the blue collar."[5]

Similar oppositions were constructed by public television's earliest conservative critics to portray public television as anti-Middle American and perhaps un-American as well. Unlike Gingrich, Nixon did not oppose public broadcasting entirely. He supported its traditional educational mission, just as he drew from rhetoric of the Great Society principles to pledge a "new quality of life in America" in his first State of the Union address. Public affairs programming was the president's bone of contention. The White House's own Office of Telecommunications Policy kept close tabs on studious talking-heads programs, precisely because they circulated information to "influential" opinion leaders. However infuriating to the president, these solemn shows tended to reinforce mainstream ideology, as was suggested by PBS president Hartford Gunn's observation that "the *Village Voice* and the White House are absolutely identical in their dislike of public broadcasting."[6] What Nixon's advisers labeled as "far-left" public television programming was, however, another story. While "masterpiece" dramas and civilized cross talk were the norm on prime-time television, exceptional programs with antiwar, antisquare, New Left, black nationalist, countercultural, or avant-garde sensibilities sometimes appeared bearing the PBS logo, much to the chagrin of watchers from the Office of Telecommunications Policy.

The contested programs frequently came from the New York City studios of National Educational Television. NET, the national hub of the educational television (ETV) system, had been passed over for the national planning and distribution role occupied by PBS. With funding from the Ford Foundation and the Corporation for Public Broadcasting, it continued to produce many early PBS programs. Since its inception in 1955, NET had sparked some resentment among the smaller local stations, particularly when its lofty program ideals undermined their pragmatic, land-grant approach to educational broadcasting. In 1959 NET moved from Ann Arbor, Michigan, to New York City, against the wishes of the stations, which opposed the relocation ten to one, believing that "somehow we'd fall into evil hands if it moved out of the heartland to the big city." NET's growing focus on general-interest programming geared to "provoking critical thinking" and cultivating taste took it further from the formal instruction and "extension services" that some local station managers saw as the center's principal public-service obligation. When NET began producing "superb cultural programming" and public affairs for national distribution, some land-grant stations clung to a mission that stressed serving local schools and adult students. While national TV critics cheered as ETV traded its "state-college, school-system" image for more polished programs, many local bureaucrats protested NET's "dictatorship," feeling that "all interests and activities were concentrated in the hands of a fairly small number of well-acquainted men." This history, as Nixon's policy advisers well knew, made NET particularly vulnerable to authoritarian-populist reform discourse.[7]

Other controversial programs often came from the largest urban stations, including WGBH-Boston and WETA-Washington in the northeast corridor and, on the other coast, KCET-Los Angeles and KQED-San Francisco. Like NET, these well-funded community-licensed stations tended to grant more cultural leeway to producers hoping to fuse television and social change as the nation became increasingly turbulent. The social and political upheavals of the late 1960s, noted the *Atlantic Monthly*, shook the accepted definition of "quality" television, causing the metropolitan centers, which received the largest percentage of public subsidies and private foundation grants, to effectively "split" along political and cultural lines. On one side was the station's power structure, which favored traditional bourgeois drama, classical music, and genteel panel discussions; and on the margins was a faction of producers and programmers who represented a generation "repelled" by such programs and prone to "artistic assaults on the values" they stood for. The divided stations were no less apt to boast the upscale viewer demographics touted by public television's marketing discourse. New York's WNET courted well-educated and affluent "members," and its viewer guide, *Image*, was modeled after a prestigious intellectual magazine like the *New Yorker*. In 1972, KQED-San Francisco's research department discovered that many people had come to perceive that city's public station as "radical" and "psychedelic" instead of "dull" and "educational." Nonetheless, the demographic makeup of its upscale audience remained more or less the same.[8] What *had* changed, as *TV Guide* observed, was that stations like WNET and KQED were attracting politicized contingencies that were "antagonistic to big business" and prone to pushing cultural and political envelopes.[9] When controversial output originating with these stations gained national visibility on PBS, Nixon's media watchers took notice. Hoping to depoliticize public television without seeming overtly hostile to people who appreciated its educational, cultural, and children's programming, they singled out PBS programming with urban origins and "subversive" attitudes as the principal source of snobbery and malaise in public television.

Before the late 1960s, conservative intellectuals feared that the upwardly mobile masses would invade and spoil high culture. A 1965 article in the *National Review* scoffed at liberal plans to spread the best throughout the land, incredulous at the prospect of blue-collar midwestern steelworkers experimenting with gourmet cooking and "tastes shaped in universities." Absolutely in sync with art critic Dwight Macdonald's opposition to "midcult," Hugh Kenner of the *National Review* protested, on aesthetic grounds, the liberal "engineering" of cultural uplift. "We mount a perilous cliff," he said of the masses clamoring to reach the "best that is enacted, thought and said," predicting that most cultural climbers would "plateau" somewhere in the superficial middle and soon drop back "into Mass Kulch."[10] By 1969, this attitude had taken a turn: civil rights, black power, student activism, the New Left, and resistance to the Vietnam War came to bear on liberal plans for culture. Under the direction of McGeorge Bundy, the Ford Foundation invested in school desegregation, civil rights, and social movements that threatened the conservative establishment in a more substantial way. That same year, a feature article in the *National Review* declared a "class war" on Ford and other private foundations, declaring them the "bedrocks" of the liberal eastern establishment. According the magazine, the foundations were using their "wealth and influence" to avert full-scale revolution, effectively funding social change to keep opposition "within the system." These changes were not acceptable to the conservative power structure, whose own tax-exempt foundations were ineffective, declared the *National Review*, when it came to managing revolutionary times. The magazine spotted in lower-middle and working-class whites a virtually untapped target for counterappeals from the Right. Promoting authoritarian populism with racist undertones, the article argued that

> the upper-middle and upper-class governing elite is attempting to carry out a social revolution under forced draft at the expense of middle and lower-middle classes–who, it is safe to say, won't put up with it, and don't have to. For the entire political/social strategy of the Establishment rests on a disastrously fallacious assumption. Desiring social stability, which they correctly estimate, is in the best interest of corporate wealth, they assume that black frustrations are a greater threat to that stability than the anger of the vast American middle-lower-middle class.[11]

Public television's susceptibility to conservative culture wars can be traced to this milieu. The declassified Nixon papers on public broadcasting reveal a concerted struggle to blunt the system's nebulous political bite. Although the records from the Office of Telecommunications Policy are not particularly concerned with politicized "minority" shows like *Soul!* and *Black*

Journal, the White House was obsessed with weeding out white-produced programming that criticized or, worse, attempted to radicalize white middle-class Middle America. Confidential memos stamped "eyes only" flew when misdemeanors like a documentary that flashed Grant Wood's painting *American Gothic* to indicate the conservative "bad guys" were found. The Office of Telecommunications Policy kept close tabs on NET's *Great American Dream Machine* (1970-1972), documenting such offenses as an "antiestablishment song and dance number," an interview with a screenwriter who "pledged himself to work against the reelection of the President," interviews with expatriates in Canada who were "fed up with life in America," and musical performances by folk singer Don McLean spoofing superpatriotism.[12] While programs like *Dream Machine* were a tiny part of the PBS schedule, they were the focus of authoritarian-populist criticism.

Nixon's principal TV adviser, Clay Whitehead, took the White House's case against public television to local station managers and politicians, protesting the jeopardized fate of educational priorities, the dangers of East Coast dictatorship, and the misuse of tax dollars for propagandizing. The declassified memos also led to "leaks" to the trade press on these issues. Whitehead complained about the Ford Foundation's fiscal generosity, comparing its grants with a "giant sponsor controlling all of commercial television." He and his staff used three authoritarian-populist strategies to push decentralization as the preferred solution to public broadcasting's shortcomings as the White House defined them. First, Whitehead and his colleagues championed the interests of Middle America against the centralized liberal establishment that was said to control public television at the national level. The credibility of the argument hinged on public television's exclusive image and imagined audience. "There is not a large viewing audience for public TV," noted Whitehead in an "eyes only" memo addressed directly to the president. As he knew, the August 1971 cover of *TV Guide* had asked in big bold letters: "Public Television: Is Anybody Watching?" Even though the magazine had supported the creation of public television, this feature story expressed deep reservations about what it now called "upper-class TV," fussed over by critics, admired by "TV's disenchanted," and practically ignored by the masses. Citing the CPB's own audience research, *TV Guide* dubbed the public television audience a tiny but apparently "very special" minority composed of the "affluent, the college-bred and, quite often, the politically liberal."[13] Whitehead and his colleagues seized on the popular resentments expressed in the magazine and elsewhere, using political and cultural complaints to implicate the national bureaucracy. In the name of so-called public broadcasting, said the White House memo, the CPB is "seeking funds and independence to create a TV network reflecting their narrow conception of what the public ought to see and hear."[14]

The second authoritarian-populist strategy the White House used was to exploit tensions within the system. The Carnegie Commission had characterized public television as a "bedrock of localism," partly to avoid the un-American trappings of a large, state-funded network, but also to combat the "mass appeal" stigma ascribed to commercial broadcasting. While PBS drew from some smaller stations to assemble the national public television programming schedule, urban centers produced the vast majority of what was shown. The Office of Telecommunications Policy discovered that some "less glamorous" regional stations resented this arrangement. Some felt that public dollars should go to local operations, not the cosmopolitan favorites allowed to dominate the PBS schedule. The apparent favoritism enjoyed by the urban stations–and the resentment it provoked within public broadcasting–spoke to Pierre Bourdieu's theory of "socially ranked geographical space." In the United States, the northeast corridor has long been ranked above Middle America as the principal locale for legitimated culture and taste.[15] The White House harnessed the tensions inherent in this hierarchy by promising to reform public television in cultural-geographical terms. Officially, Nixon's veto would combat northeastern dominance by mandating "robust" localism in public broadcasting. But the confidential paper trail tells a more complex story. Whitehead and his colleagues also believed that local control would eliminate public television's predisposition toward "liberal bias." According to Whitehead's private correspondence with the White House staff, "Public television at the national level will always attract liberal and far-left producers, writers and commentators," whereas smaller stations favored traditional education over rabble-rousing.[16]

The final authoritarian-populist strategy that the White House adopted was to establish NET as the principal cause of East Coast haughtiness and urban deviance. The symbolic coupling of New York, cultural elitism, and left-wing politics was exploited–but not entirely invented–by Nixon-era reformers. In the United States, conservative opposition to public funding for culture has long depended on ideologically inflected geographical dichotomies that pit northeastern highbrows against populist frontier people, or "wicked" cities against wholesome towns, argues Margaret Wyszomirski. New York City is a prime example in that it has come to represent the "epitome of everything that is elitist, coastal, urban and therefore, suspect." According to broadcast historian William Boddy, McCarthyites spotted a mini-Moscow there in the 1950s, putting the kibosh on commercial television's early association with the city's cultural avant-garde. *Red Channels:*

The Report on the Communist Influence in Radio and Television proclaimed "controversial" television dramas broadcast from New York to be repositories for un-Americanism, says Boddy. Commercial sponsors agreed in the name of "program taste," claiming that their urban sensibilities offended the "standards of the rest of the country." According to Lynn Spigel, modern art, the heart of New York's intellectual scene, was equally suspect, portrayed as simultaneously highbrow and treasonous by commercial television's sitcoms and documentaries. Social scientists of the era concurred: For the "man of simple artistic taste," wrote one contributor to the book *Mass, Class and Bureaucracy*, surrealist trends cannot "but appear to be morbid and unhealthy.[17]

This discursive formation reigned well into the 1960s, making it seem easier to group smaller local stations, conservative reformers, and the "silent majority" in opposition against NET, the symbol of public television's cultural, geographical, and political faults. Whitehead was aware that some station managers felt that the New York production center was less than responsive to regional differences and that others felt that its public affairs programs had grown too liberal. When congressional hearings were held in 1972 to assess public broadcasting's fate in the wake of Nixon's funding veto, NET was singled out on precisely these grounds, faulted for showing a particular tolerance for "radical or unorthodox viewpoints" and for favoring "language and ideas not shared by listeners in many areas of the country." One indignant congressman prepped by the White House typified the political, cultural, and geographical complaints against NET. Until its role in public broadcasting was downsized, he argued, the American people's exposure to culture and current events would be interpreted by a "tiny fraternity" of liberal and leftist New York City producers.[18]

In the media debate triggered by Nixon's veto and its aftermath, conservative critics with populist accents sided with "ordinary people" against public television. The authoritarian-populist strategies deployed by the White House's Office of Telecommunications Policy were magnified by the cultural debate played out in editorial pages and news magazines. Whereas Nixon's advisers strove to appear diplomatic, conservative commentators boldly declared public television's cultural, geographical, and political shortcomings. The principal argument, recorded by a congressional clipping service, was that "public broadcasting has become welfare of the airwaves for America's liberal and left-wing elite," paid for by the taxpayers for "students, academics, intellectuals, professionals and politicians." Seizing on the unspoken class biases at the heart of public television's mission, conservatives called its claim to publicness into question on the grounds that

public television regularly "distorted or attacked" the values, tastes, and beliefs of the lower classes. Fusing conservative ideology with this newfound
class consciousness, the *Wall Street Journal* contended that dramatic
changes were needed to combat the "elitist view that a self-appointed minority has a duty to decide what ideological outlook is socially beneficial."
Likewise, the publisher of commercial newspapers in Phoenix and Indianapolis took out a full-page advertisement in the *New York Times*, which
proclaimed that public broadcasting was run by an "elite group of bureaucrats" who cooperated with the "radical, the socialist and the activist element of the country." Numerous editorials echoed these assertions, as did
commercial television stations like WDAU-TV, a CBS affiliate in Scranton,
Pennsylvania, which went on the record to proclaim that public television
was "elitist and openly biased against the ideals and beliefs of the majority
of tax-paying Americans." Conservative critics championed a class-coded
image of Middle America that they were helping create, much as commercial broadcasters had created the "voting majority" to justify the vast wasteland. In so doing, they attributed conservative values to these fictional "people" and displaced legitimate concerns about culture and taste onto partisan
mudslinging. At its worst, this authoritarian-populist discourse made public television bashing a way to express hate and prejudice, as shown in a
viewer's letter to the CPB, which supported the veto because

> PBS is long on airing homosexuals, lesbians, radicals, draft dodgers,
> communists etc. or any type of program that will tear down the
> home and this country. We silent majority are very much opposed
> to this type of broadcasting. . . . I vehemently oppose paying for
> such tripe.[19]

The White House's treatment of public television was also fiercely
protested by many liberal commentators. Some argued that public television's "far-left" reputation had been grossly exaggerated, bolstered by a few
NET programs "marked by a left-wing bias" and used to convince Congress
that "*Pravda* is the bible" of East Coast producers. Others decried conservative censorship: Fred Powledge's report for the American Civil Liberties
Union criticized the White House's attempt to "starve" public broadcasting
into political obedience. Similarly, a political cartoon in the *Washington Post*
depicted a suit- and tie-clad, middle-aged white man in his living room, trying in vain to watch public television. His view of the TV set is blocked by a
paranoid-looking Nixon, with the caption reading: "I'll tell you everything
you need to know." Still others protested the grave threat to public television

posed by "robust localism." TV critic Les Brown worried that local control over public broadcasting would "mute" critical voices, just as local school boards are more apt to ban "offensive" library books than is the U.S. Supreme Court. Reproducing the same cultural and geographical hierarchies called into question by conservatives, magazines like the *New Republic* called the local stations hokey "farm clubs" and equated their influence with public television's cultural decline.[20]

Liberals who supported public television against Nixon's Middle America conceded valid populist and geographical complaints to conservative spokesmen. But most could not fathom public television as anything but a sophisticated, high-class oasis. If public television "suddenly appealed to the masses, its purpose would be defeated," said the *Boston Globe.* The *New York Times*'s TV critic, Lester Markel, defended public television without apology, claiming that he, for one, valued an eastern establishment whose sensibilities are "not accepted by the greater part of the citizenry." Powledge's American Civil Liberties Union report defended free speech but ignored the debatable dimensions of cultural policy, drawing from the discourse of the vast wasteland to support public television against both the White House and wasteland "pap." These stances did not mobilize the people on behalf of public television, nor were they expected to. As the *Globe* conceded, "The country didn't exactly rise up in rebellion when public television's funds were cut . . . there is no great constituency out there."[21]

Public television tried to rally the constituency that it did have by taking its case to loyal viewers. In 1973, an animated PBS fund-raising promotion played on public television stations nationwide, warning those who appreciated better television to hurry up and chip in. Demonstrating the class and cultural biases against which public television stood accused, the promotion depicted two blue-collar men making crude jokes as they carted Julia Child, Big Bird, a ballet dancer, and talk show host William F. Buckley to a waiting moving van. The "silent majority" furniture haulers stood in for the Nixon administration, representing a dangerous threat on public television's once bright horizon. "Public TV can no longer depend on the government or foundations for the support we once had," said a somber off-screen narrator, as the burly movers gleefully drove off with its best-known cultural icons.[22] Despite pleas for support, the 1972 veto forced changes in what viewers saw on PBS, as more than two hundred stations gained additional control over the contours of national programming. Experimentation and coverage of social issues waned, and land-grant priorities gained visibility.

For historians like James Ledbetter, the shift was an ingredient in the poison that "killed" public broadcasting. Like so many progressive scholars who write about public television, his thinking conflates ideology with cultural policy: Whatever "challenges the status quo" is believed to be good for the people when it comes to noncommercial public broadcasting. In fact, the programs scapegoated by conservative reformers drew from another set of unquestioned assumptions about mass culture and its audience. Many eschewed popular narratives for avant-garde cultural forms and reproduced authoritarian-populist stereotypes in their attempt to jar viewers out of complacency. To understand public television's vulnerability to conservative culture wars, we need to revisit the contradictory impulses of its earliest "far-left" programs.[23]

Leftist Television Revisited

In 1968, FCC Commissioner Nicholas Johnson proposed an alternative course for U.S. public broadcasting. Referencing a society torn by political protests, citizen disenfranchisement, consumer excess, and the "evil" bred by commercial television, the maverick regulator asked public broadcasters to address "controversial topics" and solve social problems. Since the advertising-sponsored networks were unwilling or unable to provide these services, Johnson demanded "courageous" television from noncommercial broadcasting.[24] Although his vision was marginalized, some people in the system shared his hope of using public television to expose injustices and remedy wrongs. During a programming conference in 1969, a dissenting faction of the funders, bureaucrats, consultants, and producers assembled did not share public television's focus on providing "quality programs for specialized audience." An alternative view, which never got more than "subliminal," according to conference transcripts, envisioned public television as the "voice of the underground and consequences be damned."

Other dissenters believed that public television should encourage more "civilized" behavior among Middle Americans, defined as the "super patriot, the red neck, the blue collar, the square." From this perspective, its purpose was to expose "people who would express the greatest discontent about our society, show the least inhibitions, sign the greatest songs of protest" to those "least willing to set aside the disciplines of the society, most afraid of apparent homosexuals, and most concerned with retaining the stability which they have inherited." In this statement, the inequalities embedded in the very structures of a white supremacist patriarchal capitalist society were reduced to attitudinal problems that could be solved by changing the minds of Middle America. It was a bit like the Ford Foundation's belief that structural racism reinforced by interlocking societal institutions could be "licked" by educational campaigns. The "civilizing" mission also mirrored the discourse of the vast wasteland, for the enlightenment of the narrow-minded masses presumed the ongoing guidance of liberal whites who failed to question their own participation in perpetuating racial hierarchies.[25]

The shortsighted arrogance of the early public television planners spoke to what the *Wall Street Journal* called the broader "Spiro Agnew phenomenon." In a 1970 editorial entitled "Assaulting the Aristocracy," the newspaper speculated on the vice-president's enormous appeal to the so-called silent majority. Using Agnew's same authoritarian-populist terminology, the *Journal* reported that a "class has sprung up in this nation that considers itself uniquely qualified ('the thinking people') and is quite willing to dismiss the ordinary American with utter contempt ('the rednecks')." The hope of using public television to "civilize" Middle America played into these complaints by failing to consider how the people might participate in public television and asking instead, in the words of one conference participant, "How can we manipulate this device to achieve the ends that we want to achieve?" It encouraged a conservative backlash by imagining Middle America in essentialist and passive terms, as a perpetually regressive "mass" to be socialized in accordance with progressive values. Some participants at the 1960 programming conference recognized as much. Anticipating Middle America's rejection of the "civilizing" mission, one planner told his colleagues that

> the people who want to communicate back and forth with each other on public broadcasting are perhaps, to use your term, the rich and intellectual on the one hand, the most obviously and grotesquely disadvantaged on the other. . . . And in the middle is a sullen, and in many ways justifiably enraged, group of forty or fifty million relatively disadvantaged white people who are saying in effect, you go ahead and have your conferences and you go ahead and plan your Brotherhood of Man and we will screw you in the ballot boxes.[26]

From the late 1960s until it was dismantled in 1972, NET was the main source of "courageous" PBS programming. Former NET Vice-President Jack Willis claims that it produced the most daring television the U.S. airwaves had ever seen. In his memoir, former NET President James Day characterizes these glory days as the peak before public television's spiral into cultural and political complacency. In his political history of public television, Ledbetter agrees that the most radical programs to feature the PBS logo emerged from the now-defunct New York production center. But NET was not always

hospitable to the leftist sentiments emphasized by Ledbetter, and its programs were evidence of some of the civilizing assumptions that circulated
during public television's planning stage. NET was an instrument of the cold
war during the 1950s and most of the 1960s, broadcasting "educational" programs like "In Common Brotherhood," the "story of labor's struggle against
world Communism." In "The Red Myth" (1960) scholars deconstruct communist dogma from a book-lined library. While unkempt actors dressed as
Marx and Lenin reenact writing and proselytizing the evil *Communist Manifesto*, experts lecture about communism spreading to Asia, Africa, and Latin
America, a portentous specter symbolized by a hammer and sickle superimposed on a globe in flames. "Great Decisions: America and Communism"
(1964), a typical panel discussion about communism, addresses extreme left-
wing politics abroad and the potential threat of socialism at home.[27] In these
programs and many like them, any value system that deviated from the United States' capitalist norms was automatically suspect.

During the late 1960s and early 1970s, NET was managed by Day, a veteran public television executive who had once worked for Radio Free Asia,
broadcasting to Communist China. During this time of unrest and activism,
NET began to address social issues like civil rights and poverty, as did the
Ford Foundation, which angered some local stations in the South. Documentaries with titles like "Where Is Prejudice," "Justice and the Poor," and
"What Harvest for the Reaper" and "Huelga!" about the grape pickers' strike
led by Cesar Chavez, brought the plight of blacks, poor whites, and migrant
workers to public television. As protests against the Vietnam War grew loud-
er, anti-imperialist sentiments also appeared in a small number of documentaries, a departure from NET's staunch anticommunist stance that generated enormous controversy. "NET Journal: Inside North Vietnam"
showed U.S. bombs raining down on North Vietnam, prompting critics (including some public television station managers) to brand the independent
British filmmaker a propagandist for Communist China and North Vietnam. A firestorm erupted, even though only a segment of the contested documentary was used, followed by a balanced debate among experts, a hall-
mark of public television. A few more NET programs were said to
sympathize with–or at least not demonize–Fidel Castro, Ho Chi Minh, and
Mao Tse-tung. "Who Invited Us" (1970), one such program, ruffled feathers
because it questioned U.S. interventions in Cuba, Latin America, and other
developing nations and interviewed a Communist poet from Chile.[28]

These NET programs were exceptional, sandwiched between opera, live
plays, concerts, prestigious BBC cultural imports, and "level-headed" documentaries. The surrounding context softened their "radicalism" along the

lines of a leftist film screened at the Harvard Faculty Club or an art-house theater in an upscale white neighborhood. The edgiest programming often took unconventional cultural forms as well, reflecting both artistic opposition to prefabricated mass tastes and the intellectual Left's political attachment to the avant-garde. In the late 1960s, the "aesthetic dimension" was seized by philosopher Herbert Marcuse as the last hope for capitalist society's transformation. As former SDS President Todd Gitlin recalls, the New Left and its sideline supporters were "drawn to books that seemed to . . . explain helplessness." Marcuse's *One-Dimensional Man* was such a book, attractive to avant-garde and countercultural leftists because it addressed "a society that had lost the very ability to think or speak opposition, and whose working class was neutered by material goods and technology." Art had the potential to cut through the haze, said Marcuse, and yet it could not be popular without losing an ability to "negate" the status quo. From satire to cinema verité, NET's most controversial programs belied the tension, attempting to fuse mass political enlightenment to the aesthetic cutting edge.[29]

Such was the case with contested segments of *Public Broadcast Laboratory* (1966-1968), the first "interconnected" public television program. According to executive producer Av Westin, *PBL* was torn between an academic board of directors who believed "nothing should appear on the air that would offend a gentleman in his living room" and young staffers who wished to "challenge the status quo" and push television toward the avant-garde. The tension made for some disjointed television. The two-hour program was laden with dry-as-dust lectures. But it also showcased minimalist theater and modern dance, avant-garde cinema, "far-out" musical compositions, contemporary poetry, experimental video, and cinema verité documentaries on social and political issues. The first program went so far as to satirize TV advertising with "noncommercials" pitching aspirin and cigarettes. The transgressions did not pass unnoticed. The "young Turks," as they were dubbed by the trade publication *Variety*, were accused by the editorial board of injecting "into the program insights, approaches, and types of thinking not normally associated with broadcasting."[30]

Since *PBL* was promoted as the "exciting" new bridge between ETV and a full-scale public television system, its episodes were taken by the stations as an indication of where that system was headed. Local station managers criticized *PBL* for political and cultural reasons. *PBL* drew fire especially in the South, where twenty-nine station managers rejected the program sight unseen, because it would present *Day of Absence*, an off-Broadway play about a racist southern town performed by black actors in "white face." Other stations labeled the show as esoteric, urbane, and confusing. *PBL*'s coverage of racial and economic inequalities was, in fact, interspersed with cultural segments addressed to intellectuals and highbrows. In one episode, a news segment addresses the Poor People's Campaign, a multiracial coalition of economic rights advocates organized by the late Martin Luther King Jr. Footage of cardboard shanty towns set up by homeless people gathered in the nation's capital was meant to evoke sympathy. So was a documentary about a black veteran, forced to move his family to a tiny substandard tenement when he could not find employment. The next segment was "Why Mozart Was a Bad Composer," a lecture/performance by famed modern pianist Glenn Gould, performing passages from Mozart's "crowd pleasers." Adopting the detached view of aesthetics that sociologist Pierre Bourdieu ascribes to a formally educated habitus, Gould deconstructs the music in detail, comparing the formal properties of Mozart's lesser "hits" with his true masterpieces. Gould speaks to an audience quite unlike the impoverished "others" revealed in the documentaries. The imagined viewer is not only schooled in classical music, but he or she is also presumed to care about intricate hierarchies of worth *within* high culture. Without batting an eyelash, Gould professes:

> The claim that the maturity of this work helped Mozart come to terms with the techniques he used in his previous 490 works seems to me like a haven for some wistful and likable themes that would have been far better off within the concertos or symphonies that he composed a few years earlier. . . . For some reason, despite all his talent and facility, Mozart was content to set down in that piece, that purported late masterpiece, an appalling collection of clichés. Let's try to find out why.[31]

PBL's cultural presentations were tailored to people who either shared or aspired to the vocabularies, museum memberships, and off-Broadway tastes of cosmopolitan intellectuals. Segments that flouted popular conventions favored what Pierre Bourdieu called acquired cultural "competencies," or the specialized knowledges and shared "codes" that make formal experimentation meaningful–and interesting–to some people. *PBL* universalized the meanings and pleasures to be found in envelope-pushing poetry, conceptual dance, and experimental video art, explaining Nam June Paik's abstract projection of colors and images with the statement, "I have treated the TV screen as a canvas." The program telecast an experimental play without subtitles, telling the viewer, "You don't need to know Polish to respond to the Polish Laboratory Theater's performance of 'Akropolis' . . . they create a poetic work that speaks directly to something very deeply hidden inside each person." When critics objected, unconventional segments became more ped-agogic, fusing the avant-garde with middlebrow traditions. One play was presented as an "experiment in clarifying a modern and controversial work for the television viewer." Each act was dissected by creators and critics, par-tially diffusing cultural competencies while enforcing assumptions about cultural worth.[32] Epitomizing Ien Ang's observation about the "irony of in-stitutionalized progressivism," *PBL*'s attempt to enlighten the public and dislodge accusations of erudite intellectualism intersected with an attempt to transform the mass audience by shaping its tastes and, implicitly, its TV-viewing practices.[33]

PBL's documentaries drew from the techniques of cinema verité, reject-ing scripted narratives for a loosely edited, impressionistic attempt to "shed new light" on problems. Cinema verité, according to film scholar Brian Win-ston, is an "ersatz style" that combines hand-held camera footage, commen-tary, interviews, and graphics with no apparent "voice of authority" to con-nect the dots. Some documentarians felt that the approach, which was inspired by "fly-on-the-wall" direct cinema, got closer to the buried truth; others felt that the radical new style challenged the stodgy status quo, with its staid look and bespectacled talking heads. Film critics now acknowledge the verité filmmaker's role in shaping "reality," from decisions about what to film, to editing, sound, and camera angles. Winston also questions cinema verité's political utility, on the grounds that its unstructured, "happenstance" form makes coherent analysis of dominant institutions and value systems difficult at best.[34] *PBL* acknowledged as much, noting in a press release that "one of the limitations and at the same time one of the glories" of cinema verité is that it leaves "little room for . . . pointmaking." *PBL*'s documentaries were also fetishized as prime examples of the artistic vanguard, a pattern not limited to known directors like Frederick Wiseman, Albert Maysles, and Jonas Mekas. Advocacy documentaries, like LeRoi Jones's film on black power, were also valorized as aesthetic innovations, components of an intel-lectual movement in cinema found in documentaries as well as in the mav-erick features of continental filmmakers like Jean-Luc Godard. Playing up the cachet, *PBL* devised a study guide for the audience entitled "What to Say to Your Friends and Loved Ones When Watching Avant-Garde Movies on Television." The publicity encouraged viewers to prioritize above all the for-mal elements of cutting-edge filmmaking, a task that included using presti-gious French New Wave terms like avant-garde, auteur, cahiers du cinéma, and mise-en-scène.

Cultural and political enlightenment were deeply intertwined on *PBL*, sending a mixed message about social change. Coupling film footage with commentary, one exposé of tax loopholes for the rich took sides with a chauffeur who paid a higher percentage of his wages to the IRS than did his millionaire employer. Just the sort of "courage" that Nicholas Johnson was calling for, the segment was followed by an erudite profile of Swedish film director Ingmar Bergman. The piece opened by pitting the cultural value of the director's art-house "classics" against that of popular Hollywood films, in a stated attempt to upgrade "movie fans." The paradox was that *PBL* also noted that Bergman's films were superior precisely because they eschewed popularity. Facing the camera, the narrator told the potential convert, "These are not easy movies . . . they are often cryptic, but profound." A cinephile's interview with the director laced with specialized knowledges underscored the warning, as did excerpts from the films, some of which were shown without subtitles. In sync with leftist intellectuals since the Frankfurt school wrote its late-1940s view of the products churned out by the "culture industries," *PBL*'s daring producers valued complex art over industrially produced mass culture and believed that once exposed, the people would, too.

Instead, the television show that promised to revolutionize the medium was ignored by 99 percent of TV viewers who, according to journalists, preferred police dramas and *Ed Sullivan*. *PBL* was not a particular hit among public television's supporters, either. Like the academic board that oversaw the "Lab," some found it too controversial, and others believed that it spoke to a narrowly conceived in-group. Some local stations resented the show's "east of the Hudson" cultural sensibilities and balked at its admitted tendency to make New York City the "center of the universe."[35] Defenders of the experiment, in contrast, blamed the lukewarm response on the public's "limited appetite" for "mindbending and experimental work." In the farewell episode, *PBL* viewers were told that unfortunately, "serious television may never command a mass audience." *PBL* carved an electronic space to occasionally challenge the status quo within a cultural framework that valorized until the end the particular cultural competencies of urban intellectuals.

NET's "social problem" documentaries, which thrived between 1968 and 1972, also harnessed the "ersatz" techniques of cinema verité style to bring the plight of the unfortunate to TV screens. Like the "victim" genre that Winston traced to John Grierson's 1930s documentaries about the British poor, many were voyeuristic in their earnest presentation of pitiable "others." While rooted in protest, the presentations tended to aestheticize poverty and evade coherent critique, as typified by "Appalachia: Rich Land, Poor People" (1968), a documentary about displaced Kentucky and West Virginia coal miners. Scenes of impoverished shacks filled with wide-eyed children in tattered clothes elicit sympathy, but they also presume that the victims are not "us," that is, the people watching the documentary on the noncommercial channel in their book-lined living rooms. Juxtaposing scenes from an anticommunist Chamber of Commerce speech with VISTA volunteers lamenting the perversion of democracy, the documentary subtly implies that free enterprise and the liberal welfare state perpetuate poverty. The unstructured vignettes defy clarity and structural explanations, however. The conflict is between the businessmen who symbolize Middle America and the rabble-rousing filmmakers, disparaged as "filthy beatniks" by one polyester-clad local businessman who appeared in the documentary.[36]

"Banks and the Poor" (1970) implicated members of Congress in reprehensible banking practices. The documentary critiques discrimination against the poor, using loosely edited footage, montages, and interviews. Savings and loan institutions are shown to perpetuate slum housing, while respectable banks channel money to dingy storefront operations that prey on low-income people, charging exorbitant interest rates and repossessing property for late payments. "Banks and the Poor" was indeed courageous. Taking on powerful institutions was, as *Life* magazine observed, "the sort of thing only noncommercial television will dare to do." Footage of people forced to live in dilapidated conditions is juxtaposed with commercials for luxury resorts financed by major lending institutions, leaving viewers to put two and two together. The Chase Manhattan Bank's president, David Rockefeller, presents his side of the story while close camera shots (as opposed to point-by-point analysis) visually question its veracity. The credits close with a list of 124 congressmen who have dealings with banks, as "The Battle Hymn of the Republic" plays in the background.

"Banks and the Poor" challenged the status quo, but its rejection of narrative structures and conventions made it hard to follow. Like "Rich Land, Poor Land," it relies on unedited footage, subtle juxtapositions, and voyeurism. The point was not to help people exploited by banks but to plead their case and radicalize well-placed viewers in their living rooms. From a cultural studies vantage point, "Banks and the Poor" reproduced public television's narrow address to the educated middle class. Documentaries like "Banks and the Poor" were prone to "speaking to the converted," in terms of not just politics but also education and intellectual cultural competencies. PBS President Hartford Gunn noted as much when the broadcast sparked bitter controversy, fueling the conservative assault on public broadcasting and prompting some banks to cancel grants to local stations. "Let us not use techniques that . . . give somebody a handle not just to club us with, but what's worse: That the whole damn point of doing the program is destroyed because nobody will remember what it was about," said the frazzled bureaucrat.[37]

The same year that "Banks and the Poor" appeared, the documentary "Factory" (1970) addressed the everyday lives of blue-collar factory workers. Curious public television viewers who presumably did not work in factories were promised a "sympathetic study of the blue-collar worker, his interests, life aspirations and political views." The opening five minutes are devoid of dialogue, a stylistic novelty publicized by PBS. Only the din of industrial machines can be heard as the camera documents the "mechanical movements of the workers as they performed their perfunctory tasks." Visually stunning, the exotic world of manual labor is filmed from an educated gaze. At one point, an extreme close-up of a time clock lingers on the screen for more than thirty seconds, joined by the shrill sound of the factory bell. For people who actually work on an assembly line, or wash dishes, haul boxes, enter data, flip burgers, or whatever, the aestheticization of the capitalist drill offers few insights and little pleasure. "Factory" speaks about "have-nots," just as NET spoke about social problems but disparaged people who were not suitably hip, educated, and cultured.[38]

Studying the "forgotten Americans for whom punch out and punch in are a way of life," the documentary probes their psyches for puzzled liberals. Accepting the stereotype of bigoted blue-collar laborers ensconced in media-induced false consciousness, the documentary addresses, in impressionistic and unstructured fashion, why factory workers accept their lot and espouse conservative ideologies.[39] The off-screen filmmaker grills the workers about their leisure time, eating habits, financial situations, resistance to the New Left, and refusal to "rebel against the bosses." "Factory" vaguely indicts consumer capitalism, but its disjointed format and tendency to cast manual workers as dupes undermines the critique. Jump cuts drive this point home. In one scene, footage of the factory workers segues into footage of male wrestlers, encouraging the viewer to draw parallels. Later, the film cuts from workers laughing about why they do not "seize control of the factories" to these men at home plopped down on the couch, smoking cigarettes, snacking on convenience foods, and watching television. The director demands to know why they like TV, but he does not accept that watching a Western or comedy after a hard day's work can be enjoyable. Cutting between the drone of the factory and an extreme close-up of the TV screen, the director explains to the savvy viewer that the "ordinary man" depicted in the documentary has been "hypnotized."

The Nader Report (1970), another NET program mired in controversy, was shown on PBS for one season. Produced with the consumer rights advocate Ralph Nader, it angered big business for investigating shady corporate practices and bolstered advertising claims. In "Red, White and Blue," documentarians explore why workers at Cannon Mills, a huge textile factory in North Carolina, are resistant to unionization. The episode is introduced by Nader himself, who delivers a rapid-fire lecture from a book-filled office. Using the language of a sociologist, Nader explains that "the object of the student studying company towns . . . is to go down to grassroots community level and analyze how power is structured." He thus sets up the film as a scholarly case study in democracy run amok, and the documentary that follows blends satire, muckraking, and "happenstance" cinema verité.

Images of the small company town where the factory is situated are juxtaposed with scenes featuring employees with heavy southern accents, torn clothes, and rotting teeth. Snatches of dialogue and facts flashed on the screen eventually add up to a disturbing scenario: The townspeople people have no union, no town government, no pensions, and hazardous working conditions. Interspersed on the sound track is the official company song, used ironically against the flashing facts to present the documentary's impressionistic critique. The program was not intended for those whose abysmal situation it documents. Shown to be victims of false consciousness, most workers say of the company, "It's OK, I guess," while the information on screen tells the sympathetic viewer how things really were. The point was not radical pedagogy or the provision of cultural resources to help economically exploited groups. It was to radicalize Middle America, yet this gesture fails too, for the film is so aestheticized and disjoined, it is hard to come away with a coherent understanding of the stakes involved. Like other programs accused of "far-left" sympathies, it made disempowered others visible, in a form geared to people who preferred art-house cinema to movies and read Marcuse in graduate school.[40]

Satirizing the American Dream

The most celebrated "far-left" PBS program was *Great American Dream Machine* (1970-1971), produced for NET by a creative team that included Jack Willis (producer of "Rich Land, Poor People") and Al Perlmutter (executive producer of "Banks and the Poor" and "Factory"). Funded by the Ford Foundation and the Corporation for Public Broadcasting, *Dream Machine* combined documentary, commentary, satire, and cultural performances at an unusually (for public television) swift pace, calculated to hold the attention of modern television viewers. According to Day, who oversaw the show as the president of NET, it was conceptualized as an alternative to public television's "ponderous and humorless, excessively highbrow" offerings. Developed "before money came to public TV with strings attached," *Dream Machine* was entirely "producer led," says Willis. Approved as an amorphous concept that lacked both pilot and script, the first program was completed just hours before it was broadcast. Day and Willis concur that *Dream Machine*'s cultural and political "edge" was an anomaly born of late 1960s turmoil, Ford's noblesse oblige, and the newness of public television itself, which meant that the approval of "red-tape committees," corporate underwriters, and local stations was not required to get a "program on the air." Immediately vulnerable to authoritarian-populist conservative criticism, *Dream Machine* was a sacrificial lamb to the Nixon conflict. It invited controversy, for the show's politically savvy address tended to snub mass culture and trade on stereotypes of suburbanites, working- and lower-middle-class people, and Middle American squares.[41]

The series opened with a mime making loud vomiting sounds, a prelude to its take on mainstream America. As a techno-rendition of the national anthem played on the sound track, cartoon images of a soldier with flowers in his gun, a rainbow wiping out smog, the Capitol, and a scale being calibrated to balance black and white human heads flash on screen. According to its publicity, the show would probe the "broad range of American life" by exploring "people's goals, ideas of themselves, their country, their hopes, their dreams." It also promised to take on powerful institutions, including advertising industry, the culture industries, and commercial television. "Our basic theme is the gulf between promise and performance in American life," stated the producers of *Dream Machine*'s rabble-rousing mission. "We're trying to show what a great country this could be if we got rid of the false values sold to us by hucksters and con men who have contempt for the public."[42]

For this, the show was branded leftist, antiestablishment propaganda, both behind closed doors at the White House and by conservative critics in public forums. *Dream Machine*'s journalistic segments drew the most fire. One ten-minute news story by advocacy journalist Paul Jacobs accused FBI agents of infiltrating the New Left and generated enormous controversy in the process. Jacobs did not come off as a suit- and tie-clad Dan Rather type, which made any story he produced immune from the established signifiers of "objectivity" and "expertise." In an earlier *Dream Machine* critique delivered on a bare stage filled with U.S. flags, the completely bald, black turtleneck-clad New Yorker challenges the space race. His satirical assessment touches on everything from the patriotic fervor surrounding the *Apollo 13* drama to the probability of astronauts' hawking "Mars" candy bars but requires a thorough understanding of the government's space program to follow. The critique spoke to the well informed who shared his skepticism and his cultural competencies. Jacob's story on the FBI apparently went too far, however. Protested by FBI Director J. Edgar Hoover, it was deleted from *Dream Machine* by PBS and later broadcast with a disclaimer, followed by a scholarly debate on its journalistic credibility. The Nixon papers make no mistake about the president's extreme displeasure with this broadcast, despite its peacemaking gestures. An internal memo called Jacobs an admitted "radical" who did not pretend to hide leftist viewpoints and, worse, who had run for public office in California on a ticket with Black Panther Eldridge Cleaver.[43] The incident catapulted *Dream Machine* into the fray engulfing NET, coinciding with Clay Whitehead's campaign to decentralize public television in the name of localism.

Dream Machine's "formless format" juxtaposed news segments, spoofs, short films, animation, and musical presentations without a narrator to explain the flow, which rendered the program somewhat "confusing," or so said *TV Guide*. It addressed a sophisticated liberal audience, incorporating countercultural sentiments while also struggling to make "establishment" high culture appear relevant and hip. A one-act play entitled *Bach to Bach* illustrates this tension perfectly. The scene opens to a young couple in bed, ruminating on a Bach sonata playing on the phonograph. As they converse, dropping casual references to philosophers from Huxley and Nietzsche, the camera pans the surroundings of the room and lingers on several Picasso prints on the wall. Soon this tasteful scenario takes an unexpected turn, as the couple lament growing up in a "stuffy bourgeois" family and reveal, at the end of the play, that they had met only a few hours earlier in a singles bar. Infusing the legitimated cultural habitus represented by classical music, literature, and art with signifiers of rebellious youth, the segment invites the imagined viewer to identify with the young white couple and the social worlds negotiated by the play.

The mass culture of "others" was alternately presented from a distance, with great irony. The opening theme song to a regular segment that profiled "American heroes" from Evil Knievel to a black roller derby queen exemplified the detached mockery by declaring the IQs of the people profiled "next to zero." Another segment on "Big Daddy Roth," an amateur car builder, makes a spectacle of an exotic blue-collar other for the bewildered amusement of urban intellectuals. Big Daddy is called a modern folk artist by *Dream Machine*, despite his own understanding of himself as a "worker." While asked explain the nuances of car parts, accessories, and body design, his detailed answers to these questions are mocked by the camera, which shows Big Daddy in close-up, driving around Detroit in one of his customized creations as country tunes blare on the radio. Daddy's "obsessive" knowledges and seeming creative talents are offered as amusement to those with hipper tastes and competencies. The segment was not meant for big-car aficionados; it was tailored to those apt to appreciate an ironic, disembodied British voice explaining, "Big Daddy Roth seems to have achieved a remarkable synthesis of variations on the mechanistic folk theme . . . so hip, so cool, so right on, so rank, so vile, so exquisitely repulsive." The off-screen commentary spoofed might have been interpreted as a send-up of overinflated art criticism, but the satirical vantage point still casts Daddy and his vernacular creations as low "others" to the sophisticated viewer addressed by *Dream Machine*'s new wave films, literature readings, experimental dance, original compositions, and acoustical performances by Joan Baez and Peter, Paul, and Mary. The vocational student who dared call hamburger making an "art" in a profile of McDonald's Hamburger University was similarly mocked. What seems serious soon turns ironic, as the camera zeroes in on scenes of patties frying and asks a class struggling with burned buns if hamburgers "are an academic subject." The joke proceeds as the filmmaker asks whether "student revolt is a problem." The members of the graduating class that are interviewed express pride in their accomplishment, but to *Dream Machine* viewers they are merely low-paid workers, fodder for an amusing "statement" on the consumer culture.

Dream Machine skewered advertising, mass culture, and consumer values. Humorist Marshall Ephron appeared regularly in a segment called "Better Living," taking potshots at everything from frozen foods to inflated product claims. Unfortunately, the jokes were aimed at the lowly feminized masses who fell for the hoaxes. The spot constructed an "us versus them" binary between savvy people who were not fooled and millions of people in the far reaches of suburbia who swallowed the bait. In a skit on proprietary drugs, Ephron flatters those in the "know" when he snidely tells those who are not: "Brand X does the same thing as more expensive products advertised on TV. Read the labels, nitwits!" An experimental New York theater group called the Groove Tube similarly satirized sitcoms, soap operas, and even public television's own "hit," the *French Chef*. A performance piece called the "The House That Jack Built" makes fun of suburban lifestyles built on credit, complete with ice crushers, backyard barbecues, washing machines, and domestic icons. It questions the premise that consumption equals happiness, but it displaces consumer ideology onto the masses of consumers, leaving us not with a coherent critique but a stereotypical image of Jack the Sap, keeping up with the Joneses and stuck with a lifetime of credit card bills.

Feeding Nixon's authoritarian-populist complaints, *Dream Machine* grouped conservative businessmen, suburbanites, and blue collars under the disparaged sign of Middle America. In the spoof "My, My More My Lais," a bigoted, overweight man gets annoyed when his wife turns on the TV news. The middle-aged white Spiro Agnew supporter does not feel like seeing a "lot of hairy hippies crying about how tragic Vietnam is." Unfazed by vets talking about massacres and burning villages, the couple eats banana ripple ice cream and cheese dip, wondering whether the man will get a raise anytime soon and reminiscing about their 1968 beach vacation. "I'm bored with this talk of killing innocent people," the gluttonous, self-absorbed man insists as war-torn images appear on his TV screen. Confirming the image of the hedonistic and apathetic mass audience circulated by the discourse of the vast wasteland, he professes: "Television ought to entertain you—they ought to put on more Westerns."

From time to time, "regional" segments appeared on *Dream Machine* to signal the program's awareness of geographical diversity. Places like the "conservative Republican" town of Clyde, Ohio, were voyeuristically presented to cosmopolitans with predisposed ideas about the heartland. In this short documentary, filmmakers quiz high-school cheerleaders about their perceptions of New York City, Chicago, and Detroit and get the expected response about "everyone killing one another." Business elites proudly show their conservative colors, while the local head-shop owner and the long-haired, tie-dyed hippies are asked how they get on in a small town where there is obviously little tolerance of different ideas. The segment does not represent geographical differences as much as it constructs them from existing assumptions and iconographies. The filmmakers constructed a stereotypical image of conservative Middle America, reiterating the very same "us versus them" opposition circulated by conservatives. Although this image offers an alternative view of who was right and who was wrong, the one-dimensional caricature is the same.

A profile of Lebanon, Indiana, juxtaposes "America the Beautiful" on the soundtrack with frenetic footage of flag-waving townspeople filmed on the Fourth of July. In this documentary, interviews with the mayor and other influentials confirm, as shown by the visuals, the community's "archconservative" makeup. Much as expected, the viewer learns that the people of Lebanon support the war in Vietnam and voted "heavily for Barry Goldwater." There are no racial tensions or antiwar demonstrations in this patriotic small town, which keeps controversial books like *Everything You Always Wanted to Know About Sex* hidden away under the counter at the public library. Articulating the provincial mentality that made some critics cringe at the decentralization of public television, a man explains that "our biggest concerns aren't in Washington but are right in Lebanon." While the chief of police has handled a few "dope" incidents, Lebanon is generally filled with "well-groomed" homes and churchgoing citizens.

In the context of *Dream Machine*, "in-the-know" viewers were encouraged to read the boosting and the "wholesome" positive portrait of Middle America as parody. Another segment, a visual collage called "Middle America," has the national anthem on the soundtrack while images of dirt roads, oil wells, highways, cowboys, pigs, farms, small-town street corners, and a map of the United States superimposed by the word *ordinary*. Newspaper headlines with the words *business, official, cars, dandruff,* and *God Bless America* are interspersed with cartoon people and images of overweight children. Having conveyed that Middle America is traditional and rural, the collage affirms taken-for-granted conservatism with an image of Nixon on television and a pro-Nixon political sign. From here, the visual commentary spirals into a dystopian scenario that equates rodeos, police officers with bully clubs, wounded victims, God Bless America superimposed over a globe, and Nixon reading the newspaper with the flashing descriptor "Middle America." *Dream Machine* was not geographically biased as much as it perpetuated a construction of place that reinforced authoritarian-populist discourse. Another documentary about the retirement community of Sun City, Arizona, worked in similar ways. The filmmaker used candid statements captured by letting the camera roll to critique the community's conservative values with ironic close-ups, camera angles, and editing. Not just a political exposé, the film also characterizes and satirizes an unsophisticated taste culture through the use of aerial footage of suburban tract houses, close-ups of mass-produced paintings and artificial hibiscus plants, and unflattering shots of flabby seniors attending group exercise classes in their bathing suits. Combining subtle critique with pretentious mockery, films like these buttressed complaints about NET's big-city arrogance.

Disadvantaged people were not ridiculed on *Dream Machine*, but they often were presented as pitiable "others." Poor people—especially poor people of color—appear as victims without voices, as typified by a visual essay on slum housing in New York City. The piece provides no narration. Modeled on a slide show, it projects a series of black-and-white photographs aestheticizing ghetto poverty. Run-down tenement apartments, garbage strewn about the streets, and black families watching television in decimated interior settings are made visible by the images, eliciting sympathy but offering no critique. The visual essay frames the plight through a voyeuristic lens that accentuates the pleasure of anonymously peeping at "others," appreciating the artistry of the photographs themselves, and seeing one's identity affirmed by *Dream Machine*'s sympathetic liberalism. While few poor people have speaking roles on the program, white middle-class angst about "have-nots" is pervasive, as shown in another essay, this one read by the author on stage with no images. The commentary contrasts air-conditioned suburbia with poor urban neighborhoods. Addressing *Dream Machine* viewers as "haves," it traces white middle-class perceptions of poverty up to the 1950s, when "the hungry, angry have-nots were out of sight in their part of town." The author then describes the "discovery" of poor people amid middle-class affluence in the 1960s. "Our castles have become our jail as we wait for the hungry man," he laments, eliciting guilt while evading structural, institutional criticism. Using words instead of pictures, the segment aestheticizes poverty. In a larger sense, it presumes that the viewer is more like the essayist than the "hungry man." Like most public television, *Dream Machine* simply assumed that its audience was white, educated, and materially comfortable.

Dream Machine provoked conservative criticism expressed with a populist accent. It is not hard to see how white blue-collar viewers might have perceived the show as an assault, had they tuned in to public television regularly. The show's condescending edge echoes the liberal "know-it-all" attitude discussed by Barbara Ehrenreich in her cogent critique of class stereotyping in the late 1960s and early 1970s. Ehrenreich argues that the working- and lower-middle-class "silent majority" did not resent liberal reformers because they advocated civil rights, racial integration, and other progressive causes. Working people, she says, were turned off by an "air of moral superiority and contempt." Behind their anger was a feeling that few well-placed liberals cared about unprivileged people who were not protesting. According to Ehrenreich, it was this broader sentiment (quoted by Robert Cole in his 1971 study *The Middle Americans*) that motivated a woman to say, "If we even try to explain our problems, they start telling us how wrong we are, and how we need to be more 'open.'"[44]

Ehrenreich rejects the Archie Bunker stereotype that also emerged in the early 1970s as grossly one-dimensional, but she does acknowledge that many so-called Middle Americans were resentful of middle-class student countercultures and protesters. This, too, had its basis in economic and cultural hierarchies. The New Left's rejection of consumer culture did not make sense to people who were not "drowning" in their parents' affluence and who had just acquired the material comforts ascribed to the American Dream, Ehrenreich notes. Shaggy hippies and hip liberal bohemians came across as somewhat arrogant because they "appeared so disdainful of the consumer options–the tract house, the matching furniture sets, the second car–that the working class still aspired to." In addition, the assault on conspicuous consumption was–and continues to be–hypocritical. While some people lived in communes and made their own granola, most ultimately traded mass-produced goods for a more subtle variation of high culture. *Dream Machine*'s repeated parodies of "Mr. and Mrs. Consumer" speak to a quest for social differentiation that is no less presumptuous and divisive than the claims of superiority attached to "prestigious" programs like *Masterpiece Theatre*. As Ehrenreich contends, the "gap" between the classes was

> beginning to take a new form: Not simply more, and more expensive, things for the more fortunate but the contrived appearance of less. For the middle class, a search for tasteful authenticity in red wine and unprocessed food . . . for the working class, the affordable comforts of Budweiser, tuna casserole, and TV dinners.[45]

Class resentments of *Dream Machine*'s "know-it-all" attitude popped up on the show itself. The first season featured an ongoing conversation among oral historian Studs Terkel, author of *Hard Times*, and blue-collar commentators gathered for beer in a Chicago saloon. Terkel's respectful, nonironic chats with the "gang" counter stereotypes of the "silent majority." So too do the men and women of different ages and races who share their views on issues from taxes to the Vietnam War and, in so doing, demonstrate that people without college degrees are not inherently conservative, apathetic, or uninformed. Terkel's gang also challenge *Dream Machine*'s spoofs of middle-class consumption. For the "gang," an ideal society is one that provides more colleges, more food, more housing, more conveniences, and more material comforts for more people. There is not "a damn thing wrong with wanting a comfortable material life [or] wanting to buy a color TV," said one participant about the rejection of conspicuous consumption. Authoritarian-populist sentiments are revealed as well. In one episode, a steelworker fantasizes about a bowling game in which liberal intellectual Arthur Schlesinger Jr. is the pin boy and Spiro Agnew drops by to "bowl a few frames." While packed with tension, the discussions are critical of the war in Vietnam, economic inequality, racism, and other important issues, showing that if blue collars resent educated liberals and New Left activists, it is not because they reject progressive plans for social change.

Terkel's working-class segment was out of place on *Dream Machine* and awkwardly handled by PBS publicity, which framed the "ordinary citizens" as exotic specimens. After one season, the segment was dropped entirely. According to the executive producer, Al Perlmutter, the gang took too long to work up to an "articulate" conversation. By that point, conservatives were casting *Dream Machine* as a "mouthpiece for the eastern liberals on controversial issues." Even the *New York Times*, a staunch supporter of public television, complained that *Dream Machine* favored the radical chic "in-group." Producers admitted as much and said it had been "done deliberately to attract the young, hip audience turned off by commercial TV." Next season, "we'll give more attention to the views of Middle America," Perlmutter promised the readers of *TV Guide*. It was too late for amends, however sincere they might have been. Pressured by the White House, the Corporation for Public Broadcasting dramatically reduced the flow of funds to NET, and *Dream Machine* was canceled.[46]

Handicrafts, Hobbies, and Farm Clubs

Richard Nixon eventually approved congressional funding for public broadcasting, contingent on the reforms he advocated. The most apparent change was the allocation of public dollars. A bigger piece of the pie went to the more than two hundred stations, which for the first time were allowed to "vote" on pitches for the upcoming PBS schedule. The "cooperative" system depended on telephone hookups to a mainframe computer that logged each station's choices, tabulated the results, and–in the words of one newspaper–"belched out" the winners. Critics said the spectacle smelled of ratings and therefore the unenlightened "cultural democracy" that had ruined commercial television. Unfortunately, "the price for grassroots democracy has always been reduced quality," said one insider alarmed by the new PBS. Former NET president James Day has also dismissed local station input in programming as a force for blandness and mediocrity, believing that decisions should be made by a centralized leadership, not by "referendum or vote." This attitude deserves pause, for it hinges on familiar anxieties about the fictitious Middle American masses.[47]

What both supporters and appalled observers described as "grassroots cultural democracy" was in fact a decentralized operation based on executive perceptions of what the local community wanted and needed. Only people who gave donations to public television were "ascertained" with questionnaires, and station managers accountable to private boards were drawn from a "narrow circle of high-ranking people" in business, and local politics made the final calls.[48] This is not to say that the push toward regional control did not challenge what counts as television worthy of public support even today, when a national programmer sets the PBS schedule. According to critics, "robust localism" failed to materialize from Nixon's reforms because most local stations spent their new allowances to purchase national PBS programs instead of creating local ones. This argument essentializes physical locales (where programs come from) and neglects culture (what programs communicate). As John Hartley argues, cultural diversity neither requires nor is guaranteed by geographical dispersion.[49] Stations might not have produced more local programs, but they did affect public television culture at the national level. What some dubbed the "shopping list" approach infused the PBS schedule with regionally coded tastes and priorities based on the land-grant mission of stations associated with state universities created with federal financing in the nineteenth century and mandated to serve the people of the state. To the delight of *TV Guide* but to the chagrin of cosmopolitan TV critics and stations like WNET-New York, the stations brought hobbies and nature, consumer advice, preventive health, popular science, and even pet care to prime-time television. Having dismissed this as ideological co-optation, historians and critics have failed to recognize its cultural significance.

Land-grant broadcasting developed in the Midwest, fueled by the promise that the "borders of the university were the borders of the state." Educational radio stations licensed to universities presented instruction and extension services, attempting to provide useful programs for the "farmers, housewives, workers, and businessmen across their states." They may have touted high culture and university knowledge, but they also believed it their duty to provide practical programs for women and men of different socioeducational backgrounds. Operated by the University of Wisconsin, the first educational radio station broadcast weather reports, farm information, and lectures on subjects from art appreciation to aluminum cooking utensils. When ETV stations went on the air in Texas, Nebraska, Minnesota, Iowa, and other midwestern states, most presented televised state university courses alongside applied knowledge, from homemaking and agricultural shows to hobbies and crafts. The University of Oklahoma's *Open Windows* typified the fusion of practical education and everyday life, broadcasting lectures on topics like income taxes, football, beer brewing, and plant growing. Stations broadcast local choirs, band music, and sports events when they were not presenting education or classroom assistance. Quite literally a "university of the air," the Midwest Program in Airborne Television Instruction symbolized the land-grant approach, transmitting courses to schools and colleges over a two-hundred-mile radius from a circulating airplane.[50]

The Nixon controversy can be better understood through a closer look at one of the early land grant-oriented stations, KTCA-Minneapolis-St. Paul. KTCA's station manager John Schwarzwalder applauded the 1972 veto as a self-defined liberal, not a conservative, which makes for an interesting case study of authoritarian populism. KTCA was licensed to a local nonprofit corporation overseen by civic, cultural, and business elites. But unlike similarly structured community stations in New York, Boston, San Francisco, and other urban locales, KTCA was modeled on the land-grant mission. The station had relationships with the University of Minnesota, private colleges, and vocational schools, using their courses (some available for credit toward diplomas) as programming. Under Schwartzwalder's direction, KTCA embodied "local" public broadcasting, drawing minimally from NET and PBS and breaking ties with the national bureaucracy altogether for a short period in the early 1970s.

Schwarzwalder, a former chorus singer, had managed KUHF-Houston, the first ETV station on the air, in the early 1950s. In an interview, part of an oral history of public broadcasting housed at the University of Maryland, he recalled brushing up against the Ford Foundation from the start, denied grants, he says, because the University of Houston used the new technology to provide conventional education—including courses beamed to TV-equipped dorm rooms—rather than showing the uplifting national programming focused on culture and public affairs. In 1957, he started KTCA with funds from the James J. Hill Foundation, the local charity of an Upper-Midwest railroad mogul, as well as Ford, schools and universities, and, eventually, income from credit courses. Schwarzwalder clashed with NET, refusing to join the network (although he did broadcast some programs) and believing that local stations could and should operate independently, extending the reach of colleges and universities. He was "skeptical" about the 1967 Public Broadcasting Act but signed papers authorizing public television, only to become "outraged" over the direction in which it was heading. Schwarzwalder protested the concentration on "uplifting TV" over educating in the land-grant tradition, as well as the "pinko" undertones he detected in occasional PBS documentaries about Cuba, Vietnam, and other cold war enemies.[51]

Schwarzwalder wrote "memos upon memos" to politicians and public television bureaucrats, referring to his mailing list as the "favored few," which included the presidents of the CPB, PBS, and NET. He was not taken seriously until the Nixon fiasco, when Schwarzwalder circulated a memo demanding the resignation of public television's national leadership and was visited personally by Clay Whitehead. Just after Nixon's veto in 1972, Schwarzwalder published an article in *TV Guide* arguing that "public television has taken it as its mission to bring to an important segment of the American public an extreme left-wing view." Seconding the White House's motion for decentralization, he spelled out PBS's faults as he saw them, in

TV Guide as well as trade publications geared to public television professionals. Believing that public television's purpose was to educate the populace broadly, Schwarzwalder questioned what he saw as an overemphasis on the high-culture crowd, mostly interested in "symphony music, classical theater, and the ballet." Unlike Nixon's team, he also protested public television's "tokenized" attention to women, ethnic minorities, teenagers, the elderly, and the blue-collar employed. Schwarzwalder's objections show how authoritarian-populist reform discourse could and did unite political, geographical, and cultural tensions irreducible to party politics.[52]

KTCA did not experiment or attempt to liberate the people it served. It eschewed the avant-garde for straightforward education delivered by local instructors and professors. The station did not aggressively solicit corporate underwriting but it was solidly pro-business, willing when asked to broadcast shows like *Money Matters*, the "fascinating story of money in our daily lives," presented as a public service by the local Farmers & Mechanics Savings Bank. But KTCA did recognize class differences rooted in education and programmed accordingly, which made it more encompassing in cultural policy terms than NET's "far-left" programming. *From Our Heritage* (1958), an ambitious series for ETV standards, was the station's first hurrah. A combination of narrative documentary, studio guests, and archival photographs and hosted by a female professor, the program set the tenor for the station by defining both the importance of education and the meaning of culture. The opening theme hails the audience as Minnesotans who need to keep learning "what's round the bend," to keep the state strong economically. Images of farmers and livestock, lakes and grasslands construct the state's regional identity, as does the governor, who wishes he could take "great leaders" to 4-H, homecoming parades, and grain elevators. ETV is quickly situated in the postwar "education boom." According to the narrator, industry needs trained personnel to accommodate the state's shift from an economy based on farming and mining to one based on technology and information. In addition, thousands of people are clamoring for televised driver education, "home and living instruction," and vocational training, she tells the broadly conceived audience. KTCA's mission, according to the introductory program, was not to enlighten or to provoke "critical thinking" but to help enhance the state's human resources while providing a range of university extension services.[53]

KTCA's interpretation of culture differed from NET's quest to serve intellectual viewers while simultaneously uplifting the habits and tastes of "others." In a segment of *From Our Heritage* called "How We Look at Culture," the station negotiated a "we ought to" respect for high culture with a preference for less prestigious crafts and do-it-yourself projects. This part of the program begins by showing a group of casually dressed visitors at the Walker Art Museum in Minneapolis, where a tour guide with a pointer offers a lesson on a modern sculpture. Having established the state's pedagogic relationship with the art museum, the narrator subverts the reverence ascribed to the legitimated habitus, explaining, "We come to places like this wearing shorts and jeans and have a great time." The camera cuts to the fairgrounds, where crafts, food preservation, livestock, and machines take central stage. "We come to look at great art," says the narrator about the museum, "but we go to state and country fairs to see what we ourselves have made." Refusing boundaries between artists and amateurs, it proves the point with housewives and farmers who paint landscapes in their spare time. With respect and enthusiasm, the narrator insists that "anyone can do this." Culture does not signify good taste or social superiority, according to this program. "We live with the arts," says the narrator while the camera pans the grasslands. That's what makes us a little different."

KTCA emphasized concrete gains—a new skill, credits toward a diploma—over cultural uplift. An early brochure boasts that "thousands of Minnesotans have been taught to read more effectively, how to study, how to manage their personal finances better, how to encourage creativity in themselves and in others, how to speak more effectively." Until the mid-1970s, the station presented three distinct levels of programming that corresponded roughly to distinct class formations: "Private School of the Air," "University of Minnesota Hour," and "Vocational Instruction." The station did not question the implications of these "levels," but it did attempt to serve audiences of different social/educational backgrounds within its own unquestioned educational parameters. Class pluralism was undermined, however, by business control over "vocational" programming. "Minnesota School of the Air," a "service to businesses and their employees," was permeated by disciplinary logic. "Nine to Five: Secretarial School" taught skills and behavior modification, instructing women how to "adjust" to superiors with abusive behavior, for a "good listener puts forward a better effort when faced with an indifferent or unlikable boss." Other programs, however, besides the formal hours, did cross class lines. The Boy Scouts, the Dental Society, 4-H clubs, the Kiwanis, and the Highway Safety Department had shows on KTCA. Universities provided general education on preventive health ("Ill Effects of Smoking"), consumer advice ("Best Food Buys"), homemaking and gardening ("Yard 'n' Garden"), animals and nature ("Minnesota Moose"), and hobbies and crafts ("American Craftsman," "Busy Knitter"), serving a broader range of interests and tastes than NET did.

KTCA aired some national PBS programs, including *Civilisation*, *Sesame Street*, and episodes of *Masterpiece Theatre*, *Black Journal*, *Soul!* and *The French Chef*. But many were rejected, including *Great American Dream Machine*, as it was "impossible" to schedule in light of the more pressing "needs of local educational institutions," said Schwarzwalder.[54] The station did not care much for controversial documentaries, but it did cover city issues and offer labor education. On these practical shows, viewers learned what was happening at their children's schools and step-by-step instructions for organizing a strike or consumer boycott. In 1970, KTCA broadcast "Roots of Reform," a local documentary tracing the history of political protest in the Upper Midwest. With scenes of small-town farmers bringing starving livestock to the state capital to protest agricultural policies, it constructed an alliance, not antagonism, between Middle America and activists. Shows by and for Minnesota's Native American communities appeared on KTCA, as did courses on African American history and ethnic cultures common to the region, a finding that does not support the presumption that Middle America was, by definition, the source of public television's racism. While mass-produced entertainment had no place on the educational channel, preindustrial "folk" culture–from traditional storytelling to sing-alongs–was as common as violin concerts and university drama performances.

Wishing to preserve KTCA's commitment to land-grant education, Schwarzwalder promoted his station as the face of localism in public broadcasting. The tables turned when in 1974, local critics and civic leaders waged a successful campaign to revamp KTCA. The *Minneapolis Star*, which had periodically complained about KTCA's refusal to broadcast national material, published several newspaper columns protesting the station's unslick, stodgy educational format and refusal to follow the national PBS schedule. One critic got personal and scrutinized "Your World This Week," a news analysis program hosted by Schwarzwalder, in which the camera was said to focus on the blackboard the entire time, and Schwarzwalder to use his pointer "six times in 30 minutes." A cartoon on the newspaper's editorial page also lampooned the station manager, showing him waving the pointer at a TV set on which "Adventures in Arithmetic" was playing. Schwarzwalder was forced to join PBS officially and purchase its programs, but the gesture was not enough to curb the reform efforts. In a much-publicized report, the Citizens League protested KTCA's dull, "supremely educational" ethos and inattentiveness to the "ascertainment" of community needs. The civic leaders wanted KTCA to be more like PBS, a high-quality alternative to the vast wasteland. This meant dropping amateurish local lectures (including those aimed at the "vocational" pupil), broadcasting prestigious PBS programs, and developing local cultural and

KTCA Programs, 1970-1971

"Tree Care: Caring for Your Christmas Tree"
"Nine to Five: Secretarial School"
"National 4-H Week"
"Yard 'n' Garden"
"Ed Grant's Stove and Other Stories of the Maine Woods"
"For Every Man Who Wants Power Tools: Buying Guide"
"General Household Pest Control"
"Efficient Reading"
"Irish Folklore"
"Public Employee Bargaining"
"Strikes and Boycotts"
"Dental Health"
"The Frontier of the Dime Novel"
"Applying for a Permanent Job"
"Minnesota State Fair"
"Services for Senior Citizens"
"Minnesota Snowmobile Safety Training"
"Fishing"
"Ill Effects of Smoking"
"Tax Relief for the Elderly"
"Basic Electricity"
"The People Ojibway"
"Your Schools Today"
"Busy Knitter"
"Afro-American History"
"Evening at Pops: Sing Along"
"The World of the American Craftsman"
"Minnesota Moose"
"Latvian Tunes and Songs"
"Recycling Cans"
"Best Food Buys"
"Heart Risks: What Are They?"
"History of the Iron Mining Industry in Minnesota"
"Automobile Accidents: First Aid Procedures"[55]

public affairs programs with funds donated by local viewers and local corporate underwriters.[56] Despite another round of memo writing, Schwarzwalder, like Nixon, was eventually forced to resign; a new station manger was recruited from the East Coast; and KTCA lost its state-college image.

The history of KTCA problematizes geographical essentialism by revealing some of the conflicts over the meaning of culture and public service at the local level. A powerful segment of the Twin Cities composed of civic and business leaders, newspaper columnists, Citizen League members, and KTCA's private trustees preferred the cosmopolitan approach to public broadcasting over a locally produced land-grant schedule. Calling for national PBS presentations and local variations of them, the reformers conflated the "needs" of an educated, upper-middle culture–their own–with those of the local community. To facilitate KTCA's transformation, the "Middle American" station brought in executives and programmers from PBS and the BBC, a move that valorized geographically inflected cultural credentials and provoked complaints about the station's East Coast elitism: They have "an attitude over there that anyone from the Midwest who didn't have credentials with the public TV establishment could be dismissed," said one local critic.[57] Despite such accusations, the station's "updated" view of public broadcasting bore recognizable traces of land-grant populism, as was demonstrated by "100% Freeze Dried Minnesota" (1976), a local production created not long after Schwartzwalder's resignation. Coupling self-conscious awareness of the state's provincial image with an irreverent attitude toward high culture and the East Coast, local comedians perform exaggerated stereotypes of Minnesotans, lampooning their tastes, hobbies, and regional phrases ("You betcha"). One skit revolves around an escape artist named Eddy, a machinist *and* a state representative, who tries throughout the program to wrangle free from a double-knit leisure suit. Other gags probed the state's awkward relationship to high culture. In one scenario, unkempt men dressed in giant parkas beat rugs with badminton rackets to the classical tune of Beethoven's Fifth Symphony, performed live by tuxedoed musicians. In another, a couple dressed up for a night at the opera reveal regional difference by ordering a lowbrow drink–"orange pop"–at the intermission. In another spoof, martini-drinking Minnesotans who mimic East Coast tastes and customs are gently skewered for putting on airs. Satirical but not critical of culturally inflected geographical hierarchies, the program implies that "natural" sophistication was beyond the reach of all Minnesotans, however well educated. In so doing, it reproduced anxious assumptions about local input in public broadcasting that continue to circulate.

Critics tend to dismiss local stations in inherently conservative terms. According to some historians, the "voting" system forced into being by the Nixon White House institutionalized public television's programmatic focus on the "safe, the cheap, and the known" and undermined its capacity for political and cultural risk taking. Such assessments fail to recognize the extent to which local stations reconstituted land-grant priorities. When the station "votes" were in and the new PBS schedule appeared in 1974, practical instruction on topics ranging from preventive health to caring for house pets found a national forum. Whatever cultural power was granted to the local stations extended public television's reach, for as *TV Guide* observed at the time, applied education encompassed a broader range of tastes and interests than had been served by PBS during its infancy. While PBS programs like "Burglar Proofing Your Home" and "Consumer Survival Kit," which traded *Dream Machine*'s satirical approach to consumer culture for advice on "coping with today's high cost of living," are easy to dismiss as political compromises, they were also modernized (and often corporate-sponsored) versions of the statewide "extension services" that originated with educational radio, as were *Nova*'s applied science, Jacques Cousteau's aquatic excursions, how-to and hobby programs, nature documentaries, and *National Geographic*.[58]

The tendency to dismiss the land-grant legacy as apolitical and therefore not authentically "public" requires consideration. How-to and nature programs, for example, are among public television's most popular offerings, across sociodemocratic lines. Rather than rejecting these practical genres or relegating them to the upscale cable channels that now provide them as well, reformers might lobby for social, ethnic, and class differences within them. KTCA and stations that shared its priorities acknowledged class differences to the extent that they provided practical instruction and folk culture for the "vocational" audience. When residual land-grant priorities entered the PBS schedule, however, middle-class culture was normalized. Public television began to address the upwardly mobile, middle-class audience for "self-improvement" anticipated by the Carnegie Commission's viewer profile. In so doing, it was forced to reject the ingrained social biases that underscored the commission's anxious perception that any sustained service to such people might "repel" cultural, intellectual, and political elites from the public television audience. At the same time, PBS ignored the interests and desires of diverse working-class populations by equating practical instruction with a mostly white, middle-class curriculum. The new PBS presented practical advice on "frugal" gourmet cooking and grand-home restoration, but nothing on casserole cooking or low-budget apartment dwelling.

Anti-Television and the Cultural Left

Critical scholars tend to recall the Nixon's era's decentralizing reforms in narrow ideological terms, while the cultural contradictions of "far-left" television are currently displayed in the productions of the Independent Television Service (ITVS). ITVS was created by Congress in the 1980s, with a mandate to diversify public television by funding independent producers and serving "unserved" audiences. Its capacity to democratize public television has been limited by a devotion to "anti-television," an operational motto that reflects more than its stated attempt to "shake up" the stodgy public television system and "engage creative risks, advance issues and represent points of view not usually seen on public or commercial television." Defined as the perpetual opposite of television, ITVS also rejects popular pleasures, tastes, and leisure practices. In its attempt to "expand viewers' horizons" with cutting-edge television that bears little formal resemblance to popular commercial programming, it has reproduced the intellectual Left's distrust of prefabricated "mass appeal" culture and its addicted viewers. By conflating political and cultural enlightenment, it has practically ensured a limited audience for its publicly funded programs, and not just because PBS can and does reject "controversial" content. While ITVS supports programming about people excluded from public television's white, upper-middle-class profile, its preoccupation with "changing" television itself does little to close the gap between public culture and the commercialized media environment in which most people live.[59]

Like mainstream public broadcasting, this corrective agency was conceptualized for the people, not by them. The normative approach to alternative television developed by ITVS reflects the sensibilities of the activists and artists who defined its purpose and lobbied for its creation. NET's collapse in the 1970s–coupled with the downsizing of the largest urban stations–put the kibosh on programming that "challenged the status quo" ideologically and aesthetically. Producers who were hoping to develop public television in directions that did not interest station managers or corporate sponsors were left without a national forum. ITVS's advocates recognized the undemocratic nature of public television's increasingly corporatized model but shared with their "far-left" predecessors a set of assumptions about what better TV would look like and what it would accomplish. Favoring unconventional and often nonlinear cultural forms, avant-garde cultural "competencies," and the advancement of causes over the development of noncommercial popular culture, ITVS emerged as a marginalized service susceptible to the same conservative accusations that plagued NET's courageous programs.

Supporters tend to overlook the limitations of this self-imposed cultural niche when defending ITVS from its conservative opponents. On the one hand, we need to denounce conservative attacks on ITVS-sponsored programs like "Tongues Untied," an early 1990s documentary about black male homosexual identity that was singled out as evidence of public television's alleged "subversive" tendencies. Likewise, it is important to protest when PBS stations decide not to air them. It also is important to recognize that ITVS reinforces social and cultural hierarchies–and invites authoritarian-populist accusations of elitism–by equating progressive television with unconventional documentaries and avant-garde artistry only. While mandated to serve the "unserved," ITVS undermines diversity in public television when it reinforces the assumption that popular culture has no place there. While it has supported projects like "Dottie Gets Spanked," an experimental documentary about the family sitcom as perceived through the detached eyes of filmmaker Todd Haynes, it has not provided alternative sitcoms for ill-represented people who find pleasure in popular television. Defined as "anti-television," ITVS cannot reinterpret the sitcom without transcending the perceived inadequacies of mass-produced infotainment. Like earlier manifestations of "far-left" television, ITVS has conceptualized "television for a change" within proscribed boundaries.

While ITVS attempts to serve "minority" audiences and facilitate "community building" with its programs, it does so within the parameters of a sophisticated taste culture, as demonstrated by the fanfare that surrounded its tenth anniversary. Marking the celebration were prestigious "film festival screenings" and "museum retrospectives" far removed from the everyday lives of most television viewers. Where ITVS has specifically addressed class differences, it has tended to follow the voyeuristic, aestheticized approach established by NET documentaries. Programs about the poor tend to explore their plight from the sympathetic vantage point of a well-placed independent filmmaker who wishes to raise the consciousness of an equally well-placed middle-class audience. ITVS programs like "No Place Like Home," a cinema verité profile of a homeless family, do not emerge from an impetus to address the cultural desires of "unserved" audiences on the wrong end of class inequalities. They make "have-nots" visible in moving and innovative formats but reflect little consideration of what poor people–the least served of any audience in commercial terms–might like to watch on television. The same can be said of "People Like Us," an ITVS documentary about "social class in America." Although the program studies different class cultures under the slogan "Bud or Bordeau," it does not challenge or change public television's own cultural niche in a capitalist society in which "the choices

you make reveal your class." However well intentioned, tokenized representations of poor and working-class "others" cannot compensate for ITVS's
avant-garde priorities and failure to develop popular programming with
class equality in mind.

Larry Daressa, a longtime media activist who participated in the struggle to create ITVS, now questions its approach to "anti-television." In retro-
spect, Daressa recognizes an enormous divide between the independent program makers who receive ITVS's resources and the underrepresented people
they claim to serve. For him, the problem is not the elevation of avant-garde
art over mass culture but, rather, the failure to provide practical education
for diverse communities, along the lines of the early land-grant broadcasting.
According to Daressa, disadvantaged groups "consistently express the need
for programs on education, jobs and health issues." Independent producers,
however, are primarily interested in exploring "cultural politics." Their failure to connect with audiences is typically blamed on the addictive effects of
mass culture, a rationale that has been evoked since *PBL*'s bitter farewell program. According to Daressa,

> Independent producers have, by and large, been able to avoid taking
> a hard-headed look at the social impact of their work by blaming the
> blockbuster. They can always assert that a large and enthusiastic au-
> dience exists for their production if only programmers weren't too
> timid, inept or reactionary to air them. This evasion . . . discounts the
> real possibility that much independent work does not appear very
> relevant to the urgent needs of underserved audiences. . . .We must
> question our assumption that merely producing and broadcasting
> programs about diverse communities is an efficient or effective con-
> tribution to helping these communities become more powerful pub-
> lic actors.[60]

Just as the Left has essentialized the radicalizing nature of cultural experimentation, Darnessa presumes that concrete instruction for diverse communities is progressive. Both claims situate public television in a narrow slot that
precludes popular entertainment. Although there should be room for many
different forms of programming on noncommercial public channels, none
should be advocated at the expense of pleasure. From a cultural studies vantage point, helping "communities become public actors" is not unrelated to
embracing popular culture and the recognitions that it offers. Until public television can provide "excellence and diversity" in popular culture, it will be
vulnerable to charges of elitism. So far, public television's progressive factions

have stressed class privilege as much as they have tried to dismantle it. Neither left-leaning "anti-television" nor practical instruction can alter the course of public television until its cultural priorities are addressed.

Public Television and the Culture Wars

Richard Nixon won the first battle in the public television culture wars, but the victory did not prevent future battles. Since then, conservatives have often cast public television as an arrogant and politically subversive enemy of the so-called common people. In 1975, on just these grounds, conservative analyst Kevin Phillips lobbied against a "long-term" financing bill for public television. Echoing earlier reformers, his prominent *TV Guide* article claimed that public subsidies were unwarranted because public television catered to the "radical chic," offering sociological films about Eskimos, Zen Buddhism, staged abortion debates, and "obscure" fare that was "contemptuous of everyday America." Drawing from the same cultural, political, and geographical oppositions established by the White House and its conservative allies, Phillips claimed that

> even though "public" television has become the plaything of the Manhattan and Washington Mercedes crowd, a lot of it is still being paid for by the Middle Americans who drive two-year-old Chevrolets and live in the Maine-to-California equivalents of Rego Park. Public television represents a subsidy by the lower-middle-class people, who pay the bulk of Federal taxes, to the super-income groups, and a subsidy of the many to the few. . . . If there's anything on for Rego Park, Levittown or Boise Idaho, it's well-hidden.[61]

The next year, in another *TV Guide* article, former Nixon aide Pat Buchanan called into question public television's claim to publicness. Reminding readers why Nixon had "rightly" vetoed its funds some years earlier, Buchanan pointed out that public television was still elitist and liberally biased, providing "handsomely subsidized" culture and opinions to the privileged few.[62] Throughout the 1980s, the Reagan administration echoed these claims in its attempt to reform public broadcasting. In the 1990s, conservative politicians from Bob Dole to Newt Gingrich took up the cause, connecting complaints about cultural elitism and left-liberal bias in an attempt to privatize public television. Conservatives love to attack public television when they wish to characterize themselves as the true friends of the common people, no matter that its radical late 1960s sensibilities are today confined to an occasional ITVS documentary and the appearance of Peter, Paul, and Mary during pledge week. While their complaints are often disingenuous, it says something about the cultural limitations of the Left when conservative faces take up its natural role.

However opportunistic, conservative accusations of left-wing elitism are part of the "truths" that have formed U.S. public broadcasting. That is, they are part of a recurring debate in which conservative opponents speak for the snubbed mass audience, presume its conservatism, flatten its diversity, and profess its devotion to commercial channels that trade in pleasure but stereotype or ignore populations outside the white, upper-middle-class audience sought by advertisers. The democratization of public television will require new ways of conceptualizing commercial culture's limitations and new ways of characterizing public television's own deep-seated cultural biases. It will demand learning from–as opposed to glorifying–the failure of leftist television to connect with audiences. Cultural studies can help unravel the cultural construction of public television, but it cannot dictate correct templates. If public television is what it promises–television for and *by* the people–then the people must be consulted in its creation.

Let us climb to the highest figurative mountain top and proclaim, with all the vigor and shrillness that made *Roseanne* a household name, that TV is good.
—ABC promotion

EPILOGUE:
PUBLIC TELEVISION, POPULARITY, AND CULTURAL JUSTICE

In 1995, in the wake of conservative pressures to dismantle public broadcasting, the Public Broadcasting Service hired an advertising agency to revamp its "brand" image. While the campaign was new, the assumptions on which it relied spoke to a cultural history. In one promotion, a fortysomething white woman defines public television as the *only* television worth watching. The spokeswoman has quit her professional job and moved from the urban northeast to live on a remote Western ranch. Shown riding a horse and performing rural chores, she explains that the superficialities of modern life have given way to "real people and challenges." So, too, has this woman's television viewing, which was limited to PBS. Only "public television feels real to me," she explains. "It's like being invited to dinner where there's a good cook: You don't worry about what they're cooking." Even though the spot tries to dislodge public television's contested ties to East Coast cultural elitism with the iconography of the working ranch, it conveys the cultural divide between PBS and the "vast wasteland" in another way, by defining public television as a pocket of quality, authenticity, and seriousness in an otherwise shallow and hedonistic mass-produced television culture. The tagline "Real TV for Real People" identifies its anticipated audience against the faceless millions drawn to trivial television on commercial channels. Nearly three decades after the passage of the Public Broadcasting Act, the promotion "brands" public television as good television, the exception to the rule.

Other promotions used the tagline "If PBS doesn't do it, who will?" In one, the assumptions that dictate what public television considers "worth doing" are clarified by the image of a TV set perched atop the spotlighted stage of an empty art-house theater on which experts from upcoming PBS programs are playing. By placing public television in a fancy setting normally associated with live performances, the promotion conveys its affinity with high culture. At the same time, it situates public television outside the everyday contexts in which television is usually watched. The theatrical costume dramas, documentaries, and sedate newscasts emanating from the screen reiterates the extent to which public television is tied to the socially legitimated cultural tastes and practices of the educated upper-middle class. Even programs that do not on automatically convey prestigious cultural associations—nature specials and *Sesame Street*, for example—are situated in this meaning system, ascribed value precisely because they appeared in public television's selective cultural environment. Charged with affirming public television's importance at a time when the "cultural branch of the welfare state" that it represents is under attack, the advertising blitz underscores a fundamental paradox.[1] Created against the grain of mass culture, public television's claim to excellence hinges on its limited popular appeal. No amount of promotion can radically change public television's image until this contradiction is addressed.

The same year that Congress debated Newt Gingrich's plans for public broadcasting, ABC developed an advertising campaign based on the premise that "TV is good." Parodying the liberal reform discourse that gave birth to public television and defended its case in the news media and in Washington, ABC's yellow promotions defended the medium from high-minded critics who sought to impose their social, cultural, and moral standards on "others." Anxieties about television's role in cultivating lowbrow taste, unproductive leisure, mindless relaxation, and "instant gratification" were turned on their head and positively celebrated. As ABC's prominent display in *TV Guide* explained,

> For years the pundits, moralists and self-righteous, self-appointed preservers of our culture have told us that television is bad. They've

stood high on their soapbox and looked condescendingly on our in-
nocuous pleasures. They've sought to wean us from our harmless
habit by derisively referring to television as the Boob Tube, or the
Idiot Box. Well, television is not the destroyer of all that is right in
the world. In fact, and we say this with all the disdain we can muster
for the elitists who purport otherwise, TV is good.

Mocking those who wished to "uplift" television and its imagined audience, the promotion invited television viewers to embrace their "cerebral-
free non-activity."[2] In another promotion, ABC announced its intention to
"convert the unconverted" to joys of habitual television viewing. "No American will be left unfulfilled and un-entertained," promised the commercial
network in an irreverent play on the progressive assumption that broadcasting is best used for self-improvement and edification. Turning the ideology
of mass culture upside down by addressing heavy television viewers as the
socially legitimated "in-group," it went on to declare: "Just think of the
pleasure that will come to these wayward citizens who will marvel at TV's
awesome power to entertain for the very first time."[3] ABC poked fun at some
of the problematic assumptions that have shaped U.S. public broadcasting,
but it also reproduced the corporate myth of "cultural democracy." Like the
commercial broadcasters of the 1960s who defended the "vast wasteland" on
the grounds that they were providing what the people wanted, the network
pitted snooty critics against pleasure-seeking common people, obscuring its
own role as a powerful culture broker. ABC is part of a giant media con-
glomerate owned by Walt Disney, a corporation that has long capitalized on
mass fun. Its defense of television failed to note that the power to produce
television culture is concentrated among a small—and shrinking— number
of similar media giants. It conflated cultural democracy in television with the
power to consume what these corporations are willing to provide. Still, ABC
managed to convey the idea that the culture industries are more in touch
with popular tastes and desires than are the "do-gooders" at public television—a claim that most people will recognize as true.[4]

Trapped in the ideology of mass culture, public television clings to the
perch it was assigned in the 1960s instead of pursuing broader rationales for
public investment in television culture. Conceived as the antidote to the vast
wasteland, it refuses to rethink the "values and ideals" that positioned public television against the "callous commercial market" and its derided cultural products. As public television scholar Robert Avery notes, this idealist
mission has lost its currency to an expanded television marketplace. New
media technologies now address fragmented consumer niches, while culture

and education—once the exclusive hallmarks of public television— are "successful commercial commodities."[5] Today, cable and satellite channels—Arts & Entertainment, Bravo, CNN, Discovery Channel, Learning Channel, Home and Garden, MSNBC, HBO, Lifetime—also claim to serve "selective" viewers with "specialized" television programming that is said to be a "cut above" mass culture. With profits in mind, these commercial venues compete for the same predominantly white, upper-middle-class viewers that public television has courted through its "excellent" and "diverse" programming priorities. The fictional mass audience so anxiously derided by 1960s broadcast reformers can no longer be claimed to "rule" the major networks. As Eileen Meehan points out, ever refined ratings instruments care only about the "community audience" coveted by advertisers.[6] The well-placed "minorities" deemed least served by the "vast wasteland" of the 1960s are now construed as the medium's favored customers. Those least served by the expanded television marketplace are people without money and education and the cultural power that it buys.

Public television is needed precisely because it can remediate cultural inequalities based on intersections of class, race, and gender that were ignored or marginalized by its founders. The cultural justice that I am proposing does not involve "uplifting" people to white, educated, upper-middle-class ideals. Nor does it mean "raising" the level of television programming in a perpetual attempt to escape its derided mass cultural connotations. Cultural justice will not be served by utopian notions of "anti-television" that conceives of public television as a means to greater political ends or by alternative programs conceived against the grain of popular practices and conventions. As cultural studies scholars have argued, television occupies an important place in the everyday lives of most people, for social reasons that early reformers tended to judge and discredit. However, commercial broadcasters are not in the business of cultivating cultural democracy in television. Cultural justice means nurturing the mediated popular cultural environment in which we live, with pragmatic, noncommercial goals that unregulated market forces tend to undermine, such as representational equity, ethical accountability, diversity that is not contingent on upscale consumption, and opportunities for popular access and participation.[7] While commercialized popular culture is a contradictory business offering pleasures, meanings, and recognitions, it is constrained by its economic priorities and devotion to consumption as the organizing principle in popular cultural expression. Simply put, people who do not "fit" the commercial impetus to sell consumers, and consumer lifestyles, are ignored, stereotyped, marginalized, and/or discredited. Public television can facilitate cultural justice by allocating its resources to people in their full complexity, a goal that must include and, indeed, prioritize an institutional commitment to people that popular television in its commercialized form is unwilling or unable to serve.

The Public Television Problem

The forces working against popular cultural justice in public broadcasting— and, in fact, any form of public culture—are formidable. While the commercialization of public television itself is a barrier, market pressures alone cannot be blamed for its elevated marginality. Public television was conceptualized *for* the people, not *by* people, because the terms of its existence presumed their failure as citizens and cultural arbiters. Its development in the United States was a response to the postwar "TV problem" and reflected its tendency to conflate commercial hegemony with unquestioned assumptions about the social, cultural, and moral inadequacies of "mass appeal." Presuming that the people's untutored hedonistic choices were responsible for the medium's homogeneity and lowness as they perceived it, reformers placed their own white, upper-middle-class cultural tastes and democratic ideals at the center of public television's corrective mission to facilitate "excellence and diversity." In so doing, they created what might be called the "public television problem," for they could not serve the universal public interest and simultaneously avoid the "perils of popularity" blamed for commercial television's shortcomings.

The social and political movements of the 1960s came to bear on public television's "rationality" in ways that emphasized its impulse to enlighten and avoid the fictional masses, and to recognize and classify "unserved" minorities according to unquestioned hierarchies of knowledge and power. Public television professed a commitment to pluralism, equality, and democratic participation but conceptualized those goals within its overall mission to cultivate an "enlightened" culture. If public television was positioned in the "habitus" of the well-educated professional middle class, its biases were tempered by its Great Society ethos to raise the people—particularly disadvantaged populations—via the televised display of particular tastes, knowledges, behaviors, and dispositions. However humanitarian, the liberal presumption that public television could and should disseminate socially approved "cultural capital" across divides of race and class tended to conflate service to "others" with logocentric notions of self-improvement and, in some cases, with social management orchestrated from above.

Public television's inability to deliver the progressive promises it represented was immediately apparent. Seized as worthwhile, "high-class" television by critics, well-placed viewers, and corporate sponsors, it was vulnerable to a delegitimation crisis triggered by conservative reformers who established themselves as the people's ally in the recurring culture wars. The Nixon White House denounced public television's tenuous claim to publicness, raising questions about geographical, class, and cultural biases for reasons that had little to do with facilitating popular cultural justice. Motivated by political reasons, conservatives targeted a marginalized strand of "leftist" programming made possible by the turbulent climate of the late 1960s. This contested material rejected "prefabricated" mass culture and its "distracted" audience for its own reasons, a stance that was compatible with public television's cultural logic and susceptible to conservative scapegoating. In the name of the common people who paid the bill for public television, conservative reformers set into motion economic, institutional, and geographical reforms. While such pressures have come to bear on public television's founding ideals, its claim to existence still depends on what Tony Bennett calls the deployment of culture as a "reformer's science," a problem that has not been addressed by its advocates and supporters. Until the assumptions that shaped public television are examined, the deployment of culture will be vulnerable to the populist complaints of conservative reformers who wish to abolish any notion of noncommercial public culture.

Broadcast reform discourse in the United States has historically conflated the limitations of commercial ownership with unexamined cultural hierarchies and a perceived need to improve and manage "others." *Viewers Like You?* has shown public television to be the product of this legacy, which influenced its "commonsense" priorities and conflicted relationship with the people it claims to serve and represent. Because public television has embraced humanist principles, has rejected blatant commercialism, and has been partially responsive to social movements and disenfranchised populations, it has been championed as a progressive institution to be protected from market mechanisms. This defensive stance, however, has short-circuited thinking about its contested limitations. During the 1995 debate started by Newt Gingrich, liberals defended federal funding on the grounds that public television alone can maintain cultural standards, uplift taste, curb delinquency, improve morals, encourage self-improvement, and transform TV viewers into responsible citizens. While critics on the Left were quick to point out that public television had been corrupted by "creeping commercialism," most agreed that its role was to combat trivial amusements and cheap infotainment with better programming better suited to serious public-interest goals. For different reasons, both responses accepted the restrictive terms of the discourse of the vast wasteland and, in so doing, accepted the contradictions that have positioned public television outside the cultural habitus in which most people live.

The "public interest" in broadcasting is a social construct inflected with meanings and power dynamics that serve some interests more than others. The ideals of public television and its supporters coexist with cultural value systems and residual "governmental" aims that are not inherently beneficial to all people. With the exception of children's programming that was mandated to reach a broad audience and therefore permitted to embrace popular multicultural conventions, public television has not "trickled down," for just these reasons. Cultural studies has identified this problem across public culture and has offered more workable solutions. Bennett, for example, has argued that economic fixes alone cannot foster a more democratic approach to the negotiation of multiple public interests. Public culture, for him, will not be made democratic until issues of "access, equity, empowerment and the divination of opportunities to exercise appropriate cultural leadership" are prioritized.[8]

Public television has not ignored the issues that Bennett raises. *Black Journal* and *Soul!* were early examples of public television programming that was committed to cultural empowerment by and for blacks. Yet "special-interest" minority programs were deeply marginalized and conflated in pluralist service to well-placed taste cultures whose whiteness and class privilege were unstated and therefore normalized. Public television's tenuous commitment to empowerment waned as the political turbulence of the late 1960s subsided, and its conventional approach to enlightenment limited opportunities for cultural leadership outside its white, upper-middle-class "center." Even the leftist programs targeted by conservative reformers tended to join cultural to political enlightenment, privileging intellectual cultural ideals over achievable priorities, to use Justin Lewis's terminology. Undoing these legacies will require rethinking subsidized cultural leadership, envisioning it not as a top-down process or as a recruitment process but as a way to serve needs established by communities.

By revisiting public television's cultural history, I have shown how its status as the "exception" to the rule draws from and perpetuates uneven hierarchies of cultural power. In so doing, I have attempted to move critical debate beyond narrowly conceived political economic problems to a broader consideration of the discourses that positioned public television as a technology for cultural enlightenment. "Changing how cultural resources function in the context of relations of power," writes Bennett, "usually involves modifying the ways in which cultural forms and activities are governmentally deployed

as parts of programs of social management."[9] Until public television's cultivating "rationality" is critically addressed, its cultural resources will be un-
equally distributed and open to conservative complaints that posit the free
market as the only solution to undemocratic tendencies.

Political economist Nicholas Garnham acknowledges a pattern prevalent in the United States. Although Garnham advocates public culture in
principle, he also concedes that "the only alternative to the market which we
have constructed" has tended to "subsidize the existing tastes and habits of
the better-off or create a new form of public culture which has no popular
audience."[10] Rejecting the popular aesthetic colonized by commercial broadcasters, public television's architects welcomed elevated marginality in the
name of cultural progress. Imbued with high-minded cultural respectability,
their solution to the "TV problem" was praised but mostly ignored by TV
viewers, including the "influential" tastemakers and opinion leaders who
were widely believed to have comprised its natural audience. At the same
time that public television valorized the "selective" nature of its small and
sporadic viewership, it was forced to embrace elements of popularity as it became more reliant on market forces. Because popularity was a function of
economic pressures, however, it was manifested in upscale terms that failed
to foster cultural democracy in public broadcasting.

Public television's desire to win audiences who can be counted on to
watch its sponsored programs—and contribute to public television financially—has tempered its cultural idealism and founding commitment to reforming the people so that they might "better perform their democratic
rights and duties."[11] Accommodating well-placed viewers who seek pleasure
as well as edification from television, stations now provide a slate of entertaining programs that connect popularity to the signifiers of cultural and educational legitimacy that define the public television "brand." The negotiations paved by ExxonMobil's *Masterpiece Theatre* have brought "hit"
programs like *Antiques Roadshow* as well as Hollywood "classics," documentaries about mass culture (hot dogs, Coney Island, baseball) and vintage
acoustical rock music performances imbued with canonical status to public
television. Conceptualized in relation to market goals, the "quality" pleasures that public television offers are typically upscale in nature, a limitation
that reinscribes its place in a particular habitus. PBS may declare *I Love
Lucy*—a sitcom vilified by early reformers—worthy of attention by its *American Masterpiece* series, but it will not allocate public resources to the production of popular sitcoms for unserved populations who are of less interest
to sponsors and pledge-drive coordinators. It will educate viewers about the
history of jazz, but it will not provide a home for contemporary urban hip-

hop culture. Public television's marketing logic allows for popularity in the same demographic terms that govern commercial broadcasting.

Critics who protest public television's encroaching marketing logic tend to conflate its upscale orientation with the presumed perils of popularity itself. In the aftermath of Gingrich's attempt to dismantle public broadcasting, PBS developed an educational game show in an attempt to disprove conservative charges of cultural elitism. The attempt to adapt one of television's most popular—and critically derided—genres was controversial in public broadcasting, and the appearance of *Think Twice* generated incredulity in the national press. The *New York Times* was typical of this response when it conflated concerns about commercialism with judgments about the "lowbrow" format. According to the *Times*, the "intelligent" person's alternative to *Wheel of Fortune* was inherently wrong for public television, not because it situated the game show in an upscale context signified by well-placed contestants, "intelligent" questions, and class-coded prizes like computers and investments in a mutual fund, but because it "lowered" public television's cultural standards. Reinforcing the ideology of mass culture that the experiment in some ways had tried to escape, the *Times* protested the cultural transgression seen in the spectacle of an "ebullient M.C. and players childishly applauding their own right answers." Insisting that public television was by nature "not the same as popular broadcasting," the newspaper rejected market pressures because they undermined an essentialist notion of cultural standards not because they excluded populations outside the niche courted by corporate and station appeals. For the *New York Times*, as for many idealist supporters, the problem with marketing is that PBS has come to depend on compromising commercials, "tedious fund appeals," and growing audiences filled with "contributing members" who appreciate tawdry fare cloaked in portentous claims to cultural respectability.[12]

The Left has protested public television's marketing logic in broader terms that underscore its undemocratic tendencies. For most critics and scholars, however, concerns about "creeping commercialism" are limited to the decline of controversial programming with a capacity to "challenge the status quo" and an overall diminished focus on "information exchange" in the privileged spheres of news and public affairs. Critical studies of public broadcasting tend to reject any attempt to address the popular cultural space where most people live as an "subversion" of public television's authentic difference. Michael Tracey's chronicle of *The Decline and Fall of Public Broadcasting* typifies the critical paradigm in its rejection of mass culture and all that that represents. Tracey acknowledges the paternalism that Raymond Williams once attributed to public broadcasting, but like many progressive supporters, he is unable to envision a better model without pitting a feminized, lowbrow, hedonistic commercial culture against a enlightened, masculine, upper-middle-class public culture. Protesting market forces with an "absolute" notion of what constitutes "good culture" in mind, Tracey dismisses commercial television not just because it is privately controlled by corporations but also because he considers its popular programming inherently "crass, trivial, shallow, exploitative" and corrosive to what is "rational, informed, and enriching"[13]

Cultural Studies and Public Television

Cultural studies has challenged social, aesthetic, and moral judgments of mass culture by demonstrating that cultural value is arbitrary: "commonsense" hierarchies always speak to social inequalities, however unconscious that process may be. Cultural studies lends itself to a more democratic approach to public culture that respects popular culture and protests its relegation to the commercial market alone. A cultural studies approach to public culture, as Ien Ang has argued, departs from the Left's promotion of a "politics of progressive television" involving a "wholly new constellation of television production and consumption."[14] It rejects the discourse of the vast wasteland—and its politicized variations within leftist criticism—and seeks simply to nurture noncommercial public culture in relation to "competing assertions of cultural value."[15] As Ang notes, cultural studies does not advocate cultural "relativism" but, rather, a recognition of socially situated cultural differences and a concern to bring those differences to bear on the allocation of public cultural resources. This means recognizing that people's relationship to TV (and particular TV programming) intersects with social differences of class, gender, race, age, and lifestyle. To use her example, the point is not that soap operas are "just as good as" or better than Shakespeare but that the value of the soap opera, as a potential venue for public cultural investment, "should be looked at within the context of viewers' experiences and understandings of their lives." This is an approach to quality that

> emphasizes different criteria of value from the discourse of high culture, one that leads to different judgments and assessments. Accepting such a point of view emphatically does not imply a declaration of bankruptcy to the project of public service broadcasting as such (as is often suggested), but it does mean that its cultural legitimatization needs to be rethought and argued over in light of the emergent contestations over "value."[16]

Justin Lewis has proposed a "cultural industries" approach to public culture that has much to offer PBS. Lewis questions the extent to which popular culture has fallen outside the parameters of government subsidies, not just in broadcasting, but in museum culture and "community arts" as well. In one sense, he says, it is because the industries that produce popular culture are prosperous. Because corporations like Disney are so financially secure, the conventional wisdom asserts that the mass-produced culture in which they trade does not need public support. Ideological understandings of cultural legitimacy are the principal culprits, however. The "goods" distributed by the culture industries are not considered particularly valuable, authentic, enduring, enlightening, or uplifting, which is why they are "naturally" left to the hands of the market. Subsidies are closely aligned with a cultural value system defined by academic canons, upper-middle-class patrons, and bureaucrats who reproduce their own educated cultural capital. While avant-garde expression, preindustrial "folk" culture, and multicultural approaches to the high arts are sometimes supported, public resources are not channeled into contemporary mass culture, even though this is our dominant cultural environment.[17] Any attempt to foster cultural democracy will require expanding the boundaries of what counts as public culture, says Lewis.

What would a "cultural industries" approach to public television entail? Instead of conceptualizing public television as a patch of excellence in a sea of mediocrity, it would develop existing forms of popular culture with proven audience appeal outside the pressures of advertising sponsorship. Daytime talk shows, for example, present a popular forum in which members of subordinated social groups—women, the working class, people of color—discuss issues and ideas on television.[18] The format allows for emotion, pleasure, and the exchange and debate of everyday information, and despite being condemned by many critics, the shows are meaningful and valued by their viewers. At the same time, the daytime talk show is constrained by its commercial format, which restricts the nature of the topics addressed and imposes expected roles on the participants. On public television, talk shows could be developed according to noncommercial goals like equity, accountability, innovation, and diversity.

Freed from commercial pressures, public television might democratize the range of pleasures, meanings, knowledges, and social recognitions that circulate within mediated culture. Popular television genres—soap operas, serial dramas, sitcoms, television movies—that rely on accessible narrative conventions to build audiences could benefit from public subsidies. While these genres in their commercial form have broad cultural appeals, they follow television's tendency to overrepresent and affirm powerful groups. As many scholars have observed, commercial television entertainment constructs a fictional social world that is disproportionately white, male, professional, economically well-off, and heterosexual.[19] On public television, programs that people like to watch could be mandated to represent racial, class, gender, and sexual diversity; to address topics and situations that do not interest commercial advertisers; and to maintain standards of social and ethical accountability that are negotiated by audiences themselves. Rather than rejecting the people's wants as unimportant or corruptive to culture, public television could help realize them.

Public television might extend to a broader range of publics the multiple forms of knowledge on which cultural citizenship depends. The binary between public television's *The NewsHour* and tabloid journalism like *Hard Copy* needs to be questioned, for it is dependent on the tastes and expertise of white, upper-middle-class male "opinion leaders," on one hand, and the myth of consumer sovereignty, on the other. If democracy is for all people, it follows that the presentation of public affairs on television should be accountable to social and cultural differences. Commercial television offers popular formats—including "infotainment" genres that blur the artificial line between reality and fiction, seriousness and triviality—but it does not embrace less profitable social goals like representational equity and attention to the specific informational needs of subordinated populations, as decided by them. A cultural industries model would begin by recognizing the multiple forms that exchanges of information can and do currently take and proceed by making these programs more accountable, relevant, and useful to the audiences that watch them.

Music videos, prime-time animation, and comedy are other areas that public television could develop in conjunction with their audiences. This is not to suggest that literary dramas, the performing arts, serious discussions, and documentaries have no place on noncommercial channels or that avant-garde culture deserves no public support. Ideally, public television could provide all these things. Since its creation in the late 1960s, however, public television overemphasized these priorities, at the expense of the popular culture that most people—including most "unserved" audiences—actually consume. People denied social power are the least apt to embrace public television's "enlightened" schedule, and public television as it currently exists does more to perpetuate cultural injustices than to ameliorate them. Public television will never be by and for the people until it embraces "excellence and diversity" *within* popular culture.

Introduction

1. Pierre Bourdieu, *Distinction: A Social Critique of the Judgment of Taste* (Cambridge, Mass.: Harvard University Press, 1984).

2. Justin Lewis, *Art, Culture, and Enterprise* (London: Routledge, 1990), p. 11.

3. Robert Avery, introduction to *Public Service Broadcasting in a Multichannel Environment*, ed. Robert Avery (New York: Longman, 1993), p. xiii.

4. "The Promise of Television" (New York: Museum of Television and Radio, July 3, 1988).

5. According to the CPB, the best predictor of public television "membership" is a college education and a professional occupation/income. According to PBS figures, only 30 percent of all television viewers tuned in to public television for more than five minutes during a sample week during the spring of 1995. The average rating for PBS hovered around 2, which means that the typical PBS program is watched by approximately 2 percent of television viewers. During the same period in 1995, ABC, CBS, and NBC drew about 30 percent of viewers; Fox attracted 11.5 percent; basic cable 16 percent; and pay cable 3.2 percent. Public Broadcasting Service, "1990 Public Television National

Image Survey," PBS Station Independence Program, unpublished report, September 1990; Public Broadcasting Service, "1990 Public Television Member Study," PBS Station Independence Program, unpublished report, September 1990; Public Broadcasting Service, "National Audience Report," unpublished report, Spring 1995. For an overview of mainstream audience research on public television, including the huge gap between the child and adult audience, see David LeRoy, "Who Watches Public Television," *Journal of Communication* 30 (1980): 157–63. Many local public television stations circulate to potential underwriters upscale audience profiles similar to the one quoted here. For an up-to-date collection of institutional discourse on the PBS audience, see "Current Briefing: Listeners and Viewers," available online at *www.current.org*.

6. Michel Foucault, *The Archaeology of Knowledge* (New York: Pantheon, 1972), p. 135.

7. Avery, introduction, p. xiv.

8. The drop in public broadcasting's funding allocations is covered by the trade publication *Current*, which also maintains an online database of policy briefings. See "Current Briefing: What Can Be Done–And Is Being Done–To Raise Support from Nonfederal Sources," available at *www.current.org*.

9. Quoted in Karen Everhart Bedford, "What to Kill First," *Current* online, January 16, 1995, *www.current.org*.

10. See, for example, "To Be or Not to Be Civilized: That Is the Question," House, *Congressional Record*, February 24, 1995, p. H22218.

11. Nicholas Garnham, "Concepts of Culture: Public Policy and the Cultural Industries," *Cultural Studies* 1 (1987): 24.

12. Max Frankel, "PBS's Wheel of Fortune," *New York Times*, January 8, 1995, p. 16.

13. Tom Shales, "The Misguided Missiles Aimed at Public TV," *Washington Post*, February 27, 1995, p. B1.

14. Senator Robert Byrd, Senate, *Congressional Record*, January 23, 1995, Thomas Legislative online.

15. My focus on discourse as a mode of historiography is indebted to Michel Foucault, who broke with the Marxist "base/superstructure" understanding of ideology to consider specific discourses on their own terms as productive forces in the social construction of reality. In *The Archaeology of Knowledge*, Foucault describes a discursive formation as follows: "Whenever one can describe, between a number of statements, such a system of dispersion, whenever, between objects, types of statement, concepts, or thematic choices, one can define a regularity (an order, correlations, positions and functionings, transformations) we will say, for the sake of convenience, that we are dealing with a *discursive formation*" (p. 38). Elaborating on Foucault's definition, John Fiske argues that discourses are "systems of representation" that develop socially "in order to make and circulate a coherent set of meanings about an important topic area." Discourses are ideological insofar as their "meanings serve the interests of that section of society within which the discourse originates and which works ideologically to naturalize those meanings into common sense," but they are not conspiratorial or "produced" by individual authors or speakers. Rather, discourses are socially produced and often institutionalized ways of making sense of

topics (like culture or public television) that "preexist their use in any one discursive practice." See John Fiske, *Television Culture* (New York: Routledge, 1987), pp. 14–15. Following Fiske, I see the purpose of discourse analysis as uncovering "the processes of discursive contestation by which discourses work to repress, marginalize, and invalidate others; by which they struggle for audibility and for access to the technologies of social circulation and by which they fight to promote and defend the interests of their respective social formations." See John Fiske, *Media Matters: Race and Gender in U.S. Politics* (Minneapolis: University of Minnesota Press, 1996), pp. 3–4.

16. Jim McGuigan, *Culture and the Public Sphere* (London, Routledge, 1996), p. 5.

17. Robert Avery, "Contemporary Public Telecommunications Research: Navigating the Sparsely Settled Terrain," *Journal of Broadcasting and Electronic Media* 40 (1996): 132–39.

18. James Ledbetter, *Made Possible by . . . the Death of Public Broadcasting in the United States* (New York: Verso, 1997), p. 217.

19. William Hoynes, *Public Television for Sale* (Boulder, Colo.: Westview Press, 1994), p. 43. Garnham's position can be found in Nicholas Garnham, "Public Service Versus the Market," *Screen* 24 (1983): 6–27.

20. Patricia Aufderheide, "Public Television and the Public Sphere," *Critical Studies in Mass Communication* 8 (1991): 168–83; and Patricia Aufderheide, *The Daily Planet* (Minneapolis: University of Minnesota Press, 2000).

21. Willard Rowland, "Public Service Broadcasting in the United States: Its Mandates, Institutions and Conflicts," in *Public Service Broadcasting in a Multichannel Environment*, ed. Robert Avery (New York: Longman, 1993), pp. 162–63; Willard Rowland, "Public Involvement: The Anatomy of a Myth," in *The Future of Public Broadcasting*, ed. Douglass Cater and Michael J. Nyhan (New York: Praeger, 1976), pp. 113–14; Willard D. Rowland and Michael Tracey, "Worldwide Challenges to Public Service Broadcasting," *Journal of Communication* 40 (1990): 8–27. Similar patterns can be observed in Ralph Engelman's *Public Radio and Television in America* (Thousand Oaks, Calif: Sage, 1996), and James Day's *The Vanishing Vision: The Inside Story of Public Television* (Berkeley and Los Angeles: University of California Press, 1995). Engelman protests foundation and corporate involvement in the development of public television against an idealized alternative based on advocacy, serious information, and debate. Day, a former public television bureaucrat, states a concern with public television's marginalized place in television culture, but his "inside story" does little to explain the problem. Day also equates commercial television with a "legal narcotic blocking out the pain and pressures of the real world" (350), a stance that limits any consideration of what popular public television would entail.

22. Engelman, *Public Radio and Television in America*, p. 39.

23. Lewis, *Art, Culture, and Enterprise*, p. 25.

24. Ien Ang, *Desperately Seeking the Audience* (New York: Routledge, 1991), p. 103; Robert Blakely, *To Serve the Public Interest: Educational Broadcasting in the United States* (Syracuse, N.Y.: Syracuse University Press, 1979), p. 28.

25. Quoted in Ang, *Desperately Seeking*, p. 28.

26. Ibid., pp. 28–29, 106.

27. Stuart Hall, "What Is This Black in Black Popular Culture?" in *Black Popular Culture,* ed. Gina Dent (Seattle: Bay Press, 1992), p. 26.

28. Lawrence Grossman, "Programming, Programming, Programming," *Current,* November 3, 1987, p. 2.

29. Laurie Ouellette and Justin Lewis, "Moving Beyond the Vast Wasteland: Cultural Policy and Television in the U.S.," *Television and New Media* 1 (February 2000): 91–113.

30. Charlotte Brudson, "Television: Aesthetics and Audiences," in *Logics of Television,* ed. Patricia Mellencamp (Bloomington: Indiana University Press, 1990), p. 69. For a critique of populism in cultural studies, see Michael Schudson, "The New Validation of Popular Culture: Sense and Sentimentality in Academia," in *Critical Perspectives on Media and Society,* ed. Robert K. Avery and David Eason (New York: Guilford Press, 1991), pp. 49–68; and Jim McGuigan, *Cultural Populism* (London: Routledge, 1992).

31. Tony Bennett, *Culture: A Reformer's Science Culture:* (London: Sage, 1998); see also Tony Bennett, "Putting Policy into Cultural Studies," in *Cultural Studies,* ed. Lawrence Grossberg, Cary Nelson, and Paula A. Triechler (New York: Routledge, 1992), pp. 23–50; Tony Bennett, "Useful Culture," *Cultural Studies* 6 (1992): 395–408; and Tony Bennett, *The Birth of the Museum* (London, Routledge, 1995).

32. McGuigan, *Culture and the Public Sphere,* p. 17.

33. Bennett, *Culture,* p.104.

34. Bennett develops this argument in *The Birth of the Museum,* a critical historical analysis of public museum culture. I have found this case study useful for making sense of the cultural reform logics that gave rise to PBS.

35. Toby Miller, *The Well-Tempered Self: Citizenship, Culture and the Postmodern Subject* (Baltimore: Johns Hopkins University Press, 1993), p. 136.

36. James Baughman, *Television's Guardians: The FCC and the Politics of Programming, 1958–1967* (Knoxville: University of Tennessee Press, 1985). I have adapted the phrase "TV Problem" (coined in 1958 by Walter Lippman) from Baughman's study of critical and regulatory responses to commercial television.

37. Carnegie Commission on Educational Television, *Public Television: A Program for Action* (New York: Bantam, 1967), p. 9.

1. Oasis of the Vast Wasteland

1. Corporation for Public Broadcasting, *From Wasteland to Oasis: A Quarter Century of Sterling Programming* (Washington, D.C.: CPB, 1992); Robert Avery, introduction to *Public Service Broadcasting in a Multichannel Environment,*" ed. Robert Avery (New York: Longman, 1993), p. xii. For a critique of the "vast wasteland" metaphor in relation to television policy, see Laurie Ouellette and Justin Lewis, "Moving Beyond the Vast Wasteland: Cultural Policy and Television in the U.S.," *Television and New Media* 1 (February 2000): 91–113.

2. Newton Minow, "The Vast Wasteland," Address to the thirty-ninth annual convention of the National Association of Broadcasters, Washington, D.C., May 8, 1961, in

Frank J. Kahn, *Documents of American Broadcasting* (Englewood Cliffs, N.J.: Prentice-Hall, 1984), pp. 207–17.

3. This is the principal argument made by former *Village Voice* media critic James Ledbetter in *Made Possible by . . . the Death of Public Broadcasting in the United States* (New York: Verso, 1997). In *Public Television for Sale* (Boulder, Colo.: Westview Press, 1994), William Hoynes also attributes U.S. public television's shortcomings largely to increased commercialism. Ralph Engelman's *Public Radio and Television in America: A Political History* (Thousand Oaks, Calif.: Sage, 1996) is more critical of the private foundations who got public television off the ground. He, too, however, emphasizes the doings of individuals and institutions with little attention to social, cultural, and political contexts. The term "safely splendid" was coined by Erik Barnouw in *The Sponsor* (New York: Oxford University Press, 1978), p. 50.

4. In *Watching Dallas*, Ien Ang posits that public discourses situated the prime-time soap opera *Dallas* in an ideologically charged "mass culture" debate, guiding the way people assessed its social/cultural value. The discourse of the vast wasteland worked in a similar way, extending ideological assumptions about mass culture to the social/cultural evaluation of "good" and "bad" TV. The discourse guided policymakers, social scientists, TV critics, and viewers in their interpretation of the remedy–the wasteland "oasis"–informing not just PBS's commonsense priorities but also the meanings, expectations, and evaluative frameworks used to make sense of the new channels. Ien Ang, *Watching Dallas: Soap Opera and the Melodramatic Imagination* (London: Routledge, 1982), pp. 92–93.

5. Peter Stallybrass and Allon White, *The Politics and Poetics of Transgression* (Ithaca, N.Y.: Cornell University Press, 1968), pp. 2–3.

6. Ang, *Watching Dallas*, pp. 94–95.

7. Michelle Hilmes, "Desired and Feared: Women's Voices in Radio History," in *Television, History, and American Culture: Feminist Critical Essays*, ed. Mary Beth Haralovich and Lauren Rabinovitz (Durham, N.C.: Duke University Press, 1999), pp. 17–35; Robert McChesney, *Telecommunications, Mass Media and Democracy: The Battle for Control of U.S. Broadcasting, 1928–1935* (New York: Oxford University Press, 1994).

8. William Boddy, *Fifties Television: The Industry and Its Critics* (Champaign-Urbana: University of Illinois Press, 1990); Brian G. Rose, *Television and the Performing Arts* (New York: Greenwood Press).

9. Boddy, *Fifties Television*; James Baughman, *Television's Guardians: The FCC and the Politics of Programming, 1958–1967* (Knoxville: University of Tennessee Press, 1985); commentator quoted in Gary Steiner, *The People Look at Television* (New York: Knopf, 1963), p. 235.

10. Barbara Ehrenreich argues that the "new consumer ethic" promoted by advertisers and the "fun morality" scrutinized by sociologists were one and the same. Likewise, the hedonism ascribed to the childlike masses by the discourse of the vast wasteland was not a character flaw but a complex economic and cultural phenomenon. The postwar consumer boom was fueled in part by business campaigns designed to direct the "average American" accustomed to traditional values like thrift and hard work toward a new "life of pleasurable consumption." Seeking to "demonstrate that

the hedonistic approach" to life was moral, corporations and advertisers contributed to the anxieties routinely blamed on television. Barbara Ehrenreich, *The Hearts of Men: American Dreams and the Flight from Commitment* (Garden City, N.Y.: Doubleday, 1983), pp. 44–45.

11. Jackson Lears, "A Matter of Taste: Corporate Hegemony in a Mass-Consumption Society," in *Recasting America: Culture and Politics in the Age of Cold War*, ed. Larry May (Chicago: University of Chicago Press, 1989), pp. 44, 46–48; Andrew Ross, *No Respect: Intellectuals and Popular Culture* (New York: Routledge, 1989), p. 43.

12. Vance Packard, *The Status Seekers: An Exploration of Class Behavior in America* (New York: McKay, 1959), pp. 327–28.

13. August Heckscher, "The Quality of American Culture," in *President's Commission on National Goals, Goals for Americans*, ed. U.S. President's Commission on National Goals (New York: Prentice-Hall, 1960), pp. 127–48.

14. Michael Curtin, *Redeeming the Wasteland: Television Documentary and Cold War Politics* (New Brunswick, N.J.: Rutgers University Press, 1995), p. 22; Heckscher, "The Quality of American Culture," p. 131.

15. John A. Andrew III, *Lyndon Johnson and the Great Society* (Chicago: Ivan R. Dee, 1998), p. 178.

16. Pierre Bourdieu, *Distinction: A Social Critique of the Judgment of Taste* (Cambridge, Mass.: Harvard University Press, 1984) especially pp. 7, 102.

17. Stuart Hall, "What Is This 'Black' in Black Popular Culture," in *Black Popular Culture*, ed. Gina Dent (Seattle: Bay Press, 1992), pp. 21–22, 26.

18. Minow, "The Vast Wasteland," p. 209. Andreas Huyssen argues that mass culture has historically been coded as feminine and low and thus worthless. See his "Mass Culture as Woman: Modernism's Other," in *Studies in Entertainment: Critical Approaches to Mass Culture*, ed. Tania Modleski (Bloomington: Indiana University Press, 1986), pp. 188–208. Cultural studies have observed similar patterns in relation to television. See Caren J. Demming, "For Television-Centered Television Criticism," in *Television and Women's Culture*, ed. Mary Ellen Brown (Newbury Park, Calif.: Sage, 1990), pp. 37–60; Jane Feuer, Paul Kerr, and Tise Vahimagi, eds., *MTM "Quality Television"* (London: BFI Publishing, 1984); Ien Ang, *Watching Dallas* (London: Routledge, 1988).

19. Lynne Joyrich, "All That Television Allows: TV Melodrama, Postmodernism and Consumer Culture," *Camera Obscura* 16 (1988): 145.

20. Baughman, *Television's Guardians*, p. 58; Minow, "The Vast Wasteland," p. 212; Newton Minow, "ETV Takes a Giant Step," *New York Times Magazine*, September 16, 1962, pp. 32–33.

21. Minow, "The Vast Wasteland," p. 212.

22. Minow, "The Vast Wasteland," p. 210; John Hartley, *Tele-ology* (London: Routledge, 1992), p. 118, 111.

23. Hartley, *Tele-ology*, pp. 101–19.

24. Minow, "The Vast Wasteland," p. 212; critic quoted in Yale Roe, *The Television Dilemma: Search for a Solution* (New York: Hastings House, 1962), p. 84.

25. Minow, "The Vast Wasteland," p. 211; Curtin, *Redeeming the Wasteland*, 237; Jack Gould, quoted in Steiner, *The People Look at Television*, 239;.Walter Armbruster, "Not Until You Finish Your Vegetables," *TV Guide*, September 1, 1962, pp. 2–5.

26. Baughman, *Television's Guardians*, p. 170; Robert Lewis Shayon, "When Everybody Loses," *Saturday Review*, Frebruary 25, 1967, p. 60.

27. "Rating the Audience," *Newsweek*, April 12, 1965, p. 70; Stallybrass and White, *Politics and Poetics of Transgression*; Steiner, *The People Look at Television*, pp. 222, 233. See also Gary Steiner, "The Steiner Report: The People Look at Television," *TV Guide*, February 23, 1963, pp. A5–A7, and March 2, 1963, pp. A2–A5.

28. Steiner, *The People Look at Television*, pp. 72, 288.

29. CBS Reports, "The Ratings Game" (New York: Museum of Radio and Television, July 12, 1965). For an influential cultural studies view of ratings as a social construct and a controlling device, see Ian Ang, *Desperately Seeking the Audience* (New York: Routledge, 1991). Ang's poststructuralist approach to ratings as a disciplinary technology has much in common with Hartley's characterization of the paedocratized audience. For a cultural studies critique that draws from political economy, see Eileen R. Meehan, "Why We Don't Count: The Commodity Audience," in *Logics of Television*, ed. Patricia Mellencamp (Bloomington: Indiana University Press, 1990), pp. 117–37.

30. Vance Packard, "New Kinds of Television," *The Atlantic*, October 1963, pp. 51–53, 69.

31. Boddy, *Fifties Television*, pp. 235–239; Hartley, *Tele-ology*, p. 118.

32. Hubbell Robinson, "You, the Public, Are to Blame," *TV Guide*, November 26, 1960, p. 14. For parallel arguments in trade publications, see Victor M. Ratner, "The Freedom of Taste," *Television Magazine*, November 1969, pp. 54–55, and "Public Taste Molds TV," *Broadcasting*, September 18, 1961, p. 26; Edgar Dale, *Can You Give the People What They Want?* (New York: Cowles Education, 1967), p. 4; Murrow quoted in Baughman, *Television's Guardians*, p. 30.

33. Baughman, *Television's Guardians*, p. 173; Toby Miller, *The Well-Tempered Self: Citizenship, Culture and the Postmodern Subject* (Baltimore: Johns Hopkins University Press, 1993), pp. 129–172; Charles A. Siepmann, "What Is Wrong with TV–And with Us," *NAEB Journal*, September-October 1964, p. 4.

34. Arthur Schlesinger Jr., "Notes on a Cultural Policy," in *Culture for the Millions?* ed. Norman Jacobs (Princeton, N.J.: Van Nostrand, 1961), p. 149; John Fischer, "TV and Its Critics," *Harper's*, July 1959, pp. 12–18.

35. Walter Lippmann, "The TV Problem," *New York Herald Tribune*, October 27, 1959, p. 26.

36. Louis Hausman, "Television and the Pursuit of Excellence," speech to the American Council for Better Broadcasts," Ohio State University, April 26, 1961, in *Vital Speeches of the Day*, July 1, 1961, p. 568; Paul F. Lazarsfeld, "Some Reflections on Past and Future Research on Broadcasting," forward to Steiner, *The People Look at Television*, p. 414; Thomas Streeter, *Selling the Air: A Critique of the Policy of Commercial Broadcasting in the United States* (Chicago: University of Chicago Press, 1996) p. 140.

37. Dale, *Can You Give the People What They Want?* p. 3; Henry and Keppel quoted in "ETV's Job: Close the Culture Gap," *Broadcasting*, December 14, 1964, p. 42; Ellen Condliffe Lagemann, *The Politics of Knowledge: The Carnegie Corporation, Philanthropy, and Public Policy* (Middletown, Conn.: Wesleyan University Press, 1989), pp. 7, 224. For more discussion, see John Edward Burke, *Historical-Analytical Study of the Legislative and Political Origins of the Public Broadcasting Act of 1967* (New York: Arno Press, 1979), p. 88.

38. Wilbur Schramm, "Educational Broadcasting: Its Aims and Responsibilities," mimeo, July 15, 1949, Morris Novik papers, Institute of Communication Research Meetings, series 1, box 1, National Public Broadcasting Archive, College Park, Md.; William Kenneth Cumming, *This Is Educational Television* (Ann Arbor, Mich.: Edwards Brothers, 1954), p. xxii.

39. Murray Schumach, "15 Women Know They Hate TV: Took It 12 Hours a Day for a Week," *New York Times*, January 11, 1951, p. 3; John Walker Powell, *Channels of Learning: The Story of Educational Television* (Washington, D.C.: Public Affairs Press, 1962), p. 48; Dallas W. Smythe, "A National Policy on Television?" *Public Opinion Quarterly* 14 (Autumn 1950): 461–74; Dallas W. Smythe, "An Analysis of Television Programs," *Scientific American*, July 1951, pp. 15–17.

40. Denise C. Buss, "The Ford Foundation in Public Education: Emergent Patterns," in *Ford Foundation: Philanthropy and Cultural Imperialism, the Foundations at Home and Abroad*, ed. Robert F. Arnove (Bloomington: Indiana University Press, 1982), pp. 331–62; Fund for Adult Education, "1951–1961 Ten Year Report," Scott Fletcher papers, series 2, subseries 11, box 4, file 1, National Public Broadcasting Archive, College Park, Md.

41. Tony Bennett, *The Birth of the Museum* (London: Routledge, 1995); Arnold quoted in Joan Shelley Rubin, *The Making of Middlebrow Culture* (Chapel Hill: University of North Carolina Press, 1992), p. 15; Dwight MacDonald, *The Ford Foundation: The Men and the Millions* (New York: Reynal, 1956), p. 57; Fund for Adult Education, "Continuing Liberal Education, Report for 1955–1957," Scott Fletcher papers, series 2, subseries 11, box 4, file 1, National Public Broadcasting Archive, College Park, Md.

42. *Omnibus*, Museum of Television and Radio; Cooke quoted in MacDonald, *The Ford Foundation*, p. 90; Ford Foundation, *Ford Foundation Activities in Noncommercial Broadcasting* (New York: Ford Foundation, 1980), p. 3.

43. John Walker Powell, *Channels of Learning: The Story of Educational Television* (Washington, D.C.: Public Affairs Press, 1962), p. 63; this phrase was coined by *TV Guide*. See Richard K. Doan, "Educational TV Looks Ahead to a Promised Land," *TV Guide*, November 5, 1966, p. 28; "Ford for Better TV," *Newsweek*, June 24, 1951, p. 53; Jim Robertson, *TeleVisionaries* (Charlotte Harbor, Fla: Tabby House Books, 1993), p. 94; Powell, *Channels of Learning*, p. 53; Scott Fletcher, "Capitalism Versus Totalitarianism," Scott Fletcher papers, series 2, box 5, subseries 2, file 3, National Public Broadcasting Archive, College Park, Md.

44. Curtin, *Redeeming the Wasteland*, p. 27; quotations from the Fletcher papers.

45. NET, "The Face of Russia" (approx. 1960), Library of Congress, Washington, D.C.

46. NET, "Power Elite and Creative Elite" (1962), *The Age of Overkill*, Library of Congress, Washington, D.C.

47. Jack Gould, "The WNYC Imbroglio," *New York Times*, December 14, 1952, p. 14; "I Love Lucidity," *Newsweek*, May 14, 1956, p. 114; "Educational TV: What Is It and Where's It Going," *Changing Times*, February 1963, n.p., National Public Broadcasting Archive reference; Gordon A. Sabine, "ETV for a People Who Will Travel to the Moon," *NAEB Journal*, November 1958, pp. 16–178.

48. Rowland, "Public Service Broadcasting," p. 159.

49. Doan, "Educational TV," pp. 29–30.

50. Shayon quoted in Ralph Lewis Smith, *A Study of the Professional Criticism of Broadcasting in the United States 1920–1955* (New York: Arno Press, 1979), p. 384; Powell, *Channels of Learning*, pp. 6, 25; Richard M. Elman, "Educational TV," *The Nation*, March 1, 1965, p. 217.

51. National Educational Television, "A True Fourth Network: Why and How," brochure, John White papers, series 1, box 1, folder 10, National Public Broadcasting Archive, College Park, Md.; John F. White, "We Will Guide but You Must Push," *TV Guide*, May 5, 1962, p. 23; Samuel Grafton, "Educational Television: Boor or Boondoggle?" *TV Guide*, October 1962, p. 9; Bourdieu, *Distinction*, p.57; Lynn Spigel, *Make Room for TV* (Chicago: University of Chicago Press, 1992), p. 85.

52. Wilbur Schramm, "The Audiences of Educational Television," in *The Impact of Educational Television*, ed. Wilbur Schramm (Champaign-Urbana: University of Illinois Press, 1960), p. 23; Henri Lefebvre, *Critique of Everyday Life* (London: Verso, 1991), pp. 33–34; Wilbur Schramm, Jack Lyle, and Ithiel de Sola Pool, *The People Look at Educational Television* (Stanford, Calif.: Stanford University Press, 1963), p. 46; Barbara Ehrenreich, *Fear of Falling: The Inner Life of the Middle Class* (New York: HarperPerennial, 1990), p. 132.

53. Samuel Grafton, "Who Watches ETV," *TV Guide*, October 1962, p. 24; NET, "The Return of Prometheus," *Basic Issues for Man* (1960), Library of Congress, Washington, D.C.; NET, *Invitation to Art* (1958), Library of Congress, Washington, D.C.; NET, *Pablo Casal's Master Class at Berkeley* (1961), Museum of Television and Radio, New York.

54. Kai Bird, *Color of Truth: McGeorge Bundy and William Bundy* (New York: Simon & Schuster, 1998), pp. 102, 378; McGeorge Bundy, *The Strength of Government* (Cambridge, Mass.: Harvard University Press, 1968). According to Bird, Bundy had difficulties with the update, which was never completed.

55. Quoted in Elman, "Educational TV," p. 217.

56. Streeter, *Selling the Air*, especially pp. xii, 43; Willard Rowland, "Public Service Broadcasting in the United States: Its Mandates, Institutions and Conflicts," in *Public Service Broadcasting in a Multichannel Environment*, ed. Robert Avery (New York: Longman, 1993), p. 157.

57. Richard Flacks, "Is the Great Society Just a Barbecue?" in *Thoughts of the Young Radicals*, ed. New Republic (New York: Pittman, 1966), pp. 48–56.

58. Frank A. Darknell, "The Carnegie Philanthropy and Private Corporate Influence on Higher Education," in *Philanthropy and Cultural Imperialism, the Foundations*

at Home and Abroad, ed. Robert F. Arnove (Bloomington: Indiana University Press, 1982), p. 386; David E. Weischadle, "The Carnegie Corporation and the Shaping of American Educational Policy," in *Philanthropy and Cultural Imperialism,* pp. 363–84; Ellen Condliffe Lagemann, *The Politics of Knowledge: The Carnegie Corporation, Philanthropy, and Public Policy* (Middletown, Conn.: Wesleyan University Press, 1989), pp. 7, 18, 258.

59. Robertson, *TeleVisionaries,* pp. 231–34; Buss, "Ford Foundation," p. 333; Lagemann, "Politics of Knowledge," p. 224; Ralph Engelman, *Public Radio and Television in America* (Thousand Oaks, Calif.: Sage, 1996), pp. 156–157.

60. "The Architects of CPTV," *Broadcasting,* January 30, 1967, p. 24; Weischadle, "The Carnegie Corporation," p. 366; Martin Meyer, "Whatever Happened to Educational Television? *Change,* March 1972, pp. 51–52; Robertson, *TeleVisionaries,* pp. 233–36; James R. Killian, "Toward a Research-Reliant Society: Some Observations on Government and Science," in *Science as a Cultural Force,* ed. Harry Wolfe (Baltimore: Johns Hopkins University Press, 1964), pp. 9–34; "Educational Ecumenist: James Rhyne Killian Jr.," *New York Times,* January 26, 1967, n.p., Wisconsin State Historical Society, Madison, Carnegie Commission papers, box 6, file 2, press clippings.

61. Letter from John Fischer to James Killian, November 22, 1966, Carnegie Commission papers, box 1, file 1; Programming Panel minutes, June 20–21, 1966, box 2, file 1; Proceedings, Carnegie Commission on Educational Television, March 17–19, 1966, box 1, file 9; Proceedings and Statement to Carnegie Commission by William G. Harley, April 14–16, 1966, box 1, file 10, Wisconsin State Historical Society, Madison.

62. Stephen White, unpublished draft, May 11, 1966, Carnegie Commission papers, box 2 file 8, Wisconsin State Historical Society, Madison.

63. "Heyday for Intellectuals," *U.S. News & World Report,* July 21, 1969, pp. 74–75.

64. Letter from John P. Cunningham to Hymin Goldin, July 7, 1966, Carnegie Commission papers, box 1, file 2, Wisconsin State Historical Society, Madison.

65. "Architects of CPTV," *Broadcasting,* p. 24; Carnegie Commission on Educational Television, *Public Television: A Program for Action* (New York: Bantam, 1967), pp. 16, 90.

66. Carnegie Commission, *A Program for Action,* pp. 13–15, 204.

67. White, unpublished draft; Carnegie Commission, *A Program for Action,* p. 1; Letter to James Killian from Frank Stanton, January 27, 1967, Carnegie Commission papers, Box 1 file 4, Wisconsin State Historical Society, Madison.

68. Dwight Newton, "Seeking Excellence, Not Just Acceptability," *San Francisco Examiner,* January 29, 1967, n.p.; see also Erwin D. Canham, "The Quality of Viewing," *Christian Science Monitor,* January 27, 1967, n.p., Carnegie Commission papers, press clippings, box 6, file 2.

69. Burke, *Historical-Analytical Study,* p. 150.

70. "Educational Television," *Washington Post,* February 5, 1967, p. E6; "Subsidized TV Easy Prey for Politicians," *Seattle Daily Times,* January 27, 1967, p. 27. See also "Beauty and the Beast," *Wall Street Journal,* February 20, 1967, n.p., Carnegie Commission papers, press clippings, box 6, file 2.

71. Lagemann, *The Politics of Knowledge*, p. 222.

72. "Distasteful Caviar," *Milwaukee Sentinel*, January 27, 1967, n.p.; Percy Shain, "New Public TV System Proposed," *Dallas Morning News*, January 26, 1967, n.p., Carnegie Commission papers, press clippings, box 6, file 2; Burke, *Historical-Analytical Study*, p. 129.

73. Lawrence Laruent, "Carnegie Study Proposes New TV Deal," *Washington Post*, January 27, 1967, n.p.; Lagemann, *The Politics of Knowledge*, 225; Burke, *Historical-Analytical Study*, p. 201; Representative Brock Adams, House Committee on Interstate and Foreign Commerce, *Public Television Act of 1967:Hearings on H.R. 6736*, p. 151; Rosel Hyde, *Hearings on H.R. 6736*, p. 180, 199; McGeorge Bundy, *Hearings on H.R. 6736*, pp. 371–72, all in 90th Cong., 1st sess., July 11–21, 1967.

74. Frank Stanton, *Hearings on H.R. 6736*, pp. 244–45; John W. Gardner, *Hearings on H.R. 6736*, pp. 20–24.

75. Hyde, *Hearings on H.R. 6736*, p. 197; Joseph Beirne, *Hearings on H.R. 6736*, p. 668; William G. Hartley, *Hearings on H.R. 6736*, p. 446; William F. Fore, *Hearings on H.R. 6736*, p. 362.

76. Killian, *Hearings on H.R. 6736*, pp. 130, 148; Fred Friendly, *Hearings on H.R. 6736*, p. 378; House Committee on Interstate and Foreign Commerce, 90th Cong., 1st sess., July 11–21, *Report No. 572, to accompany H.R. 6736*, p. 16; John P. Witherspoon and Roselle Kovitz, "A Tribal Memory of Public Broadcasting Missions, Mandates, Assumptions, Structures," unpublished report, Corporation for Public Broadcasting, July 1986, p. 169, National Public Broadcasting Archive, reference. In the final version of the bill, section 397(9) was amended to define an educational program as "one designed for educational or cultural purposes."

77. "Public TV: A Wasteland Oasis, *Life*, February 17, 1967, p. 4; "TV's Fourth Network," *U.S. News and World Report*, Oct. 12, 1970, p. 45.

78. Public Broadcasting Service, "A Chance for Better Television," press release, 1970, National Public Broadcasting Archive, reference.

79. Alistair Cooke, "Public Television," *TV Guide*, October 3, 1970, pp. 20–23; Jack Gould, "What's a 12-Letter Word for Extraordinary," *New York Times*, October 18, 1970, n.p.; Bernie Harrison, "This Little Show Will Grow on You," *Evening Star*, January 27, 1971, n.p.; Judith Crist, "This Week's Movies," *TV Guide*, December 5, 1970, n.p.; Julia Inman, "Mama Mia! No Commercials? Thatsa Breaking All the Rules," *Indianapolis Star*, October 10, 1970, n.p., PBS collection, public information, press clippings 1970, box 8, National Public Broadcasting Archive, College Park, Md.

80. Terrence O' Flaherty, "PBS–The Cinderella Network," *Reader's Digest*, November 1971; Marvin Kitman, "The Big Sell Goes Public," *Newsday*, October 8, 1970, n.p.; Marquis Childs, "TV Is Much More Than Distraction," *Washington Post*, December 1970, n.d., n.p.; Dave Simms, "New Shows Erupt with Relevancy," *Washington Post*, December 1970, n.d., n.p.; Diana Loercher, "PBS Woos Youth with Demanding Mix," *Christian Science Monitor*, October 9, 1970, n.p.; Fred Ferretti, "TV: An Enriching San Francisco Mix," *New York Times*, December 19, 1970, PBS collection, public information, press clippings 1970, box 8, National Public Broadcasting Archive, College Park, Md.

81. Simms, "New Shows."

82. George Leonard, "Television Is Alive and Well in San Francisco," *Look*, November 17, 1970, n.p., PBS collection, public information, press clippings 1970, box 8, National Public Broadcasting Archive, College Park, Md.; Kitman, "The Big Sell Goes Public."

83. "Educational TV Great," *Des Moines Register*, December 29, 1970, n.p., PBS collection, public information, press clippings 1970, box 8, National Public Broadcasting Archive, College Park, Md.; study reported in Daniel Boorstein, "Television," *Life*, September 10, 1971, p. 43.

84. Ien Ang, "Understanding Television Audiencehood," in *Television: The Critical View*, ed. Horace Newcomb (New York: Oxford University Press, 1994), p. 372.

85. Letter, PBS collection, Mary Aladj papers, viewer mail, box 1, National Public Broadcasting Archive, College Park, Md.

86. McGraw Hill Research, "National Educational Television Survey," unpublished report, October 1969, WNET collection, box 8, National Public Broadcasting Archive, College Park, Md.

87. Les Brown quoted in "TV: Is the Bloom Off the Old Rose," *Forbes*, October 15, 1970, p. 29.

88. Feuer, Kerr, and Vahimagi, eds., *MTM "Quality Television,"* p. 56.

89. "Transcript of Proceedings: Kettering Conference on Public Television Programming," unpublished report, pp. 25–28, June 1969, Wingspread, Wisconsin, 19, CPB collection, box 34, National Public Broadcasting Archive, College Park, Md.; Corporation for Public Broadcasting, "The Viewing of Public Television," unpublished report, 1971, pp. 32–34, CPB collection, Audience Research 1971, box 54, National Public Broadcasting Archive, College Park, Md.; Richard K. Doan, "The Doan Report," *TV Guide*, June 17, 1972, p. A1.

90. PBS commercials 1973, videotape collection, National Public Broadcasting Archive, College Park, Md.; Clarke Williamson, "Let TV Be 'Vast Wasteland,' Plurality of Voters Decide," *Charleston Gazette*, October 8 1970, n.p., PBS collection, public information, press clippings 1970, box 8, National Public Broadcasting Archive, College Park, Md.

2. The Quest to Cultivate

1. Al Gore, "Address on Public Broadcasting Before American University," Washington, D.C., March 3, 1995, White House Office of the Press Secretary; Duggan quoted in David Zurawik, "America Wants Good Old Elitism, Insists PBS Boss," *Baltimore Sun*, July 29, 1994, p. 1D.

2. Representative Samuel N. Friedel, Secretary of Health, Education and Welfare John W. Gardner, James R. Killian, Representative Claude Pepper, and Thomas P. F. Hoving, House Committee on Interstate and Foreign Commerce, *Public Television Act of 1967: Hearings on 6736*, 90th Cong., 1st sess., July 11–21, 1967, pp. 108, 28, 122, 109, 139.

3. Heather Hendershot, *Saturday Morning Censors: Television Regulation Before the V-Chip* (Durham: Duke University Press, 1998), p. 191. Hendershot refers to "educational" cartoons, but her arguments applies to cultural policy as well.

4. Joan Shelley Rubin, *The Making of Middlebrow Culture* (Chapel Hill: University of North Carolina Press, 1992), pp. 1–33; John Kasson, *Amusing the Million: Coney Island at the Turn of the Century* (New York: Hill & Wang, 1978), pp. 3–9; Tony Bennett, *The Birth of the Museum* (London: Routledge, 1995), esp. pp. 21–24, 89–91; Tony Bennett, "Useful Culture," *Cultural Studies* 6 (1992): 395–408; Rubin, *Middlebrow Culture*, p. 14.

5. Morgan quoted in Rubin, *Middlebrow Culture*, p. 272; Joy Elmer Morgan, "A National Culture–By-Product or Objective of National Planning," *School and Society*, July 28, 1934, p. 114.

6. Janice Radway, *A Feeling for Books: The Book of the Month Club, Literary Taste and Middle Class Desire* (Chapel Hill: University of North Carolina Press, 1997), p. 15; Dwight MacDonald, "A Theory of Mass Culture," in *Mass Culture: The Popular Arts in America*, ed. Bernard Rosenberg and David Manning White (Glencoe, Ill.: Free Press, 1957), pp. 59–73.

7. John Kasson, *Amusing the Million: Coney Island at the Turn of the Century* (New York: Hill & Wang, 1978), p. 4; Garth Jowett, "The Emergence of the Mass Society: The Standardization of American Culture, 1830–1920," in *Prospects: The Annual of American Cultural Studies*, ed. Jack Salzman (New York: Burt Franklin, 1982), p. 212; Wilbur Schramm, "The Audiences of Educational Television," in *The Impact of Educational Television*, ed. Wilbur Schramm (Champaign-Urbana: University of Illinois Press, 1960), pp. 26–27.

8. Wilbur Schramm, Jack Lyle, and Ithiel de Sola Pool, *The People Look at Educational Television: A Report of Nine Representative ETV Stations* (Stanford, Calif.: Stanford University Press, 1963), pp. 46–47, 65–69, 85–86.

9. Todd Gitlin, *The Sixties: Years of Hope, Days of Rage* (New York: Bantam, 1993), p. 21; Hulett C. Smith, Governor of the State of West Virginia, *Hearings on H.R. 6736*, p. 430; Fritz Machlup, *The Production and Distribution of Knowledge in the United States* (Princeton, N.J.: Princeton University Press, 1962), p. 56; John W. Macy, "The Critics of Television: A Positive Answer," Speech to the National Press Club, January 15, 1970, in *Vital Speeches of the Day*, February 15, 1970, pp. 268–88.

10. Jim Robertson, *TeleVisionaries* (Charlotte Harbor, Fla.: Tabby House Books, 1993), p. 62.

11. David E. Weischadle, "The Carnegie Corporation and the Shaping of American Educational Policy," in *Philanthropy and Cultural Imperialism, the Foundations at Home and Abroad,* ed. Robert F. Arnove (Bloomington: Indiana University Press, 1982), p. 367; John Gardner, *Excellence: Can We Be Equal and Excellent Too?* (New York: Harper & Row, 1961), pp. 73, 105, 133.

12. Gardner, *Excellence*, pp. 71, 133; Weischadle, "Carnegie Corporation," p. 367.

13. Vance Packard, *The Status Seekers: An Exploration of Class Behavior in America* (New York: McKay, 1959), p. 130.

14. John Fiske, *Television Culture* (New York: Routledge, 1987), p. 266.

15. Randal Johnson, editor's introduction to *The Field of Cultural Production*, by Pierre Bourdieu (New York: Columbia University Press, 1993), p. 23.

16. Lyndon B. Johnson, "Full Educational Opportunity," in *The Great Society Reader: The Failures of American Liberalism*, ed. Marvin E. Gettleman and David Mermelstein (New York: Vintage Books, 1967), p. 186.

17. Barbara Ehrenreich, *Fear of Falling: The Inner Life of the Middle Class* (New York: HarperPerennial, 1990) pp. 48–51; Oscar Lewis, "The Culture of Poverty," *Scientific American* 215 (October 1966): 19–25; Casey Hayden, "Raising the Question of Who Decides," in *Thoughts of the Young Radicals*, ed. *New Republic* (New York: Pittman, 1966), p. 44.

18. Statement to Carnegie Commission by William G. Harley, Proceedings, April 14–16, 1966, Carnegie Commission papers, box 1, file 10, Wisconsin State Historical Society, Madison.

19. Gardner, *Excellence*, p. 12.

20. Quoted in American Enterprise Institute for Public Policy Research, *Educational Television: Who Should Pay?* (Washington, D.C.: American Enterprise Institute, 1968), p. 9.

21. Terrence O'Flaherty, "PBS—The Cinderella Network," *Reader's Digest*, November 1971, n.p., PBS collection, public information, press clippings 1970, box 8, National Public Broadcasting Archive, College Park, Md: Hendershot, *Saturday Morning Censors*, p. 161.

22. Carnegie Commission on Educational Television, *Public Television: A Program for Action* (New York: Bantam, 1967), p. 95; "Joan Ganz Cooney," *Current Biography 1970* (New York: H. W. Wilson, 1970), pp. 97–99; Thomas D. Cook et al., eds., *Sesame Street Revisited* (New York: Russell Sage, 1975), p. 35; Museum of Television and Radio, "Museum of Television and Radio Seminar: The Children's Television Workshop 25th Anniversary," Museum of Television and Radio, New York.

23. Cook et al., eds., *Sesame Street Revisited*, pp. 22, 30; John Culhane, "Report Card on Sesame Street," *New York Times Magazine*, May 24, 1970, p. 44.

24. John A. Andrew III, *Lyndon Johnson and the Great Society* (Chicago: Ivan R. Dee, 1998), p. 57; Culhane, "Report Card," 34.

25. CTW quoted in "Cooney," *Current Biography 1970*, p. 98; Museum of Television and Radio, *Sesame Street* (1969 debut and early episodes), Museum of Television and Radio, New York.

26. Culhane, "Report Card," pp. 50, 51; Byron Scott, "Turning on Tots with Educational TV," *Today's Health*, November 1969, pp. 30–31, quoted in Terrence O'Flaherty, "PBS–The Cinderella Network," *Reader's Digest*, November 1971, rprt., n.p.; O'Flaherty, "Cinderella Network," n.p.; "'Sesame' Has City Specials," *San Antonio Express and News*, September 11, 1970, PBS collection, public information, press clippings 1971, box 8; *San Francisco Chronicle*, quoted in "Sesame Street," *Educational Broadcasting Review*, August 1969, p. 67.

27. Linda Francke, "The Games People Play on Sesame Street," *New York Times*, April 5, 1971, n.p., PBS collection, press clippings 1970–71, box 7, National Public Broad-

casting Archive, College Park, Md.; Cooney quoted in "Sesame Street Report Card," *Time*, November 16, 1970, p. 70; Robert Blakley, *The People's Instrument: A Philosophy of Programming for Public Television* (Washington, D.C.: Public Affairs Press, 1971), pp. 67–68; John Holt, "Big Bird, Meet Dick and Jane," *The Atlantic*, May 1971, pp. 72–74.

28. "Brightening the Boob Tube," *Newsweek*, April 1, 1968, p. 67, *Time* quoted in Cook, *Sesame Street Revisited*, p. 37; Blakley, *The People's Instrument*, p. 64; John W. Macy, *To Irrigate a Wasteland* (Berkeley and Los Angeles: University of California Press, 1974), p. 22.

29. Brown, quoted in Cooney, *Current Biography 1970*, p. 98; Francke, "Games," n.p.

30. Untitled article, *Image*, June 1971, p. 14, WNET collection, program guides, box 4, National Public Broadcasting Archive, College Park, Md.

31. Francke, "Games," n.p.; Richard K. Doan, "Backing a Network of a Different Color," *TV Guide*, February 20, 1971, n.p., PBS collection, public information, press clippings 1971, box 8, National Public Broadcasting Archive, College Park, Md.; Don Monaco, "Cooney & The Kids: Here's TV Your Child Can Watch," *Look*, November 18, 1969, pp. 100–2.

32. Dede Compagno, "This 'Most Pervasive Medium,'" *Image*, June 1971, pp. 11–14, WNET collection, program guides, box 4, National Public Broadcasting Archive, College Park, Md.

33. John A Niemi and Darrell V. Anderson, "Television: A Viable Channel for Educating Adults in Culturally Different Poverty Groups?" unpublished report, ERIC Clearinghouse on Adult Education, April 1971, Richard Meyer papers, series 2, box 5, National Public Broadcasting Archive, College Park, Md.

34. Ien Ang, *Desperately Seeking the Audience* (New York: Routledge, 1991), p. 105.

35. "Breeding Ground for Riots," *Saturday Review*, April 20, 1968, p. 66; Howe quoted in *Tenth Anniversary Program of KTCA-TV*, September 17, 1967, unpublished transcript, National Public Broadcasting Archive, reference; Hubert Humphrey, "Remarks to the Convention," *NAEB Journal*, January–February 1966, p. 49.

36. Mendelsohn quoted in memo to promotion directors from Fritz Jacobi, July 10, 1970, National Public Broadcasting Archive, PBS collection, public information, box 7; Stuart Hall, "The Whites of Their Eyes: Racist Ideologies and the Media," in *The Media Reader*, ed. Manuel Alvarado and John Thompson (London: British Film Institute, 1990), pp. 8–23.

37. Niemi and Anderson, "Television," p. 14; Richard J. Meyer and Chalmers H. Marquis, "Report on ETV in the Ghetto," submitted to Vice-President Hubert Humphrey, in Meyer, "ETV and the Ghetto," *Educational Broadcasting Review*, August 1968, pp. 19–24.

38. "Final Report of WETA-TV, Channel 26," for Social and Rehabilitation Service, U.S. Department of Health, Education and Welfare, March 1970, James Karyn papers, series 1, box 1, file 2, National Public Broadcasting Archive, College Park, Md.

39. "Final Report of WETA-TV, Channel 26"; Charlie Cobb, "Whose Society Is This?" in *Thoughts of the Young Radicals*, p. 21.

40. "Final Report of WETA-TV, Channel 26."

41. Meyer, "ETV and the Ghetto," p. 24.

42. Richard M. Uray, "*Job Man Caravan*," *Educational Broadcasting Review*, October 1970, p. 60.

43. "Transcript of Proceedings: Kettering Conference on Public Television Programming," June 25–28, 1969, Wingspread, Wisconsin, unpublished report, p. 126, CPB collection, box 34, National Public Broadcasting Archive, College Park, Md.

44. Walter Benjamin, "The Work of Art in the Age of Mechanical Reproduction," in *Illuminations*, ed. Hannah Arendt (New York: Schocken Books, 1985), pp. 217–52.

45. British Broadcasting Corporation, *Civilisation* (1969), Museum of Television and Radio, New York. Also available from PBS video marketing, which calls *Civilisation* the "greatest cultural program" ever produced.

46. Robertson, *TeleVisionairies*, p. 158; John Edward Burke, *An Historical-Analytical Study of the Legislative and Political Origins of the Public Broadcasting Act of 1967* (New York: Arno Press, 1979), p. 180; "ETV Goes Commercial," *Sponsor*, June 17, 1963, pp. 29–30; "TV's Highbrow Wing Feeds on Business Cash," *Business Week*, January 19, 1963, p. 112.

47. Galbraith says the "small yet significant revolt" was mainly concentrated among the professional middle class. Much like Bourdieu, he says that this social class formation is defined by education and a "feeling of social superiority," as opposed to concentrated wealth. John Kenneth Galbraith, *The Affluent Society* (Boston: Houghton Mifflin, 1958–69), pp. 165, 307; Herb Schmertz, *Goodbye to the Low Profile* (Boston: Little, Brown, 1986), p. 216; Roland Marchand traces discreet image marketing to the 1920s, when radio advertisers wishing to impress the "class within the mass" turned to sponsorship of "elevated" programs presented as a "public service," largely because the publicity was considered less "debasing" and more appealing to a well-educated and affluent consumer base. By the 1960s, commercial network television's quest for high ratings had squelched such appeals. Roland Marchand, *Advertising the American Dream* (Berkeley and Los Angeles: University of California Press, 1985), p. 64.

48. Russell Lynes, *The Tastemakers: The Shaping of American Popular Taste* (New York: Dover, 1980), p. 310; Ehrenreich, *Fear of Falling*, pp. 18, 37–38; Packard, *The Status Seekers*, p. 3.

49. Packard, *The Status Seekers*, pp. 8–9, Alvin Toffler, *The Culture Consumers, A Study of Art and Affluence in America* (New York: St. Martin's Press, 1964), pp. 51–54; Packard, *The Status Seekers*, p. 62; Fiske, *Television Culture*, p. 266.

50. "Programs Must Have an Over-Purpose," *Xerox World*, September 25, 1970, p. 3; "Television Has Been Good to Xerox," *Xerox World*, September 25, 1970, p. 3; "It Took the Mona Lisa to Top Civilisation," *Xerox World*, September 25, 1970, p. 2, PBS collection, program files, *Civilisation*, box 22, National Public Broadcasting Archive, College Park, Md.; Robert Lewis Shayon, "When Everybody Loses," *Saturday Review*, February 25, 1967, p. 60; Rex Polier, "Public TV," *Philadelphia Sunday Bulletin*, December 13, 1970, n.p., PBS collection, public information, press clippings 1970, box 8, National Public Broadcasting Archive, College Park, Md.

51. Opinion Research Corporation, "Opportunities for Business in Educational Television," unpublished report, June 1964, National Public Broadcasting Archive,

reference shelf; Ford Foundation, "Profit Making Ventures and Public Television Stations: A Report to the Ford Foundation," unpublished report, November 1970, National Public Broadcasting Archive, reference; Corporation for Public Broadcasting, "Auction and Underwriting Special," unpublished report, July 1972, CPB collection, box 53, National Public Broadcasting Archive, College Park, Md.

52. Packard, *The Status Seekers*, pp. 129–30.

53. *Civilisation* (British Broadcasting Corporation, 1969); Jerry Buck, "Silent Sponsors: What's Making Public TV Run?" *Columbus Dispatch*, November 29, 1970, n.p.; O'Flaherty, "Cinderella Network," n.p.; Frank Judge, "A Special TV Night," *Detroit News*, September 9, 1970, n.p., PBS collection, program files, *Civilisation*, box 22, National Public Broadcasting Archive, College Park, Md.;"Civilized Offerings," *News-Press*, October 3, 1970, n.p., PBS collection, public information, press clippings 1971, box 8, National Public Broadcasting Archive, College Park, Md.; letter to the editor, *Image*, March 1971, p. 3, WNET collection, program guides, box 4, National Public Broadcasting Archive, College Park, Md.

54. Macy, *To Irrigate a Wasteland*, pp. 57, 60; Harry Bowman, "Civilisation Is Fascinating," *Dallas Morning News*, October 9, 1970, n.p., PBS collection, program files, *Civilisation*, box 22, National Public Broadcasting Archive, College Park, Md.; Marquis Childs, "TV Is Much More Than Distraction," *Washington Post*, December 1970, n.d., n.p., PBS collection, public information, press clippings 1970, box 8, National Public Broadcasting Archive, College Park, Md.

55. "PTV," *TV Guide*, September 12, 1970, p. 69; Cathy Coffey, "Comments by Cathy," *Courier-Gazette* (Rockland, Md.), October 9, 1970, n.p., PBS collection, program files, *Civilisation*, box 22, National Public Broadcasting Archive, College Park, Md.

56. Cleveland Amory, "Civilisation," *TV Guide*, December 12, 1970, n.p., PBS collection, public information, press clippings 1970, box 8, National Public Broadcasting Archive, College Park, Md.

57. Laurence Jarvik, "Masterpiece Theatre and the Politics of Quality: A Case Study" (Ph.D. diss., University of California at Los Angeles, 1991), pp. 1–9. Jarvik makes a similar argument in reference to the BBC import *Masterpiece Theatre*. He argues that the televised display of "imported" cultural capital enabled Mobil to ingenuously target the cream of the consumer crop. Referring to C. Wright Mills, Jarvik attributes the "need to import European culture" to the lack of an official aristocracy and the high culture traditions that go with it in the United States. I agree more or less on these points, but Jarvik fails to address public television's uplifting promises and how the promise of meritocracy intersected with mobility narratives and cultural longings in a particularly American way. Finally, this is the time to reiterate my disagreement with Jarvik's activism to "zero out" funding for PBS. His argument mirrors the thrust of his study: Mobil's unhampered success in crafting a well-educated, upscale public television subculture proves the viability of privatization. I argue that we need to revisit the discourses that Mobil used as part of a much-needed cultural policy overhaul in which the people participate. Likewise, I believe that public funding is necessary to create a truly public television alternative. For an overview of

Jarvik's conservative free-market position on the funding of public television, see David Horowitz and Laurence Jarvik, eds., *Public Broadcasting and the Public Trust* (Los Angeles: Second Thought Books, 1995); and Laurence Jarvik, *PBS: Behind the Screen* (Rocklin, Calif.: Forum, 1997).

58. Richard K. Schull, "Learning About Ourselves from a 'Civilized' Guy," *Indianapolis News*, October 8, 1970, n.p., PBS collection, program files, *Civilisation*, box 22, National Public Broadcasting Archive, College Park, Md.

59. Advertisement, *Life*, September 10, 1971, n.p., PBS collection, program files, *Civilisation*, box 22, National Public Broadcasting Archive, College Park, Md.; advertisement, *Image*, January 19, 1971, WNET collection, program guides, box 4, National Public Broadcasting Archive, College Park, Md.

60. J. Carter Brown, "Civilisation," *Renaissance*, October 1970, p. 40, PBS collection, program files, *Civilisation*, box 22, National Public Broadcasting Archive, College Park, Md.

61. Quoted in Public Broadcasting Service, "Festival 1975," unpublished report, Mary Aladji papers, box 1, June 1975 conference, National Public Broadcasting Archive, College Park, Md.

62. Marvin Kitman, "A New Racehorse," *Newsday*, October 21, 1970, n.p., PBS collection, public information, press clippings 1970, box 8, National Public Broadcasting Archive, College Park, Md.

63. Gardner, *Excellence*, p. 13; Charles Kadushin, *The American Intellectual Elite* (Boston: Little, Brown, 1974), p. 289; Ehrenreich, *Fear of Falling*, p. 59.

64. Jack Lyle, *The People Look at Public Television 1974* (Washington, D.C.: Corporation for Public Broadcasting, 1974), pp. 29–31, 37.

65. Quoted in Robert Blakely, "Rethinking the Dream: A Copernican View of Public Television," *NAEB Journal* 3 (1975): 32.

3. TV Viewing as Good Citizenship

1. Quoted in *Journal of the Committee on Media Integrity* Summer 1992, p. 1; the cartoon appeared on the cover of the June 1992 issue of FAIR's media watch newsletter *Extra!*. This chapter draws from my article "TV Viewing as Good Citizenship? Political Rationality, Enlightened Democracy and PBS," *Cultural Studies* 13 (January 1999): 62–90 (www.tanafico.uk).

2. DuPont-Columbia survey, quoted in "Hoked up Conspiracy," *New Republic*, July 22, 1972, p. 23; Public Broadcasting Service, *PBS on Record: The Public Service Programming October 1971–October 1972* (Washington, D.C.: Public Broadcasting Service, 1971), National Public Broadcasting Archive, College Park, Md.

3. Michael Tracey, *The Decline and Fall of Public Broadcasting* (New York: Oxford University Press, 1998); Graham Murdock, "Citizens, Consumers, and Public Culture," in *Media Cultures: Reappraising Transnational Media*, ed. Kim Christian Schroder and Michael Skovand (London: Routledge, 1992), p. 18; Ralph Engelman, *Public Radio and Television in America* (Thousand Oaks, Calif.: Sage, 1996), p. 39; Ien

Ang, *Desperately Seeking the Audience* (New York: Routledge, 1991). For studies that protest corporate underwriting against an idealized democratic alternative to the marketplace of ideas, see David Croteau, William Hoynes, and Kevin Caragee, "The Political Diversity of Public Television," *Journalism and Mass Communication Monographs* 157 (1996); and William Hoynes, *Public Television for Sale* (Boulder, Colo.: Westview Press, 1994). For a critique of the corporatization of U.S. public television, see James Ledbetter, *Made Possible by . . . the Death of Public Broadcasting in the United States* (New York: Verso, 1997).

4. Day Thorpe, "A Political Bonanza for Viewers," *Evening Star*, June 2, 1972, n.p., National Public Broadcasting Archive, PBS collection, program files, *The Advocates*, box 2.; Raymond Williams, *Communications* (London: Chatto & Windus, 1966); Tony Bennett, *The Birth of the Museum* (London: Routledge, 1995), p. 89.

5. Colin Gordon, "Governmental Rationality: An Introduction," in *The Foucault Effect: Studies in Governmentality*, ed. Graham Burchell, Colin Gordon, and Peter Miller (Chicago: University of Chicago Press, 1991), p. 3. See also Michel Foucault, "Governmentality," pp. 87–104, in the same volume.

6. Graham Burchell, "Liberal Government and the Techniques of the Self," in *Foucault and Political Reason: Liberalism, Neo-Liberalism and Rationalities of Government*, ed. Andrew Barry, Thomas Osborne, and Nikolas Rose (Chicago: University of Chicago Press), p. 19.

7. Theodore J. Lowi, *American Government: Incomplete Conquest* (Hinsdale, Ill.: Dryden Press, 1977), p. 45.

8. Bennett, *Birth of the Museum*, pp. 21, 24, 47, 89–91, 98. I took the term *political rationality* from Bennett's cultural analysis of the nineteenth-century public museum.

9. Toby Miller, *The Well-Tempered Self: Citizenship, Culture and the Postmodern Subject* (Baltimore: Johns Hopkins University Press, 1993), pp. 129–130, 136; Ang, *Desperately Seeking*, p. 21.

10. Representative Samuel N. Friedel, House Committee on Interstate and Foreign Commerce, *Public Television Act of 1967: Hearings on H.R. 6736*, 90th Cong., 1st sess., July 11–21, p. 103; Senate Report quoted in Jim Karayn, "In Defense of Public Television," *Wall Street Journal*, November 15, 1972, n.p., National Public Broadcasting Archive, PBS collection, NPACT, box 2; Johnson quoted in Miller, *The Well-Tempered Self*, p. 136; Robert Blakely, *The People's Instrument: Philosophy of Programming for Public Television* (Washington, D.C.: Public Affairs Press, 1971), p. 55.

11. Quoted in John W. Macy, *To Irrigate a Wasteland* (Berkeley and Los Angeles: University of California Press), p. 29; and in Miller, *The Well-Tempered Self*, p. 136.

12. Joan Shelley Rubin, *The Making of Middlebrow Culture* (Chapel Hill: University of North Carolina Press, 1992); Stanley Aronowitz, "Is a Democracy Possible? The Decline of the Public in the American Debate," in *The Phantom Public Sphere*, ed. Bruce Robbins (Minneapolis: University of Minnesota Press, 1993), pp. 75–83.

13. Garth Jowett, "The Emergence of the Mass Society: The Standardization of American Culture, 1830–1920," in *Prospects: The Annual of American Cultural Studies*, ed. Jack Salzman (New York: Burt Franklin, 1982), pp. 212, 218; John Kasson, *Amusing*

the Million: Coney Island at the Turn of the Century (New York: Hill & Wang, 1978), pp. 101–2. My understanding of this reform history also comes from John and Barbara Ehrenreich's important essay "The Professional-Managerial Class," in *Between Labor and Capital*, ed. Pat Walker (Boston: South End Press, 1979), pp. 5–48.

14. Aronowitz, "Is a Democracy Possible," pp. 78–80; Walter Lippmann, *Public Opinion* (New York: Macmillan, 1922).

15. Elihu Katz and Paul Lazarsfeld, *Personal Influence* (Glencoe, Ill.: Free Press, 1955), pp. 273, 276, 285–86.

16. Leo Cherne, "Biggest Question on TV Debates," *New York Times Magazine*, March 2, 1952, p. 14; Armand L. Hunter, "The Way to 1st-Class Educational Citizenship," *NAEB Journal*, July–August 1961, pp. 19–23; Ford Foundation, *Ford Foundation Activities in Noncommercial Broadcasting*, 1951–1975 (New York: Ford Foundation, 1980), p. 2; Newton Minow, "Our Common Goal: A Nationwide ETV System," *NAEB Journal*, January–February 1962, p. 9; John C. Schwarzwalder, "Educational Television and the Sense of Urgency," commencement address to the University of Minnesota, July 16, 1959, unpublished transcript, National Public Broadcasting Archive, College Park, Md.

17. "A Panel Speaks on Public Affairs Programming," *NAEB Journal*, January–February 1966, pp. 54–66; Harold Lasswell, "The Future of Public Affairs Programs," in Institute for Communication Research, *Educational Television: The Next Ten Years* (Stanford, Calif.: Institute for Communication Research, 1962), pp. 97–102; Wilbur Schramm, Jack Lyle, and Ithiel de Sola Pool, *The People Look at Educational Television: A Report of Nine Representative ETV Stations* (Stanford, Calif.: Stanford University Press, 1963), pp. 67–70.

18. Fred Friendly, *Due to Circumstances Beyond Our Control* (New York: Vintage, 1967); Harold Howe, "The Tenth Anniversary Program of KTCA," unpublished transcript, September 17, 1967, p. 13, National Public Broadcasting Archive, College Park, Md.

19. August Heckscher, "The Quality of American Culture," in President's Commission on National Goals, *Goals for Americans* (New York: Prentice-Hall, 1968), pp. 127–28; Patricia Aufderheide, "Public Television and the Public Sphere," *Critical Studies in Mass Communication* 8 (1991): 168–83; Stokely Carmichael, "Who Is Qualified?" in *Thoughts of the Young Radicals*, ed. *New Republic* (New York: Pitman, 1967), pp. 26–34; McGeorge Bundy, *The Strength of Government* (Cambridge, Mass.: Harvard University Press), pp. 85, 103–104; Douglass Cater, *Power in Washington* (New York: Random House, 1964), p. 253.

20. Carnegie Commission on Educational Television, *A Report for Action* (New York: Bantam, 1967), p. 18; Blakely, *The People's Instrument*, pp. 55–57, 175.

21. Quoted in "Committee for the National Friends of Public Television," unpublished proceedings, May 5, 1970, National Friends collection, box 2.

22. "Goals and Operating Principles of PBL," December 15, 1967, Av Westin papers, box 6, file 10; Murry Frymer, "He'll Put Meaning into a Test Tube," *Newsday*, August 15, 1967, n.p., Av Westin papers, box 8, file 11, *PBL* press clippings, Wisconsin State Historical Society, Madison.

23. NET, *PBL*, "The Whole World Is Watching," December 22, 1968, Library of Congress, Washington, D.C.; "Symposium on *PBL*," *Educational Broadcasting Review*, December 1967, pp. 70–71.

24. John W. Macy, "The Critics of Television: A Positive Answer," speech delivered to the National Press Club, January 15, 1970, rpt. in *Vital Speeches of the Day*, February 15, 1970, pp. 286–88.

25. Blakely, *The People's Instrument*, p. 115; Michael Harris, "TV's First Real Paper," *The Nation*, March 18, 1968, p. 377; Ford Foundation, "*Newsroom:* A Report," unpublished report, 1970; Corporation for Public Broadcasting, "*Newsroom:* An Audience Evaluation for KQED-TV," unpublished report, 1969, National Public Broadcasting Archive, College Park, Md.

26. John Hartley, *Popular Reality: Journalism, Modernity and Popular Culture* (New York: St. Martin's Press, 1996); Daniel Hallin, "The Passing of the 'High Modernism' of American Journalism," in *The Media & The Public*, ed. Casey Ripley Jr. (New York: H. W. Wilson, 1994), pp. 81–83.

27. Advertisement, *TV Guide*, December 16, 1971, p. A–29; Quoted in Jim Karayn, "In Defense of Public Television," *Wall Street Journal*, November 15, 1972, n.p, PBS collection, NPACT, box 2, National Public Broadcasting Archive, College Park, Md.; Robert MacNeil quoted in "Public Television: In the Balance," *Congressional Record*, February 5, 1973, p. E653, PBS Collection, NPACT, box 2, National Public Broadcasting Archive, College Park, Md.

28. Pierre Bourdieu, *Distinction: A Social Critique of the Judgment of Taste* (Cambridge, Mass.: Harvard University Press, 1984), pp. 444–45.

29. Lawrence Laurent, "Vanocur-MacNeil Start a New Kind of News," *Washington Post*, September 3, 1972, n.p.; Ron Dorfman, "Gelding Public TV," *Chicago Journalism Review*, April 1973, p. 3, PBS collection, NPACT, box 2; *Museum of Broadcasting Seminar: Wall Street Week in Review*, Museum of Television and Radio, New York; Norma Franklin, "This Week 1972," *Educational Broadcasting Review*, April 1972, p. 128.

30. Public Broadcasting Service, "PBS on Record: The Public Broadcasting Service Programming, October 1971–October 1972," unpublished report, p. 115, National Public Broadcasting Archive reference; Blakely, *People's Instrument*, p. 123.

31. Statistical Research Inc., "Public Broadcasting Audience Analysis," unpublished report, May 31, 1974, p. 15, National Public Broadcasting Archive, College Park, Md.

32. Blakely, *People's Instrument*, p. 165; Michael Schudson, *Discovering the News* (New York: Basic Books, 1978), pp. 7–8.

33. John Kasson, *Rudeness and Civility* (New York: Hill & Wang, 1990), p. 3; Jürgen Habermas, *The Structural Transformation of the Public Sphere* (Cambridge, Mass.: MIT Press, 1989); see Hoynes, *Public Television for Sale*, for a good example of the idealization I'm talking about. I have found the volume *The Phantom Public Sphere*, ed. Bruce Robins (Minneapolis: London, 1993), helpful for understanding the limitations and possibilities of the "public sphere." See especially Nancy Fraser's essay in this volume, "Rethinking the Public Sphere: A Contribution to the Critique of Actually Existing Democracy," pp. 1–32.

34. Aufderheide, "Public Television and the Public Sphere," p. 180; Peter Stally-brass and Allon White, *The Politics and Poetics of Transgression* (London: Methuen, 1986), quoted in Bennett, *Birth of the Museum*, p. 27.

35. Aronowitz, "Is a Democracy Possible?" p. 90.

36. Blakely, *People's Instrument*, p. 90; Macy, "The Critics of Television," p. 286; Todd Gitlin, *The Whole World Is Watching* (Berkeley and Los Angeles: University of California Press, 1980); "Farewell to Razzmatazz," *Newsweek*, August 21, 1972, p. 61.

37. Mobil promotion, PBS Collection, program files, *National Town Hall Meeting*, box 61, National Public Broadcasting Archive, College Park, Md.; "Transcript of Proceedings: Kettering Conference on Public Television Programming," pp. 25–28, June 1969, Wingspread, Wisconsin, unpublished report, p. 35, CPB collection, box 34, National Public Broadcasting Archive, College Park, Md.

38. Macy, "Critics of Television," p. 286.

39. "Final Report of WETA-TV, Channel 26" for Social and Rehabilitation Service, U.S. Department of Health, Education and Welfare, March 1970, pp. 37–38, James Karayn papers, series 1, box 1, file 2, National Public Broadcasting Archive, College Park, Md.

40. Quoted in "Symposium on *PBL*," p. 71.

41. Clarence Peterson, "Drug Series Starts Here with a Dud," *Chicago Tribune*, January 27, 1971, n.p., PBS collection, public information, press clippings 1971, box 8; PBS collection, program files, *The Turned-on Crisis*, box 74, National Public Broadcasting Archive, College Park, Md.

42. *The Turned-on Crisis* (1971), Library of Congress, Washington, D.C.

43. *VD Blues* (1972), Museum of Television and Radio, New York; Henry S. Resnik, "Putting VD on Public TV," *Saturday Review of Education*, October 14, 1972, pp. 33–38; PBS collection, program files, *VD Blues*, box 76, National Public Broadcasting Archive, College Park, Md.; "VD Blues," *Educational Broadcasting Review*, December 1972, pp. 447–50.

44. PBS Collection, program files, *The Just Generation*, box 49, National Public Broadcasting Archive, College Park, Md.

45. *The Advocates* (1970–74), Museum of Television and Radio, New York. My analysis is based on archived episodes as well as detailed program summaries and guest lists, publicity, materials sent to public officials and the media, and newspaper and magazine reviews collected in the unpublished report "The Critics Respond to *The Advocates*." Quotations are from materials collected in PBS program files, *The Advocates*, boxes 1 and 2.

46. Blakely, *The People's Instrument*, p. 171.

47. "Advocates Define Their Terms," *Image*, WNET-TV, May 2, 1971, n.p., WNET collection, program files, box 4, National Public Broadcasting Archive, College Park, Md.

48. Percy Shain, "Hot TV Debate on *Advocates* Debut," *Boston Globe*, October 13, 1970, n.p., PBS collection, program files, *The Advocates*, box 1, National Public Broadcasting Archive, College Park, Md.

49. Michael Harrington, "The Mystical Militants," in *Thoughts of the Young Radicals*, p. 68.

50. John and Barbara Ehrenreich, "The Professional Middle Class."

51. Max Gunther, "The Thinking Man's Fight of the Week," *TV Guide*, April 14, 1973, pp. 7–10.

52. "Television Review," *Alhambra California Post*, October 5, 1970, n.p., PBS collection, program files, *The Advocates*, box 1, National Public Broadcasting Archive, College Park, Md.

53. Gunther, "Thinking Man's Fight," p. 7.

54. Richard J. Meyer, "ETV and the Ghetto," *Educational Broadcasting Review*, August 1968, pp. 19–24; Bird, *The Color of Truth* (New York: Simon & Schuster, 1998), pp. 377–78; Ed Dowling, "Color Us Black" *New Republic*, June 8, 1968, p. 13.

55. *Black Journal*, Museum of Television and Radio, New York, and Library of Congress, Washington, D.C.; PBS collection, program files, *Black Journal*, box 13, National Public Broadcasting Archive, College Park, Md.

56. "The New Black TV," *Ebony*, September 1969, p. 88.

57. St. Clair Bourne, "Bright Moments," *Independent Film and Video Monthly*, May 1988, pp. 10–13.

58. Karen G. Gray, "*Black Journal*: An Overview," *Educational Broadcasting Review*, April 1972, p. 231.

59. Jannette L. Dates, "Public Television," in *Split Image: African Americans in the Media*, ed. Janette L. Dates and William Barlow (Washington, D.C.: Howard University Press, 1990), p. 306.

60. Robert A. Carlson, "Reply to R. J. Blakley," *Educational Broadcasting Review* 6 (1972): 230–31; Gray, "*Black Journal*," p. 231; Jack Gould, "A Black Critic for a Black Show?" *New York Times*, October 11, 1970, n.p., PBS collection, program files, *Black Journal*, box 13, National Public Broadcasting Archive, College Park, Md.

61. Joel Dreyfuss, "Revamping *Black Journal*," *Washington Post*, January 11, 1975, n.p., PBS collection, program files, *Black Journal*, box 13, National Public Broadcasting Archive, College Park, Md.

62. Brown changed the name of the program to *Tony Brown's Journal*. After some years on commercial television, it is now shown on public television, in a low-budget interview format reminiscent of other PBS public affairs programs.

63. Publicity, PBS collection, program files, *Black Perspective on the News*, box 13, National Public Broadcasting Archive, College Park, Md.

64. PBS collection, Mary Aladj papers, viewer mail, box 1, National Public Broadcasting Archive, College Park, Md.

65. C. Edward Wotring and David J. LeRoy, "The Decline of the Watergate Audience," *Public Telecommunication Review* 2 (1974): 28–33; James E. Fletcher, "Commercial Versus Public Television Audiences: Public Activities and the Watergate Hearings," *Communication Quarterly* 25 (1977): 13–16; see also David Leroy, "Looking Back: The Audience for Impeachment," *Public Telecommunication Review* 3 (1975): 23–25.

66. Paul Duke, "Public Affairs: The Commitment We Need," *Public Telecommunications Review* 2 (1974): 24.

67. Lauer, Lalley & Associates, "Perceptions of Balance and Objectivity in Public Broadcasting," November 1993, unpublished report, Corporation for Public Broadcasting.

68. Karen Everhart Bedford, "Social Capital: Purpose or Just a Slogan?" *Current,* June 11, 2001, n.p.; David and Judith LeRoy, "By Human Nature: Fund Drives Should Initiate a Social Relationship," *Current,* March 26, 2001, n.p.; both articles are found online, *www.current.org.* For more on "social capital," see Robert Putnam, *Bowling Alone: The Collapse and Revival of American Community* (New York: Simon & Schuster, 2000).

69. Aronowitz, "Is a Democracy Possible," p. 77.

4. Something for Everyone

1. Robert Bianco, "New PBS President Defends Programming," *Pittsburgh Post-Gazette,* July 27, 1994, p. C9. Duggan has since resigned.

2. Tim O' Sullivan, "Pluralism/Liberal Pluralism," in *Key Concepts in Communication and Cultural Studies,* ed. Tim O' Sullivan et al. (London: Routledge, 1994), pp. 230–31.

3. Andrew Ross, *No Respect: Intellectuals and Popular Culture* (New York: Routledge, 1989), p. 55.

4. Stuart Hall, "The Rediscovery of 'Ideology': Return of the Repressed in Media Studies," in *Mass Media & Society,* ed. James Curran, Michael Gurevitch, and Janet Woollacott (London: Methuen, 1982), p. 59.

5. John Guillroy, *Cultural Capital: The Problem of Literary Canon Formation* (Chicago: University of Chicago Press, 1993), p. 14.

6. James R. Killian, House Committee on Interstate and Foreign Commerce, *Public Television Act of 1967: Hearings on 6736,* 90th Cong., 1st sess., July 11–21, 1967, pp. 123, 130, 148.

7. Hyman Goldin, *Hearings on H.R. 6736,* p. 149.

8. E. G. Eichholtz, *Hearings on H.R. 6736,* p. 113.

9. "Transcript of Proceedings: Kettering Conference on Public Television Programming," unpublished report, June 25–28, 1969, Wingspread, Wisconsin, p. 5, CPB collection, box 34, National Public Broadcasting Archive, College Park, Md.

10. Ibid., p. 131.

11. Quoted in "TV's Fourth Network Comes into Its Own," *U.S. News & World Report,* October 12, 1970, n.p., PBS collection, public information, press clippings 1970, box 8, National Public Broadcasting Archive, College Park, Md.

12. "Public Television . . . What Is It?" (Washington, D.C.: Public Broadcasting Service, 1970), PBS collection, Karen Aides papers, public information, box 1; Public Broadcasting Service, *PBS on Record: The Public Service Programming October 1971–October 1972* (Washington, D.C.: Public Broadcasting Service, 1971); PBS program guides inventory, National Public Broadcasting Archive, College Park, Md.

13. Dwight Newton, "A Boost for Black Pride," *San Francisco Examiner*, September 29, 1970, n.p., PBS collection, public information, press clippings 1970, box 8, National Public Broadcasting Archive, College Park, Md.

14. David Abrahamson, *Magazine Made America: The Cultural Transformation of the Postwar Periodical* (Cresskill, N.J.: Hampton Press, 1996), pp. 48–49.

15. Ford Foundation, "Profit Making Ventures and Public Television Stations: A Report to the Ford Foundation," unpublished report, November 1970, p. 16, National Public Broadcasting Archive, reference; Corporation for Public Broadcasting, "Auction and Underwriting Special," unpublished report, July 1972, CPB collection, box 53, National Public Broadcasting Archive, College Park, Md.

16. Marquis Childs, "TV Is Much More Than Distraction," *Washington Post*, December 1970, n.p., PBS collection, public information, press clippings 1970, box 8, National Public Broadcasting Archive, College Park, Md.

17. Minority Programs, editor's introduction, *Educational Broadcasting Review* 6 (1968): 271; Dave Berkman, "Minorities in Public Broadcasting," *Journal of Communication*, Summer 1980, pp. 179–88.

18. Herman Gray, *Watching Race: Television and the Struggle for Blackness* (Minneapolis: University of Minnesota Press, 1995); Gray also develops this critique in the film *Color Adjustment*, directed by Marlon Riggs (San Francisco: California Newsreel, 1991); "New Black TV," *Ebony*, September 1969, pp. 88–90.

19. Jacqueline Bobo, "The Politics of Interpretation: Black Critics, Filmmakers, Audiences," in *Black Popular Culture*, ed. Gina Dent (Seattle: Bay Press, 1992), p. 65.

20. St. Clair Bourne, "Bright Moments," *Independent Film and Video Monthly*, May 1988, pp. 10–13.

21. PBS collection, program guides, *Black Journal*, box 13, National Public Broadcasting Archive, College Park, Md; *Black Journal* (1969–1974), Museum of Television and Radio, New York and Library of Congress.

22. *Soul!* (1969–1972), Library of Congress, Washington, D.C., and Museum of Television and Radio, New York; PBS collection, program files, *Soul!*, box 70, National Public Broadcasting Archive, College Park, Md.

23. Martin Meyer, "Whatever Happened to Educational Television?" *Change*, March 1972, p. 50.

24. Michael Eric Dyson, *Material Witness: Race, Identity and the Politics of Gangsta Rap*, directed by Sut Jhally (Northampton, Mass.: Media Education Foundation, 1995).

25. Anita L. Washington, "*Soul!*" *Educational Broadcasting Review*, October 1972, p. 273.

26. Publicity and program descriptions, PBS Collection, program files, *On Being Black*, box 63, National Public Broadcasting Archive, College Park, Md.

27. "Soul Opera," *Newsweek*, February 22, 1970, p. 68; PBS Collection, program files, *Bird of the Iron Feather*, box 12, National Public Broadcasting Archive, College Park, Md; See *Color Adjustment* for a critique of the commercial "ghetto" sitcoms and their constraints.

28. "Soul Drama," *Time*, February 23, 1970, pp. 59–60.

29. "Public TV Going Places," *Parade*, November 1, 1970, n.p., PBS collection, public information, press clippings 1970, box 8;"Public Television Wants You," *Milwaukee Journal*, October 4, 1970, n.p., PBS collection, public information, press clippings 1970, box 8; "Burghardt, Roach on *Soul!*" *Amsterdam News*, October 30, 1971, n.p., PBS collection, program files, *Soul!*, box 70, National Public Broadcasting Archive, College Park, Md.

30. Jannette L. Dates, "Public Television," in *Split Image: African Americans in the Media*, ed. Janette L. Dates and William Barlow (Washington, D.C.: Howard University Press, 1990), p. 302.

31. "Transcript of Proceedings," p. 50.

32. Dave Berkman, "Minorities in Public Broadcasting," *Journal of Communication*, Summer 1980, pp. 179–88; National Analysts, "Attracting Minority Audiences to Public Television" (Washington, D.C.: Corporation for Public Broadcasting, 1981), p. 22; Public Broadcasting Service, "You Belong to Us, We Belong to You," undated memo, PBS collection, public information conference, June 1975, box 1.

33. Quoted in John A. Andrew III, *Lyndon Johnson and the Great Society* (Chicago: Ivan R. Dee, 1998), p. 51.

34. Stuart Hall, "What Is This 'Black' in Black Popular Culture?" in *Black Popular Culture*, ed. Gina Dent (Seattle: Bay Press, 1992), p. 25.

35. Pierre Bourdieu, *Distinction: A Social Critique of the Judgment of Taste* (Cambridge, Mass.: Harvard University Press, 1984), p. 445.

36. Richard Dyer, "White," *Screen* 28 (1988): 45–46.

37. *The French Chef* (1963–1973), Museum of Television and Radio, New York; PBS collection, program files, *The French Chef*, box 38, National Public Broadcasting Archive, College Park, Md.

38. Charles Kadushin, *The American Intellectual Elite* (Boston: Little, Brown, 1974), pp. 283–84.

39. "Vulnerable Civilizations," *Rutland Herald*, October 9, 1970, n.p., PBS collection, program files, *Civilisation*, box 22, National Public Broadcasting Archive, College Park, Md.

40. Erik Barnouw, *The Sponsor: Notes on a Modern Potentate* (New York: Oxford University Press, 1978), pp. 66–67; Laurence Jarvik, "PBS and the Politics of Quality: Mobil Oil's Masterpiece Theatre," *Historical Journal of Film, Radio and Television* 3 (1992): pp. 253–74.

41. Ross, *No Respect*, p. 63.

42. *The Forsyte Saga* (1969), Museum of Television and Radio, New York; *Forsyte Saga* program descriptions, Museum of Television and Radio Catalog; PBS collection, program files, *The Forsyte Saga*, box 38, National Public Broadcasting Archive, College Park, Md.

43. "Talk of the Town," *New Yorker*, January 10, 1970, pp. 15–17.

44. Ross, *No Respect*, p. 60

45. John W. Macy, *To Irrigate a Wasteland* (Berkeley and Los Angeles: University of California Press, 1974), p. 58.

46. Sedulus, "Television: Forward with *Forsyte*," *New Republic*, November 1970, n.p., PBS collection, program files, *The Forsyte Saga*, box 38, National Public Broadcasting Archive, College Park, Md.

47. Macy, *To Irrigate a Wasteland*, p.58; "The Public Season, *Time*, October 18, 1971, p 78; C. J. Screen, "Sound Idea," *Seattle Daily Times*, October 6, 1969, n.p., PBS collection, public information, press clippings 1970, box 8, National Public Broadcasting Archive, College Park, Md.

48. Herb Schmertz, *Goodbye to the Low Profile* (Boston: Little, Brown, 1986), p. 225.

49. Bourdieu, *Distinction*; *Masterpiece Theatre* (1971), Museum of Television and Radio, New York; PBS collection, program guides, *Masterpiece Theatre*, box 55, National Public Broadcasting Archive, College Park, Md.

50. Museum of Broadcasting Seminar Series: *Masterpiece Theatre*, 15 Years of Excellence, parts 1 and 2, January 21, 1986, Museum of Television and Radio, New York; "A Sparkling Start for *Masterpiece Theatre*," *Philadelphia Inquirer*, January 11, 1971, n.p., PBS collection, program guides, *Masterpiece Theatre*, box 55;. Terrence O'Flaherty, "The Thunder of History Marks PTV Schedule," *Baltimore Sun*, September 5, 1971, n.p.; Terrence O'Flaherty, "English Court Opulent Setting for Series," *Dallas Morning News*, January 10, 1971, n.p.; Betty Utterback, "A Fiery, Romantic Tale," *Rochester Statesman*, January 9, 1971, n.p., PBS collection, program files, *Masterpiece Theatre*, box 55, National Public Broadcasting Archive, College Park, Md.

51. Arthur Burgess, "Seen Any Good Galsworthy Lately?" *New York Times Magazine*, November 16, 1969, p. 57; Michael Arlen, "The Air," *New Yorker*, March 24, 1975, pp. 76–83.

52. Schmertz, *Goodbye to the Low Profile*, p. 226; Museum of Broadcasting, Seminar Series, *Masterpiece Theatre*.

53. Timothy Brennan argues that the program's success was attributable less to its popularizing tactics or its snobbery than to the larger appeals of cultural colonization, which he defines as an "attempt to fuse together the apparently incompatible national myths of England and the United States in order to strengthen imperial attitudes in an era of European and North American decline." Looking at *Masterpiece Theatre*'s shift to the use of original screenplays as opposed to literary "classics" exclusively, he suggests that its central message involves the promotion of British and North American unity. While Brennan considerably downplays *Masterpiece Theatre*'s relationship to whiteness and class difference within the United States, I agree that the program promoted Anglo superiority, a consequence he attributes to global power inequities as much as to local ones. See Timothy Brennan, "*Masterpiece Theatre* and the Uses of Tradition," in *American Media and Mass Culture: Left Perspectives*, ed. Donald Lazere (Berkeley and Los Angeles: University of California Press, 1987), pp. 373–83.

54. Tom Shales, Television Review, *Washington Post*, October 14, 1976, n.p., PBS collection, program files, *Masterpiece Theatre*, box 55, National Public Broadcasting Archive, College Park, Md.

55. "Hoving Committee," *Television Digest*, Sept. 30, 1969, n.p.; National Citizens Committee for Public Television, mission statements and press releases, Scott Fletcher Papers, series 2, subseries 3, box 6, file 6, National Public Broadcasting

Archive, College Park, Md; Ralph Engleman, *Public Radio and Television in America* (Thousand Oaks, Calif.: Sage, 1996), p. 176; Willard Rowland, "Public Involvement: The Anatomy of a Myth," in *The Future of Public Broadcasting,* ed. Douglass Cater and Michael J. Nyham (New York: Praeger, 1976), p. 116.

56. "Report to National Friends of Public Television on Station Membership Procedures, KQED-San Francisco," 1970, unpublished report, National Friends of Public Broadcasting, box 1, National Public Broadcasting Archive, College Park, Md; Willard D. Rowland, "Tension Among Friends: Dilemmas Facing the Volunteer Movement in Public Broadcasting," *Public Telecommunications Review* 4 (1976): 24–28.

57. Unpublished remarks of Ward B. Chamberlin Jr., executive vice-president, National Friends of Public Broadcasting, first annual conference, Waldorf Astoria Hotel, May 4–6, 1970, National Friends collection, box 1, National Public Broadcasting Archive, College Park, Md.

58. Minutes of Planning Meeting for a National Friends of Public Television, May 12, 1969, National Friends collection, box 2, National Public Broadcasting Archive, College Park, Md.

59. Letter, PBS collection, Mary Aladj papers, viewer mail, box 1, National Public Broadcasting Archive, College Park, Md.

60. National Friends of Public Broadcasting Statement of Purpose, n.d., National Friends of Public Broadcasting collection, box 1, National Public Broadcasting Archive, College Park, Md.

61. "Carnegie Corporation to Fund National Friends," press release, October 30, 1970, National Friends collection, box 1, National Public Broadcasting Archive, College Park, Md.

62. Quoted in *National Friends of Public Television Newsletter,* March 1–2, 1970, National Friends of Public Broadcasting collection, box 1, National Public Broadcasting Archive, College Park, Md.

63. Untitled memo, June 27, 1971, PBS collection, public information, Promotions and Fund Raising Conference, box 1, National Public Broadcasting Archive, College Park, Md.

64. Dede Compagno, "This 'Most Pervasive Medium,'" *Image,* March 1971, pp. 4–8, April 1971, pp. 10–12, and June 1971, pp. 10–13, WNET collection, program guides, box 4, National Public Broadcasting Archive, College Park, Md.

65. Alvin Toffler, *The Culture Consumers, A Study of Art and Affluence in America* (New York: St. Martin's Press, 1964), p. 167.

66. "News from the Friends of Channel 13," *Image,* February 1970, p. 20, WNET collection, program guides, box 4, National Public Broadcasting Archive, College Park, Md.

67. Public Broadcasting Service, "They Got It Together: A Collection of 100 Outstanding Public Television Promotion Ideas," unpublished report, PBS collection, public information, box 7, National Public Broadcasting Archive, College Park, Md.

68. Bourdieu, *Distinction,* pp. 71–72.

69. Advertisement, *Image,* December 1970, n.p., WNET collection, program guides, box 4, National Public Broadcasting Archive, College Park, Md.

70. "TV Made Book Best Seller," *Miami Herald*, January 27, 1971, n.p., PBS collection, program files, *Civilisation*, box 22, National Public Broadcasting Archive, College Park, Md.

71. Advertisement, n.d., PBS collection, Mary Aladj papers, box 1, National Public Broadcasting Archive, College Park, Md.

72. "PTV's Biggest Bake Sale Yet," *Broadcasting*, October 21, 1974, p. 36.

73. Mimi White, *Tele-Advising: Therapeutic Discourse in American Television* (Chapel Hill: University of North Carolina Press, 1992).

74. "Get a Piece of the Auction," press release, WTVS Detroit, n.p., CPB collection, auction announcements, box 53, National Public Broadcasting Archive, College Park, Md.

75. Station Independence Project, "Auction" (1974–1975), videotape collection, National Public Broadcasting Archive, College Park, Md.

76. Sally Bedell, "Why Public Television Keeps Rattling Its Cup," *TV Guide*, February 11, 1978, pp. 24–29.

77. Ien Ang, "Understanding Television Audiencehood," in *Television: The Critical View*, ed. Horace Newcomb (New York: Oxford University Press, 1994), p. 368; William Hoynes, *Public Television for Sale: Media, the Market, and the Public Sphere* (Boulder, Colo.: Westview Press, 1994); Willard D. Rowland and Michael Tracy, "Worldwide Challenges to Public Service Broadcasting," *Journal of Communication* 40 (1990): 8–27.

78. Arlen, "The Air," p. 80; Dates, "Public Television," p. 316; John O'Conner, "Does WNET Cater Only to Rich White Intellectuals?" *Public Telecommunications Review* 3 (1975): 38–39.

79. The multiple "taste cultures" advocated by Herbert Gans is a prime example of pluralist ideology's conflation of difference with power. Gans provided an early critique of the mass culture debate and the presumed superiority of high culture on which it hinges. Recognizing the policy implications of his work, he charted the parameters of a pluralist alternative in which cultural differences were recognized and valued. Gans did not address the close relationship between taste and power, and he did not question whiteness and upper-middle class privilege as the normalized center from which "other" taste cultures must be recognized and accepted. While he rejected the paternalistic presumption that taste cultures outside this center require "uplift," Gans's model left fundamental inequities of cultural power intact. See Herbert Gans, *Popular Culture and High Culture* (New York: Basic Books, 1974).

5. Radicalizing Middle America

1. Stuart Hall, *The Hard Road to Renewal* (London: Verso, 1990). For more on conservative authoritarian populism and public television, see Laurie Ouellette and Justin Lewis, "Moving Beyond the Vast Wasteland: Cultural Policy and Television in the U.S.," *Television and New Media* 1 (February 2000): 91–113.

2. See, in particular, Ralph Engelman, *Public Radio and Television in America* (Thousand Oaks, Calif.: Sage, 1996); and James Ledbetter, *Made Possible by . . . the Death of Public Broadcasting in the United States* (New York: Verso, 1997).

3. Michael Kazin, *The Populist Persuasion: An American History* (New York: Basic Books, 1995), pp. 252–53; "Assaulting the Aristocracy," *Wall Street Journal*, January 12, 1970, p. 12; Jeffrey Hart, "The New Class War," *National Review*, September 9, 1969, p. 896.

4. Benedict Anderson, *Imagined Communities* (London: Verso, 1998).

5. Kazin, *Populist Persuasion*, p. 253. My analysis draws from Kazin's thorough account of the political and cultural construction of Middle America.

6. Quoted in Fred Powledge, *Public Television: A Question of Survival* (Washington, D.C.: Public Affairs Press, 1972), p. 24.

7. John Walker Powell, *Channels of Learning: The Story of Educational Television* (Washington, D.C.: Public Affairs Press, 1962), p. 36; Jim Robertson, *TeleVisionaries* (Charlotte Harbor, Fla.: Tabby House Books, 1993), p. 178; John P. Witherspoon and Roselle Kovitz, "A Tribal Memory of Public Broadcasting," unpublished report, Corporation for Public Broadcasting, July 1986, pp. 163–65, National Public Broadcasting Archive, reference; Martin Meyer, "Whatever Happened to Educational Television?" *Change*, March 1972, p. 50.

8. Leonard Chazen, "The Price of Free TV," *Atlantic*, March 1969, p. 223; Dwight Newton, "Public Television," rprt. in KQED program guide, n.d., PBS collection, public information, press clippings 1972, box 8, National Public Broadcasting Archive, College Park, Md.

9. Edith Efron, "Boston: Home of the Bean, the Cod and WGBH," *TV Guide*, December 18, 1971, p. 40.

10. Hugh Kenner, "Lingering Tastemakers," *National Review*, November 30, 1965, p. 1098; MacDonald, who wrote for the *New Yorker*, spells out his position in Dwight MacDonald, "A Theory of Mass Culture," in *Mass Culture: The Popular Arts in America*, ed. Bernard Rosenberg and David Manning White (Glencoe, Ill.: Free Press, 1957), pp. 59–73.

11. Hart, "The New Class War," p. 896.

12. White House memo from Alvin Snyder to Peter Flanigan, November 22, 1971, Ralph Rogers Papers, series 1, box 2, White House Office of Telecommunication Policy, National Public Broadcasting Archive, College Park, Md. My analysis of the Office of Telecommunication Policy draws details from memoranda contained in this collection as well as declassified documents summarized in U.S. National Telecommunications and Information Administration, *Nixon Administration Public Broadcasting Papers 1969–1974* (Washington, D.C.: National Association of Educational Broadcasters, 1979). Some details are drawn from Richard Stone, *Nixon and the Politics of Public Television* (New York: Garland, 1975); and Powledge, *Public Television*.

13. Richard K. Doan, "Public Television: Is Anybody Watching?" *TV Guide*, August 21, 1971, p. 5.

14. Memo to the president from Clay Whitehead, September 28, 1971, Ralph Rogers Papers, series 1, box 2, White House Office of Telecommunication Policy, National Public Broadcasting Archive, College Park, Md.

15. Pierre Bourdieu, *Distinction: A Social Critique of the Judgment of Taste* (Cambridge, Mass.: Harvard University Press, 1984), p. 124.

16. U.S. National Telecommunications and Information Administration, *Nixon Papers*, pp. 32–33; memo to Clay Whitehead from Peter Flanigan, October 7, 1970, and memo to Pat Buchanan from Clay Whitehead, May 17, 1972, Ralph Rogers Papers, series 1, box 2, White House Office of Telecommunication Policy, National Public Broadcasting Archive, College Park, Md.

17. Margaret J. Wyszomirski, "Controversies in Arts Policymaking," in *Public Policy and the Arts*, ed. Kevin V. Mulcahy and C. Richard Swain (Boulder, Colo.: Westview Press, 1982) pp. 18–20; William Boddy, *Fifties Television: The Industry and Its Critics* (Champaign-Urbana: University of Illinois Press, 1990), pp. 99–101; Lynn Spigel, "High Culture in Low Places: Television and Modern Art, 1950–1970," in *Disiplinarity and Dissent in Cultural Studies*, ed. Cary Nelson and Dilip Parameshwar Gaonkar (New York: Routledge, 1996), pp. 313–46: Joseph Bensam and Bernard Rosenberg, *Mass, Class and Bureaucracy* (Englewood Cliffs, N.J.: Prentice-Hall, 1963), p. 346.

18. Memo to Clay Whitehead from Peter Flanigan, October 30, 1969, Ralph Rogers papers, series 1, box 2, White House Office of Telecommunication Policy, National Public Broadcasting Archive, College Park, Md.; Robert Pepper, *The Formation of the Public Broadcasting Service* (New York: Arno Press, 1979), pp. 113–17; U.S. National Telecommunications and Information Administration, *Nixon Papers*, p. 67.

19. Yorick Blumenfeld, "Public Broadcasting in Britain and America," *Editorial Research Reports*, October 25, 1972; "New Direction for Public TV," *Wall Street Journal*, October 24, 1972, pp. 810–11, PBS collection, public information, press clippings 1972, box 8, National Public Broadcasting Archive, College Park, Md.; advertisement, "We Can't Tolerate Government Control of TV," *New York Times*, October 3, 1972, PBS collection, Mary Aladji papers, Institutional Factbook, box 1, National Public Broadcasting Archive, College Park, Md.; WDAU-TV press release, PBS collection, public information, press clippings, 1972, box 8, National Public Broadcasting Archive, College Park, Md.; Letter to President Richard Nixon, January 24, 1973, PBS collection, Mary Aladji papers, viewer mail, box 1, National Public Broadcasting Archive, College Park, Md.

20. Lester Markel, "Will It Be Public or Private TV?" *New York Times Magazine*, rprt, n.d. 1972; Powledge, *Public Television*; cartoon, *Washington Post*, July 2, 1972, n.p., PBS collection, public information, press clippings 1972, box 8, National Public Broadcasting Archive, College Park, Md.; "Hoked up Conspiracy," *New Republic*, July 22, 1972, p. 23; the degradation of local public TV was also expressed in "The Nixon Network," *Newsweek*, January 1, 1973, p. 59.

21. Nina McCain, "Public Television in the U.S.: A Fuzzy Picture," *Boston Globe*, June 10, 1973, p. 9; Mort Young, "Who Really Controls Public Broadcasting," *Sunday Herald Traveler*, July 16, 1972, n.p.; Markel, "Will It Be Public or Private

TV?" PBS collection, public information, press clippings, 1972, box 8, National Public Broadcasting Archive, College Park, Md.; memo to Clay Whitehead from Henry Goldberg, February 22, 1972, Ralph Rogers Papers, series 1, box 2, White House Office of Telecommunication Policy, National Public Broadcasting Archive, College Park, Md.

22. PBS Commercials, 1973, PBS videotape collection, National Public Broadcasting Archive, College Park, Md.

23. James Ledbetter, *Made Possible By*.

24. Nicholas Johnson, "The Financing of Educational Broadcasting," in National Association of Educational Broadcasters, *Convention Report* (Washington, D.C.: National Association of Educational Broadcasters, 1968), pp. 13–14.

25. "Transcript of Proceedings: Kettering Conference on Public Television Programming," unpublished report, June 25–28, 1969, Wingspread, Wis., pp. 127–28, CPB collection, box 34, National Public Broadcasting Archive, College Park, Md.; Kai Bird, *Color of Truth: McGeorge Bundy and William Bundy* (New York: Simon & Schuster, 1998), p. 380.

26. "Assaulting the Aristocracy," p. 12; "Transcript of Proceedings," pp. 55, 96.

27. Willis quoted in "Museum of Broadcasting Seminar: *The Great American Dream Machine*," February 16, 1988, Museum of Television and Radio, New York; James Day, *The Vanishing Vision: The Inside Story of Public Television* (Berkeley and Los Angeles: University of California Press, 1995); NET, "The Red Myth" (1960) and NET, "Great Decisions" (1964), Library of Congress, Washington, D.C.

28. Robertson, *TeleVisionaries*, p. 144; Pepper, *Formation*, pp. 112–13; NET program descriptions, National Public Broadcasting Archive, College Park, Md.; *Who Invited Us* (1970), Library of Congress, Washington, D.C.; Ledbetter, *Made Possible By*, p. 45.

29. I'm referring to the general position outlined in Max Horkheimer and Theodor Adorno, "The Culture Industry: Enlightenment as Mass Deception," in their *The Dialectic of Enlightenment* (New York: Continuum, 1990), pp. 120–67; Todd Gitlin, *The Sixties: Years of Hope, Days of Rage* (New York: Bantam, 1993), p. 246; Herbert Marcuse, *One-Dimensional Man* (Boston: Beacon Press, 1969).

30. Av Westin quoted in "Museum of Radio and Television Seminar: Television 1968," January 1, 1998, Museum of Television and Radio; "Come What May from Affils, PBL Must Have Last Word," *Variety*, April 24, 1968, n.p., Av Westin papers, box 8, file 11, *PBL* press clippings, Wisconsin State Historical Society, Madison; Pepper, *Formation*, p. 45.

31. NET, *Public Broadcast Laboratory* (1968–1960), Museum of Television and Radio, New York; Av Westin papers, *PBL* program summaries, box 7, file 1, Wisconsin State Historical Society, Madison.

32. Bourdieu, *Distinction*; my analysis of *PBL* draws from archived episodes, publicity, and program summaries in PBS collection, NET program files, *Public Broadcast Laboratory*, box 21, National Public Broadcasting Archives, College Park, Md.

33. Ien Ang, "The Vicissitudes of Progressive Television," *New Formations* 2 (1987): 100.

34. Brian Winston, *Claiming the Real: The Griersonian Documentary and Its Legitimations* (London: British Film Institute, 1995), pp. 210–11.

35. John Schwarzwalder, "Symposium on *PBL*," *Educational Broadcasting Review*, December 1967, pp. 70–71; Bill Greeley, "PBL Folds Old School Tie," *Variety*, April 24, 1968, n.p., Av Westin papers, box 8, file 11, *PBL* press clippings, Wisconsin State Historical Society, Madison.

36. Winston, *Claiming the Real*, p. 40; NET, "Appalachia: Rich Land, Poor People" (1968), Museum of Television and Radio, New York.

37. NET, "Banks and the Poor" (1970), Museum of Television and Radio, New York; John Leonard, "Does Money Think You're Dead?" *Life*, November 6, 1970, n.p., CPB collection, "Banks and the Poor"controversy, box 69, National Public Broadcasting Archive, College Park, Md.

38. NET, "Factory" (1970), Museum of Television and Radio, New York; PBS collection, program files, "Realities," "Factory," box 68, National Public Broadcasting Archive, College Park, Md.

39. Barbara Ehrenreich critiques this stereotype in her "The Discovery of the Working Class," *Fear of Falling: The Inner Life of the Middle Class* (New York: HarperPerennial, 1990), pp. 97–143.

40. NET, *The Nader Report* (1970), Museum of Television and Radio, New York.

41. NET, *The Great American Dream Machine* (1970–1972), Museum of Television and Radio, New York and Library of Congress; PBS collection, program files, *The Great American Dream Machine*, box 40, National Public Broadcasting Archive, College Park, Md.; Day and Willis quoted in "Museum of Broadcasting Seminar: *The Great American Dream Machine*," February 16, 1988, Museum of Television and Radio, New York.

42. Stanley Frank, "The Brat Is Back," *TV Guide*, November 27, 1971, p. 26.

43. White House memo from Alvin Snyder to Peter Flanigan, November 22, 1971, Ralph Rogers Papers, series 1, box 2, White House Office of Telecommunication Policy, National Public Broadcasting Archive, College Park, Md.; "PBS, NET and the FBI," *Newsweek*, October 18, 1971, p. 127.

44. Ehrenreich, *Fear of Falling*, p. 130.

45. Ibid., pp. 131–32. For an overview of intellectual responses to popular and consumer culture and the class dimensions of their critique, see Andrew Ross, *No Respect: Intellectuals and Popular Culture* (New York: Routledge, 1989).

46. Frank, "The Brat Is Back," p. 28; Powledge, *Public Television*, p. 28.

47. Michael J. Conner, "Public TV Is Viewing Its Long Term Future with More Optimism," *Wall Street Journal*, August 23, 1974; Paul Duke, "Public Affairs: The Commitment We Need," *Public Telecommunications Review* 2 (1974): 27; James Day, *The Vanishing Vision* (Berkeley and Los Angeles: University of California Press, 1995), pp. 358–59.

48. Willard Rowland, "Public Involvement: The Anatomy of a Myth," in *The Future of Public Broadcasting*, ed. Douglass Cater and Michael J. Nyham (New York: Praeger, 1976), p. 114.

49. John Hartley, *Tele-ology* (London: Routledge, 1992), pp. 193–201.

50. Witherspoon and Kovitz, "A Tribal Memory of Public Broadcasting," pp. 157, 162; William Kenneth Cumming, *This Is Educational Television* (Ann Arbor, Mich.: Edwards Bros., 1954), pp. 37, 165.

51. Transcribed interview with John Schwarzwalder by Donald McNeil, January 6, 1992, National Public Broadcasting Archive, College Park, Md.

52. Irv Letofsky, "KTCA Founder Says Officials of U.S. Public TV Should Quit," *Minneapolis Tribune*, July 22, 1972, n.p., John Schwarzwalder papers, series 2, box 2, press clippings, KTCA, National Public Broadcasting Archive, College Park, Md.; John C. Schwarzwalder, "Public Broadcasting Must Clean House," *TV Guide*, September 30, 1972, pp. 6–9; John C. Schwarzwalder, "Educational Television: The Dream That Failed," *Educational and Industrial Television*, mimeo, n.d., National Public Broadcasting Archive, reference.

53. "'Money Matters' of Highschoolers to Feature New TV Channel," *Commercial West: The Magazine of Banking and Business*, September 14, 1957, p. 49, John Schwarzwalder papers, series 2, box 2, press clippings, National Public Broadcasting Archive, College Park, Md.; KTCA, *From Our Heritage* (1959–1960), Minnesota State Historical Society, St. Paul.

54. Quoted in *"The Great American Dream Machine," Educational Broadcasting Review*, April 1971, p. 58.

55. This list is based on KTCA's program guide *Scene* between January 1970 and December 1971, KTCA-TV, Minneapolis-St. Paul.

56. "Educational TV Flunking Here?" *Minneapolis Star*, February 2, 1967; "Let's Get All the Facts," *Minneapolis Star*, June 10, 1974; Irv Letofsky, "Fresh Trouble Brewing over KTCA Avoiding PBS," *Minneapolis Tribune*, June 7, 1974, p. 1B; Peter Vaughan, "KTCA May Be Premature in Its Self-Congratulations," *Minneapolis Star*, May 12, 1976, p. 4B; "Working Together for Better Public TV," *Minneapolis Tribune*, December 10, 1976, John Schwarzwalder papers, series 2, box 2, press clippings, National Public Broadcasting Archive, College Park, Md. Minneapolis-St. Paul Citizens League Committee on Realizing the Potential of Community Television, "Serving Diversity: A New Role for Channel 2," unpublished report, August 27, 1975, Richard Meyers papers, series 2 box 6, National Public Broadcasting Archive, College Park, Md.

57. "Channel 2," *Minneapolis Star*, November 27, 1979, n.p., John Schwarzwalder papers, series 2, box 2, press clippings, National Public Broadcasting Archive, College Park, Md.

58. Michael G. Reeves and Tom W. Hoffer, "The Safe, Cheap and Known: A Content Analysis of the First (1974) PBS Program Cooperative," *Journal of Broadcasting* 20 (1976): 549–65; "Public TV," *TV Guide*, September 7, 1974, p. 67.

59. Quotations describing the mission of the Independent Television Service come from the ITVS web site, *www.itvs.org*, and from Joel Engardio, "Might See TV," *SF Weekly*, October 20, 1999, n.p., available online at *www.sfweekly.com*.

60. Larry Daressa, "Television for a Change: To Help Us Change Ourselves," *Current*, February 12, 1996, p. 20.

61. Kevin Phillips, "Should Federal Money Support Public Television?" *TV Guide*, July 12, 1975, p. A7.

62. Patrick Buchanan, "Of Public TV, Public Affairs and Politics," *TV Guide*, May 15, 1976, p. A3.

Epilogue

1. Jim McGuigan, *Culture and the Public Sphere* (London: Routledge, 1996), p. 20.

2. Advertisement, *TV Guide*, August 9, 1997, back cover.

3. Advertisement, *TV Guide*, October 25, 1997, back cover.

4. Quoted in "TV Is Good," ABC-TV promotion, distributed in New York City.

5. Robert Avery, introduction to *Public Service Broadcasting in a Multichannel Environment*, ed. Robert Avery (New York: Longman, 1993), p. xiv.

6. Eileen Meehan, "Why We Don't Count: The Commodity Audience," in *Logics of Television*, ed. Patricia Mellencamp (Bloomington: Indiana University Press, 1990), pp. 117–37.

7. Justin Lewis, *Art, Culture and Enterprise* (London: Routledge, 1990) pp. 26–32.

8. Tony Bennett, "Useful Culture," *Cultural Studies* 6 (1992): 396.

9. Tony Bennett, *Culture: A Reformer's Science* (London: Sage, 1998), p. 61.

10. Nicholas Garnham, "Concepts of Culture: Public Policy and the Culture Industries," *Cultural Studies* 1 (1987): 34.

11. Ien Ang, *Desperately Seeking the Audience* (New York: Routledge, 1991), pp. 28–29.

12. Max Frankel, "PBS's Wheel of Fortune," *New York Times*, January 8, 1995, p. 16.

13. Michael Tracey, *The Decline and Fall of Public Broadcasting* (New York: Oxford University Press, 1998), p. 34. The "absolute" stance referred to here is critiqued by Ien Ang in "The Performance of the Sponge: Mass Communication Theory Enters the Postmodern World," in *The Media in Question: Popular Cultures and Public Interests*, ed. Kees Brants, Joke Hermes, and Liesbet van Zoonen (London: Sage, 1998), p. 81–83. To be fair, Tracey does critique U.S. public television's exceptionally upscale interpretation of public broadcasting.

14. Ien Ang, "The Vicissitudes of 'Progressive Television,'" *New Formations* 2 (1987): 93.

15. Ang, "The Performance of the Sponge," p. 82.

16. Ibid., p. 82.

17. Lewis, *Art, Culture and Enterprise*, pp. 50–86. See also Laurie Ouellette and Justin Lewis, "Moving Beyond the Vast Wasteland: Cultural Policy and Television in the U.S.," *Television and New Media* 1 (February 2000): 91–113.

18. Paulo Carpigano et al., "Chatter in the Age of Electronic Reproduction: Talk Television and the 'Public Mind,'" *Social Text* 25–26 (1990): 33–55; Jane Shattuc, *The Talking Cure* (New York: Routledge, 1997).

19. Gail Dines and Jean M. Humez, eds., *Gender, Race and Class in Media* (Thousand Oaks, Calif.: Sage, 1995); Justin Lewis, *The Ideological Octopus* (New

York: Routledge, 1991); Herman Gray, "Television, Black Americans and the American Dream," in *Television: The Critical View*, ed. Horace Newcomb (New York: Oxford University Press, 1994), pp. 176–87; E. Ann Kaplan, "Feminist Criticism and Television," in *Channels of Discourse, Reassembled*, ed. Robert C. Allen (Chapel Hill: University of North Carolina Press, 1992), pp. 247–83; Susan Douglas, *Where the Girls Are: Growing up Female with the Mass Media* (New York: Times Books, 1995); Ian Angus and Sut Jhally, eds., *Cultural Politics in Contemporary America* (New York: Routledge, 1989). Michele Hilmes traces this pattern to the development of commercial radio, showing how popular programming incorporated and reconstructed race, class, and gender biases. See her *Radio Voices: American Broadcasting, 1922–1952* (Minneapolis: University of Minnesota Press, 1997).

ABC-TV, 218–19

Abrahamson, David, 144–45

activism, 12, 101; black, 106, 122, 132, 148, 151, 153, 155, 156, 178, 180, 191; and ITVS, 212; on local stations, 208; and NET, 188; student, 106, 129–30, 143, 180, 201. *See also* political unrest

advertising: of ABC-TV, 218–19; and black programming, 151; of British dramas, 160–61; and citizenship, 113; and class, 65, 93; and consumerism, 71; control of audiences by, 84; and cultural fragmentation, 144–45; and *Dream Machine*, 196, 198; and mass audience, 26–27, 65; and membership culture, 169; niche, 66, 94, 146; of PBS, 217–18; on public television, 59, 62; to upscale audience, 92–97, 102, 145–46. *See also* commercialism; consumerism

advocacy, 10, 18, 20, 133, 134

The Advocates (TV series), 125–31, 137

aesthetics: of black programming, 133, 134, 148–49, 151; and cultural competencies, 190; of documentaries, 191–95; educational, 126; of empowered class, 139; and ITVS, 212; of leftist programming, 188–89; popular, 117, 124, 125, 151, 224; print-derivative, 19, 46, 106, 116–17, 118, 119; of public affairs programming, 115, 124, 125; of public sphere, 121; of *Sesame Street* vs. *Civilisation*, 98–99, 102

African Americans: activism of, 106, 122, 132, 148, 151, 153, 155, 156, 178, 180, 191; and authoritarian-populist discourse, 180; and Carnegie Commission, 52, 164; and commercial television, 56, 64, 135, 137, 152; cultural empowerment of, 223; culture of, 88–89, 90, 147–49, 153, 154; on *Dream Machine*, 200; and leftist programming, 188; on local stations, 208; on *PBL*, 122, 189; as PBS volunteers, 165–66; and personal and social development programming, 86–88, 89; programming for, 20, 56, 132–37, 143, 144, 146–53, 163; and *Sesame Street*, 81–82; tokenization of, 154, 167

The Age of Kings (TV series), 49, 92, 155
The Age of Overkill (TV series), 45
Agnew, Spiro, 177, 187, 199, 202
Ain't Supposed to Die a Natural Death (musical), 149–50
All-African People's Revolutionary Party, 132
All in the Family (TV series), 65
American Civil Liberties Union (ACLU), 184, 185
American Masterpiece (TV series), 224
American Mercury (magazine), 38
American Playhouse (TV series), 162
Anderson, Benedict, 177
The Andersonville Trial (televised play), 161
Ang, Ien, 25, 64, 172, 191, 226; on controlling the audience, 84, 107, 109; on European public television, 13–14, 16
Antiques Roadshow (TV series), 11, 170, 224
"Appalachia: Rich Land, Poor People" (TV program), 192–93, 195
Arendt, Hannah, 39
Arlen, Michael, 160, 161

Arnold, Matthew, 16, 17, 30, 43, 51, 70, 110
Aronowitz, Stanley, 110, 139
Atlantic Monthly (magazine), 36
audience: and ABC advertising campaign, 219; and advertising, 26–27, 65; and authoritarian-populist discourse, 179, 181; black, 134, 152–53; for British dramas, 157, 158–59, 163; building of PBS, 80, 164, 166; for cable and satellite television, 137, 145; and Carnegie Commission, 53, 211; and citizenship, 20; and class, 66, 103, 144–45, 162, 216; commodity, 35; as community, 167, 168; and consumerism, 119; contempt for, 34–35; control of, 14, 35, 84, 107, 109; cultivation of, 19, 39–41, 91, 103, 191; and cultural democracy, 37, 60; and culture wars, 216; and decline of cultural standards, 16; and democracy, 12–13, 110, 120; disadvantaged, 19; donations from, 92; for *Dream Machine*, 197; economic constraints of, 59; educated, 19, 35; elite minority, 53–55, 56, 62, 65–66; elitism of PBS, 118–19; and equality of opportunity, 77; for ETV, 46, 102; and excellence, 25; expected, for PBS, 4–5; feminized, 33, 80, 198; fictionalized, 57, 98, 99; fragmented, 53–54, 59, 80, 143, 144–45, 169, 219–20; idealized, 95; imagined, 102, 103, 138, 146, 147, 158–59, 163–69, 181, 190, 211, 219, 226; infantilization of, 32–33; as institutional creation, 53; for ITVS, 213; and leisure pursuits, 145; for local programming, 207; mass, 4, 16, 17, 19, 24, 25, 40–41, 55, 56, 59–60, 64, 65–66, 103, 136, 186, 192, 199, 220, 226; for *Masterpiece Theatre*, 162; maximization of, 18,

27, 32, 93, 109; and meritocracy, 77,
100–103; middle-class, 102–3; myth
of power of, 38; niche, 137; of
opinion leaders, 54, 110, 117–18, 119,
122; passive, 13; for *PBL*, 190; for
PBS, 5, 53–56, 103, 119, 131, 162, 171;
and PBS membership community,
163–69; and PBS promotion, 62–63,
218; and pluralism, 142–46; prime-
time, 80, 102; for public affairs
programming, 117–18, 130–31, 134;
and ratings, 33, 95, 101, 145; and
reform, 25, 64, 106, 118–19;
regulation of, 32; research on, 15,
64, 66, 102–3, 119, 145, 181; selective,
35, 59, 63–64, 66, 93, 95, 102–4, 136,
137, 145; for *Sesame Street*, 79, 84;
sovereignty of, 108–9; and
technology, 219–20; and TV
auctions, 170–71; and TV problem,
27, 116; underserved, 212, 214;
upper-middle-class, 54, 56, 66, 103,
119; upscale, 5, 92–97, 102, 145–46,
173, 179, 223; and "vast wasteland"
discourse, 64; viewing patterns of,
35, 37, 47; white, 5, 146, 147, 173
Aufderheide, Patricia, 12, 13, 113, 120
authoritarian-populist discourse: and
censorship, 184–85; and class, 177,
180, 183–84; and *Dream Machine*,
196, 199, 200, 202; and funding,
175–76; and ITVS, 213; and leftist
programming, 187; and local
stations, 181–82, 183, 205, 206; and
media debate, 177, 183–84; and
NET, 179, 181; and social
movements, 176–77
avant-garde, 189, 191, 226; on ITVS, 212,
213, 214; *vs.* popular entertainment,
183, 186
Avery, Robert, 24, 219

Bach to Bach (televised play), 197

Baez, Joan, 198
"Banks and the Poor" (TV program),
193, 194, 195
Baraka, Amiri (LeRoi Jones), 149, 191
"Basic Issues of Man" (TV program), 48
Baughman, James, 31, 34, 38
behavior, 130, 139; psychology of,
84, 85
Benjamin, Walter, 91, 99
Bennett, Tony, 121, 222; on
governmentality, 42–43, 107, 111,
125; on museums, 70, 108, 127; on
public culture, 16–17, 223
Bergman, Ingmar, 192
Bernstein, Leonard, 164
The Beverly Hillbillies (TV series), 2, 35,
65, 137
Bird of the Iron Feather (TV series),
150–51, 156, 162
The Black Frontier (TV series), 146
Black Horizons (TV series), 147
Black Journal (TV series), 132–35, 137,
144, 147–48, 151, 152, 223; on local
stations, 208; political content of,
133, 134, 180–81
Black Panthers, 132, 151, 155
Black Perspective on the News (TV
series), 135–37, 152
black power, 106, 122, 153, 156, 178, 180,
191. *See also* African Americans
Blakely, Robert, 114, 121, 127
Bobo, Jacqueline, 147
Boddy, William, 37, 182–83
Bonanza (TV series), 57
Book Beat (TV series), 144
Book of the Month Club, 70
Bourdieu, Pierre, 3, 16, 47, 117, 190; on
class, 53, 153, 158; on culture, 29, 75,
168; on geography, 182
*Bowling Alone: The Collapse and
Renewal of American Community*
(Putnam), 138, 139
Bristol Meyers Company, 92

British Broadcasting Corporation (BBC), 11, 14; audience for, 157, 158–59, 163; and class, 99, 163; and local programming, 210; and PBS fund-raising, 166; programming from, 49, 92, 141, 144, 155–63. See also *Civilisation*

broadcast reform discourse, 61, 64, 93, 218, 222; and citizenship, 112; and cultivation, 68; and democracy, 70, 111; and funding, 66, 92, 203, 204. *See also* reform

Brown, Les, 81, 159, 185

Brown, Tony, 134, 135

Brundson, Charlotte, 15

Buchanan, Pat, 177, 215

Buckley, William F., 185

Bundy, McGeorge, 23, 49–50, 59, 113, 180

Bush, George H. W., 6

Byrd, Robert, 8–9

cable and satellite television, 6, 68, 93, 103, 106, 220; and access for poor, 7–8; audience for, 137, 138, 145

Cancion de la Raza (TV series), 86

Can We Be Excellent and Equal Too? (Gardner), 73–74, 75

Can You Give the Public What It Wants? (Dale), 38

capitalism: and citizenship, 17, 109; and corporate liberalism, 50, 51; cultural contradictions of, 41, 70; and leftist programming, 186; liberal, 49, 50; and mass culture, 27, 30–31; and meritocracy, 100; and NET, 188; and personal and social development programming, 88, 90; and private control, 26; and productivity, 47–48, 71–72; and social problems, 193, 194

Carmichael, Stokely, 113, 133, 153, 154

Carnegie, Andrew, 51

Carnegie Commission on Educational Television, 18, 50–59; and African

Americans, 52, 164; on children's programming, 78; elitism of, 53, 54–56, 114; and imagined audience, 211; on localism, 182; and mass audience, 53; and pluralism, 141, 142, 164; report of, 55–59, 78

Carnegie Corporation, 18, 50, 51, 52, 79, 164

Carroll, Diahann, 135

Castro, Fidel, 188

Cater, Douglass, 53, 113

Chamberlin, Ward, 144, 165

Channels of Learning: The Story of Educational Television (Powell), 47

Chavez, Cesar, 188

Child, Julia, 154, 168, 185

children's programming, 4, 5, 6, 19, 78–84; and cultivation, 103, 104; and equality of opportunity, 76–77, 78; funding for, 9; multiculturalism of, 223; *vs.* prime-time programming, 97–99, 102. See also *Sesame Street*

Children's Television Workshop (CTW), 78–80

cinema verité, 189, 191–95, 213

citizenship, 10, 14, 18–20; and automobile, 113; and *Black Journal*, 134; in capitalist state, 17, 109; and civility, 120–21, 125–31; and cultural capital, 106, 117; and deviants, 122–25; and education, 109, 112, 114, 117, 121; and experiential knowledge, 120; and governmentality, 107–8; and public television bias, 138–39; as social construct, 108; viewing as, 11, 12, 13, 105–39

civil disobedience, 18, 106, 121. *See also* political unrest

Civil Disorders, National Commission on, 146

Civilisation (BBC documentary), 77, 91–99, 102, 144; companion book to, 168; culture in, 101, 154, 155; on local stations, 208; *vs. Sesame Street*, 97–99

civil rights movement, 75, 154, 180, 188, 201

Clark, Kenneth, 92, 96–99, 100, 101, 102, 155

class, 1–3; and advertising, 65, 96; and aesthetic hierarchies, 14; and audience fragmentation, 144–45; and authoritarian-populist discourse, 177, 180, 183–84; and behavior, 120–21, 127; and black programming, 150; and British dramas, 99, 161, 163; and Carnegie Commission, 53, 56; and children's programming, 102; in commercial television, 226; and consumerism, 72, 93–94; and cultivation, 103, 104; and culture, 29–30, 59, 71, 99, 141–46, 156, 220, 226; and democracy, 139, 226; denial of, 20, 28, 29, 94, 166, 171; and equality of opportunity, 19, 76–77; and heritage, 156, 158, 168, 171; and infantilization of audience, 33; on ITVS, 213–15; and journalistic hierarchies, 117; and leisure, 47–48; and local programming, 206, 207, 210, 211; and meritocracy, 72, 75, 100; normalization of privileged, 223; and PBS audience, 66, 69, 103, 221, 222; and PBS bias, 185; and PBS membership community, 164–66, 170–73; and personal and social development programming, 88; and popularity, 225; and prime-time audience, 102; and programming policy, 145, 226; and ratings, 36; on *Sesame Street*, 79–80, 83, 98–99; stereotyping of, 201–2; and taste cultures, 93, 170, 180, 182–83, 184, 218, 223; and upward mobility, 54–55, 69

class, lower-middle, 3, 177, 180, 196, 201. *See also* class, working

class, middle: and advertising, 93; anxieties of, 34; black, 134, 151, 152; and Cold War ideology, 28; and commercial television, 56; and confrontational TV, 122, 127–28; and cultivation, 104; and cultural fragmentation, 144–45; and cultural hierarchies, 29, 71, 101, 179–80; educated, 55, 73, 104; and expertise, 129; and ITVS, 213; and leisure, 48, 71–72; and meritocracy, 75; of Middle America, 181, 184; normalization of, 211; as opinion leaders, 112; as PBS audience, 102–3; and PBS programming, 128, 201; and personal and social development programming, 87, 89, 91; and producer values, 71–72; professional, 48, 54, 119; radicalization of, 181, 193; and self-culture, 69–70; and *Sesame Street*, 79, 81, 82, 83; stereotypes of, 202; upwardly mobile, 30, 99, 100; white, 104, 119

class, upper-middle, 2–3, 5, 7, 16; and advertising, 65, 93; and authoritarian-populist discourse, 177; and cable television, 220; and civil unrest, 84; in commercial television, 226; and corporate liberalism, 51; and cultural fragmentation, 144–45; as cultural hierarchies, 29–30, 71, 173–74; and culture industries, 226; and culture wars, 216; and ETV, 42; and expertise, 129; and ITVS, 212; and local programming, 210; normalization of, 167, 173–74; as opinion leaders, 111; and PBS advertising campaign, 218; as PBS audience, 54, 56, 66, 103, 119; and PBS membership, 164–66, 168; and PBS problem, 221; and PBS programming, 67; and personal and social

class, upper-middle *(continued)*
development programming, 87;
professional, 54, 65, 66, 71, 87, 93,
103, 111, 119, 129, 144–45, 164–66, 221,
226; as universal, 153; and "vast
wasteland," 33–34; white, male, 32,
137, 138, 139, 226

class, working: aestheticization of, 194;
and authoritarian-populist
discourse, 177, 180; and Carnegie
Commission, 52; and children's
programming, 102; and
commercial television, 34, 64, 119;
and consumerism, 189, 201–2; and
emotionality, 119; and leisure, 48;
and local programming, 206, 211;
marginalization of, 141; neutering
of, 189; and opinion leaders, 111;
and PBS programming, 194, 196,
197–200, 201; programming for,
144, 174, 226; and ratings, 36;
reform of, 110; resentment of, 202;
and self-culture, 70; and *Sesame
Street*, 80; stereotyping of, 201, 202;
tokenization of, 214

Cleaver, Eldridge, 148, 197
Cleaver, Kathleen, 134, 148
Cobb, Charlie, 88
Cold War, 28, 31, 44, 112, 188, 205
Cole, Robert, 201
commercialism: of commercial
television, 8, 63; and cultural
decline, 96–97, 98, 225; and cultural
justice, 220; and culture, 13, 22, 51,
92; and gender, 31; of mass culture,
9, 24; on PBS, 6–7, 10, 20, 21, 25,
176, 221, 222, 225; and popularity,
63, 64–65, 172; and private
ownership, 29, 31; and public affairs
programming, 225; and public
culture, 12, 172; and self-culture, 70;
and viewer funding, 169, 172–73
commercial television: advertising on,
94, 95, 96; and African Americans,

56, 135–37, 152; audience of, 55,
59–60, 65–66, 168, 220, 226; and
authoritarian-populist discourse,
184; and capitalism, 31; and
Carnegie Commission, 52, 53;
changes in, 65; and citizenship, 130;
consumer sovereignty on, 107;
control of, 34, 42, 113, 226; and crisis
in democracy, 108–9; criticism of,
24, 27, 61; cultural democracy of,
35–38, 106, 220; and cultural justice,
220–21; cultural power of, 37–38, 57,
219; defenders of, 58; economic
constraints on, 59; and education,
40, 73, 220; and elevated reform
logic, 39–40; genres in, 31, 32;
golden age of, 26, 29, 31, 49, 161; and
high culture, 98, 143, 183; *vs.* ITVS,
212; and leftist programming, 186;
and local stations, 182, 203; and
McCarthyism, 182; marketing of, 37,
93; pay, 53; *vs.* PBS, 4, 14, 50, 162,
196, 203; and PBS advertising
campaign, 218; pluralism on, 142;
policy on, 42; and popularity, 225;
profit motive of, 4, 60; public
affairs programming on, 115–16, 117,
118; regulation of, 32–33, 58, 109;
and socialization, 85; support of
public television by, 57; as "vast
wasteland," 7, 13, 17, 18, 23–24, 26,
27, 31, 32–34; and viewing habits, 47,
64; *vs. Sesame Street*, 80
Committee on Media Integrity, 105
Communications Act (1934), 26
communism, 45–46, 54, 75, 94, 96, 142,
182–83, 188
Communist Manifesto (Marx), 188
community: black, 165–66; and class,
170–73; imagined, 167, 168, 177; PBS
membership, 163–69, 170–73; and
social capital, 138, 139
Congress, U.S., 36, 109, 193; and *The
Advocates*, 125, 126, 130; and ETV,

46, 73; and ITVS, 212; and PBS
funding, 6, 9, 58–59, 67; and
pluralism, 142–43; and Public
Broadcasting Act, 50, 59, 175
conservatives: on *The Advocates*, 125,
126, 127, 131; and authoritarian-
populist discourse, 176, 177, 183;
backlash from, 187; and class
consciousness, 184; and cultivation,
68; on cultural democracy, 15; in
culture wars, 6–10, 20, 215–16; and
Dream Machine, 196, 201, 203; on
free market, 224; and funding for
culture, 182–83; on funding social
change, 180; and geographical
hierarchy, 185; and ITVS, 212, 213;
and leftist programming, 115, 193,
223; *vs.* liberals, 6–10, 13, 14, 106–7;
and local stations, 211; and Middle
America, 200; opposition to PBS
from, 14, 58, 66, 105, 118, 138, 217,
222; on privatization, 169, 172; in
working class, 194
consumerism: and citizenship, 113; and
class, 72, 93–94; and cultural
justice, 220; feminization of, 31;
and fund-raising, 20; and fun
morality, 27, 46; leftist rejection of,
194, 201–2; and local programming,
211; and mass culture, 28; passive,
33, 100; *vs.* political order, 17, 38,
109; and popularity, 173; and
producer values, 71; and public
television audience, 119; and radio,
26; socially acceptable, 30, 56; and
social mobility, 68; and TV
auctions, 170, 171–72; upscale,
171–72, 173; working-class, 189,
201–2
consumers, 4, 17; sovereignty of, 9–10,
107, 110, 226; stereotypes of, 198;
viewers as, 11, 12, 13
Contract with America, 7
Cooke, Alistair, 43, 158–59, 160, 162, 163

Cooney, Joan Ganz, 78, 79, 80, 81
corporate liberalism, 50–51, 57, 109, 119
corporate sponsors, 6–7, 12, 24, 107, 222;
and ETV, 43; and high culture, 120,
155; and ideology, 10–11; and ITVS,
212; and liberalism, 105–6; and local
programming, 206, 207, 210, 211;
and PBS programming, 92–97, 122,
161, 176, 196; and pluralism, 145–46;
public images of, 93; and *Sesame
Street*, 79, 83; and urban taste, 183
Corporation for Public Broadcasting
(CPB), 23, 85, 143; audience
research of, 66, 102–3, 119, 145, 152,
181; commercial donations to, 57;
creation of, 21, 59; funding from,
79, 122, 125, 136, 161, 195, 203; and
liberal bias, 138; and NET, 178; and
prohibition of entertainment, 61;
and racial crisis, 132, 152; underwriting guidelines of, 96
counterculture, 18, 101, 177, 189; and
class resentment, 201; and PBS
programming, 106, 143, 144, 178,
197; as social problem, 122–25. *See
also* the Left: New
Cousins, Norman, 31
Cousteau, Jacques, 211
CPB. *See* Corporation for Public
Broadcasting
Cuba, 188
cultivation, 18, 39–41, 44, 60, 67–104;
and ABC advertising campaign,
219; and cultural justice, 220; and
disciplinary logics, 103; and
funding, 103, 222; and leftist
programming, 186–87; and local
programming, 205, 206–7, 211; and
PBL, 192; self-, 100, 101; and *Sesame
Street*, 80–81, 102–3; and social
mobility, 68–69, 103, 104; *vs.*
structural inequalities, 103–4; and
"vast wasteland," 91. See also
Civilisation; self-improvement

cultural capital, 3, 22; and citizenship, 106, 117; and class, 30; and culture industries, 226; and meritocracy, 75; and PBS programming, 79, 99; of PBS volunteers, 165; and public television problem, 221; and social capital, 138–39; and upward mobility, 69

cultural competencies, 190, 191, 192, 193, 197, 198, 212

cultural policy, 10; and authoritarian-populist discourse, 186; and Carnegie Corporation, 51; and citizenship, 107, 109; and commercialism, 8, 13; and cultural reform, 16–17; in Europe, 104; and race, 90, 154, 155; and social hierarchies, 91, 174; and "vast wasteland" discourse, 24, 185

cultural relativism, 226

cultural standards, 16, 17, 29–30, 225

cultural studies, 14–18, 226–28

culture: accessibility of, 30–31; American, 28; black, 88–89, 90, 147, 148, 149, 153; and capitalism, 70; and class, 94, 120, 143–46, 153; commercialized, 22, 31, 51, 92, 108, 172, 216; corporate control of, 47, 149; and cultivation of disadvantaged, 68; and culture industries, 226–27; definitions of, 30–31; democratization of, 70, 77, 103, 108; differences of, 19, 22; European, 20, 98, 153–63, 168; experimentation with, 214; female volunteer, 164–66; folk, 208, 211, 226; fragmented, 53–54, 144–45; fund-raising, 20; vs. geographical origin, 204; hierarchies of, 5, 15, 29, 99, 190; high, 99, 101, 145, 163, 166, 179–80, 190, 197, 202, 204, 206–7, 210, 218, 226; homogenization of, 29; idealized tastes in, 42; intellectual, 45; and justice, 217–21, 222, 226; legitimated, 43, 75, 104, 143, 153–63,

182, 224, 226; and local programming, 206–7, 210; middle-class, 70–71, 77, 179–80, 191, 211; and normalization, 154–55, 156; and PBS advertising campaign, 218; and PBS bias, 185; PBS membership, 163–69; political, 108; popular, 12–15, 69, 108, 163, 223, 226–28; of poverty, 19, 81, 82, 83, 84, 86–87, 90; public, 9, 12–15, 16, 20, 172, 212, 221–24, 226–28; public vs. popular, 12, 13, 14–15; and race, 150; and radio, 26, 204; and rebellion, 101–2; reform of, 16–17, 111; and rejection of consumerism, 202; television, 4, 37, 42, 50, 62, 132, 142, 165, 218, 219–20; transmission of, 16–17; upper-middle-class, 99, 156, 226; and upward mobility, 69; white, 156, 158. See also counter-culture; mass culture; taste cultures

culture wars, 5–10, 16, 18, 20–22, 66, 69, 106; and authoritarian-populist discourse, 176, 180; and funding, 215–16; PBS's vulnerability to, 139, 186, 222; and public interest, 104; and Sesame Street, 78

Curtin, Michael, 29, 33, 44

Dale, Edgar, 38

Dallas (TV series), 157

Daressa, Larry, 214

Darknell, Frank, 51

Dates, Jeanette, 134, 152

Davis, Miles, 149

Day, James, 157, 187, 188, 195–96, 203

Day of Absence (televised play), 189

The Decline and Fall of Public Broadcasting (Tracey), 225–26

the Delfonics, 149

the Dells, 149

democracy, 11–14, 70, 216, 221; and commercial television, 9–10, 27, 58, 106, 220; crisis of, 107–10; and cultivation, 104; cultural, 15, 19,

35–41, 58, 60, 65, 104, 106, 203, 219, 220, 224, 226; and cultural standards, 17; and culture industries, 226; as defense of public television, 7–8; and education, 74; and elite audience, 119; "enlightened," 19, 121, 125, 138–39; and expertise, 106, 121, 129; and industrialism, 110; and ITVS, 212; and local station input, 203; and market forces, 14, 224; and mass audience, 24, 60; and media, 110–14; and meritocracy, 100; participatory, 107, 126; and personal and social development programming, 90, 91; and population growth, 110; and public affairs programming, 117, 131–37; radical, 101, 113, 131–37, 139; and ratings, 65; threats to, 17, 109, 120, 129; trickle-down approach to, 106; two-tier, 139; and urbanization, 110

Dewey, John, 110, 121

disadvantaged, 18, 19; cultivation of, 67–104. *See also* class, working; minorities; poverty

Disney Corporation, 3, 219, 227

diversity: cultural, 56–57, 62, 69, 132, 141–42, 204, 221, 226; ethnic, 141; and geography, 204; *vs.* normalization of whiteness, 141–42, 154–55; *vs.* popularity, 56–57; racial, 141–42, 154–55, 163

documentaries: cinema verité, 189, 191–95, 213; on local stations, 208; political, 12, 188; and popularity, 224; social-problem, 192–95

Dole, Bob, 215

"Dottie Gets Spanked" (TV program), 213

Douglass, Frederick, 135, 148, 150

Dream Machine. See Great American Dream Machine

Duggan, Ervin, 67, 141

Dyer, Richard, 153–54

Dyson, Michael Eric, 149

Ebony (magazine), 133, 145, 147, 148

economy: and class, 2, 145; and culture industries, 226; free-market, 6, 13, 15, 17, 44; and inequality, 190, 202; and popular culture, 9, 12, 13, 224; and public culture, 224; *vs.* public service, 11, 14. *See also* funding; poverty

Ed Sullivan (TV series), 192

education: and black programming, 132, 134, 148; and Carnegie Corporation, 51; and children's programming, 9, 78, 80–81; and citizenship, 109, 112, 114, 117, 121; and class, 1, 30, 93, 94, 119, 145; and commercial television, 40, 73, 220; and cultural fragmentation, 144–45; and debate on public television, 6, 7–8, 18; disciplinary approach to, 107; equality in, 74, 76; labor, 208; and leisure, 47; levels of, 48, 54, 72–73; liberal, 44; and local stations, 181, 182, 205, 206, 211; of mass audience, 16, 40–41; and museums, 108; Nixon's support for, 178; of opinion leaders, 16, 111; and PBS audience, 53–54, 66, 146; and PBS programming, 85, 98–99, 128; political, 136, 138; preschool, 78, 80–81; and prime-time audience, 102; public, 30, 54, 55, 75; and public affairs programming, 120–21; and race, 85, 132, 186–87; on radio, 70, 204, 211; and ratings, 36; and self-culture, 18, 70; and social mobility, 69, 75–76; and technology, 41, 81; universal, 110; and "vast wasteland," 34–35; vocational, 88, 132, 146, 206, 207, 211, 214, 215. *See also* cultivation; educational television; National Educational Television

Education, U.S. Department of, 41
educational television (ETV), 6, 19,
    41–50; audience for, 46, 102; and
    Carnegie Commission, 52; and
    citizenship, 112; and class, 42, 45, 71,
    72; and Congress, 46, 73; and early
    public television, 62, 68, 84; and
    Ford Foundation, 42–45, 48, 49, 50,
    112; and Friends of Public
    Broadcasting, 164; funding of, 41,
    43, 46, 73, 92; and government, 41,
    49, 50; and local stations, 20, 46,
    204, 206; and NET, 178–79, 189;
    paternalism of, 42–44;
    programming on, 48–49; as public
    service, 23; report on, 89, 132; and
    upscale marketing, 95; and "vast
    wasteland" discourse, 42, 49. *See
    also* National Educational
    Television
Educational Testing Service (ETS),
    80–81
effects: art of, 14, 17; of *Sesame Street*,
    80–81
Ehrenreich, Barbara, 48, 76, 93, 129,
    201–2
Ehrenreich, John, 129
Eisenhower, Dwight D., 28, 52
Eliot, T. S., 24
elites: and corporate liberalism, 51; as
    cultural center, 173–74; diploma,
    54; and ETV, 45; intellectual, 54, 55;
    leadership of, 113–14; male, white,
    educated, 137, 138, 139, 226; *vs.* mass
    culture, 1–5, 8, 9; and *Masterpiece
    Theatre*, 159, 162; and meritocracy,
    100; as minority, 53–55, 56, 62,
    65–66, 95, 146; paternalism of, 32;
    as PBS audience, 53–54; *vs.*
    pluralism, 141; political, 55; self-
    made, 71, 72
elitism: and ABC advertising campaign,
    218–19; and authoritarian-populist
    discourse, 180, 184; of Carnegie

Commission, 53, 54–56, 114;
    criticism of, 6, 7, 14; and
    cultivation, 60, 104; cultural, 2–3,
    21, 28, 54, 55, 118, 159, 175–76, 184,
    217–19, 225; and cultural demo-
    cracy, 36–37; and funding, 67; of
    ITVS, 213–15; leftist, 215–16; and
    local programming, 210, 211; and
    PBS advertising campaign, 217–18;
    vs. populism, 175–76; and
    privatization, 172; and public
    interest, 38; and *Sesame Street*, 78;
    of urban centers, 182–83; volunteer,
    164–66. *See also* class
Elizabeth R (TV series), 160
Ellison, Ralph, 52, 164, 165
the Enlightenment, 119–20
entertainment, popular: *vs.* avant-garde
    culture, 183, 186; in black
    programming, 135, 147, 148, 163; and
    British imports, 166; in children's
    programming, 223; on commercial
    television, 65; and consumerism,
    172–73; and cultivation, 69; as
    deviance, 131; *The Forsyte Saga* as,
    156–58; and fun morality, 27, 46; *vs.*
    high culture, 163; and ITVS, 212,
    214; *Masterpiece Theatre* as, 158–63;
    and Middle America, 177; and
    minority programming, 174; and
    personal and social development
    programming, 84, 87, 88, 89; and
    private funding, 169; *vs.*
    productivity, 71–72; prohibition of,
    61; and public affairs programming,
    116, 117, 124, 125; and reform, 111; on
    Sesame Street, 79–80, 81, 98–99; and
    televised live theater, 161–62
Ephron, Marshall, 198
equality: economic, 190, 202;
    educational, 76; *vs.* excellence, 102;
    lack of, 77, 103–4, 190, 202, 220, 221;
    social, 81, 98; structural, 103–4. *See
    also* democracy

equality of opportunity: in children's programming, 76–77, 78, 83, 100; and class, 19, 76–77; and cultivation, 68, 104; *vs.* egalitarianism, 75, 83; and meritocracy, 74, 100

ethnicity, 141, 144, 211. *See also* race

ETV. *See* educational television

"ETV and the Ghetto" (Meyer), 89, 132

Europe: aesthetic models from, 149; and American culture, 30–31; cultural influence of, 20, 98, 144, 153–63, 168; cultural policy in, 104; high culture of, 98; public television in, 13, 14, 16, 25, 107

excellence, 18, 22, 25, 31, 141, 221; cultivation of, 68, 74, 91; and culture industries, 226; definitions of, 66, 104; *vs.* equality, 102; and meritocracy, 77; *vs.* popularity, 58, 76–77, 226; professional, 133

experts: on *The Advocates*, 125–31; on *Black Journal*, 132, 134; on Carnegie Commission, 52; and culture wars, 106; and democracy, 19, 70, 106, 113, 121, 129; on *Dream Machine*, 196; *vs.* experiential knowledge, 129; female, 130, 132; and personal and social development programming, 87, 89, 91; and public affairs programming, 111, 114–25

"The Face of Russia" (documentary), 45

"Factory" (TV program), 194, 195

Fairness and Accuracy in Reporting (FAIR), 105–6, 118

Family Ties (TV series), 6

Federal Bureau of Investigation (FBI), 196–97

Federal Communications Commission (FCC), 29, 32–33, 41, 44

feminization: and consumerism, 31; of mass audience, 33, 38, 80, 198; of mass culture, 31, 59, 157, 198, 226

Feuer, Jane, 65

film, 32, 62, 71, 95, 189, 191–95, 213

Film Odyssey (TV series), 95

The First Churchills (TV series), 158–59, 160

Fischer, John, 39

Fiske, John, 94

Flacks, Richard, 51

Fletcher, C. Scott, 44, 52

Ford, Gerald, 121

Ford, Henry, 43–44

Ford Foundation, 18, 51, 181; and black programming, 151, 152; and ETV, 42–45, 48, 49, 50, 112; funding from, 79, 125, 136, 158, 161, 195, 196; and leftist programming, 188; and local programming, 205; and membership community, 164; and NET, 178; and PBS audience, 119, 145; and personal and social development programming, 86, 89; and public affairs programming, 114, 116, 136; and social problems, 113, 132, 177, 180, 186–87

The Forsyte Saga (TV series), 154, 155–58, 159, 160, 163, 166, 168

Foucault, Michel, 10, 14, 16, 42, 107

Frankel, Max, 8

Frankfurt school, 192

Frasier (TV series), 170

The French Chef (TV series), 144, 154–55, 168, 198, 208

Friendly, Fred, 60–61, 112–13, 114–15

From Our Heritage (TV series), 206

"From Wasteland to Oasis: A Quarter Century of Sterling Programming" (CPB report), 23

funding: and authoritarian-populist discourse, 175–76; and avoidance of controversy, 24–25; and Carnegie Commission report, 57–58; and class, 170–72; and commercialism, 172–73; from CPB, 21, 79, 122, 125, 136, 161, 195, 203;

funding *(continued)*
and cultivation, 103, 222; and
culture wars, 215–16; of ETV, 41, 43,
46, 73, 92; from Ford Foundation,
79, 125, 136, 158, 161, 195, 196; and
Gingrich, 1, 67, 69, 103; government, 1, 3–4, 6–7, 8, 9, 18, 41, 72–73;
for minority programming, 134,
146–47; and Nixon administration,
24, 136, 169, 183; and populism, 67;
private, 11, 66, 67, 169; and
prohibition of entertainment, 61;
for public affairs programming,
136, 137; and reform, 66, 92, 203,
204; taxes for, 57–58; viewer, 10,
163–73. *See also* corporate sponsors
fund-raising, 20, 66, 166, 168, 169,
170–72

Galbraith, John Kenneth, 93
Galsworthy, John, 155–56, 157, 159
Gardner, John, 52, 53, 60, 83, 92; on
Great Society values, 73–74, 75, 77,
91, 101
Garnham, Nicholas, 8, 11, 224
gender, 32, 33, 47, 117, 119; and Carnegie
Commission, 52, 53; and cultural
democracy, 220, 226. *See also*
feminization
geographical hierarchies, 182, 199–200,
204, 210, 217, 222
GI bill, 72
Gilligan's Island (TV series), 35
Gingrich, Newt, 4, 9, 21, 138, 178, 218,
225; and culture wars, 215; defenses
against, 68, 222; and funding, 1, 67,
69, 103; populism of, 7, 58, 175; on
public culture, 15
Giovanni, Nikki, 149
Gitlin, Todd, 72, 121, 189
Goals for America (1960), 28, 29
Godard, Jean-Luc, 191
Goldin, Hymin, 52, 143

Goldwater, Barry, 199
Gomer Pyle (TV series), 57
The Good Society (Lippmann), 49
Good Times (TV series), 151, 152
Gore, Al, 67, 78
Gould, Glenn, 190
Gould, Jack, 31, 33, 45, 58, 62, 122, 135
government: and Carnegie
Commission, 52; and citizenship,
107–8; and corporate liberalism, 51;
elites in, 113–14; and ETV, 41, 49,
50; funding from, 1, 3–4, 6–7, 8, 9,
18, 41, 72–73; and liberal capitalism,
49, 50; paternalism of, 16; policies
of, 42, 178, 180–81, 182, 183; and
public affairs programming, 122;
and social control, 19, 108–10
governmentality, 42–43, 70, 85, 125; and
citizenship, 107–11; and culture,
223–24
Graves, Robert, 160
Gray, Herman, 147
Great American Dream Machine (TV
series), 181, 195–203, 208, 211
"Great Decisions: America and
Communism" (TV program), 188
Great Performances (TV series), 162
Great Society, 7, 18, 22; and corporate
liberalism, 51; criticisms of, 129;
and cultivation, 67, 68, 72, 75, 76,
77, 91; and democracy, 40, 41, 101;
and education, 73, 74; and
founding of public television, 50,
52, 175; Nixon's support for, 178;
and PBS programming, 78, 88; and
public/private alliance, 92; and
public television problem, 221; and
selective audience, 95
Greaves, William, 133, 134, 152
The Green Berets (film), 177
Greene, Petey, 88
Grierson, John, 192
Groove Tube (theater group), 198

Grossman, Lawrence, 15
Guillroy, John, 142
Gunn, Hartford, 178, 193

Habermas, Jürgen, 120, 121
habitus (legitimated social space), 3, 30, 32, 197
Haizlip, Ellis, 148, 150
Hall, Stuart, 14, 30, 85, 142, 153, 176
Hallin, Daniel, 117
Hampshire, Susan, 158
Hard Copy (TV series), 226
Hard Times (Terkel), 202
Harley, William, 53, 76
Harper's (magazine), 145
Harrington, Michael, 129
Hartley, John, 32, 37, 53, 117, 204
Hayden, Casey, 76
Haynes, Todd, 213
Head Start, 75
Health, Education and Welfare, U.S. Department of (HEW), 18, 58, 74, 86, 87; and *Sesame Street*, 79, 83
Heckscher, August, 28, 29, 31
hegemony theory, 108
Hennock, Frieda, 73
Henry, William, 35, 40
Henson, Jim, 79
Heritage Foundation, 7
hierarchies: aesthetic, 14, 149; of citizenship, 130; cultural, 29–30, 32, 60, 71, 92, 101, 134, 138, 163, 173–74, 179–80, 201–2, 213, 222, 223, 226; geographical, 182, 183, 185, 210; within high culture, 190; journalistic, 117; of leadership, 111; power/knowledge, 16, 82, 108, 221; racial, 187; social, 91, 117, 138, 174; and women's movement, 130
Highway Beautification Act, 29
Hilmes, Michele, 26
Hispanics, 144, 173, 174, 188; Mexican American, 146, 152

Hobby, Oveta Culp, 52
Ho Chi Minh, 188
Hollywood, 32, 62, 71
Hollywood Television Theater (TV series), 161–62
Holt, John, 81
Home Shopping Network (HSN), 170
homosexuals, 124, 184, 186, 213
Hooker, John Lee, 133
Hooks, Benjamin, 173
Hoover, J. Edgar, 197
House, Lou, 133
Howe, Harold, 85
Howe, Howard, 113
Hoynes, William, 11, 172
"Huelga!" (TV program), 188
Humble Oil, 92, 155
Humphrey, Hubert, 85, 86, 88, 132
Hyde, Rosel, 60

I, Claudius (TV series), 160
identity, 53, 201; black, 147; and class, 3, 154; cultural, 61, 156, 168
I Dream of Jeannie (TV series), 137
I Love Lucy (TV series), 224
Image (magazine), 167–68, 179
immigrants, 110, 111
"In Common Brotherhood" (TV program), 188
Independent Television Service (ITVS), 12, 212–15, 216
individualism, 77, 130; competitive, 83, 92, 94, 102
"Industry on Parade" (TV program), 92
influentials, 92, 97, 119, 139, 155; primary, 19, 110, 111, 131
Institute for Communication Research (University of Illinois), 41
intellectuals, 71, 94, 177; conservative, 179–80; and ITVS, 212; leftist, 189, 192, 223; and *PBL*, 190, 191; urban, 197

Invitation to Art (TV series), 48–49
ITVS. *See* Independent Television
Service

Jackson, Jesse, 135
Jacobs, Paul, 196–97
James J. Hill Foundation, 205
Jefferson, Thomas, 110
The Jeffersons (TV series), 152
Job Man Caravan (TV series), 89–90, 91
Jobs 26 (TV series), 87–88
Johnson, Lady Bird, 29
Johnson, Lyndon B., 18, 49, 68, 77, 113;
    and Carnegie Commission, 52, 53;
    and education, 73, 74, 75–76; and
    Great Society programs, 175; and
    public television, 40, 57, 58, 109, 110
Johnson, Nicholas, 186, 192
Jones, LeRoi (Amiri Baraka), 149, 191
journalism, 114–15, 117, 118, 132. *See also*
    newspapers
Jowett, Garth, 71
Joyrich, Lynn, 31
Jude the Obscure (TV series), 160
Julia (TV series), 150
Just Generation (TV series), 124–25
justice, cultural, 217–21, 222, 226
"Justice and the Poor" (TV
    program), 188

Karayn, Jim, 117
Kasson, John, 71, 111, 120
Katz, Elihu, 111
KCET-Los Angeles, 45, 86, 179
Kennedy, John F., 29, 45, 49, 118
Kenner, Hugh, 180
Keppel, Francis, 40, 76
KERA-Dallas, 171
Kerner Commission, 132, 135
Kettering Foundation, 143
Killian, James, 52, 60, 141, 142
King, B. B., 149
King, Martin Luther, Jr., 87, 133,
    149, 190

Knight, Gladys, 149
knowledge: and black programming,
    132, 147; and class, 94; and
    cultivation, 68; democratization
    of, 108; experiential, 119–20, 129,
    130; hierarchies of, 16, 82, 108,
    221; legitimated, 121, 132; and
    meritocracy, 77; and power,
    142; social construction of,
    119–20
knowledge workers, 83
KOCE-Huntington Beach, 100
KQED-San Francisco, 179
KTCA-Minneapolis-St. Paul, 20,
    204–10, 211; attacks on, 208, 210;
    programs on, 209
KUHF-Houston, 205

labor, organized, 164
Lagemann, Ellen Condliffe, 51
Land Grant Act, 68
land-grant broadcasting, 20, 178–79,
    185, 203–11, 214
Latin America, 188
Lazarsfeld, Paul, 39, 111
Lears, Jackson, 27–28
Ledbetter, James, 10–11, 185–88
the Left: and authoritarian-populist
    discourse, 184; on commercialism,
    222, 225; and consumerism, 201–2;
    cultural, 212–15, 216; elitism of,
    215–16; intellectuals of, 189, 192,
    223; liberalism on, 215–16; and local
    programming, 205; New, 101, 129,
    178, 180, 189, 194, 196–97, 201;
    politics of, 182–84, 205; on public
    culture, 226; of urban centers,
    182–83
leftist programming, 186–95, 189,
    222, 223
leisure: and capitalism, 47–48; of elites,
    55, 56, 145; and ITVS, 212; passive
    vs. active, 47; and producer values,
    71–72; productive *vs.* unproductive,

34, 47–48, 71, 98, 218; and *Sesame Street*, 79
Lerner, Max, 45
Lewis, Justin, 3, 4, 13, 223, 226
Lewis, Oscar, 76, 86
liberalism: and ABC advertising campaign, 218–19; and authoritarian-populist discourse, 177, 184; and capitalism, 49, 50; and commercial television, 38; corporate, 50–51, 57, 109, 119; and corporate sponsors, 105–6; and cultivation, 104, 179–80, 187; and education, 44, 76; on entertainment, 172; left, 215–16; and local control, 182, 205; and mass culture, 22, 28; and media debate, 183–84; of Minow, 29; of PBS programming, 78, 81, 91, 105, 115, 118, 125–27, 131, 138, 183, 197, 201, 203; and PBS's imagined audience, 181; *vs.* populism, 175–76, 185; and public television problem, 221; and reform, 110; and social activism, 180; and social control, 139. *See also* the Left
liberals: arrogance of, 201–2; on auctions, 170; *vs.* conservatives, 6–10, 13, 14, 106–7; and Middle America, 177, 181, 187; paternalism of, 14; and private funding, 169; and public ownership, 31
libraries, public, 51
Life (magazine), 144, 193
Limbaugh, Rush, 15
Lippmann, Walter, 49, 57, 115, 120, 128; elevated reform logic of, 39–40, 41; on popular democracy, 111; on public service, 23, 50, 59
local television stations: and authoritarian-populist discourse, 181–82, 183, 205, 206; and censorship, 185; and cultivation, 205, 206–7, 211; and education, 181,

182, 205, 206, 211; and ETV, 20, 46, 204, 206; input from, 182, 203–4, 205, 211; land-grant approach of, 178–79, 185, 203–11; PBS programming on, 84, 189, 192, 196, 208; and upscale marketing, 95
Locard, Jon, 147
Loevinger, Lee, 58
Lowell, Ralph, 52
Lyle, Jack, 102
Lynes, Russell, 93

McCarthyism, 182
McChesney, Robert, 26
MacDonald, Dwight, 43, 71, 180
McDonald, Jimmy, 136
MacDonald, Torbert, 59
McDonnell, Joseph, 58
McGuigan, Jim, 16–17
Machlup, Fritz, 73
McLean, Don, 181
MacNeil, Robert, 115, 117
The MacNeil/Lehrer Report (*The NewsHour*; TV series), 105, 118, 138, 226
Macy, John, 73, 81, 97, 119, 121; on PBS programming, 155, 156, 157; on pluralism, 143, 144; on public affairs programming, 115–16, 120
Made Possible by...the Death of Public Broadcasting in the United States (Ledbetter), 10–11
Malcolm X, 149
Mao Tse-tung, 188
Marcuse, Herbert, 189
marginalization: and commercial television, 220; and cultivation, 104; and high culture, 224; of ITVS, 12, 212; of leftist programming, 186; of minorities, 20, 134, 141, 223; and prestige, 25; of public television, 15, 18, 139
Markel, Lester, 185
Marx, Karl, 54

Marxism, 94, 96
Mary Tyler Moore (TV series), 65
Mass, Class and Bureaucracy (Bensam and Rosenberg), 183
mass culture: and ABC advertising campaign, 219; anxieties about, 11, 17, 22, 23; and black programming, 134, 135, 151; and British dramas, 159–63; and cable television, 220; and capitalism, 27, 30–31; and Carnegie Commission report, 56; and *Civilisation*, 92, 98; commercialism of, 9, 24, 220; commodification of, 30; and communism, 45–46; cultivation of, 39, 44; and cultural justice, 220, 226; debate on, 27–28; and democracy, 110, 139; denigration of, 13, 23–24, 27, 192, 222; documentaries on, 224; on *Dream Machine*, 196, 197–200; *vs.* elite culture, 1–5, 8, 9; and emotionality, 119; feminized forms of, 31, 59, 157, 198, 226; ideology of, 25, 29, 61–62, 186, 225; and ITVS, 212, 213–14; and liberalism, 22, 28; and museums, 109; and pluralism, 142, 144; and public affairs programming, 117–18; *vs.* public culture, 16, 121, 226; *vs.* public television, 61–62, 63, 64, 66, 218; on *Sesame Street*, 98; and TV auctions, 170, 171. *See also* audience, mass
Mastering the Art of French Cooking (Child), 168
Masterpiece Theatre (TV series), 8, 11, 93, 154, 173, 224; as high culture, 156, 158–63, 202; on local stations, 208
Maysles, Albert, 191
media: and authoritarian-populist discourse, 177, 183–84; and consumerism, 71; and democracy, 110–14; and political unrest, 106, 115, 132, 146; print, 61–65, 144–45; and reform, 106; on *Sesame Street*, 81; white, 151–52. *See also* commercial television; newspapers; public television
Meehan, Eileen, 220
Meet the Press (TV series), 118, 136
Mekas, Jonas, 191
Mendelsohn, Harold, 85–86
"Men of the Philharmonic" (TV program), 92
meritocracy: and class, 19, 72, 75, 100; and cultivation, 68; and education, 74; and personal and social development programming, 90; and public television audience, 77, 100–103; and *Sesame Street*, 79, 83
Mexican Americans, 146, 152
Middle America: civilizing of, 186–87, 188; on *Dream Machine*, 196, 199–200; and leftist programming, 186–87; and local programming, 210; *vs.* PBS, 176–86, 215; radicalizing of, 175–216; and social problems, 193, 208; *vs.* urban centers, 20, 182. *See also* class, middle; class, working
The Middle Americans (Cole), 201
Midwest Program in Airborne Television Instruction, 204
Mill, John Stuart, 110
Miller, Howard, 127
Miller, Toby, 17, 38, 109, 119
Mills, C. Wright, 113
Milton Berle (TV series), 47
minorities: and children's programming, 102; and commercial television, 34; and corporate liberalism, 51; cultural empowerment of, 223; elite cultural, 53–55, 56, 62, 65–66, 95, 146; on ITVS, 213; and local programming, 206; marginalization of, 20, 134, 141, 223;

Native-American, 144, 146, 208; and personal and social development programming, 84, 86; and pluralism, 142, 167; and political participation, 107; programming for, 134, 143, 144, 146–47, 163, 166, 173–74, 180–81, 226; on public affairs programming, 133; racial, 143, 144, 146, 152; tokenization of, 141, 152, 167; and Western European culture, 155. *See also* African Americans; Hispanics

Minow, Newton, 37, 40, 57, 93, 109; and ETV, 49, 112; and PBS, 106, 164; on "vast wasteland," 17, 23–27, 29–34, 38, 66, 73

Mr. Minority (unpublished memo), 153

Mobil Oil, 93, 121, 159, 162, 163; study guides from, 158, 160, 161

Money Matters (TV series), 206

Morgan, Joy Elmer, 70, 101

Morrison, Toni, 149

Moyers, Bill, 1, 4–5, 118

Muhammad, Elijah, 148

multiculturalism, 98, 153–54, 223, 226. *See also* diversity

Murdock, Graham, 107

Murrow, Edward R., 38, 39

Museum of Broadcasting (Museum of Television and Radio), 159

museums, 70, 108, 109, 127, 226

Nader, Ralph, 194–95

The Nader Report (TV series), 194–95

National Association for the Advancement of Colored People (NAACP), 148, 164

National Association of Manufacturers, 92

National Black Theater, 149

National Citizens Committee on Public Broadcasting, 164

National Defense in Education Act, 73

National Educational Television (NET), 45–50, 133; and authoritarian-populist discourse, 183, 184; documentaries from, 192–95; and *Dream Machine*, 195–203; education on, 188; and European high culture, 155; and ITVS, 212, 213; *vs.* land-grant local stations, 178–79, 203–11; leftist programming on, 187–89; and Nixon administration, 181, 182, 183

National Education Association, 78

National Endowments for the Arts and Humanities (NEH), 50

National Friends of Public Broadcasting, 164–66

National Geographic (TV series), 211

National Organization for Women (NOW), 164

National Program Service, 21

National Public Affairs Center for Television (NPACT), 116–17, 118, 137

National Review (magazine), 179–80

Native Americans, 144, 146, 208

NET. *See* National Educational Television

NET Journal (TV series), 133

"NET Journal: Inside North Vietnam" (TV program), 188

New Frontier, 45

New Republic (magazine), 132, 185

The NewsHour (*The MacNeil/Lehrer Report*; TV series), 105, 118, 138, 226

newspapers: and authoritarian-populist discourse, 184; black, 136, 152; and black programming, 151–52; TV versions of, 116–17, 118

Newsroom (*Newspaper of the Air*; TV series), 116

Newsweek (magazine), 34, 35, 99

Newton, Huey, 133

New York City, 20, 182–83, 192

Nielsen Corporation, 1–2, 3, 35–36

Nightline (TV series), 5

Nixon, Richard, 6, 10, 132, 210; attacks on PBS by, 107, 118, 138, 175–76, 178, 183, 222; authoritarian-populist strategies of, 180, 181–83; and culture wars, 215; and funding, 24, 136, 169, 183; and local stations, 205, 211, 212; Middle America of, 177–78, 185; and NET, 179; and PBS programming, 125, 196, 197, 199, 200; reforms of PBS by, 203, 204, 212

"No Place Like Home" (TV program), 213

Nova (TV series), 211

objectivity: in black programming, 132, 133, 136; on *Dream Machine*, 196; *vs.* emotionality, 119–20, 132, 135; in public affairs programming, 132, 133, 136; study of, 138

O'Connell, James, 77

O'Conner, John, 173

Office of Telecommunications Policy, 178, 180–81, 182, 183

Omnibus (TV series), 31, 43, 46, 71, 158–59

On Being Black (TV series), 150, 152

One-Dimensional Man (Marcuse), 189

"One Week of Commercial Television" (Smythe), 42

Open Windows (TV series), 204

"Operation Gap-Stop" (TV program), 85

opinion leaders, 130, 146, 224; male, 111, 138, 226; public affairs programming for, 111–12, 117–18, 121, 122, 137. *See also* influentials

Oppenheimer, Robert, 112

Our Kind of World (TV series), 86

Pablo Casal's Master Class at Berkeley (ETV program), 49

Pace, Frank, 114

Packard, Vance, 28, 54, 74–75, 93–94, 96

paedocracy, 32, 42

Paik, Nam June, 190

Palmieri, Victor, 128

paternalism: cultural, 12, 13, 32, 36, 148; and culture of poverty, 76; of ETV, 42–44; of European public television, 16, 107; governmental, 16; of PBS programming, 14, 88–91, 225

Patterson, Franklin, 53

PBL. See Public Broadcast Laboratory

PBS. *See* Public Broadcasting Service; public television

Pei, I. M., 164

"People Like Us" (TV program), 213

The People Look at Educational Television (Schramm), 72, 102, 103

The People Look at Television (Steiner), 34–35, 37

The People's Instrument (Blakley), 114

Pepsi Cola, 135

"Perceptions of Balance and Objectivity in Public Broadcasting" (study), 138

Perlmutter, Al, 195, 202, 203

personal and social development programming, 77, 84–91; biases of, 104; and disciplinary logics, 84, 89; *vs.* popular entertainment, 84, 87, 88, 89; and race, 85, 88, 90, 132; as socialization, 85, 86, 89, 91; and unemployment, 86–89, 91

Personal Influence (Katz and Lazarsfeld), 111

Petticoat Junction (TV series), 35

Phillips, Kevin, 215

Playhouse 90 (TV series), 26

pluralism, 20, 62, 141–74, 221; and audiences, 55–56, 142–46; and *Black Journal*, 134; and Carnegie Commission, 53, 56, 164; class, 207; and commercial television, 27; contradictions of, 173–74; cultural,

29, 36, 142, 143, 156, 163; as goal, 16, 18; ideology of, 142; and normalization of whiteness, 153–54; and political unrest, 142, 143; and tokenization of minorities, 167

Podhoretz, Norman, 164

Polaroid, 154

policy: broadcast, 138; education, 74; government, 42, 178, 180–81, 182, 183; liberal corporate approach to, 50–51; programming, 143, 144, 145, 155. *See also* cultural policy

Polish Laboratory Theater, 190

political order: *vs.* consumer economy, 17, 38, 109

political participation, 106, 107, 122, 123, 129; and experiential knowledge, 119–20; and PBS, 110, 126, 131, 221

political rationality, 108, 110, 119

political unrest: and authoritarian-populist discourse, 177; and black programming, 150, 151, 152; and cultivation, 101, 180; and democracy, 109, 113; and experts, 129–30; and leftist programming, 186; and media, 106, 115, 132, 146; and PBS, 110, 121, 146, 155, 221; and personal and social development programming, 84–85, 87, 89; and pluralism, 142, 143; and public affairs programming, 132, 135, 137; racial, 19, 84–85, 87, 89, 113, 132, 143, 150, 151, 152; and social programming, 223

politics: and black programming, 133, 134, 148, 180–81; cultural, 14, 214, 220; *vs.* depoliticization, 176, 179; in documentaries, 12, 188; education in, 136, 138; elites of, 55; and ITVS, 212, 214; leftist, 182–84, 205; and local stations, 205, 211; and race, 150; and socialization, 108

Poor People's Campaign, 190

popularity: and citizenship, 125; and commercialism, 63, 64–65, 172; *vs.* diversity, 56–57; *vs.* excellence, 58, 76–77, 226; and leftist programming, 189; and market forces, 224–25; paradox of, 13; and PBS programming, 81, 192, 221; and "vast wasteland" discourse, 66. *See also* entertainment, popular

populism: *vs.* authoritarianism, 20; and authoritarian-populist discourse, 176; and criticism of PBS, 3, 6, 7, 58, 66, 222; and cultural democracy, 37; and funding, 67; land-grant, 210; *vs.* liberalism, 175–76, 185

"The Potential Uses of Television in Preschool Education" (Cooney), 78

poverty: aestheticization of, 192–93, 200–201, 213; and capitalism, 193; and citizenship, 129; cultural, 91; culture of, 76, 77, 81; and education, 77; and NET, 188; and PBS programming, 78, 81, 85, 86–87, 90, 96, 200–201; and race, 132

power: of audience, 38; black, 106, 122, 153, 156, 178, 180, 191; of commercial television, 37–38, 57, 219; cultural, 37–38, 57, 139, 143, 219, 223; and cultural standards, 29–30; hierarchies of, 16, 82, 108, 221; social, 226; technologies of, 107; and TV viewing habits, 64

The Power Elite (Mills), 113

Power in Washington (Cater), 113

Powledge, Fred, 184, 185

privatization, 7, 8–9, 13, 26, 215; and commercialism, 29, 31; conservatives on, 169, 172; and funding, 11, 66, 67, 169

The Production and Distribution of Knowledge in the United States (Machlup), 73

A Program for Action. See Public Television: A Program for Action programming conferences, 143, 152, 186, 187

Progressive Era, 70

Project for the Republican Future, 7

"The Promise of Television" (PBS documentary), 4

psychology: behaviorist, 90, 91, 124; program, 86–87

A Public Affair (TV series), 118

public affairs programming: aesthetics of, 115, 124, 125; audience for, 117–18, 130–31, 134; and citizenship, 113; and civility, 120–21; and commercialism, 225; on commercial television, 17, 26, 115–16, 117, 118; confrontation in, 122, 127–28; and corporate sponsors, 10, 11; and cultural diversity, 226; and democracy, 19, 37, 111, 117, 131–37, 139; and education, 120–21; and ETV, 41; experts on, 111, 114–25; feminism on, 130; and founding of PBS, 109; liberalism of, 183; and local stations, 205, 210; and NET, 178; Nixon on, 178; objectivity in, 132, 133, 136; for opinion leaders, 111–12, 117–18, 121, 122, 137; and political unrest, 132, 135, 137; and popular entertainment, 116, 117, 124, 125; and social change, 136, 179; social management in, 122–25, 134; town-hall style, 121–22; for women, 130, 131–32

Public Broadcasting Act (1967), 10, 21, 23, 113; debate on, 59, 68, 109–10; and Great Society programs, 77, 175; and local programming, 205; and PBS advertising campaign, 218; on pluralism, 142–43; and prohibition of entertainment, 61

Public Broadcasting Service (PBS), 20–21, 25, 41, 61; advertising by, 217–18. *See also* public television

Public Broadcast Laboratory (*PBL*; TV series), 114–15, 189–92, 214

Public Opinion (Lippmann), 111

public service: and audiences, 33, 84; and citizenship, 113; and commercial television, 60–61; and consumerism, 172; and corporate liberalism, 50; and culture wars, 5, 104; and democracy, 13–14, 38–41, 110; vs. economy, 11, 14; and ETV, 42; and founding of CPB, 59; and Friends of Public Broadcasting, 164; interpretations of, 32, 66; and local programming, 210; vs. popularity, 23, 35–41, 57; and public affairs programming, 116, 117, 123; radio as, 26; and "vast wasteland" discourse, 31–33, 222–23

public sphere, 11, 120–21, 132

public television: and art of effects, 14, 17; "caviar," 58; corporate structure of, 113; cultural identity of, 61; effects of, 14; late development of, 11, 14; marginalization of, 15, 18, 139; as "Marshall Plan of America," 114; membership community of, 163–69; as "oasis of the wasteland," 4, 23–24, 56, 61–65, 68; political rationality of, 108, 110; promotion of, 61–65; rationalizing, 65–66; social construction of, 33; studies of, 10–15; as supplement to commercial television, 50; as universal service, 12–13

Public Television: A Program for Action (Carnegie Commission report), 55–59, 78

public television, European, 104, 107

Public Television for Sale (Hoynes), 11, 172

Puerto Rican Media Action and Educational Council, 173

Putnam, Robert, 138, 139

"The Quality of American Culture" (Heckscher), 28

quiz show scandals, 36, 39

race: and Carnegie Commission, 53, 56; and cultivation, 103, 104; and cultural center, 173–74; and cultural policy, 90, 154, 155; and democracy, 139, 220, 226; and education, 85, 132, 186–87; and emotionality, 119; and equality of opportunity, 76–77; and European high culture, 155, 156; and leftist programming, 189–90; and PBS programming, 85, 87, 88, 90, 132, 145, 221, 226; and pluralism, 142; and public affairs programming, 131–37; on *Sesame Street*, 78–79, 80, 81–82, 83, 98. *See also* African Americans; whiteness
Racine (Wisconsin) programming conference, 143, 152
racism: and authoritarian-populist discourse, 180; of commercial television, 136, 137; denial of, 166; inferential, 90, 132, 135; invisible, 144; and Middle America, 187, 208; and minority programming, 147, 173; and personal and social development programming, 85, 88, 90; structural, 146, 166, 186–87; and working class, 201, 202
radio, 55, 62, 93; and consumerism, 28, 71; and cultivation, 60, 101; educational, 70, 204, 211; and ETV, 41; public, 26, 70
Radway, Janice, 70–71
ratings: and audience, 33, 95, 101, 145; and citizenship, 113; and class, 36; and commercial television, 17, 220; and cultural democracy, 35–37, 65; and demographics, 27; and ETV, 43; and fund-raising, 169; and local station input, 203; and marketing, 93; for PBS, 1–2, 5, 57, 66, 101, 156; for public affairs programming, 115, 116; and sensationalism, 121

"The Ratings Game" (documentary), 35–36
Rauschenberg, Robert, 164
Reagan, Ronald, 6, 177, 215
Red Channels: The Report on the Communist Influence in Radio and Television, 182–83
Redd Foxx (TV series), 152
"The Red Myth" (TV program), 188
Red Skelton (TV series), 57
reform: and audience, 25, 64, 95, 106, 118–19; corporate opposition to, 37; cultural, 16–17, 19, 70; decentralizing, 203, 204, 212; disciplinary approach to, 107; dual logics of, 22, 39–41; and educational television, 19; elevated cultural, 39–40; and ETV, 41; and founding of CPB, 59; and funding, 66, 203, 204; and governmentality, 43, 110–11; and marketing, 94; and mass culture, 23–24, 25; and media, 106; pedagogic, 40–41, 45; and producer values, 71–72; public-service, 39–40; of radio, 26, 101; of "vast wasteland," 34. *See also* broadcast reform discourse
Reisman, David, 39
Report of the National Advisory Commission on Civil Disorders, 84–85
Rhoda (TV series), 171
The Ritual (televised play), 149
Rockefeller, David, 193
Rockefeller Foundation, 41
"Roots of Reform" (TV program), 208
Roseanne (TV series), 1–5, 68–69, 217
Ross, Andrew, 28, 142, 155
Rowland, Willard, 12–13, 50, 165
Rubin, Joan Shelley, 69, 70, 110
Rushner, William, 127
Russell Sage Foundation, 115

Say Brother (TV series), 147

Schlesinger, Arthur, Jr., 39, 202
Schmertz, Herb, 93, 158
Schramm, Wilbur, 41, 72, 95, 102–3, 112
Schudson, Michael, 120
Schuman, Mrs. William
("Frankie"), 166
Schwarzwalder, John, 204–10
Scientific American (magazine), 145
See It Now (TV series), 26, 38
self-improvement, 68–71, 100, 101, 222;
and ABC advertising campaign,
219; and culture of poverty, 76;
and education, 18, 70, 77; and
museums, 108; and PBS, 54–55,
75, 221. See also cultivation
sense-making discourse, 4, 18
Sesame Street (TV series), 5, 9, 77, 78–84,
166, 218; vs.Civilisation, 97–99; and
class bias, 185; and cultivation, 102,
103; effects of, 80–81; and equality
of opportunity, 100; on local
stations, 208
Shakespeare, William, 49, 92, 155
Shales, Tom, 8, 162
Shayon, Robert Lewis, 31, 46
Sid Caesar (TV series), 47
silent majority, 177, 183, 184, 185, 187,
201, 202
sitcoms, 1–5, 68–69, 213, 217, 224, 226
The Six Wives of Henry VIII (TV
series), 160
Smythe, Dallas, 42
soap opera, 160, 162; black, 150–51; and
cultural democracy, 226;
Masterpiece Theatre as, 156, 158–63;
Upstairs, Downstairs as, 161
social change: and authoritarian-
populist discourse, 180; and
documentaries, 191–95; and PBS
programming, 180, 185; and public
affairs programming, 136, 179;
working class on, 202. See also
political unrest

socialization, 47, 111; and personal and
social development programming,
85, 86, 89, 91; political, 108
social management, 17, 221; and
cultivation, 69, 76, 103; and culture,
108, 224; and governmentality, 43;
and leftist programming, 186; and
personal and social development
programming, 84, 91; and public
affairs programming, 122–25, 134;
of social problems, 69, 84, 91, 103,
122–25, 153, 186
social mobility: and class, 19, 30, 54–55,
69; and consumption, 68; and
cultivation, 68–69, 103, 104; and
cultural fragmentation, 144–45; and
education, 69, 75–76; and
meritocracy, 100; and PBS
programming, 83–84, 90, 99; and
producer values, 71
Soul! (TV series), 149–52, 154, 156, 166,
180, 208, 223
special-interest groups, 51, 142
Spigel, Lynn, 47, 183
Spotlight on Opera (ETV series), 46
Sputnik, 46
Stallybrass, Peter, 25, 34, 120–21
Stanton, Frank, 39, 57, 60
Station Independence Project, 169,
170, 172
The Status Seekers: An Exploration of
Class Behavior in America
(Packard), 28, 74–75, 93
Steambath (televised play), 161
Steiner, Gary, 34–35, 37
stereotypes: authoritarian-populist,
186; and class, 201–2; and
commercial television, 220; on
Dream Machine, 196, 198, 199; of
Middle America, 177, 185
Streeter, Thomas, 50
The Strength of Government
(Bundy), 113

Studio One (TV series), 26

talk shows, daytime, 226. *See also* public affairs programming
Task Force on Minorities in Public Broadcasting, 152
Task Force on Urban Problems, 86
taste cultures: and class, 93, 170, 180, 182–83, 184, 218, 223; fragmented, 53–54, 174; idealized, 42; and ITVS, 212, 213; legitimated, 218; and minority programming, 173; popular, 16; and public television problem, 221; regional, 200, 204; urban, 182–83
The Tastemakers (Lynes), 93
technology: and audiences, 219–20; cultural, 108, 109, 223; and democracy, 139; and education, 81; and local programming, 205, 206; and personal and social development programming, 84, 86; and public affairs programming, 115; and social control, 122; and working class, 189. *See also* cable and satellite television
Terkel, Studs, 202
Terrell, Bill, 90
theater, 4, 144, 163, 218; black, 149, 150; vs. British dramas, 161–62; on *Dream Machine*, 197, 198; on *PBL*, 189, 190–91
Think Twice (TV series), 225
This Week with Bill Moyers (TV series), 118
Time (magazine), 151, 177–78
"Tongues Untied" (TV program), 213
Tracey, Michael, 13, 106, 225–26
Trilling, Lionel, 101
The Turned-on Crisis (TV series), 122–23
Turner, Ted, 3
TV Guide (magazine), 33, 34–35, 62, 66; and ABC advertising campaign,

218–19; and authoritarian-populist discourse, 179, 181; on culture wars, 215; on ETV, 47, 48; and local programming, 204, 205, 206, 211; on PBS programming, 98, 130, 131, 197, 203; on public affairs programming, 117
TV Job Center (TV series), 86–87
TV problem, 26–35; and audience, 27, 116; and Carnegie Commission report, 56; and consumer sovereignty, 110; and corporate liberalism, 50, 57; and cultivation, 91; and cultural democracy, 37; and ETV, 42, 47, 49; and marketing, 93; PBS as solution to, 16, 18, 19, 25, 50, 59, 62, 113, 224; and public television problem, 221; and reform logic, 39
two-step flow theory, 19, 111, 119, 131

Upstairs, Downstairs (TV series), 161

Van Peebles, Melvin, 149, 150
"vast wasteland" discourse, 23–66, 226; and ABC advertising campaign, 219; and Carnegie Commission, 52–53; and commercialism, 96; and commercial television, 7, 13, 17, 18, 23–24, 26, 27, 31, 32–34, 58; and cultural democracy, 36, 38; and ETV, 42, 49; and mass audience, 64; and Middle America, 185, 187; and PBS programming, 130, 136, 160, 199; and pluralism, 142; and public interest, 66, 222–23; and public television, 4, 23–24, 50, 56, 57, 61–65, 68, 106
VD Blues (TV series), 124
Vietnam War, 101, 106, 112–13, 115; and authoritarian-populist discourse, 177, 180; in PBS programming, 129–30, 188, 199, 202

voyeurism, 192, 193, 199, 200, 213

Wall Street Week (TV series), 118
War on Poverty, 75, 79, 82
Warwick, Dionne, 89
Washington Week in Review (TV series), 105, 118, 136, 138
The Waste Land (Eliot), 24
Watergate hearings, 137
Wayne, John, 177
WCET-Cincinnati, 168
WDAU-Scranton, 184
Weathermen, 155
Weaver, Pat, 40
welfare state, 7, 50–51, 218
Westin, Av, 115, 189
WETA-Washington, D.C., 86–89, 90, 137, 179
WGBH-Boston, 48, 147, 150, 154, 161, 179
"What Harvest for the Reaper" (TV program), 188
"Where Is Prejudice" (TV program), 188
Where It's At (TV series), 88–89
White, Allon, 25, 34, 120–21
White, Mimi, 170
White, Stephen, 52, 54, 56
Whitehead, Clay, 181–82, 183, 197, 205
whiteness, 143, 163; and membership culture, 168, 171, 173; normalization of, 20, 53, 137, 141–42, 144, 145, 153–56, 167, 171, 173, 223
The Whole World Is Watching (Gitlin), 121
WHRO-Norfolk, 171
WHYY-Philadelphia, 135
Will, George, 5
Williams, Raymond, 14, 16, 23, 32, 107, 225

Willis, Jack, 187, 195, 196
Winston, Brian, 191, 192
Wiseman, Frederick, 191
WJCT-Jacksonville, 122
WMHT-Schenectady, 170
WNET-New York, 20, 82, 167, 173, 179, 204
Woman Alive! (TV series), 131–32
women: as audience, 64, 226; and Carnegie Commission, 52; and experiential knowledge, 120, 130; and leisure, 48; and local programming, 206, 207; and mass culture, 29; as opinion leaders, 111; and public affairs programming, 130, 131–32; and sexual revolution, 124; as volunteers, 164–66. *See also* feminization
women's movement, 106, 130
Wonder, Stevie, 89, 149
Wood, Grant, 181
Woodcock, Leonard, 52, 53, 56
work ethic, 71–72, 76, 87, 89, 100
WQED-Pittsburgh, 100, 147
WTTW-Chicago, 150–51
WTVS-Detroit, 171
Wyszomirski, Margaret, 182

Xerox Corporation, 92, 94, 95–96, 97, 99; and *Civilisation*, 98, 100, 101

Yeats, William Butler, 155
"Your World This Week" (TV program), 208
youth, 122–25, 143

Zazin, Michael, 177